AVIATION SECURITY

This book is dedicated to Michael Milde,
for his outstanding contributions to the field of international civil aviation

AVIATION SECURITY
LEGAL AND REGULATORY ASPECTS

RUWANTISSA I.R. ABEYRATNE

Routledge
Taylor & Francis Group
LONDON AND NEW YORK

First published 1998 by Ashgate Publishing

Reissued 2018 by Routledge
2 Park Square, Milton Park, Abingdon, Oxon OX14 4RN
711 Third Avenue, New York, NY 10017, USA

Routledge is an imprint of the Taylor & Francis Group, an informa business

A Library of Congress record exists under LC control number: 98020262

ISBN 13: 978-1-138-31911-0 (hbk)
ISBN 13: 978-0-429-45408-0 (ebk)

Contents

Preface

This book examines the offence of unlawful interference with international civil aviation and analyses critically the legal and regulatory regime that applies thereto, with a view to recommending measures that are calculated to infuse a new approach to the problem. Emphasis is laid throughout the work on action which may be taken to alleviate the problem of unlawful interference. The conclusion of this book incorporates various steps that can be taken towards achieving this objective.

Much has been written already on the various conventions which apply to the subject of unlawful interference with civil aviation. These instruments have proved effective only to the extent of nurturing existing values of international law as they are restrictively perceived through the parameters of air law. This book therefore does not attempt to analyse these conventions in depth, since such an exercise would be counter-productive in an attempt at introducing a new approach to existing principles of international criminal law. Rather, it focuses on the core of the problem which has effectively precluded significant progress into inroads that would curb the threat of terrorism in aviation. The attitude of the international community, which has sunk its roots into its belief in absolute sovereignty of states and the incontrovertibility and supremacy of municipal law, has been that an international crime should be determined, adjudicated and punished within municipal boundaries. To meet this approach, this book examines *in limine* the fundamental role of international law in the light of the United Nations Congress of International Public Law of March 1995, and its effect on international criminal law. It then determines the applicable principles of State sovereignty and examines principles of state responsibility in this context. The purpose of this work is to recommend the establishment of a new philosophy of international criminal law which transcends municipal boundaries. Academic, scholarly and judicial precedent for this thesis is adduced in support of this argument.

This book also examines the role of the International Civil Aviation Organization (ICAO) as the regulatory body responsible for civil aviation in the context of new approaches made by the international community towards the status of ICAO in aviation security. Concrete measures are recommended towards ICAO's enhanced importance in this field. Also suggested are the possibilities of the establishment of an international criminal court to address the offence of terrorism and the adoption of an international convention or code to support the court in its adjudicatory process.

The practical value of this book essentially lies in the legal recommendations it makes at its conclusion, which are based on existing principles of international law.

Ruwantissa I.R. Abeyratne
Montreal

Introduction

Recent attempts made towards attaining peace in such areas as the Arab–Israeli conflict and the Northern Ireland issue have been thwarted by the proliferation of incendiary acts against the world at large, thus amply demonstrating the inherent difficulties attendant upon such peace processes. In the context, unlawful interference with international civil aviation has become a principal area of concern to the world community both as a recognized threat to world peace and security and as a grave social malady which needs a fast cure. The bombing of a PAN-AM aircraft over the Atlantic in December 1988, the mortar attacks on London Heathrow Airport in March 1994, the bombing in London's Docklands in early February 1996 breaking a cease-fire between the British and the Irish Republican Army (IRA) and the devastating explosion which ripped the Central Business District of Colombo, Sri Lanka in January 1996 are several events which occurred over a period of eight years, graphically illustrating the effects of terrorism on international civil aviation and world peace. While the first incident caused diplomatic and legal ripples between Libya and the United States, leading up to its adjudication in the International Court of Justice, the incidents in the United Kingdom have caused a further widening of the bridge between the British Government and the IRA. This book, while identifying the offence in its many forms, will discuss international legal and regulatory measures that have so far been taken against the offence and suggest legal measures that may be taken to dissuade terrorism against international civil aviation.

Terrorism is usually the genus of the species of political discord within and between nations., The terrorist is well aware of this situation and usually exploits political disharmony among nations. Whatever laws that are enacted are rendered ineffective as they cannot be enforced with uniformity. Political asylum is a product of this anomaly and remains by and large the greatest encouragement to the proliferation of terrorism in the world today.

In the past the United Nations General Assembly has made sustained efforts to adopt collective measures to prevent terrorism[1] at national and international levels.[2] In its efforts, the United Nations has succeeded in focusing the attention of its member states to the increasing problems of terrorism and its natural corollaries such as the proliferation of arms, the emergence of mercenaries etc. The efforts of the international community, however, in entering into treaties have been rendered nugatory due to two reasons – the first being the aura of ambiguity that shrouds the nature and force of an international agreement and the second being the lack of enthusiasm on the part of most states to label terrorism as an offence against humanity. The latter, if recognized, would immediately entail the mandatory punishment of the terrorist by all states concerned.

The question as to whether international law upon which international treaties are based has the nature and force of law has aroused much debate, and indeed the concern of the United Nations and its members. This concern can be seen in the United Nations Resolution 44/23. Although 19th century Austinian thinking[3] did not consider international law to be endowed with the attributes of law, there is a strong view to the contrary.[4] The theory that international law was not enforceable law was based on the theory that law should emanate from a sovereign authority which was politically superior to those on whom such law was imposed. International law, it was claimed, did not emanate from such authority. The contrary view which is more persuasive holds that if international law had mere force of morality, such authorities as precedent and opinion of jurists would not be cited in instances of adjudication.[5] In addition, certain judicial decisions have expressly recognized the fact that international law is enforceable law and has all the attributes of law.[6]

Once it is accepted that international law is enforceable law, the second issue is whether treaties in general have the necessary obligatory force to demand adherence from their signatories. Although treaties are founded upon the expectancy of the observance of good faith under the principles of the *pacta sunt servanda,* the emergence of competent courts and tribunals and the increasing dependence upon precedent and scholastic opinion in this field are sufficiently compelling factors in support of the enforceability of treaties.[7]

There is no doubt that legislative measures, like practical measures, can be effectively adopted. All states must recognize in their legislation that terrorism is a crime against humanity and that they should punish terrorists or deport them to a country which has sufficient interest in the offence to punish them. The treatment of the offence by all states should be devoid of political ideology and the tendency to offer political asylum to terrorists. As a first step, states should at least negotiate bilaterally or in groups and enter into treaties and the provisions of these treaties should apply to third nations as well, on the analogy of the most-favoured-nation treatment clause.[8] The most important factor is to involve all states one way or another to form a composite force and not to isolate them in the face of terrorism.

Interference with civil aviation should be viewed as an extortion-oriented act committed against the international order and world peace and which is calculated to take advantage of the most susceptible human quality of seeking personal security as a priority. The offence is an immediate threat to world peace and should be treated with the utmost care. It is needless to say that any nation which views the offence differently encourages world discord. Any wilful act calculated to endanger the safety of an aircraft, its passengers or any aviation-related property should be collectively regarded as an offence against the safety of air travel.

As for the need for a more flexible approach to the extradition of offenders the establishment and recognition of a universal offence against the safety of aircraft would almost automatically nurture mutual co-operation between nations. Often, if an offender imputes politics to the offence committed by him, he is granted political asylum by the host nation merely because the latter sympathizes with the alleged motive for the offence as represented by the offender. Once this takes place it no longer remains the commission of an offence universally condemned but becomes an altercation between nations on political beliefs and convictions.

There are two fundamental measures that have to be adopted to accomplish the above. Firstly, the existing attitude of the international community towards international law, state responsibility and state sovereignty should be examined within existing principles of international law. A closer look at these factors reveal a grave inconsistency between perceptions and actual values. Secondly, international crimes must be viewed beyond the parameters of municipal legislation and litigation. In order to achieve this objective, a serious and well-thought-out approach should be adopted towards the establishment of an international court of criminal justice, which is spurred on by an international convention on terrorism. As a corollary and necessary catalyst to these procedures, the role of the International Civil Aviation Organization (ICAO) as an effective tool against unlawful interference with civil aviation should be revised.

There is a compelling need to add more teeth to ICAO – the only regulatory body which is responsible for matters relating to international civil aviation. As the world moves towards the next millennium, it becomes a compelling need to revisit the role of ICAO and introduce new measures for its sustenance and effectiveness.

This book contains six chapters, ranging from an analysis of the role of international law in aviation security to an analysis of the offence of unlawful interference and legal and regulatory issues related thereto. It culminates in recommendations of a legal nature which are calculated to radically revise the present approach towards the offence.

Notes

1 See UN Papers A/40/1003, 7 December 1985. See also, UN Papers A/40/979, 6 December 1985, 2–7. UN Papers A/C 6/40/9, 7 November 1985, at 1. Also, UN Official Records, Sixth Committee 9th Meeting A/C. 6/40/9 SR. 9, 9 October 1985, 2–16. UN Papers A/C. 6/40/SR/13, 14 October 1985, 1–5. UN Papers A/C 6/40/SR 17, 3–11 and UN Papers A/40/979., 2–3.
2 Proposal 2 UN Papers A/40/1003, 7 December 1985, *op. cit.* at 3.
3 Morrison, W.L. (1982), *John Austin*, Stanford, C.A., Stanford University Press at p. 6.
4 Starke, J.G. (1984), *Introduction to International Law*, (9th ed.), London, Butterworths, London, at p.18. See also, Lloyd, D. (1970), *The Idea of Law*, (Rev. ed.), Harmondsworth, Middlesex, London, Penguin Books, p.37 at 40. See also, Jennings, R.Y. (1990), 'An International Lawyer Takes Stock', *International and Comp. Law Quarterly*, July 1990, 513, at 514–516.
5 Starke, (1984), *op. cit.* at p.18–21.
6 See the *Charming Betsy* (1804) 2 Cranch 64 at 118, where Marshall, C.J. cited Article V1 para 2 of the United States Constitution which gives constitutional validity to international law. See also *The Paquete Habana*, (1900) 175 US 677 at 700 per Gray, J. who went on to say that international law must be ascertained and administered by the courts of justice of appropriate jurisdiction.
7 See generally, Brierly, J.L. (1963), *The Law of Nations*, (6th ed.), Oxford, Clarendon Press at pp.331–345.
8 First introduced in 1947 by the *General Agreement on Tariffs and Trade* (GATT), the most-favoured-nation treatment clause ensures that certain benefits accrue to nations other than the signatory states in instances that apply to those non-signatory states.

1 The Growth of International Law and its Applicability to Air Law

A General Overview

Early Stages of Development

The genesis of international law may well lie in the seminal European Charter – the Peace of Westphalia – which was signed in 1648. This document recognized unrestrained sovereignty of states and effectively consolidated the concept of world unity through sovereign states.

The next significant step was the Concert of Europe – a haphazard system of consultation between the great countries of Europe – which was established by the Settlement of Vienna in 1815 and followed by the Congress of Aix-la-Chapelle in 1818. The Concert emerged as a corollary to the Napoleonic Wars and provided a forum which maintained and balanced power between the European nations for a century. One of the salient features of the Concert was that although the treaty admitted of consultation and conference on the devolution of power among states, its findings or decisions had no obligatory effect on the Great Powers. This perceived inadequacy of the Concert resulted in its impotence and inability to impose adherence by states of its findings or decisions and is often attributed to states having a free hand in doing as they pleased to each other in World War I.

As history would demonstrate time and time again, the aftermath of a major disaster brings fresh thinking for reformation and revival. After World War I, states adopted the Paris Settlement of 1919, partially as atonement for the bankruptcy and inability of the Concert to ensure uniformity in international accord and also to infuse new ideas and rules of conduct for the international community. The

Paris Settlement, which retained for the most part the spirit of the Peace of Westphalia, set the tone for the establishment of the League of Nations which further strengthened the bonds of unity between states, based on the wartime collaboration between Associated and Allied Powers. The League of Nations adopted the principle that undertakings of international law would actively determine conduct among governments, without abdicating *jus ad bellum*, or the right of war. This in turn resulted in failure, as was seen in 1939, when, without reference to the League of Nations, Britain and France hastened to come to Poland's assistance when it was attacked by Germany.

At this stage in history, international law was considered as simply law binding upon States in their relations with each other. The Provisional International Court of Justice (the predecessor to the International Court of Justice) decided in the famous *Lotus* case of 1927:

> International law governs relations between independent States. The rules of law binding upon States therefore emanate from their own free will as expressed in conventions or by usages generally accepted as expressing principles of law and established in order to regulate the relations between those co-existing independent communities or with a view to the achievement of common aims. Restrictions upon the independence of States cannot therefore be presumed.[1]

The aftermath of World War II saw the advent of the United Nations and the United Nations Charter, the latter of which proclaims that the United Nations is based on the sovereign equality of all members. The Charter also provides that less powerful nations recognize the pre-eminence of the Great Powers as guardians of international peace and security.[2] With the exception of this predominant innovation of post-World War II accord, the rest of the Charter seems complacently to accord with the basic framework of international law which existed under the Peace of Westphalia. Judicial recognition of the United Nations as a subject of international law was given by the International Court of Justice (ICJ) in 1949, in the *Reparation for Injuries Case*,[3] where the ICJ pronounced the end of the old orthodoxy that states are the only subjects of international law, and advised that the United Nations, though not a state, had the capacity to bring certain kinds of claims directly against a state under the rubric of international law.

The many contributions of the United Nations to the development of international law have been both significant and sustained, ever since the United Nations General Assembly convened its first session in 1946. The General Assembly has been prolific in adopting numerous resolutions, declarations and conventions through diplomatic conferences. Guided by Article 13 of the United Nations Charter which places an obligation on the General Assembly to initiate studies and make recommendations for encouraging the progressive development of international law and its codification,[4] the Assembly, in November 1947, established the International Law Commission whose members were entrusted with the formulation of principles of international law. One of the first tasks of the Commission was to write a Draft Code of Offenses (sic) against Peace and Security of Mankind, which the Commission completed in 1954. The Draft Code provided that any act of aggression, including the employment by the authorities of a state of armed forces against another State for any purpose other than national or collective self-defence or in pursuance of a decision or recommendation of a competent organ of the United Nations, was an offence against the peace and security of mankind. The code also stipulated that any threat by the authorities of a state to resort to an act of aggression against another state was a similar offence.[5]

The sense of international responsibility that the United Nations ascribed to itself had reached a heady stage at this point, where the role of international law in international human conduct was perceived to be primary and above the authority of states. In its Report to the General Assembly, the International Law Commission recommended a draft provision which required:

> Every State has the duty to conduct its relations with other States in accordance with international law and with the principle that the sovereignty of each State is subject to the supremacy of international law.[6]

This principle, which forms a cornerstone of international conduct by states, provides the basis for strengthening international comity and regulating the conduct of states both internally – within their territories – and externally, towards other states. States are effectively precluded by this principle of pursuing their own interests untrammelled and with disregard to principles established by international law.

Development of International Law through Treaties

Treaties, conventions, agreements, protocols, exchanges of notes and other synonyms all mean one and the same thing at international law – that they are international transactions of a legal character. Treaties are concluded between states in written form and governed by international law, whether embodied in a single instrument or in two or more related instruments and whatever its particular designation.[7] Each treaty has four constituent elements: the capacity of the parties thereto to conclude agreement of the provisions of the treaty under international law; the intention of the parties to apply principles of international law when concluding agreement under a treaty; *consensus ad idem* or a meeting of the minds of the parties[8]; and, the parties must have the intention to create legal obligations among themselves. These four elements form a composite regulatory process whereby a treaty becomes strong enough at international law to enable parties to settle their differences within the parameters of the treaty, make inroads into customary international law if necessary, and, transform an unorganized international community into one which may be organized under a uniform set of rules. Treaties are based on three fundamental principles of international law: good faith; consent; and, international responsibility.[9] Since international customary law does not prescribe any particular form for consensual agreements and requirements that would make them binding, the parties to a treaty could agree upon the form of treaty they intend entering into and make it binding among them accordingly. Legal bonds are established between nations because they wish to create them and, as is seen in the Preamble to the Chicago Convention, a statement to this effect is reflected in the treaty itself.[10] The main feature of a multilateral international agreement is that absolute rights that may have existed within states before the entry into force of such treaty would be transformed into relative rights in the course of a balancing process in which considerations of good faith and reasonableness play a prominent part. However, treaty provisions must be so written and construed as best to conform to accepted principles of international customary law.[11]

Great reliance is placed on treaties as a source of international law. The international Court of Justice, whose function it is to adjudicate upon disputes of an international character between states, applies as a source of law, international conventions which establish rules that are expressly recognized by the states involved in a dispute.[12] The Court also has jurisdiction to interpret a treaty at the request of a state.[13]

The *Vienna Convention on the Law of Treaties*[14] while recognizing treaties as a source of law, accepts free consent, good faith and the *pacta sunt servanda* as universally recognized elements of a treaty.[15] Article 11 of the Vienna Convention provides that the consent of a state to be bound by a treaty may be expressed by signature, exchange of instruments constituting a treaty, ratification, acceptance, approval or accession, or by any other means agreed upon. 'Ratification', 'acceptance', 'approval', and 'accession' generally mean the same thing, that is, that in each case the international act so named indicates that the state performing such act is establishing on the international plane its consent to be bound by a treaty. A state demonstrates its adherence to a treaty by means of the *pacta sunt servanda,* which is reflected in Article 26 of the Vienna Convention — that every treaty in force is binding upon the parties and must be performed by them in good faith. The validity of a treaty or of the consent of a state to be bound by a treaty may be impeached only through the application of the Vienna Convention[16] which generally requires that a treaty could be derogated upon only in circumstances the treaty in question so specifies[17]; a later treaty abrogates the treaty in question;[18] there is a breach of the treaty;[19] a *novus actus interveniens* or supervening act which makes the performance of the treaty impossible;[20]and the invocation by a state of the *Clausula Rebus Sic Stantibus*[21] wherein a fundamental change of circumstances (when such circumstances constituted an essential basis of the consent of the parties to be bound by the treaty) which has occurred with regard to those existing at the time of the conclusion of the treaty, and which was not foreseen by the parties, radically changes or transforms the extent of obligations of a state. A state may not invoke the fact that its consent to be bound by a treaty has been expressed in violation of a provision of its internal law regarding competence to conclude treaties and seek to invalidate its consent unless such violation was manifest and concerned a rule of its internal law of fundamental importance.[22]

States or international organizations which are parties to such treaties have to apply the treaties they have signed and therefore have to interpret them. Although the conclusion of a treaty is generally governed by international customary law to accord with accepted rules and practices of national constitutional law of the signatory states, the application of treaties are governed by principles of international law. If, however, the application or performance of a requirement in an international treaty poses problems to a state, the constitutional law of that state would be applied by courts of that state to settle the problem. Although Article 27 of the Vienna Convention requires states not to invoke provisions of their internal laws as justification for failure to comply with the provisions of a treaty, states are free to choose the means of implementation they see fit according to their traditions and political organization.[23] The overriding rule is that treaties are juristic acts and have to be performed.

Every international treaty is affected by the fundamental dichotomy where, on the one hand, the question arises whether provisions of a treaty are enforceable at law, and, on the other, whether the principles of state sovereignty, which is *jus cogens* or mandatory law, would pre-empt the provisions of a treaty from being considered by states as enforceable. Article 53 of the Vienna Convention addresses this question and provides that where treaties, which at the time of their conclusion conflict with a peremptory norm of general international law or *jus cogens* are void. A peremptory norm of general international law is a norm accepted and recognized by the international community of states as a whole as a norm from which no derogation is permitted and which can be modified only by a subsequent norm of general international law having the same character. The use of the words 'as a whole' in Article 53 effectively precludes individual states from considering on a subjective basis, particular norms as acceptable to the international community.[24] Therefore, according to this provision, a treaty such as the Chicago Convention could not have derogated from principles of accepted international legal norms when it was being concluded. The Vienna Convention has, by this provision, implicitly ensured the legal legitimacy of international treaties, and established the principle that treaties are in fact *jus cogens* and therefore are instruments containing provisions, the compliance with which is mandatory.

Applicability of Treaty Law to the Chicago Convention and its Annexes

The basic principles of international conduct for the regulation of civil aviation are enshrined in the *Convention on International Civil Aviation*,[25] signed at Chicago on 7 December 1944. It would therefore not be irrelevant to examine the status of the Chicago Convention against established principles of international law and assess whether this convention has legally derived its authority as an international legal instrument from the United Nations' system.

The text of the Chicago Convention in the English language was signed at Chicago on 7 December 1944. The text of the Convention in the French and Spanish languages annexed to the protocol on the authentic trilingual text of the Convention was signed at Buenos Aires on 24 September 1968 and came into force without reservation as to acceptance on 24 October 1968 under the *Buenos Aires Protocol*. Article 1 of the Protocol makes the French, Spanish and English texts of the Chicago Convention equally authentic.[26] The Chicago Convention, in its Preamble, confirms that signatory states had agreed on certain principles and arrangements in order that international civil aviation may be developed in a safe and orderly manner and that international air transport services may be established on the basis of equality of opportunity and operated soundly and economically, and concluded the Convention to that end, thus complying with the requirement of consensual agreement that an international treaty needs to fulfil in order to gain legal recognition. Article 80 of the Convention unequivocally abrogates the preceding Paris and Havana Conventions and calls in the following provision for all aeronautical agreements which were in existence on the coming into force of the Chicago Convention that had been signed between states and airlines, states themselves or airlines, to be registered with the ICAO Council. The Convention, in Article 82, abrogates all obligations and understandings between contracting states which are inconsistent with the provisions of the Convention. Any contracting state which made arrangements not inconsistent with the provisions of the Chicago Convention, was required by Article 83 to register such arrangement forthwith with the ICAO Council, which in turn would make such arrangement public.

Article 89 stipulates that in the case of war and in emergency situations, the provisions of the Chicago Convention are not deemed to affect the freedom of action of any of the contracting states, whether as belligerents or as neutrals. Ratification of the Convention is provided for in Article 91, which requires that the instruments of ratification shall be deposited in the archives of the Government of the United States of America, which shall give notice of the date of the deposit to each of the signatory states and adhering states. The Convention, in Article 92, recognizes that it would be open for adherence by the members of the United Nations and states associated with them, and states which remained neutral during World War II. Other states could only be admitted to participate in the Convention on approval by four-fifths of the ICAO Assembly. Article 94 provides that the Convention could be amended on approval by a two-thirds vote of the Assembly and such amendment would come into force only in respect of those states which ratify the amendment at the time it is addressed by the Assembly. Denunciation of the Convention is provided for in Article 95, on the condition that such would be done three years after the coming into effect of the Convention, such denunciation to take effect one year from the date of receipt of the notification and to operate only as regards the state effecting the denunciation.

One of the most significant aspects of the Chicago Convention is the formation of the International Civil Aviation Organization (ICAO), to be comprised of an Assembly, a Council and such other bodies as may be deemed necessary. The Convention sets out in Article 44 the aims and objectives of the Organization as those that would develop the principles and techniques of international air navigation and foster the planning and development of international air transport. One of the mandatory functions of the Council, as laid out in Article 54 (l) is to adopt international standards and recommended practices and for convenience, designate them as Annexes to the Convention, with the requirement that contracting states be notified of such action taken.

It is clear that there are three significant aspects of inquiry that emerge in an analysis of the legal status of the Chicago Convention.

The first is whether the Convention is properly constituted as an international treaty. To determine this fact, it is necessary to discuss the legal requirements at international law that govern the constitution of such documents. Secondly, it is relevant to analyse the particular nature of the Chicago Convention, which formed ICAO as an international body to set standards and recommended practices on international civil aviation. The noteworthy aspect of ICAO's formation by the Convention is that while the Convention identifies ICAO's aims and objectives in Article 44, one of which later manifests itself in Article 54 (l) as the adoption of international standards and recommended practices, these standards and recommended practices are required to be contained in documents which are called 'Annexes to the Chicago Convention' for convenience. It is only arguable that this would not only take away any hint of legal legitimacy that the Annexes would have of being part of the Convention, but it would also seriously question the extent of compliance that these Annexes would be expected to draw from states, as is usual in instances of compliance with substantive tenets of international law. This anomaly seemingly gives rise to an instance where a valid international treaty forms an organ for the implementation of its policy as contained in the provisions of the treaty and thereafter, by implication, disassociates itself from the regulatory provisions adopted by that organ by refusing to recognize the documents which contain such provisions as part of the treaty itself. By this apparent abnegation of its own legitimacy, the Chicago Convention may seem to have adversely affected its validity as a treaty. A discussion of this ambiguity at international law will follow later in this chapter.

The initial issue that has to be addressed when one considers the legal status of the Chicago Convention and its Annexes is whether the Convention contains provisions which admit of law-making (legislative) powers of ICAO, and if so, to what extent such law could be promulgated under the Convention. The answer to this question lies in the extent to which the ICAO Assembly mandates the Council to exercise its quasi-legislative functions. The words 'legislative power' have been legally defined as 'power to prescribe rules of civil conduct'[27], while identifying law as a 'rule of civil conduct'. The word 'quasi' is essentially a term that makes a resemblance to another and classifies it. It is suggestive of comparative analogy and is accepted as:

> ... the conception to which it serves as an index and its connection with the conception with which the comparison is instituted by strong superficial analogy or resemblance.[28]

The question *stricto sensu* according to the above definition is therefore whether the ICAO Council now has power to prescribe rules of civil conduct (legislative power) or in the least a power that resembles by analogy the ability to prescribe rules of conduct (quasi-legislative power). Since legislative power is usually attributed to a state, it would be prudent to inquire, on a general basis, whether the ICAO Council has law-making powers in a quasi-legislative sense. Therefore, all references hereafter that may refer to legislative powers would be reflective of the Council's law-making powers in a quasi-legislative sense.

Article 37 of the Convention obtains the undertaking of each contracting state to collaborate in securing the highest practical degree of uniformity in regulations, standards, procedures and organization in relation to international civil aviation in all matters in which such uniformity will facilitate and improve air navigation. Article 38 obligates all contracting states to the Convention to inform ICAO immediately if they are unable to comply with any such international standard or procedure and notify differences between their own practices and those prescribed by ICAO. In the case of amendments to international standards, any state which does not make the appropriate amendment to its own regulations or practices shall give notice to the Council of ICAO within 60 days of the adoption of the said amendment to the international standard or indicate the action which it proposes to take.

Article 54 (l) of the Chicago Convention prescribes the adoption of international Standards and Recommended Practices (SARPS) and their designation in Annexes to the Convention, while notifying all contracting states of the action taken. The adoption of SARPS was considered a priority by the ICAO Council in its Second Session (2 September–12 December 1947)[29] which attempted to obviate any delays to the adoption of SARPS on air navigation as required by the First Assembly of ICAO.[30] SARPS inevitably take two forms: a negative form, for example, that states shall not impose more than certain maximum requirements; and a positive form, for example, that states shall take certain steps as prescribed by the ICAO Annexes.[31]

The element of compulsion that has been infused by the drafters of the Convention is compatible with the 'power to prescribe rules of civil conduct' on a *stricto sensu* legal definition of the words 'legislative power' as discussed above. This leaves no room for doubt that the 18 Annexes to the Convention or parts thereof lay down rules of conduct both directly and analogically. In fact, there is a conception based on a foundation of practicality that ICAO's international standards that are identified by the words 'contracting states shall' have a mandatory flavour (reflected by the word 'shall'). At the First Session of the ICAO Assembly, the adoption of Assembly Resolution A1–31[32] confirmed the mandatory nature of a standard with the definition contained therein:

'Standard' means any specification for physical characteristics, configuration, material, performance, personnel or procedure, the uniform application of which is recognized as necessary for the safety or regularity of international air navigation and to which Contracting States will conform in accordance with the Convention; in the event of impossibility of compliance, notification to the Council is compulsory under Article 38 of the Convention.

Recommended Practices identified by the words 'contracting States may' have only an advisory and recommendatory connotation (reflected by the word 'may'). Although the same Assembly Resolution adopted the following definition:

'Recommended Practice' means any specification for physical characteristics, configuration, material, performance, personnel or procedure, the uniform application of which is recognized as desirable in the interest of safety, regularity or efficiency of international air navigation, and to which Contracting States will endeavour to conform in accordance with the Convention.

It is interesting that at least one ICAO document[33] requires States under Article 38 of the Convention, to notify ICAO of all significant differences from both Standards and Recommended Practices, thus making all SARPS regulatory in nature.

The above definitions were later confirmed as valid and effectual by *Appendix E* to Assembly Resolution A15–6 at the ICAO Assembly's 15th Session held in Montreal in June/July 1965. This Resolution called for a high degree of stability to be maintained so that Contracting States could achieve the necessary stability in their national regulations relating to international air navigation. Another factor which the Assembly took into account when considering the role of SARPS was that in fixing the dates for their application, the Assembly laid down the requirement that sufficient time should be given for states to complete arrangements that are necessary for the implementation of SARPS and change their national regulations accordingly.

Other measures were taken by the ICAO Assembly at its 15th Session to ensure the implementation of *SARPS*. They addressed the financial and procedural problems that most states faced in the implementation of these provisions. Consequently, the Assembly established principles that were calculated to facilitate the implementation by states of SARPS, and states were requested to adapt their procedures accordingly, to ensure the implementation of SARPS, thereby ensuring secure, safe and regular air services.[34] Consideration was also given to the possibility of some states finding it difficult to keep their national regulations and operating instructions up-to-date with the Annexes. The Assembly therefore requested Council to seek measures to facilitate the task of states in instituting ICAO practices and procedures at their operating installations. For this purpose, the Assembly also authorized the Council to deviate from present policies and practices relative to the content, applicability and amendment of the Annexes, other than the provision of the Convention, if the Council found such deviation unavoidable in order to accomplish the objective.

It is clear therefore that in adopting the Annexes and including in them SARPS, the ICAO Assembly has ensured that the Council follows established customary practice at international law to ensure that SARPS had the effect of legal principles, by making inroads into the laws of states and introducing a uniform regulatory structure within a particular community of states.

Another strong factor that reflects the overall ability and power of the Council to prescribe civil rules of conduct (and therefore legislate) on a strict interpretation of the word is that in Article 22 of the Convention each contracting state agrees to adopt all practical measures through the issuance of special regulations or otherwise, to facilitate and expedite air navigation. It is clear that this provision can be regarded as an incontrovertible rule of conduct that responds to the requirement in Article 54 (l) of the Convention. Furthermore, the mandatory nature of Article 90 of the Convention – that an Annex or amendment thereto shall become effective within three months after it is submitted by the ICAO Council to contracting states, is yet another endorsement of the power of the Council to prescribe rules of state conduct in matters of international civil aviation. *A fortiori*, it is arguable that the Council is seen not only to possess the attribute of 'jurisfaction' (the power to make rules of conduct) but also 'jurisaction' (the power to enforce its own rules of conduct). The latter attribute can be seen where the Convention obtains the undertaking of contracting states not to allow airlines to operate through their airspace if the Council decides that the airline concerned is not conforming to a final decision rendered by the Council on a matter that concerns the operation of an international airline.[35] This is particularly applicable when such an airline is found not to conform to the provisions of Annex 2 to the Convention that derives its validity from Article 12 of the Convention relating to rules of the air.[36] In fact, it is very relevant that Annex 2, the responsibility for the promulgation of which devolves upon the Council by virtue of Article 54 (l), sets mandatory rules of the air, making the existence of the legislative powers of the Council an unequivocal and irrefutable fact.

Academic and professional opinion also favours the view that in a practical sense, the ICAO Council does have legislative powers. Professor Michael Milde says:

> The Chicago Convention, as any other legal instrument, provides only a general legal framework which is given true life only in the practical implementation of its provisions. Thus, for example, Article 37 of the Convention relating to the adoption of international standards and recommended procedures would be a very hollow and meaningless provision without active involvement of all contracting States, Panels, Regional and Divisional Meetings, deliberations in the Air Navigation Commission and final adoption of the standards by the Council. Similarly, provisions of Article 12 relating to the rules of the air applicable over the high seas, Articles 17 to 20 on the nationality of aircraft, Article 22 on facilitation, Article 26 on the investigation of accidents, etc., would be meaningless without appropriate implementation in the respective Annexes. On the same level is the provision of the last sentence of Article 77 relating to the determination by the Council in what manner the provisions of the Convention relating to nationality of aircraft shall apply to aircraft operated by international operating agencies.[37]

Professor Milde concludes that ICAO has regulatory and quasi-legislative functions in the technical field and plays a consultative and advisory role in the economic sphere.[38] A similar view had earlier been expressed by Buergenthal who states:

> the manner in which the International Civil Aviation organization has exercised its regulatory functions in matters relating to the safety of international air navigation and the facilitation of international air transport provides a fascinating example of international law making ... the Organization has consequently not had to contend with any of the post war ideological differences that have impeded international law making on politically sensitive issues.[39]

Paul Stephen Dempsey endorses in a somewhat conservative manner, the view that ICAO has the ability to make regulations:

> In addition to the comprehensive, but largely dormant adjudicative enforcement held by ICAO under Articles 84–88 of the Chicago Convention, the Agency also has a solid foundation for enhanced participation in economic regulatory aspects of international aviation in Article 44, as well as the Convention's Preamble.[40]

Another significant attribute of the legislative capabilities of the ICAO Council is its ability to adopt technical standards as Annexes to the Convention without going through a lengthy process of ratification.[41] Eugene Sochor refers to the Council as a powerful and visible body in international aviation.[42] It is interesting, however, to note that although by definition the ICAO Council has been considered by some as unable to deal with strictly legal matters since other important matters come within its purview,[43] this does not derogate the compelling facts that reflect the distinct law-making abilities of ICAO. Should this not be true, the functions that the Convention assigns to ICAO in Article 44 – that ICAO's aims and objectives are 'to develop the principles and techniques of international air navigation and to foster the planning and development of international air transport' – would be rendered destitute of effect.

The above discussion makes it clear that the Chicago Convention has, through the Assembly and Council of ICAO, legitimately and according to customary international law, created a regulatory framework through its Annexes to legally implement its policy. The measures taken by the Assembly in promulgating the SARPS of ICAO in order that states may not find practical and philosophical difficulties in implementing such, together with the fact that the 18 Annexes ensure the establishment of a uniform regulatory structure in international civil aviation, thus bringing ICAO member states under one regulatory umbrella, is typical of the principles of customary international law. In the face of such compelling evidence, the fact that Article 54 (l) of the Chicago Convention provides that the Annexes are named as such for convenience, becomes irrelevant at law.

Other Sources of International Law

In international law, although there is a distinction between formal and material sources, it is often difficult to maintain. What matters really is that sources, of whatever nature they may be, are the important reflectors of evidence of the existence of consensus among states concerning certain rules, regulations and practices that would obtain at international law. Ian Brownlie is of the view:

> ... decisions of the International Court, resolutions of the General Assembly of the United Nations, and 'law making' multilateral treaties are very material evidence of the attitude of States toward particular rules, and the presence or absence of consensus. Moreover, there is a process of interaction which gives these evidences a status somewhat higher than mere 'material sources'. Thus neither an unratified treaty nor a report of the International Law Commission to the General Assembly has any binding force either in the law of treaties or otherwise. However, such instruments stand as candidates for public reaction, approving or not, as the case may be: they may stand for a threshold of consensus and confront states in a significant way.[44]

The law of treaties on the one hand addresses questions relating to the content of obligations between states, and, on the other, relates to the incidence of obligations resulting from express agreement by and between states. Treaties are usually considered as falling under two headings: treaties which incorporate particular international law; and those which incorporate general international law. If one were to analyse finely the distinction between these two treaties one could assume that while the former binds a few states, the latter is more multilateral and would be considered as treaties which make law on a general basis. There is, however, no fundamental difference between the two categories as both types of treaties bind the states' parties to obligations stipulated therein.

The work of the International Court of Justice Article 38.1 of the Statute of the International Court of Justice (ICJ) provides that the ICJ, in settling international disputes, will apply: international conventions, whether general or particular; international custom; the general principles of law as recognized by civilised nations; and, judicial decisions and the teachings of the most highly qualified publicists of the various nations, as subsidiary means for the determination of the rules of law. As far as judicial decisions are concerned as binding precedents, the ICJ is constrained by Article 59 of its own statute which stipulates that the decision of the Court has no binding force except between the parties and in respect of a particular case.

Although the provisions in Article 38.1 are expressed in terms of the function of the court, and the elements therein are by no means explicitly referred to as sources, Article 38 is generally considered as a statement comprising sources of international law. Brownlie observes that these sources are not stated to represent a hierarchy, but the draftsmen intended to give an order and in one draft the word 'successively' appeared.[45] Brownlie concludes that in general Article 38 does not rest upon a distinction between formal and material sources, and a system of priority application depends simply on the order (a) to (d) in all cases.[46]

The recent ICJ hearing of the PAN-AM case is of particular relevance to the subject of the effect of ICJ decisions on air law. Although this decision will be discussed in some detail in Chapter 2, it would be relevant at this stage to examine the general position of the ICJ *vis-à-vis* the Security Council, as both are primary organs of the United Nations, and a certain clash of interests between the two organs can be perceived in the ICJ's judicial consideration of Security Council decisions.

The International Court of Justice is the principal judicial organ of the United Nations, and, therefore, it is incontrovertible that the ICJ cannot be considered subservient or subsidiary to any other organ of the United Nations.[47] The logical conclusion that would follow from this premise is that the ICJ would have principal jurisdiction or authority over judicial issues and other organs would have principal authority over political and administrative issues. Therefore, if the

ICJ should be considered in its role as the principal judicial authority of the United Nations system, then, its judicial character and integrity, as well as the integrity of the judicial system it portrays must be preserved at all costs. It is submitted that the fundamental argument in this issue should be based on the very nature of international law that the ICJ represents and uses in its adjudicatory process. If one were to impute a certain moral flavour to international law and therefore to the ICJ, then one would be impelled to treat the ICJ as the exclusive authority which administers public international law to the parties which come before it.

There is no presumption in international law that the Security Council and the ICJ cannot concurrently address an issue which is before them. In fact, the two organs did just that in the *Iran Hostages case*[48] In this case, consequent upon the ICJ entertaining a request from one of the parties to the action, the Security Council adopted a resolution of which the preamble took into consideration the order of the ICJ. The Court observed:

> ... it does not seem to have occurred to any member of the Council that there was or could be anything irregular in the simultaneous exercise of their respective functions by the Court and the Security Council. Whereas Article 12 of the Charter expressly forbids the General Assembly to make any recommendation with regard to a dispute or situation while the Security Council is exercising its functions in respect of that dispute or situation, no such restriction is placed on the functioning of the Court. The reasons are clear. It is for the Court, the principal judicial organ of the United Nations, to resolve any legal questions that may be in issue between parties to a dispute; and the resolution of such questions by the Court may be an important, and sometimes decisive factor in promoting the peaceful settlement of the dispute.[49]

The Court also addressed the compelling question of statutory provision on the subject, where Article 36 of the United Nations Charter, in Paragraph 3 provides expressly that the Security Council should also take into consideration that legal disputes should, as a general rule, be referred by parties to the ICJ in accordance with the provisions of the Statute of that court. However, the practical applicability of this principle may become an issue in some instances. Judge Bedjaoui in the PAN-AM case observed:

> ... if the concomitant exercise of concurrent but not exclusive powers has thus far not given rise to serious problems, the present case, by contrast, presents the Court not only with the grave question of the possible influence of the decisions of a principal organ on the consideration of the same question by another principal organ, but also,

> more fundamentally, with the question of the possible inconsistency between the decisions of the two organs and how to deal with so delicate a situation.[50]

Be that as it may, on an overall assessment of the subject, it would not be illogical to conclude that the ICJ could determine legal disputes that are part of a political issue that is addressed concurrently by the Security Council.

Custom as a source and issues of sovereignty Article 38.1.b. of the Statute of the ICJ refers to international custom as an evidential element that can be used as accepted law. There is a palpable difference between custom and usage in this context, where the former is a practice, the sustained use of which gives rise to obligations at law, and the latter remains a practice that is usually only of ceremonial significance. This point was brought out succinctly in the case of *Nicaragua* v. *United States*[51] where the ICJ referred to the *North Sea Continental Shelf Cases* and held:

> In considering the instances of the conduct above described, the Court has to emphasise that, as was observed in the *North Sea Continental Shelf Cases*, for a new customary rule to be formed, not only must the acts concerned 'amount to a settled practice', but they must be accompanied by the *opinio juris sive necessitatis*. Either the States taking such action or other States in a position to react to it, must have behaved so that their conduct is 'evidence of a belief that this practice is rendered obligatory by the existence of a rule of law requiring it. The need for such a belief, i.e. the existence of a subjective element, is implicit in the very notion of the *opinio juris sive necessitatis*.[52]

The application of this judicial dictum to international air law brings out several legal norms that have established themselves as fundamental principles of air law through sustained usage. Sovereignty of states over the airspace above their territories is one such concept.

Sovereignty *inter alia* involves the supreme power of a state to make and administer laws and has two attributes:

1 Internal sovereignty, whereby a state exercises its exclusive right and competence to determine the character of its own institutions and to provide for their function. Internal sovereignty also includes the exclusive power of a state to enact its own internal laws and to ensure their respect.
2 External sovereignty, whereby a state freely determines its relations with other states or entities without the restraint or control of another state.

Territorially, state sovereignty is exercised over all persons and things found on a state's territory, including its airspace.[53] Sovereignty in airspace is therefore an ineluctable characteristic of state sovereignty.

Dr. H.A. Wassenbergh lists seven objectives of a state's policy in respect of modern civil aviation. They are:

1 to contribute to the functioning of the international community of states as a total legal order by upholding and further developing the rule of international law;
2 to protect the integrity and identity of the national society;
3 to promote the nation's participation in mankind's activities in the air and space;
4 to create the best possible conditions and opportunities for use by the public of aviation and space activities;
5 to increase the benefits to be derived from the use of the air and outer space for its nationals;
6 to promote the further development of technology and the knowledge of mankind;
7 to cooperate with other states on the basis of equal rights in order to bridge conflicting national interests and achieve the aims mentioned above.[54]

Paul Steven Dempsey attributes the insistence of mankind on sovereignty to the fact that human beings are territorial beasts whose primordial imperative was to satisfy their thirst for control over a given area.[55] This view seems compatible with the early trends where the Paris Convention[56] provided that each state enjoys complete and exclusive sovereignty over the airspace above its territory.[57] Accordingly, from 1919, transit and landing rights for airlines became notionally subject to the explicit or tacit approval of the state in which the aircraft landed. Later, in August 1945, at the first meeting of the Opening Session of the Interim Council of the Provisional International Civil Aviation Organization (PICAO), the Hon. C.D. Howe, Minister of Reconstruction, Canada said :

> We (Canada) believe that there must be greater freedom for development of international air transport and that this freedom may best be obtained within a framework which provides equality of opportunity and rewards for efficiency.[58]

Dr. Edward Warner, Representative of the United States of America (later the first President of the ICAO Council) said at the same meeting:

> Our first purpose will be to smooth the paths for civil flying wherever we are able. We shall seek to make it physically easier, safer, more

> reliable, more pleasant; but I believe it will be agreed also that we should maintain the constant goal that civil aviation should contribute to international harmony. The civil use of aircraft must so develop as to bring the peoples closer together, letting nation speak more understandingly unto nation.[59]

Dr. Warner had notably stressed on the purpose of civil aviation to be the promotion of international harmony and dialogue between nations. He had also made it clear that the seminal task of civil aviation is to bring the people of the world together through understanding and interaction. It is clear that at this stage at least, civil aviation was recognized more as a social necessity rather than a mere economic factor.

In addition, through the statements of Minister Howe and Dr. Warner, one can glean the attitude of the international community towards aviation at that time:

- that civil aviation was based on equality of opportunity; and,
- that it was a social need rather than a fiscal tool.

If this early view of international civil aviation were to be applied *stricto sensu* now, there would be no need to be apprehensive of whether a state would not allow an aircraft of another state, carrying an offender on board, or whether the former would allow the aircraft to land, and grant the offender asylum in its territory without prosecuting him. Indeed, as one commentator observed:

> The simultaneous existence of many sovereign States in the international community, each one of them wishing to keep its complete sovereign authority intact, has for centuries hampered the employment of the apparatus of international law to its fullest extent. The jealousy with which States guard their complete sovereignty in their airspace is the main reason for the lack of solution of the problem ...[60]

A detailed discussion and analysis of state sovereignty will follow in Chapter 6 of this book.

Judicial decisions and scholastic views as sources Judicial decisions and learned opinions of jurists have also established themselves as significant elements of air law. The direct relevance of these elements to air law are lucidly reflected in the Chicago Convention itself, which empowers the ICAO Council with 'quasi-judicial' powers. Scholastic views attached to this concept may also considered an example of a coercive force in air law.

The Council of ICAO has the power under the Chicago Convention to adjudicate disputes between the member states of ICAO on matters pertaining to international civil aviation. The Council is a permanent body responsible to the ICAO Assembly and is composed of 33 contracting states elected by the Assembly. It has its genesis in the Interim Council of the Provisional International Civil Aviation Organization (PICAO)[61]. PICAO occupied such legal capacity as may have been necessary for the performance of its functions and was recognized as having full juridical personality wherever compatible with the Constitution and the laws of the state concerned.[62] The definitive word 'juridical' attributed to PICAO a mere judicial function, unequivocally stipulating that the organization and its component bodies, such as the Interim Council were obligated to remain within the legal parameters allocated to them by the Interim Agreement[63] and that PICAO was of a purely technical and advisory nature. A legislative or quasi-legislative function could not therefore be imputed to the Interim Council of PICAO. It could mostly study, interpret and advise on standards and procedures[64] and make recommendations with respect to technical matters through the Committee on Air Navigation.[65] The International Civil Aviation Organization (ICAO) which saw the light of day on 4 April 1947 derived the fundamental postulates of its technical and administrative structure from its progenitor – PICAO – and it would seem reasonable to attribute a certain affinity *ipso facto* between the two organizations and hence, their Councils. One of the Council's functions is to consider any matter relating to the Convention which any contracting state refers to it.[66] Since one of the distinctive features of the ICAO Council is its ability to make rules for international civil aviation, it follows incontrovertibly that the Council's dispute resolution powers are compelling.

Under the Interim Agreement[67] the PICAO Council was required to act as an arbitral body on any differences arising among member states relating to matters of international civil aviation which may be submitted to it, wherein the Interim Council of PICAO was empowered to render an advisory report or if the parties involved so wished, give a decision on the matter before it.[68] The Interim Council, which was the precursor to the ICAO Council, set the stage therefore for providing the Council with unusual arbitral powers which are not attributed to similar organs of the specialized agencies of the United Nations system.[69] *A fortiori,* since the ICAO Council is permanent and is almost in constant session, contracting states could expect any matter of dispute brought by them before the Council to be dealt with, without unreasonable delay.[70]

Chapter XVIII of the Convention formalizes the arbitral powers of the Council by stating:

> If any disagreement between two or more contracting States relating to the interpretation or application of this Convention and its Annexes

> cannot be settled by negotiation, **it shall** [emphasis added], on the application of any State concerned in the disagreement, be decided by the Council ...[71]

This provision reflects two significant points: the first is that contracting states should first attempt to resolve their disputes by themselves, through negotiation[72]; the second is that the word **shall** in this provision infuse into the decision-making powers of the Council an unquestionably mandatory character. Furthermore, a decision taken by the Council is juridically dignified by Article 86 of the Convention, when the Article states that unless the Council decides otherwise, any decision by the Council on whether an international airline is operating in conformity with the provisions of the Convention shall remain in effect unless reversed in appeal. The Council also has powers of sanction granted by the Convention, if its decision is not adhered to.[73] Schenkman states:

> The power of sanctions in this field is an entirely new phenomenon, attributed to an aeronautical body... none of the pre-war instruments in the field of aviation had the power of sanctions as a means of enforcement of its decisions.[74]

Most contracting States have, on their own initiative, enacted dispute-settlement clauses in their bilateral air services agreements wherein provision is usually made to refer inter-state disputes relating to international civil aviation to the ICAO Council, in accordance with Chapter XVIII of the Convention. In this context, it is also relevant to note that the President of the Council is empowered by the Convention to appoint an arbitrator and an umpire in certain circumstances leading to an appeal from a decision of the Council.[75]

A most interesting aspect of the ICAO Council remains to be that one of its mandatory functions is to consider any subject referred to it by a contracting state for its consideration,[76] or any subject which the President of the Council or the Secretary General of the ICAO Secretariat desires to bring before the Council.[77] Although the Council is bound to consider a matter submitted to it by a contracting state it can refrain from giving a decision as the Council is only obligated to consider a matter before it.

There seems to be an unfortunate dichotomy in terminology in the Convention since on the one hand, Article 54 (n) makes it mandatory that the Council shall merely consider any matter relating to the Convention which any contracting state refers to it, while on the other, Article 84 categorically states that any disagreement between two or more states relating to the interpretation or application of the Convention and its Annexes, that cannot be settled by negotiation shall ... be decided by the Council. The difficulty arises on a strict interpretation of Article 54 (n) where even a disagreement between two states as envisaged under Article 84 could well be considered as 'any matter' under Article 54 (n). In such an instance, the Council could well be faced with the dilemma of choosing between the two provisions. It would not be incorrect for the Council to merely consider a matter placed before it, although a decision is requested by the applicant state, since, Article 54 (n) is perceived to be comprehensive as the operative and controlling provision that lays down mandatory functions of the Council. It is indeed unfortunate that these two provisions obfuscate the issue which otherwise would have given a clear picture of the decision-making powers of the Council. A further thread in the fabric of adjudicatory powers of the Council is found in Article 14 of the Rules of Settlement promulgated by the Council in 1957[78] which allows the Council to request the parties in dispute to engage in direct negotiations at any time.[79] This emphasis on conciliation has prompted the view that the Council, under article 84, would favour the settling of disputes rather than adjudicating them.[80] This view seems compatible with the proposition that the consideration of a matter under Article 54 (n) would be a more attractive approach *in limine* in a matter of dispute between two states.

Dempsey points out that in the four decades since the promulgation of Chapter XVIII, only three disputes had been submitted to the Council for formal resolution:[81] the first involved a dispute between India and Pakistan (1952), where India complained that Pakistan was in breach of the Convention by not permitting Indian aircraft to overfly Pakistani airspace on their way to Afghanistan; the second was a complaint filed by the United Kingdom against Spain (1969), alleging the violation by Spain of the Convention by the establishment of a prohibited zone over Gibraltar; and the third was a complaint by Pakistan against India (1971), concerning a hijacking of Indian aircraft which landed in Pakistan. India unilaterally suspended Pakistan's overflying privileges, five days after the hijacking. The first complaint was amicably resolved by the parties, the second was differed by the parties *sine die*, and the third was suspended with the formation of the State of Bangladesh in 1972, even though the matter had been processed as an appeal from the Council to the International Court of Justice. Unfortunately, none of these instances was taken to its conclusion so that the world could have the opportunity to evaluate clearly ICAO's decision-making process.

Professor Milde noted in 1979:

> The Council of ICAO cannot be considered a suitable body for adjudication in the proper sense of the word – that is, settlement of disputes

> by judges and solely on the basis of respect for law. The Council is composed of States (not independent individuals) and its decisions would always be based on policy and equity considerations rather than on pure legal grounds ... truly legal disputes ... can be settled only by a true judicial body which can bring into the procedure full judicial detachment, independence and expertise. The under-employed ICJ is the most suitable body for such types of disputes.[82]

The perceived inadequacies of the ICAO Council in being ethically unsuitable to decide on disputes between states can only be alleviated by the thought that the members of the Council are presumed to be well versed in matters of international civil aviation and therefore would be deemed to be better equipped to comprehend the issues placed before them than the distinguished members of the International Court of Justice, some of whom may not be experts of international air law. Nonetheless, there is no doubt that the ICAO Council possesses juridical powers[83] and that as one commentator said:

> If ICAO did not exist, it would have to be invented; otherwise, international civil aviation would not function with the safety, efficiency and regularity that it has achieved today.[84]

The United Nations Decade of International Law

Introduction

On 17 November 1989 the United Nations General Assembly adopted Resolution 44/23 which declared that the period 1990 to 1999 be designated as the United Nations Decade of International Law. The main purposes of the Decade have been identified *inter alia* as:

- The promotion of the acceptance of the principles of international law and respect therefor;
- The promotion of the means and methods for the peaceful settlement of disputes between States including resort to the International Court of Justice with full respect therefor,
- The full encouragement of the progressive development of international law and its codification;
- The encouragement of the teaching, studying, dissemination and wider appreciation of international law.

The four main tasks of the Resolution have been based on the fact that the purpose of the United Nations is to maintain peace and security, to which end the adjustment or settlement of disputes among states is paramount. The end itself is achievable through the promotion of the principles of international law by the evolved teaching, study, dissemination and wider appreciation of international law. The sum total of the aim of Resolution 44/23 is therefore to strengthen the rule of law in international relations.

The Resolution demonstrates two facts clearly – that there is an identified lacuna in the appreciation and acceptance of the principles of international law by states and that such an inadequacy erodes the concept of international peace and security which the United Nations is pledged to maintain. It would be worthwhile therefore, to examine at the start of the decade, the position of international law in the eyes of states and how it could help achieve the goals of the United Nations if the contents of Resolution 44/23 attained fruition at the end of the decade. This article would therefore examine the legal possibilities that United Nations General Assembly Resolution 44/23 would open to persuade states to accept international law and its principles as a stronger source of dispute settlement. It would also be worthwhile to see whether more binding authority may be attributed to the principles of international law by the sustained programme of awareness planned by the United Nations over the next decade.

The United Nations General Assembly

The General Assembly is the plenary organ of the United Nations[85] comprising all member states, each with one vote. The Assembly is a deliberative organ which depends on resorting to making recommendations rather than binding decisions. Therefore, it is far from legislative in nature although its recommendatory functions often result in the Assembly being considered political, moral and persuasive. This reputation has an overall effect of United Nations General Assembly Resolutions being regarded at least as morally binding on states.[86] No international agencies however, are authorized to enforce international law[87] and to this extent the United Nations General Assembly stands bereft of legal enforcement powers *stricto sensu*. The interesting aspect of the United Nations General Assembly powers is that although, primarily, its function is to initiate studies and make recommendations for the purpose of:

> ... promoting international co-operation in the economic, cultural, educational and health fields and assisting in the realization of human rights and fundamental freedoms for all without distinctions as to race, sex, language or religion.[88]

There have been instances where such studies and recommendations have resulted in resolutions that eventually become law. For instance, the resolutions adopted by the General Assembly on principles for outer space in 1961 and 1963 were incorporated later in the 1967 Treaty on Outer Space.[89] An additional factor that stands in favour of the implementation of the United Nations General Assembly Resolution is that the Assembly may obtain the support of the Security Council of the United Nations to make a resolution applicable. One of the significant events where this practice was put into effect was in the formative stages of the United Nations when changes were sought by the General Assembly of the United Nations in 1946 in Spain and the Assembly sought the Council to exercise its responsibilities under the United Nations Charter and bring about the necessary persuasion to remedy the situation in Spain.[90]

The General Assembly usually adopts several measures to ensure that its resolutions are implemented. Firstly, it recommends the implementation of its resolutions to individual member states. Secondly, it may also enlist the support of other organs and agencies of the United Nations. Thirdly, it may even establish special machinery to perform specific functions towards implementing its resolutions. The objectives of the United Nations General Assembly in ensuring the implementation of its resolutions is to achieve ultimately its overall aim of attaining international peace and security and promoting general welfare and friendly relations among nations. In this context Resolution 44/23 has a special significance in that before the United Nations was established, the most dramatic and prominent weakness of traditional international law was in its characteristic of yielding to the use of force by individual states to compel another state or person to comply with its will[91] while international law itself stood by bereft of enforcing power or machinery. The establishment of the United Nations – a well developed international organization with competent powers to maintain peace, portended in 1945 a different outlook for the principles of international law. It is therefore incontrovertible that with the entry of the United Nations into the world arena the mere theoretical basis of the impotency of international law has indeed taken new dimensions. The establishment of the International Court of Justice (ICJ),[92] the adjudication of international disputes between states and the stringent action that may be taken by the Security Council are all steps in this direction. Resolution 44/23 could well be the final progressive step.

The Acceptance of International Law by States

The enforcement of international law is strictly the purview of the national states and each state claims sovereignty to the extent that it is its own source of authority and power. In this sense, international law has no overall application on a common basis where each state can be held responsible for the adherence to a unified set of mandatory rules that can be set and enforced by one supreme legislative body. On a juridical basis however, this primitive antithesis does not leave the world totally destitute of hope. It is now very apparent that with all its inadequacies, international law is at least an entity whose presence is felt. Indeed as a legal scholar recently stated:

> If one doubts the significance of this law, one need only imagine a world from which it were absent ... There would be no security of nations or stability of governments; territory and air space would not be respected; vessels could navigate only at their constant peril; property – within or without any given territory – would be subject to arbitrary seizure; persons would have no protection of law or of diplomacy; agreements would not be made or observed; diplomatic relations would end; international trade would cease; international organizations and arrangements would disappear.[93]

Logically speaking, it would therefore seem that international law establishes ethical and moral dimensions that have proven to be accepted and followed by the United Nations member states. A further indication that principles of international law have been accepted may be found in those instances in which an injured state resorts to self-help in response to branches of international law. For example, when its airspace is encroached upon, the state may request a forced landing of the offending aircraft in its territory or guide the aircraft out of its territory. The absence of organized sanctions does not create a hiatus that cannot be bridged.

The maintenance of international peace and security is an important objective of the United Nations,[94] which recognizes one of its purposes as being *inter alia*:

> To maintain international peace and security, and to that end: take effective collective measures for the prevention and removal of threats to the peace, and for the suppression of acts of aggression or other breaches of peace, and to bring about by peaceful means, and in conformity with the principles of justice and international law, adjustment or settlement of international disputes or situations which might lead to a breach of the peace.[95]

It is clear that the United Nations has recognized the application of the principles of international law as an integral part of maintaining international peace and security and avoiding situations which may lead to a breach of the peace.[96] The United Nations Charter from which Resolution 44/23 obtains its validity makes States fundamentally promise to settle their disputes by peaceful means and to refrain from the use of threat or force against each other.[96] The power and influence of this document has been so great that:

> ... the law of the Charter, the wide acceptance of that law by governments and peoples, and authority of the United Nations and world opinion behind the law and other political reactions (stronger because war has been outlawed) can claim substantial credit for the fact that the world has avoided major war since 1945...

The personality and character of law and the possibility of it being followed hinge firstly on the personality of the leadership from which the law emanates[97]. Therefore it is appropriate that a leadership of the stature of the United Nations endeavours to strengthen international law by its Resolution 44/23.

The extent to which the stature of international law has been enhanced by the United Nations is evident in yet another legal and political phenomenon – the international sanction. An essential corollary of international law and the moral and ethical fibres of the Charter of the United Nations, this measure, like the previously discussed measure of self-help is now widely used by one nation against another. The reasons for application of sanctions is often the same – as retaliation against the action of one state calculated to breach provisions of the United Nations Charter. The use of self-help and the imposition of sanctions are two clear and forceful instances in which both the force and the acceptability of international law are recognized by states. Although some still believe that sanctions are not effective tools of statecraft that would result in punitive action with anticipated results,[99] there is now strong contrary opinion that the application of sanctions does effectively enhance the principles of international comity.[100] While some view economic sanctions as mere tools that are used to achieve foreign policy goals,[101] the fact remains that, in the ultimate analysis, a sanction effectively punishes an offending state and to that extent supplements the punitive element in international law.[102]

Past Achievements of the United Nations

Fundamentally, the role of the United Nations in international legal affairs is to promote the peaceful settlement of disputes between states and to endeavour to develop and codify international law. Therefore, the United Nations views international law in its purest form as a set of rules to be followed by member states. Needless to say, the United Nations has nothing to do with the measures adopted by some states, either in using self-help measures or sanctions against others. Regardless, the United Nations has gone on over the past 45 years developing conventions and establishing and recommending international codes of behaviour for member states to follow. Its achievements in the field of international law are best summed up by Secretary General Perez de Cuellar when he said in 1985:

> In the past 40 years more has been done by the United Nations in codifying international law than in all previous years of history together. In 1873 when the International Law Association was founded, there were no more than 133 multilateral treaties in the whole world. As against this, the United Nations has secured the conclusion of as many as 350 multilateral agreements including some of fundamental importance. Moreover, in the past, multilateral treaties rarely had more than 10 parties. Nowadays, a typical United Nations Convention has at least 50 parties; some major ones have over 100. The diversity of subjects covered is indeed phenomenal, some of them touching on most aspects of daily life and all testifying to the variety of concerns of the international community in a world of growing interdependence.[103]

Some of the significant areas in which the United Nations has done creditable work are international terrorism, hostage-taking, mercenaries, outer space, international civil aviation and law of the sea. All treaties that are introduced by the United Nations have the entrenched principle of international law that:

> Contracting parties are always assumed to be acting honestly and in good faith. That is a legal principle, which is recognized in private law and cannot be ignored in international law.[104]

The basic premise of the international law of treaties as endorsed by the United Nations is that an obligation has to be fulfilled in good faith and not merely according to what is written in the treaty. In other words, international law is founded on considerate policy, good faith and good conduct. It is non-exploitative, however advantageous a treaty provision may seem to a state. Indeed, in the 1910 decision of the Permanent Court of Arbitration this principle has been well stated when the court said:

> Every state has to execute the obligations incurred by treaty bona fide, and is urged thereto by ordinary sanctions of international law in regard to observance of treaty obligations.[105]

All treaties are binding on the parties to the treaties on the principle *pacta sunt servanda*.[106] A treaty is a solemn compact between nations and:

> ... it possesses in ordinary the same essential qualities as a contract between individuals, enhanced by the weightier quality of the parties

> and by the greater magnitude of the subject matter. To be valid, it imports a mutual assent.[107]

International law relating to multilateral or bilateral treaties as endorsed by the United Nations dictates that a party may not unilaterally free itself from the engagement of a treaty or modify its provisions. The treaty has to be honoured without reservation as long as it remains valid, and the doctrine *clausula rebus sic stantibus* – that changed circumstances alter obligations under a contract – does not apply under the international law of treaties except in those instances where a treaty cannot be deemed to apply to circumstances not envisaged at the time the treaty was made.[108]

It is now evident that the United Nations derives its very authority and sustenance from international law and its principles. As President Nixon, addressing the United Nations General Assembly in September 1969 – on the eve of the 25th Anniversary of the United Nations – said:

> For the first time ever, we have truly become a single world community ... technological advance has brought within reach what once was only a poignant dream for hundreds of millions ... in this new age of 'first' even the goal of a just and lasting peace is a 'first' we can dare to strive for.[109]

The goal of a just and lasting peace can only be achieved through adherence to a set of mutually acceptable rules of conduct. If this fact was apparent after the first 25 years of the existence of the United Nations it is now even more prominently seen in the statement of Secretary General Perez de Cuellar:

> After 40 years we have, for the first time in history, a virtually universal world organization. We have also for the first time in history, a world of independent sovereign States ... We have achieved unprecedented economic growth and social progress ... We are making collective efforts to the new generation of global problems.[110]

Resolution 44/23 in Action

The Resolution itself consists of two main thrusts. These are the promotion and expansion of international law among states. Its promotional role consists of such elements as respect for the principles of international law, the peaceful settlement of disputes between states and the progressive development of international law and its codification. Its expansionist role includes the teaching, study and dissemination of international law. It is best for the effective implementation of Resolution 44/23 that these two areas are handled separately. The first (promotion) would essentially have to be achieved by the International Court of Justice, the International Law Commission and certain other United Nations Agencies involved with the promotion of international law.[111] The expansion of international law by the implementation of teaching programmes that bring about its wider appreciation would have to be accomplished by such United Nations assistance programmes as the United Nations Development Programme (UNDP) and United Nations Educational Social and Cultural Organization (UNESCO). The more important factor in the latter objective of teaching and studying international law is not the procedural side but the philosophical approach to the subject. Wider appreciation of and education in the international law must necessarily be approached from the standpoint of contemporary international problems and not mere conceptual values of the subject.

The Promotion of International Law

The perceived inadequacies of international arbitration were first brought to light at the Second World Peace Conference of the League of Nations held at the Hague in 1907. A draft convention was prepared, Article 14 of which established a Permanent Court of International Justice (PCIJ).[112] The Statute of the Court was drafted in 1920 and one of the main objectives of the Court was deemed to be to perform an essential function in giving the proper interpretation to the rules of international law.[113] Now called the International Court of Justice (ICJ) it is both the principle judicial limb and one of the six major organs of the United Nations.[114] The Statute of the Court is an integral part of the United Nations Charter.[115] The International Court of Justice does not have compulsory jurisdiction[116] although Article 38 of the Statute of the Court stipulates that the Court may apply international conventions, international customs and the general principles of law as accepted by civilized nations as a primary means of adjudication and the opinions of recognized teachers, scholars and jurists as a subsidiary or secondary means of adjudication. However, by virtue of Article 36 (2) of the Statute of the International Court of Justice any member state of the United Nations may declare itself bound by a decision of the Court in which case an adjudication between two such adhering states would be binding on the parties concerned. Called the optional clause, Article 36 (2) had only been ratified by 45 states in 1985 – less than one-third of the membership of the United Nations.

Article 13 of the Charter of the United Nations provides that:

> The General Assembly shall initiate studies and make recommendations for the purpose of:

a) promoting international co-operation in the political field and encouraging the progressive development of international law and its codification;
b) promoting international co-operation in the economic, social, cultural, educational and health fields, and assisting in the realization of human rights and fundamental freedoms for all without distinction as to race, six, language or religion.

This article bifurcates international cooperation into the elements of political and other fields – the latter to include all aspects of human existence other than political. The political element is therefore a prominent one as against all other common elements, and is associated with international law, making it arguably the most important developmental area of the United Nations programme. The progressive development and codification of international law is therefore the core of Resolution 44/23, affecting both the promotional and teaching aspects of the subject that are envisioned in the implementation of the Resolution.

The International Law Commission was established by the United Nations for the purpose of initiating various studies that have since resulted in the adoption of important conventions. Some of the major contributions of the Commission have been the Vienna Diplomatic and Consular Relations Conventions (1961 and 1963 respectively), the Geneva Conference on Statelessness (1959) followed by the one in New York (1961), the Vienna Convention on the Law of the Treaties (1969) and the various studies it has undertaken from time to time on such matters as the Nuremberg Trials principles, the rights and duties of states, offences against the peace and security of humankind and the definition of aggression.

There are of course other United Nations Agencies that have been appointed from time to time by the General Assembly to promote areas of international law. In 1965, under this programme, the General Assembly appointed a ten-member advisory committee on a programme of technical assistance charged with the teaching, studying and disseminating of a wider acceptance of international law. These and other organizations, such as the International Labour Organization (ILO), which has seen the ratification of more than 160 conventions on international labour law, the United Nations Development Programme (UNDP), and the United Nations Institute for Training and Research, have amply demonstrated the relevance of threads of international law which have run consistently through the fabric of the United Nations Organization.

The Expansion of International Law

The expansion or the teaching of international law is the second limb of Resolution 44/23. In view of the already established machinery for the promotion of international law, it is arguably the one that needs more attention. If a teaching and expansion programme of international law over the 1990s is to succeed, the subject itself must be approached from both its proactive and reactive bases. In other words, world awareness, both scholastically and professionally, should focus on the positive achievements of which international law is capable and the responsive contribution it can make to the world community. On its positive or proactive side are the prevention of war and on its responsive or reactive side are dispute settlement and international adjudication. If the teaching of international law were to have its desired effect of obtaining more acceptance and world awareness, however, a third element, that of obtaining world consensus and agreement on its binding force would be the most important element.

The teaching of international law should therefore be devoid of the shackles of conceptualism, to the extent that basic principles should address current problems. For example, the concept of international war as analysed by early western philosophers[117] should be expanded to envelope modern exigencies of war and invasion. The early concepts of naturalism, positivism and socialism should be studied in the context of modern day exigencies. The role of international law in its positive sense should then be seen to enforce a machinery that is internationally credible. The element of credibility comes not only in the establishment of the sanction-carrying machinery but also in the logicality of international law as it has evolved over the years. It is crucial to the study of international law to avoid dissent on the concepts by following either the positivist, naturalist or eclectic schools and instead enunciate one common value judgement as the fundamental postulate that:

> The human race though divided into different nations and states still has a certain unity, not only as a species but, as it were, politically and morally as is indicated by the precept of mutual love and charity which extends to all, even to strangers of any nation whatsoever.[118]

The commonality of nations is the most crucial binding thread in the fabric of international law without which the world would end in chaos.[119] This principle should be the most fundamental in any law student's mind and would form a firm basis for the implementation of Resolution 44/23. Students of international law should be exposed to the various levels of discourse affecting international relations today, be it in outer space matters, civil aviation or maritime issues *inter alia*. They should be made totally aware of and be informed of the positive achievements of international law through the United Nations. They should be made to understand that non-violent sanctions have in the past succeeded in being tools that prevent the success of belligerence or aggression rather than being modes of punishment.[120] As important for study are the reasons for the failure of multilateralism at a time when it is needed most[121] and the widespread claim that international law remains a toothless tiger due to its lack of punitive powers. Above all, a study programme under Resolution 44/23 should contain an analytical study of the development of the positive aspects of international law in the environment of today's world in order that these positive elements be further developed. The study of international law should therefore be developed into being the following of a creative set of principles which, within its sphere evokes a steady evolution into new rules to cope with emerging world problems.

Subsequent United Nations Resolutions

The United Nations General Assembly followed up its Resolution 44/23 by adopting Resolution 45/40[122] which expressed its appreciation to states and international organizations for taking the initiative to sponsor conferences on various subjects of international law. The Resolution also invited international organizations and institutions to undertake the relevant activities outlined in Resolution 44/23 and appealed to states, international organizations and non-governmental organizations working in this field and to the private sector to make financial contributions in kind for the purpose of facilitating the implementation of the programme. The Annex to Resolution 45/40 invited states to consider, if they had not already done so, becoming parties to existing multilateral treaties; providing assistance and technical advice to states together with international organizations; and reporting to the Secretary General on ways and means, as provided by the multilateral treaties to which they are parties, regarding the implementation of international treaties.

The General Assembly has underlined in Resolution 45/40 that the fundamental postulate on which the success of the implementation of the programme of the United Nations Decade of International Law is based is the maintenance of international peace and security.[123] The impact of this focus and consideration of whether the total approach to international law should hinge on the maintenance of peace and security would depend on the coercive legal effect that General Assembly Resolutions may have on the international community as a whole and states separately.

The Charter of the United Nations contains no provisions on the legal status of General Assembly Resolutions. Nevertheless, the international community places great emphasis on these resolutions as being the collective will of the international community. But, although there is uncertainty about the status of the resolutions, one cannot deny that resolutions, which are in some measure expression of the wills of most nations, will be considered to be of great weight by the international community. Lauterpacht observed:

> Whatever may be the content of the Resolution and whatever may be the nature and circumstances of the majority by which it has been reached, it is nevertheless a legal act of a principal organ of the United Nations which Members of the United Nations are under a duty to treat with a degree of respect.[124]

Notwithstanding Lauterpacht's somewhat cautious approach in not ascribing to the General Assembly the full status of a legislative body, it must be inferred by his words that in the presence of special tools that the General Assembly is endowed with – such as sanctions – he ascribes to the General Assembly full legal status as a coercive body which cannot be easily dismissed by the international community.

It is also worthy to note that M. Alejandro,[125] a former judge of the International Court of Justice, takes the extreme view that resolutions of the United Nations are binding upon states. Kelsen[126] however, is of the view that these resolutions are only of a recommendatory nature.

The United Nations General Assembly, however, serves other intents and purposes as well as its coercive role. They are generally considered to express the moral conscience of mankind and the General Assembly is therefore capable of exerting moral coercion on the international community. Arguably, there are situations which precipitate international crises where it may be desirable to depend on moral force alone, which is one of the major attributes of General Assembly Resolutions. They have exhibited an ability to infuse an aura of authority to states in the absence of an international enforcement authority. There General Assembly resolutions act as a means of insuring the endorsement of states of the intent of the international community the refusal of which may result in at least a moral reprobation by the rest of the international community.

In the light of the above, it is somewhat disappointing that the dedication of the current decade to international law has been narrowed down to the elements of peace and security, although the primary importance of these elements in the modern context cannot be denied.

Resolution 45/40 also mandated the committee implementing the programme to consider strengthening the use of means and methods for the peaceful settlement of disputes (with particular attention to the role played by the United Nations); ways and means of encouraging greater recognition of the role of the international court of justice and its wider use in the peaceful settlement of disputes; and the enhancement of co-operation of regional organizations within the United Nations system in respect of the peaceful settlement of disputes. States were invited to submit their observations on these issues.[127] At the same meeting, the General Assembly considered the Report of the International Law Commission, wherein the Assembly recalled the main purposes of the decade, that is, the promotion of the maintenance of peace and security among nations and noted with appreciation the work of the Commission on the Draft Code of Crimes against the Peace and Security of Mankind.[128]

At its 67th Plenary Meeting in December 1991, the General Assembly adopted Resolution 46/53,[129] which recalled the seminal Resolution 44/23 and encouraged states and relevant international organizations and institutions to update or supplement information on activities they had undertaken in the implementation of the programme. At the same session the Assembly also adopted Resolution 46/54[130] on the Report of the International Law Commission and expressed its appreciation to the Commission on its work *inter alia* on the possible establishment of an international criminal jurisdiction.

In November 1992 the General Assembly adopted Resolution 47/32[131] which further mandated the Sixth Committee of the United Nations which was given the task to implement work on the programme to consider the following:

- strengthening the use of means and methods for the peaceful settlement of disputes, with particular attention to the role to be played by the United Nations, as well as methods for early identification and prevention of disputes arising in specific areas of international law;
- establishing procedures for the peaceful settlement of disputes arising in specific areas of international law;
- introducing ways and means of encouraging greater recognition of the role of the International Court of Justice and its wider use in the peaceful settlement of disputes;
- enhancing cooperation of regional organizations with the United Nations' system of organizations in respect of the peaceful settlement of disputes; and,
- using the Permanent Court of Arbitration in a wider context.[132]

At its 48th Session in 1993, the General Assembly adopted Resolution 48/30[133] which, *inter alia*, decided that a United Nations Congress on Public International Law should be held in 1995.[134]

At the time of writing, the most recent General Assembly resolution on the subject was Resolution 49/50 which was adopted in February 1995 at the 49th Session of the Assembly, and which *inter alia* requested the Secretary General to proceed with the organization of the United Nations Congress on Public International Law to be held from 13–17 March 1995. The resolution also urged the Advisory Committee on the United Nations Programme of Assistance in the Teaching, Study, Dissemination and Wider Appreciation of International Law to continue to formulate, as appropriate and in a timely manner, relevant guidelines for the programme's activities in relation to the Decade of International Law.[135]

The United Nations Congress on Public International Law

The United Nations Congress on Public International Law, which was held on 13–17 March 1995 within the framework of the United Nations Decade of International Law attracted about 1000 people from 146 countries. Participants included practising lawyers, corporate counsel, ministry officials, judges, arbitrators, teachers of law, diplomats and members of academia.[136] The congress was organized on the general theme 'Towards the twenty-first century: international law as a language for international relations'.

Under-Secretary General for Legal Affairs of the United Nations Hans Corell observed at the opening session of the meeting that international law was not the exclusive interest of a few specialists, but an important ingredient in daily decision-making. As such, Mr. Corell was of the view that decision-makers must ensure that international law was applied and that legal advice was sought before important decisions were made in foreign policy matters; their actions stayed within the boundaries of international law; and that ratification of international treaties were not empty gestures but reflected a genuine determination to comply.[137]

Former Governor General of Australia, Sir Ninian Stephen, in his address to the meeting, observed:

> Today we have grown perfectly accustomed to the prospect of nations around the world assuming obligations and undertaking burdens internationally that would have been unthinkable in the climate of 60 or 70 years ago. The world of the 1920s and 30s, its politicians and its peoples, could not have imagined today's spending of vast sums from national resources, albeit much less than is needed, on foreign aid or the achievements of United Nations agencies in so many areas of

> human welfare ... Today, and essentially through the agency of the United Nations, we have moved far from that stance and when the generations now living look to the future, as we are called upon to do here today, we do so with minds surely more accustomed to change than those of any earlier generation before us.[138]

Sir Stephen focused his delivery on dispute settlement and sustained the view that all the tools of international law as vital parts of one system of preventive diplomacy was a vital concept. He lauded the United Nations dispute settlement process as enshrined in Article 33[139] of the United Nations Charter, which enjoined nations in dispute to have recourse to the whole range of available dispute resolution process, from negotiation to judicial settlement.

Another commentator was of the view that international law was weak in its former manifestation of a set of rules which applied to an anarchic international society. The transformation in recent times of this international order into a more organized, coherent world society which was interdependent has added to the new dynamism of international law.[140] He said:

> This change may be described as a movement from classical international law to world law. If international law is geared toward the co-existence of States in the age of nationalism, then world law refers to a system for the co-operation of States in the age of globalism ... World law is a human value-oriented system. In this context, human dignity as the key value provides the political and legal framework within which economic well-being and ecological balance are to be promoted.[141]

Interventions and sanctions as provided by the United Nations Charter were, in this commentator's view, essential, and effective enforcement of world law was critical. It was therefore essential that sanctions were available at diplomatic, economic and military levels.

One of the points stressed by the Permanent Representative of Slovenia to the United Nations, Danilo Türk was that the creation of *ad hoc* international criminal tribunals by the Security Council which tried persons responsible for serious violations of international criminal law was a major innovation of the United Nations system.[142] In his view, the Security Council has, by this innovation, assumed an important responsibility for the effectiveness of justice in these cases and, indirectly in all its efforts for maintenance of international peace and security.

Donald E. Buckingham, an academic, speaking on the subject of 'International Law as a Language for International Relations', stressed the need to introduce students to international law earlier than at university level. He was of the view that a more educated and internationally literate public will assist the goal of recognizing international law as the language of international relations. It was far too late a stage to leave the learning of international law to chance or to higher education. One of the measures suggested was familiarizing secondary school teachers with international law and by that process, introducing the teaching of international law in the secondary school educational curriculum.[143]

Regarding the authoritativeness of international law norms, the moderator of the panel on 'New Approaches to Research, Education and Training in the Field of International Law', Edward A. Laing said:

> Regarding authoritativeness, I have already intimated the normative significance of consensus resolutions is enhanced by the decline in international relations of polarities. And, speaking about authority, let me suggest that lawyers should stop pretending that the authority of a legal norm exclusively derives from the stature of the formal or other source. We, the interpreters and applicators, whether in Assembly, Chancery or Secretariat, must own up to being the high priests of the legal order. What we say is the law often comes close to being oracular. Thankfully, we are at the dawn of an era in which electronic communications and changing forensic techniques make instant armchair lawyers of the average citizen. When this trend eventually reaches the international legal system, its inherent democracy will provide the antidote to apparent excesses in my 'high priest' position.[144]

Laing underlined what he called 'humanitarian universalism' which related to humanitarian intervention by states or groups of states or by the United Nations itself as a body, where the role of international law in the modern context was identified as a more proactive and involved one than its counterpart in the 1960s and 1970s.

Another thought that emerged from the conference related to making international law 'user friendly' or, in other words, more readily applicable in practical situations which bring to bear on the law, exigencies of modern life. International law, according to this premise, must make life easier for individuals, while promoting democracy; protecting human rights and the environment; establishing common labour standards; providing new air routes between cities; facilitating the use of new communications systems and techniques unknown to previous generations; permitting instantaneous international mail through the electronic media; and providing warnings and reports on weather patterns, to name a few.[145]

Arguably, one of the most relevant contributions at the meeting was made by the President of the International Court of Justice, Mohammed Bedjaoui, who observed that because the court's advisory function was not dramatic, little was heard about it, although the advisory opinions of the court were an effective tool of preventive diplomacy and served to prevent conflict and deflate tension.[146] Judge Bedjaoui also said the Court had been giving advisory opinions since the days of the League of Nations and that, in most cases, such opinions were immediately accepted by states involved in a dispute. He suggested that access to the advisory opinions of the Court be extended to more organizations and states, as the reasons for the limitations on such access were not well founded.[147]

Dispute Settlement in the United Nations System and its Applicability to Air Law

The Decade of International Law, as proclaimed by the United Nations, has underscored the exclusive focus on the maintenance of international peace and security as the single element to address in the programme implementation of the decade. Thus, dispute settlement, which was also a focal point in the United Nations Congress on Public International Law, inextricably links the decade and its programme to the role played by the United Nations dispute settlement process in the field of international civil aviation. In this context, the 1993 adjudication in the International Court of Justice of the PAN-AM disaster sheds light on the relationship between the principles of international law and air law in the modern context.

In addition to the foregoing propositions that establish the crucial role played by international law, there is now no question that international law on which international treaties are based has the nature and force of law. Although 19th century Austinian thinking[148] stringently maintained that international law was not endowed with the attributes of law, that theory has since been refuted.[149] The earlier view was predicated upon the claim that enforceable law should originate from a sovereign authority which was politically more superior to those to whom it applied. International law, it was claimed, did not emanate from such authority. The later view, which is both logically and intellectually more coercive, holds that if international law was based on mere morality and had the force of morality only, such authorities as precedents and juristic opinion would not be cited in instances of adjudication.[150] *A fortiori,* certain judicial decisions have explicitly recognized the fact that international law is enforceable and consequently has all the attributes of law.[151]

Although the United Nations Decade of International Law is seemingly focused on the maintenance of international peace and security, it is a compelling fact that now is an opportune time to address principles of international law in a much wider context. This affects not only the promotion of international law, but also its expansion or teaching, particularly in the context that the past achievements of the United Nations and its specialized agencies have shown the many achievements of international law in spite of its alleged impotence. Resolution 44/23 is therefore not an antithetical impracticality. On the contrary it is a further step towards total acceptance and appreciation of international law by the world community. As for the mission of the United Nations Decade of International Law, whatever its parameters, the following measures are recommended in order that the role of international law as effective 'world law' would serve the next century more efficiently:

- Optional Clause 36(2) of the Statute of the International Court of Justice should be made more acceptable to more member states;
- International forums should be devoid as much as practicable of political polemics;[152]
- Support as far as practicable from such important judicial bodies as the European Court of the European Union should be available for the collective effort of international law-making in accordance with the Charter of the United Nations;
- Such organs of international law as the Commission of Jurists (Inter-American Conference) should be actively involved in the promotion and expansion of international law;
- More evolved programmes of world disarmament should be introduced and followed by those nations that are capable of arms proliferation and extended use to the detriment of humanity;
- More conciliatory or mediatory judicial tribunals should be established to ensure peaceful arbitration of international disputes;
- Disparities of the economic conditions of under-privileged nations must be obviated or controlled by a duly established world order that is followed by consensus;
- A world-wide basis for law and order must be established in unequivocal terms by consensual agreement within the United Nations; and,
- the teaching of international law must be undertaken by states in their territories to make the legal profession, politicians and students more aware of the international responsibility of states towards each other in the promotion of international trade and preservation of the environment, peace and security and the advancement of scientific technology.

With the above measures and the sensibility of Resolution 44/23, tempered with the immense potential and achievement that the United

Nations has achieved and is capable of, international law could certainly take a new dimension in the next decade.

Notes

1 *PCIJ* (1927) Ser. A, No. 9 at 18.
2 Article 24 of the United Nations Charter provides that the members of the United Nations confer on the Security Council primary responsibility for the maintenance of international peace and security and recognizes that the Security Council would act on behalf of all member States of the United Nations. Article 23 of the Charter provides that the Security Council shall consist of 15 members of the United Nations. The Republic of China, France, Russian Federation (the then USSR), the United Kingdom of Great Britain and Northern Ireland and USA are permanent members. Article 25 provides that members of the United Nations agree and accept to carry out the decisions of the Security Council in accordance with the provisions of the Charter.
3 *ICJ Report* (1949) 174.
4 See *Charter of the United Nations and Statute of the International Court of Justice*, United Nations: New York, Article 13.1.a.
5 Article 2 of the Draft Code at 64–65.
6 *Report of the International Law Commission to the General Assembly on the Work of the 1st Session*, (1949) *A/CN.4/13*, June 9, at 21.
7 *Vienna Convention on the Law of Treaties* (1969), United Nations General Assembly Document *A/CONF.39/27*, 23 May.
8 There are instances where states may record their reservation on particular provisions of a convention while signing the document as a whole. The International Court of Justice in its examination of the *Gcnocide Convention* has ruled:

> The object and purpose of the Convention ... limit both the freedom of making reservations and that of objecting to them. It follows that it is the compatibility of a reservation with the object and purpose of the Convention that must furnish the criterion for the attitude of a State in objecting to the reservation. 1 *I.C.J Rep.* (1951) at 15.

9 Schwarzenberger, G. and E.D. Brown (1976), *A Manual of International Law*, (6th ed.), Oxon, Professional Books Limited at 118.
10 The Preamble to the Chicago Convention states:

> ... the undersigned governments having agreed on certain principles and arrangements in order that international civil aviation may be developed in a safe and orderly manner and that international air transport services may be established on the basis of equality of opportunity and soundly and economically; have accordingly concluded this Convention to that end.

11 Greig, D.W. (1976), *International Law* (2nd ed.), London, Butterworths at 8.
12 *Statute of the International Court of Justice, Charter of the United Nations and Statute of the International Court of Justice*, United Nations: New York, Article 38.1.(a).
13 *Id.*, Article 36.2 (a).
14 *Supra*, note 7.

15 *Vienna Convention*, Preamble.
16 *Id.*, Article 42. 1.
17 *Id.*, Article 57.
18 *Id.*, Article 59.
19 *Id.*, Article 60.
20 *Id.*, Article 61.
21 *Id.*, Article 62.
22 *Id.*, Article 46.
23 Reuter (1989), *Introduction to the Law of Treaties*, London and New York, Pinter Publishers at 16.
24 See von der Dunk, F.G. (1992), 'Jus Cogens Sive Lex Ferenda: Jus Cogendum', *Air and Space Law: De Lege Ferenda*, Essays in Honour of Henri A. Wassenbergh, (ed Tanja L. Masson-Zwaan and Pablo M.J. Mendes De Leon), Dordrecht, Martinus Nijhoff, 219 at 223–224.
25 *Convention on International Civil Aviation*, which was signed at Chicago on 7 December 1944. See ICAO *Doc 7300/6* (6th ed.) 1980. Although the Chicago Convention had its predecessors, they were not considered adequate to address the question of air transport and aerial navigation that were required in the second half of the 20th century. The Chicago Convention, on the other hand, which came into force upon ratification by 26 states, laid down, by mutual agreement among the delegates of the participating nations of the Chicago Conference, certain principles and arrangements which ensured that international civil aviation may be developed in a safe and orderly manner and that international air transport services may be established on the basis of equality of opportunity and operated soundly and economically. For this purpose, 12 draft sets of regulations, dealing with technical subjects were initially adopted as draft Technical Annexes and later incorporated into the Convention. At its golden jubilee which fell on 7 December 1994, the Chicago Convention still remained a steadfast proponent of these principles.
26 See *Protocol on the Authentic Trilingual Text of the Convention on International Civil Aviation* (1944), Article IX, ICAO *Doc 7300/6* Chicago, at 41. *supra* at note 4.
27 *Schaake* v. *Dolly* 85 Kan. 590., 118 Pac. 80.
28 *People* v. *Bradley* 60 Ill. 402, at 405. Also, *Bouviers Law Dictionary and Concise Encyclopedia* (1914) (3rd ed.) Vol 11, New York, Vernon Law Book Co.
29 *Proceedings of the Council's 2nd Session* 2 September–12 December 1947, Doc. 7248-C/839 at 44–45.
30 See ICAO *Resolutions A–13 and A–33* which recommended that SARPS relating to the efficient and safe regulation of international air navigation be adopted.
31 *Annex 9, Facilitation*, (9th ed.), July 1990, Foreword.
32 ICAO, Doc. 7670, vol 1.
33 *Aeronautical Information Services Manual*, ICAO, *Doc. 8126-0 AN/872/3*.
34 ICAO, Doc. 8528, A15-P/6.
35 Article 86 of the Convention.
36 Article 12 stipulates that over the high seas, the rules in force shall be those established under the Convention, and each contracting state undertakes to insure the prosecution of all persons violating the applicable regulations.
37 Milde, M., The Chicago Convention – After Forty Years, 1X *Annals Air and Space L.* 119, at 126. See also Schenkman, J. (1955), *International Civil Aviation Organization*, Geneve, at 163.
38 Milde, *id.* at 122.
39 Buergenthal, T. (1969), *Law Making in the International Civil Aviation Organization*, Kluwer, Dordrecht at 9.

40 Dempsey, p. 5 (1987), *Law and Foreign Policy in International Aviation*, Dobbs Ferry: New York, Transnational Publishers Inc., at 302.
41 Sochor, E. (1991), *The Politics of International Aviation*, London, Macmillan at 58.
42 *Ibid.*
43 Tobolewski, A. (1979), 'ICAO's Legal Syndrome', *IV Annals Air and Space Law*, 349 at 359.
44 Brownlie, I. (1990), *Principles of Public International Law*, (4th ed.), Oxford, Clarendon Press 4 ed. at 2.
45 See Id., at 3.
46 *Id.* at 4. Also, *Right of Passage Case*, (1960), ICJ Reports at 90.
47 See Rossenne, S. (1989), *The World Court* (4th ed), Dordrecht, M. Nijhoff at 28.
48 *Case Concerning United States Diplomatic and Consular Staff in Tehran (United States of America* v. *Iran*) [1980] *ICJ Rep.* 3.
49 *Id.* at 21–22.
50 *Libyan Arab Jamahiriya* v. *United States of America; Libyan Arab Jamahiriya* v. *United Kingdom*), Provisional Measures, Order of Apr. 14 1992 [1992] *ICJ Reports* 114 at 143.
51 *ICJ Reports* (1986), 14.
52 *ICJ Reports* (1969), 44 at para 77.
53 See the Chicago Convention *supra*, Article 1. See also, Cooper, J.C. (1968), *Exploration in Aerospace Law*, (ed. I.A. Vlasic), Montreal, McGill University Press, 104–202.
54 Wassenbergh, H.A. (1978), 'Reality and Value of Air and Space Law', *Annals Air & Space Law* III 323 at 352.
55 Dempsey, P.S. (1987), *Law and Foreign Policy in International Aviation*, Dobbs Ferry, New York, Transnational Publishers Inc. at 7.
56 *Convention Relating to the Regulation of Aerial Navigation*, signed 13 October 1919, (hereafter referred to as the Paris Convention).
57 *Paris Convention*, Article 1.
58 *PICAO Documents*, (1945), Montreal, Volume 1, Doc. 1, at 3.
59 *Id.*, Doc. 2, at 2.
60 Zussman, E.A. (1970), *International Law Regulating Unlawful Seizure of Aircraft*, LL.M. Thesis, Montreal, McGill University, September at 23.
61 Hereafter referred to as PICAO. See Interim Agreement on International Civil Aviation, opened for signature at Chicago, 7 December 1944, Article 3. Also in Hudson, *International Legislation*, vol IX (1942–1945, New York) at 159.
62 PICAO, *Id.* Article 1 Section 4. It is interesting to note that PICAO was established as a provisional organization of a technical and advisory nature for the purpose of collaboration in the field of international civil aviation. *Vide* Article 1, Section 1.
63 *Ibid.*
64 Ibid., Interim Agreement, Section 6.4.b (1).
65 Ibid., Section 6.4.b (6). Also, Buergenthal (1969), supra, note 39, at 4, where the author states that PICAO's functions were merely advisory, which precludes any imputation of legislative or quasi-legislative character to its Interim Council.
66 Chicago Convention, *op. cit.*, Article 54.
67 See note 88.
68 Interim Agreement, Article 111, Section 6 (i).
69 Schenkman, (1955) *op. cit.*, 160.
70 See statement of R. Kidron, Israeli Head Delegate, Statement of the Second Plenary Meeting of the 7th Assembly on 17 June 1953, reported in *ICAO Monthly Bulletin* (1953), August–October, at 8.
71 Article 84.

72 Hingorani, H. 'Dispute Settlement in International Civil Aviation' (1959), *Arb J* 14, at 16. See also, *Rules of Procedure for the Council,* (1980) (5th ed.) Article 14.
73 Article 87.
74 Schenkman, supra, notes 69, 162.
75 Article 85.
76 Rules of Procedure for the Council, *op. cit.,* Section 1V, Rule 24 (e). Also, Article 54 (n) stipulates that one of the mandatory functions of the Council is to consider any matter relating to the Convention which any contracting state refers to it.
77 Rules of Procedure for the Council, *op. cit.,* Section 1V Rule 24 (f). The two additional multilateral agreements stemming from the Convention and providing for the exchange of traffic rights – the Air Services Transit Agreement and the Air Transport Agreement, also contain provisions that empower the ICAO Council to hear disputes and 'make appropriate findings and recommendations... ' see Air Services Transit Agreement, Article 11, Section 1, and the Air Transport Agreement, Article 1V, Section 2.
78 Rules for the Settlement of Differences, (1975) (2nd ed.), *ICAO Doc.* 7782/2.
79 *Id.,* Article 14(a).
80 Buergenthal, *op. cit.,* at 136.
81 Dempsey, *op. cit.,* at 295.
82 Milde, M. (1979), 'Dispute Settlement in the Framework of the International Civil Aviation Organization (ICAO)', *Settlement of Space Law Disputes,* 87, Martins Nijhoff, Dordrecht, at 88.
83 Sampayo de Lacerda, J.C. (1978), 'A Study About the Decisions of the ICAO Council'... 111, *Annals of Air and Space Law,* McGill, Montreal, at 219.
84 Fitzgerald, G.F. (1976), 'ICAO Now and in the Coming Decades', *International Air Transport Law, Organization and Politics for the Future,* (ed. N.M. Matte), 47 at 50.
85 See Elmandjra, M. (1973), *The United Nations System, An Analysis,* London, Faber, p. 32 for a descriptive analysis of the United Nations System.
86 Johnson, D.H.N. (1955–1956), 'The Effect of Resolutions of the General Assembly of the UN', Vol. 32, *B.Y.B.I.L.,* p. 97, Lauterpacht, J. (1955), 'South Africa – Voting Procedure', *ICJ. Reports,* pp. 118–119. See also Sloane, B. (1948), 'The Binding Force of a Recommendation of the General Assembly of the UN', *B.Y.B.I.L.,* Vol. 25, p. 1. See also generally Goodrich, L.M. and Simons, A.P. (1955), *The United Nations and the Maintenance of International Peace and Security,* Washington, Brookings Institution, pp. 248–249.
87 Bennet, L.B. (1983), *International Organizations, Principles and Issues* (43rd ed.), Englewood Cliffs, New Jersey, Prentice Hall, p. 171.
88 Charter of the United Nations, Article 13.
89 Bennet, L.A. (1983), *International Organizations, Principles and Issues* (43rd ed.), Englewood Cliffs, New Jersey, Prentice Hall, p. 195.
90 Res. 39 (1) December 1946 and Res. 114 (11) 17 November, 1947.
91 3 Hyde 1686 as quoted in Jessup, P.C. (1948), *A Modern Law of Nations,* New York, The Macmillan Co., p. 157.
92 The International Court of Justice is discussed in this chapter on page 14.
93 Henkin, L. (1979), *How Nations Behave: Law and Foreign Policy,* New York, (published for the Consular Foreign Relations), F.A. Prawger, pp. 22–23.
94 *Charter of the United Nations and Statute of the International Court of Justice,* Department of Public Information, United Nations, New York, *DPI/511– 40108 (3–90),* 100M at 1.
95 *Id.* at 3.
96 On 17 November 1989 the United Nations General Assembly adopted Resolution 44/23 which declared that the period 1990–1999 be designated as the

United Nations Decade of International Law (the full text of Resolution 44/23 is annexed as Appendix 1 at the end of this book). The main purposes of the decade have been identified *inter alia* as:

a the promotion of the acceptance of the principles of international law and respect therefor;
b the promotion of the means and methods for the peaceful settlement of disputes between states including resort to the International Court of Justice with full respect therefor;
c the full encouragement of the progressive development of international law and its codification;
d the encouragement of the teaching, studying, dissemination and wider appreciation of international law.

The four tasks of the Resolution have been predicated upon the fact that the purpose of the United Nations is to maintain peace and security. See Resolutions and Decisions Adopted by the General Assembly During its 44th Session, Vol. 1, 19 Sept–29 Dec 1989, *General Assembly Official Records*: 44th Session, Supplement No. 49 (A/44/49), United Nations, New York, 1990, 31. For a detailed discussion on Resolution 44/23 see Abeyratne, R.I.R. (1992), The United Nations Decade of International Law, *International Journal of Politics, Culture, and Society*, Vol. 5, No. 3, Human Sciences Press, Inc., New York, 511–523.

97 See Charter of the United Nations Article 1. See also Kelsen, H. (1951), *Recent Trends in the Law of the United Nations*, London: London Institute of World Affairs, Stevens, p. 953. For a commentary of the Charter of the United Nations see generally, Goodrich, L.M. and Hambro, E. (1949), *Charter of the United Nations, Commentary and Documents*, Boston, World Peace Foundation.

98 Henkin, L. (1979), *How Nations Behave: Law and Foreign Policy*, New York, F.A. Prawger, p. 137.

99 Carlston, K.S. (1962), *Law and Organization in World Society*, Urbana, University of Illinois Press, p. 135.

100 Daoudi, M.S. and Dajni, M.S. (1983), *Economic Sanctions: Ideals and Experience*, London; Boston: Routledge & Kegan Paul, p. 187.

101 Nossal, R.K. (1989), 'International Sanctions as International Punishment', *International Organization*, vol. 43, no. 2, Spring, p. 302.

102 Nossal, *id.*, p. 304.

103 Knorr, K. (1975), *The Power of Nations: The Political Economy of International Relations*, New York, Basic 12 Books, Chapters 1 and 6.

104 *Id.*, pp. 151–156.

105 PCIJ: *Lighthouse Case* (1934), France/Greece, S.O. by Seferiades A/B 62 p. 47.

106 *North Atlantic Coast Fisheries Case* 1 HCR p. 143 at p. 167.

107 Kelsen, H. (1944), *Peace Through Law*, Chapel Hill, The University of North Carolina Press, p. 30.

108 Cheng, B. (1953), *General Principles of Law as Applied by International Courts and Tribunals*, London, Stevens, p. 112.

109 *Id.*, p. 113.

110 United Nations (1970), *The United Nations: The Next Twenty-five Years* – Twentieth Report of the Commission to Study the Organization of Peace, Dobbs Ferry, New York, Oceana Publications Incl, pp. 2–3.

111 United Nations (1985), *The United Nations at Forty, A Foundation to Build on*, New York, United Nations, V.

112 Lissitzyn, O.J. (1951), *The International Court of Justice – Its Role in the Maintenance of International Peace and Security*, New York, Carnegie Endowment for International Peace, p. 11.

113 United Nations (1946), *The United Nations Conference on International Organization, Selected Documents*, Washington, Government Printing Office, p. 883. 11.
114 The other five are the Economic and Social Council (ECOSOC), the Trusteeship Council, the Security Council, the General Assembly and the Secretariat.
115 Charter of the United Nations, Article 33.
116 Bennet, L.A. (1983), *International Organizations, Principles and Issues*, (43rd ed.), Englewood Cliffs, New Jersey, Prentice Hall, p. 178. The International Court of Justice has a dual role – of a tribunal and a counsellor. See Sohn, L.B. (1956), *Cases on United Nations Law*, Brooklyn, The Foundation Press, p. 20.
117 See generally, *Great Books of the Western World* (vol. 6), Chicago, Encyclopedia Britannica Inc., by William Benton, 1990; vol. 6, Herodotus, *Melpomene*, pp. 102–107 and Thucydides, *The Peloponnesian War*, pp. 434–438, (vol. 7), Plato, *Dialogues of Plato*, pp. 806–807 (vol. 14), Plutarch, *The Lives of the Noble Grecians and Romans* – Pompey, p. 533 and also *Otho* at p. 875, (vol. 23), Machiavelli, *The Prince*, p.31 and Hobbes, *Leviathan* Part 1, Chapter 8, pp. 68–69.
118 Walker, T.A. (1899), *A History of the Law of Nations*, Cambridge, Cambridge University Press, p. 333, Nussbaum, A. (1947), *A Concise History of the Law of Nations*, New York, Macmillan Co., p. 104, Scott, J.B. (1934), 'The Modern Law of Nations and its Municipal Sanctions,' *Georgetown Law Journal*, pp. 139–206.
119 Supra. See also Olmstead, C.J. (ed.) (1984), *Extra Territorial Application of Laws and Responses Thereto*, Oxford, ILA (and) ESC, p. 38 where the Federal Republic of Germany is cited as a country which makes rules of general international law prevail over any domestic statutory law except its constitution on the premise that any infringement of a rule of international law entails international responsibility.
120 RIIA (1957), *International Sanctions*, London, Royal Institute of International Affairs, p. 13.
121 United Nations (1985), *The United Nations at Forty – A Foundation to Build on*, New York, United Nations, p. 1. See Secretary General Perez de Cuellar's statement.
122 United Nations (1990), *Resolutions and Decisions Adopted by the General Assembly during its Forty-fifth Session*, Vol. 1, 18 September–21 December 1990, General Assembly Official Records: Forty-fifth Session Supplement No. 49 A (A/45/49).
123 *Id.*, Annex, 1.1.
124 ICJ (1955), *Voting Procedure on Questions Relating to Reports and Petitions Concerning the Territory of South-West Africa*, International Court of Justice Report 67, p. 118.
125 Willcox, N. and Marcy, M. (1955) *Proposals for Change in the United Nations*, New York, p. 106.
126 *Id.*, p. 106.
127 *Id.*, Annex, III.2.
128 See United Nations (1990). General Assembly Resolution 45/51, *Resolutions and Decisions Adopted by the General Assembly during its Forty-fifth Session*, Volume 1, 18 September–21 December 1990, General Assembly Official Records: Forty-fifth Session Supplement no. 49 A (A/45/49).
129 See United Nations (1991), *Resolutions and Decisions Adopted by the General Assembly during its Forty-sixth Session*, Volume 1, 17 September–20 December 1991, General Assembly Official Records: Forty-sixth Session Supplement no. 49 (A/46/49), at 285.
130 *Id.*, at 286.
131 United Nations (1992), *Resolutions and Decisions Adopted by the General Assembly During the First Part of its Forty-seventh Session*, 15 September–23 December 1992, United Nations Department of Public Information, at 491.

132 *Id.*, Annex to Resolution 47/32, at 493.
133 United Nations (1993), *Resolutions and Decisions Adopted by the General Assembly during its Forty-eighth Session*, Volume 1, 21 September–23 December 1993, General Assembly, Official Records, Forty-eighth Session Supplement No. 49(A/48/49) at 327.
134 *Id.*, at 328.
135 A/RES/49/50, 17 February 1995.
136 *L/2699*, 10 March 1995, at 1.
137 *L/2702*, 13 March 1995, at 1.
138 See Address by Sir Ninian Stephen: 'Meeting Expectations Through Process and Practice', 95-07436 at 2.
139 Article 33 provides that the parties to any dispute, the continuance of which is likely to endanger the maintenance of international peace and security, shall, first of all, seek a solution by negotiation, enquiry, mediation, conciliation, arbitration, judicial settlement, resort to regional agencies or arrangements or other peaceful means of their own choice. The provision also requires the Security Council of the United Nations to call upon the parties to settle their dispute by the above means, when it deems necessary.
140 Chi Young PAK, C.Y. (1988), 'The Changing Role of International Law in World Society', 95-07377, at 3.
141 *Ibid.*
142 See opening remarks by the Moderator, Ambassador Danilo Türk, *95–07429*, at 2.
143 Buckingham, D.E. (1990), 'International Law as a language for International Relations', Law Book Company, Sydney, *95-07282*, at 12–13.
144 Moderator's Presentation by Edward A. Laing, 'United Nations Congress on Public International Law, Panel on New Approaches to Research, Education and Training in the Field of International Law and its Wider Application', New York, 16 March 1995, at 5.
145 Sohn, L.B. (1989), 'Making International Law User-friendly', Butterworths, London *95-07418*, at 11.
146 L/2704, 14 March 1995.
147 L/2704 *Ibid.*
148 Morrison, W.L. (1982), *John Austin*, Stanford, California, Stanford University Press, p. 78.
149 Starke, J.G. (1984), *Introduction to International Law*, (9th ed.), London, Butterworths, p. 18. See also Lloyd, D. (1970), *The Idea of Law* (revised ed.), Harmondsworth, Middlesex, Penguin Books, pp. 37–40.
150 Starke (1984), *op. cit.*, pp. 18–21.
151 See *The Charming Betsy* (1804) 2 Cranch p. 64 at p. 118 where Marshall, C.J. cited Article VI para 2 of the United States Constitution which gives constitutional validity to international law. See also *The Paquete Habana* (1900) 175 US 677 at 700 per Gray J., who went on to say that international law must be ascertained by the Courts of Justice of appropriate jurisdiction.
152 See Corbett, P.E. (1971), *The Growth of World Law*, Princeton, New Jersey, Princeton University Press, pp. 51–51.

2 The Elements of the Offence and Current Situation

Introductory Comments

It is also necessary to examine the elements of the offence of unlawful interference with international civil aviation and analyse the status of international law in the context of the offence. To that end, this chapter will remain a scholastic exploration, and will set the pace for the chapters to follow, to examine, analyse and recommend legal measures to deal with the offence.

The maintenance of international peace and security is an important objective of the United Nations,[1] which recognizes one of its purposes as being *inter alia*:

> To maintain international peace and security, and to that end: take effective collective measures for the prevention and removal of threats to the peace, and for the suppression of acts of aggression or other breaches of peace, and to bring about by peaceful means, and in conformity with the principles of justice and international law, adjustment or settlement of international disputes or situations which might lead to a breach of the peace.[2]

It is clear that the United Nations has recognized the application of the principles of international law as an integral part of maintaining international peace and security and avoiding situations which may lead to a breach of the peace.[3] The purpose of this book is to discuss the evolution of the problem of unlawful interference with civil aviation and analyse the purpose of the law in the task of alleviating and eventually eradicating the problem.

The first task of this work is to examine the meaning and significance of the words 'unlawful interference' in the context of civil aviation. 'Unlawful interference' is clearly a generic term of the expression 'acts of aggression or other breaches of peace' used in the

United Nations Charter.[4] The Chicago Convention of 1944[5] – the seminal document which sets out the principles of international civil aviation – recognizes that the abuse of international civil aviation can lead to a threat to 'general security'[6] and that international civil aviation may be developed in a safe and orderly manner.[7] The Provisional International Civil Aviation Organization (PICAO) which was formed as a consequence of the Chicago Conference of December 1944 (which later resulted in the Chicago Convention) and its interim agreement which was agreed upon, in order that PICAO was in operation until a permanent Convention was summoned[8], records the first official international response to aviation security.

In its preparation for the PICAO Assembly, the Council in its 7th Session inserted an agenda item which called for:

> Consideration of the action taken and to be taken by the Organization and Member States with respect to safety in the air.[9]

At its 7th Session in 1947, mention was also made of safety of life in the air.[10] By then, the Operational Studies Section of PICAO had already been charged with the task of studying *inter alia,* factors conducive to the provision of safe, regular and efficient air services.[11] Although there is no direct reference to aviation security in the annals of PICAO meetings, it is reasonable to impute to the PICAO Council the characteristic that it was concerned with the overall safety of human life in the air, whether it be ensured through mechanical efficiency of aircraft or the prevention of adverse human conduct. This intent was more clearly brought out in 1977 by the ICAO Council when, at its 92nd Session, the ICAO Council referred to UN General Assembly Resolution 32/8 on Safety of International Civil Aviation[12] and referred *in contextu* to 'Strengthening of Measures to Suppress Acts of Unlawful Interference with Civil Aviation'.[13] The interaction between 'safety', 'security', and 'unlawful interference with civil aviation' is now clearly established. The consolidated statement of continuing ICAO policies related to the safeguarding of international civil aviation against acts of unlawful interference, appearing in ICAO Resolution A 26–7 now in force, which resolves:

> ... the unlawful seizure of aircraft and other unlawful acts against the safety of civil aviation, particularly the threat of terrorist acts, have a serious adverse effect on the safety, efficiency and regularity of international air transport and undermine the confidence of the peoples of the world in the safety of international civil aviation ...
>
> ... acts of unlawful interference with civil aviation continue to have an adverse effect on the safety and efficiency of international air trans-

> port and endanger the lives of aircraft passengers and crews engaged in air transport ...[14]

The concern of the international community would therefore lie in the fact that unlawful interference with international civil aviation erodes the safety and security of international civil aviation.

Unlawful Interference

Under general legal principles, unlawful interference of civil aviation can be regarded as a crime. A crime has been identified as:

> A wrong which affects the security or well being of the public generally so that the public has an interest in its suppression.[15]

The word 'wrong' in this definition could be considered as presupposing an act that is perpetrated against the law. Since interference with civil aviation is in itself a wrong, and therefore definitively against the law, the question arises whether the word 'unlawful' is tautologous. Tautology in the phrase 'unlawful interference' was judicially discussed in England in 1981 in a case which involved indecent assault on a mental patient. Justice Hodgson observed:

> ... it does not seem to me that the element of unlawfulness can properly be regarded as part of the definitional element of the offence. In defining a criminal offence the word 'unlawful' is surely tautologous and can add nothing to its essential ingredients.[16]

Lord Justice Lawton, in a later case analysed Justice Hodgson's reasoning and observed:

> We have found difficulty in agreeing with this reasoning, even though the judge seems to be accepting that belief in consent does entitle a defendant to an acquittal on a charge of assault. We cannot accept that the word 'unlawful' when used in a definition of an offence is to be regarded as tautologous. In our judgment the word unlawful does import an essential element into the offence. If it were not there, social life would be unreasonable.[17]

Lord Lane in the 1987 case of *R.* v. *Williams*[18], citing with approval Lord Justice Lawton's analysis went on to say:

> ... the mental element necessary to constitute guilt is the intent to apply unlawful force to the victim. We do not believe that the mental element can be substantiated by simply showing an intent to apply force and no more.[19]

Lord Lane seems to impute to the defendant a knowledge of going against applicable law, making the word 'unlawful' *sui generis* and mutually exclusive from the term 'interference'.

This line of cases seems to suggest by analogy that 'unlawful interference' constitutes an act whereby the perpetrator knows that his or her interference of an activity is clearly contrary to the law. Unlawful interference with civil aviation forms no conceivable exception to this logicality.

Another significant fact emerges from the judgement of Lord Lane when His Lordship said:

> What then is the situation of the defendant in labouring under a mistake of fact as to the circumstances? What if he believes, but believes mistakenly, that the victim is consenting, or that it is necessary to defend himself, or that a crime is being committed which he intends to prevent? He must then be judged against the mistaken facts or circumstances and if the prosecution fails to establish his guilt, then he is entitled to an acquittal.[20]

By analogy therefore, if a person interferes with civil aviation, but does not believe he or she is contravening the law, he or she is not guilty of an offence and the mental element in an offence becomes as important as the physical element of the offence of unlawful interference with civil aviation. The criminal element[21] that is thus infused into the offence of unlawful interference makes the offence, like any other, hinge on the criminal policy that is created in the jurisdiction to which it applies. In other words, an act of interference would be considered unlawful and thereby an offence only in jurisdictions whose criminal policies determine such acts to be unlawful. Although a crime has so far not been coherently defined by any writer[22], the characteristics of a crime, that is, the *actus reus* (physical act forbidden by law) and the *mens rea* (the intention to commit the act and to understand the reasonable and natural consequences of the act) have been identified.[23] The identification of these elements has given rise to the maxim *Actus non facit reum (hominem) nisi mens sit rea,* meaning that whatever deed a man may have done, it cannot make him criminally punishable unless his doing of it was activated by a legally blameworthy attitude of mind. Usually, each prohibited deed is legally specified and defined and the legal definition identifies the essential facts which must be present to constitute the forbidden deed. As will be discussed later, the offence of unlawful interference with international civil aviation forms no exception to this practice.

Elements of the Offence

The offence of the unlawful interference with international civil aviation broadly comprises: hijacking of aircraft; aviation sabotage such as the causing of explosions in aircraft on the ground and in flight; missile attacks against aircraft; armed attacks on airports, passengers and other aviation-related property; and the illegal carriage of narcotics by air and its criminal ramifications.

Often, the heart of the offence is dignified with a core of legitimacy on the grounds that the actions of the offender are justified. Some states have acquiesced in this approach by giving the offender a safe haven to conduct his or her activities and consequent political refuge. Accordingly, there exists now a dichotomy in some minds that the need for a solution to the problem does not arise in the absence of a problem. Professor Michael Milde addresses this dichotomy and observes current trends:

> How did the international community respond to these acts? The applause and 'hero's welcome' for the perpetrators did not last too long beyond the first bizarre incidents and the international community realised that, in the dangerous game of unlawful seizure of aircraft and the acts of sabotage, there are no winners – the security of civil aviation is an overriding interest because international air transport is an indivisible part of international economy and co-operation which must be protected in the common interest.[24]

Despite this clear view, in a general sense, confusion has been worse confounded with the paucity of a clear definition of the offence itself and the lack of recognition of the principles of international law as universally enforceable laws against the offender. The blatant incompatibility between the heinous quality of the offence and the tepid judicial attitudes of some jurisdictions marks an insouciance that needs the urgent attention of the world community.

This book will also address the definitive and logistical aspects of the problem of the unlawful interference with international civil aviation from a legal perspective, examine and critically analyse the legal measures taken so far to control the problem and its effects, and propose new legal measures where necessary. Also included will be an examination of issues related to international criminal law which bring to bear the need for revision of the fundamental philosophy applicable to the notion of a crime committed internationally.

It would also be relevant to examine the ramifications of a crime in the determination of its nature. Modern criminal law should apply circumstances rather than elements to determine the nature of a crime. In this perspective, although a crime may be committed within a domestic jurisdiction, it may be motivated and deigned to result in injury that would transcend borders of countries. For example, a bomb explosion by terrorists in a city may only affect local citizens. However, the bomb may have been manufactured by material provided internationally by delinquent states or entities. The very act of an international entity aiding and abetting the crime would *ipso facto*, make such a crime international.

Criminal law in such instances would transcend local boundaries, making it illogical and indeed, iniquitous for states concerned to take matters of adjudication of crimes involving an international flavour into their own hands. It is therefore time for states to infuse an element of international responsibility to their constitutional jurisprudence so that collective responsibility of states would be woven into a uniform fabric of law, with entrenched and internationally recognized legal principles. Moreover, it is essential that states should recognize their duties towards their citizens as one in which domestic responsibility is complemented harmoniously with a more widespread international responsibility. This philosophy would succeed in extending principles of State responsibility towards the international community on a more global level. *A fortiori*, it would also introduce a new element of domestic state responsibility towards citizens that would give citizens of a state the right to expect of it an international obligation to protect them from international wrongs.

In order to accomplish this new goal, a new structure of international law should be introduced through innovative legislation. A universally accepted convention or code should address issues of international criminal justice. To complement this legislative process, an effective judicial process is necessary, whereby an international court would adjudicate on international criminality. To achieve this, states should consensually abdicate myopic notions of sovereignty and egregious values of independence.

International Responses to the Offence

In January 1991, the Secretary General of the International Civil Aviation Organization (ICAO)[25] addressed a State Letter[26] to all ICAO-contracting states wherein he informed them that the ICAO Council had identified the major challenges facing international civil aviation. The subject of unlawful interference had been defined by the 27th Session of the ICAO Assembly as the overriding priority in ICAO's work programme[27] and the Secretary General requested that all contracting states provide their comments on the challenges, priorities and action that they think ought to be taken to meet those challenges.[28] The responses of states were consensual in that such measures as the implementation of ICAO policy on unlawful interference, world-wide enhancing of security measures and the development of aviation security assistance programmes were unanimously acceptable as those most desirable to combat the challenge.[29] In this context, one of the more significant decisions taken by the ICAO Council was to proceed, with the highest priority, with the development of a comprehensive and detailed ICAO aviation security training programme for world use.[30] Accordingly, ICAO has been very active in the field of aviation security in the recent past. The Committee on Unlawful Interference had held 17 meetings in 1990 and considered the review of the reports of the *ad hoc* Group of Specialists on the Detection of Explosives, the initial development of the ICAO Aviation Security (AVSEC) training programme and *inter alia*, the comprehensive revision of the ICAO Security Manual.[31]

Aviation security is by no means a recent concern of ICAO. The President of the ICAO Council, Dr. Assad Kotaite cautioned the world of this danger in 1985 when he said:

> ... the last two decades witnessed the emergence of an alarmingly wide scale of a new type of danger to international civil aviation ... This new type of danger is man-made and is manifested in violent human acts against the safety of civil aviation, use of threat or force, unlawful seizure of aircraft and other forms of unlawful interference with civil aviation ... These violent acts which constitute a world-wide problem, are not limited by geographic or political boundaries and no nation and no airline of the world is immune to such acts ...[32]

Professor Michael Milde, Director of ICAO's Legal Bureau (as he then was) focused attention on the importance attributed by ICAO to the problem of aviation security when he said:

> In 1980, the 23rd Session of the ICAO Assembly adopted what is considered to be a 'landmark' decision concerning the general work programme of the Legal Committee: it decided that only subjects of sufficient magnitude and practical importance requiring urgent international action should be included in the work programme ... problems of aviation security have been predominant and have commanded overriding priority for several years, thus reflecting the highest priority accorded, by members of the Organization, to problems of security against unlawful interference.[33]

There are however, two major obstacles to the enthusiasm shown so far in taking concerted action in this field:

1 The implementation of measures taken relating to the threat against aviation security in the face of the absence of the acceptance of the principles of international law and respect therefor – a concern reflected in a) of UN Resolution 44/23[34] ; and,

2 The subject of aviation security is too vast for one organization to handle on its own.[35]

While there have been various practical measures recommended to combat acts of unlawful interference such as: the training of personnel to detect a threat beforehand; intensifying security on such susceptible targets as airports; and the surveillance of all persons who are seen in such areas,[36] the threat against aviation security can only be effectively curbed if it is recognized *in consensu* by the international community as an offence against humanity. The lack of resources only makes the offence of interference of civil aviation subject to the punitive sanctions of diverse municipal laws.[37] World consensus on punitive sanctions against the offence and a more cohesive international structure to combat the offence are therefore necessary tools that would obviate this threat.

Nature of the Offence

The offence of unlawful interference with civil aviation, whether it be a direct attack on an airline, its passengers and crew or on other related properties or an act of seizure of an aircraft for the illegal carriage of narcotics by air, is a criminal act and can be broadly identified as an act of terrorism. One interpretation of terrorism given by the courts is that terrorism does not violate international law on the grounds that accusations of terrorism are often met not by a denial of the fact of responsibility but by a justification of the challenged actions.[38] This judgement clearly shows that there is no consensus among the world community that terrorism is an offence against established principles of law. It also infuses to the heart of the offence a core of legitimacy that is often considered incontrovertible, giving rise to the dichotomy that the need for a solution does not arise in the absence of a problem.[39]

The term 'terrorism' is seemingly of French origin and is believed to have been first used in 1798.[40] 'Terrorism' gave connotations of criminality to one's conduct and was later explicitly identified with the 'reign of terror' of the French Revolution. It is now generally considered a system of coercive intimidation[41] brought about by the infliction of terror or fear. The most frustrating obstacle to the control of unlawful acts against international civil aviation is the paucity of clear definition of the offence itself. Many attempts at defining the offence have often resulted in the offence being shrouded in political or national barriers.

In 1980 the Central Intelligence Agency (CIA) of the United States of America adopted a definition of terrorism which read:

> Terrorism is the threat or use of violence for political purposes by individuals or groups, whether acting for or in opposition to established governmental authority, when such actions are intended to shock, stun or intimidate victims. Terrorism has involved groups seeking to overthrow specific regimes, to rectify perceived national or group grievances, or to undermine international order as an end in itself.[42]

This all-embracing definition underscores the misapprehension that certain groups such as the French Resistance of Nazi-occupied France during World War II and the Contras in Nicaragua would broadly fall within the definitive parameters of terrorism. In fact, this formula labels every act of violence as being 'terrorist' engulfing in its broad spectrum such diverse groups as the Seikigunha of Japan and the Mujahedeen of Afghanistan, although their aims, *modus operandi* and ideologies are different. James Adams prefers a narrower definition which reads:

> A terrorist is an individual or member of a group that wishes to achieve political ends using violent means, often at the cost of casualties to innocent civilians and with the support of only a minority of the people they claim to represent.[43]

Even this definition, although narrower than the 1980 definition cited above, is not sufficiently comprehensive to cover the terrorist who hijacks an airplane for personal gain.[44] The difficulty in defining the term seems to lie in its association with political aims of the terrorist as is found in the definition that terrorism is really:

> Terror inspired by violence, containing an international element that is committed by individuals or groups against non-combatants, civilians, States or internationally-protected persons or entities in order to achieve political ends.[45]

The offence of terrorism has also been defined as one caused by:

> ... any serious act of violence or threat thereof by an individual. Whether acting alone or in association with other persons which is directed against internationally protected persons, organizations, places, transportation or communication systems or against members of the general public for the purpose of intimidating such persons, causing injury to or the death of such persons, disrupting the activities of such international organizations, of causing loss, detriment or damage to such places or property, or of interfering with such transportation and communications systems in order to undermine friendly relations among States or among the nationals of different States or to extort concessions from States.[46]

It is time that terrorism is recognized as an offence that is *sui generis* and one that is not always international in nature and motivated by the political aims of the perpetrator. For the moment, if terrorism were to be regarded as the use of fear, subjugation and intimidation to disrupt the normal operations of humanity, a more specific and accurate definition could be sought, once more analysis is carried out on the subject. One must always be mindful however, that without a proper and universally acceptable definition, international cooperation in combatting terrorism would be impossible.[47]

A terrorist act is one which is *mala in se* or evil by nature[48] and has been associated with the political repression of the French Revolution era where, it is said, the word terrorism was coined.[49] A terrorist is a *hostis humani generis* or common enemy of humanity. Generally, terrorist attacks that are calculated to interfere with civil aviation are four-fold:

1 Hijacking (or 'skyjacking'), which in the late 1960s started an irreversible trend which was dramatized by such incidents as the skyjacking by Shiite terrorists of the TWA flight 847 in June 1985. The skyjacking of Egypt Air flight 648 in November 1985 and the skyjacking of a Kuwait Airways Airbus in 1984 are other examples of this offence;
2 Aviation sabotage, where explosions on the ground or in mid-air destroy whole aircraft, their passengers and crew. Recent dramatizations of this type have been the Air India flight 182 over the Irish Sea in June 1985 and PAN-AM flight 103 over Lockerbie, Scotland in 1988, and the UTA explosion over Niger in 1989;
3 Missile attacks, where aircraft are destroyed by surface-to-air missiles (SAM). The destruction of the two Viscount aircraft of Air Rhodesia in late 1978/early 1979 are examples of this offence;
4 Armed attacks on airports and airline passengers where terrorists open fire in congested areas in the airport terminals. Examples of this type of terrorism are: the June 1972 attack by the Seikigunha (Japanese Red Army) at Ben Gurion Airport, Tel Aviv; the August 1973 attack by Arab gunmen on Athens Airport; and the 1985 attacks on Rome and Vienna Airports.) The illegal carriage by air of narcotics and other psychotropic substances and crimes related thereto such as the seizure of or damage to aircraft, persons and property.

International terrorism has so far not been defined comprehensively largely due to the fact that owing to its diversity of nature the concept itself has defied precise definition. However, this does not preclude the conclusion that international terrorism involves two factors. They are:

1 The commission of a terrorist act by a terrorist or terrorists: and,
2 The 'international' element involved in the act or acts in question, that is, that the motivation for the commission of such act or acts or the eventual goal of the terrorist should inextricably be linked with a country other than that in which the act or acts are committed.

Perhaps the oldest paradigm of international terrorism is piracy which has been recognized as an offence against the law of nations and which is seen commonly today in the offence of aerial piracy or hijacking.[50]

Acts of international terrorism that have been committed over the past two decades are too numerous to mention. Suffice it to say that the most deleterious effect of the offence is that it exacerbates international relations and endangers international security. From the isolated incidents of the 1960s, international terrorism has progressed to becoming a concentrated assault on nations and organizations that are usually susceptible to political conflict, although politics is not always the motivation of the international terrorist. International terrorism has been recognized to engulf acts of aggression by one state on another as well as by an individual or a group of individuals of one state on another state. The former typifies such acts as invasion, while the latter relates to such individual acts of violence as hijacking and the murder of civilians in isolated instances. In both instances, the duties of the offender-state have been emphatically recognized. Such duties are to condemn such acts and take necessary action.

The United Nations gave effect to this principle in 1970 when it proclaimed that:

> Every State has the duty to refrain from organizing or encouraging the organization of irregular forces or armed bands, including mercenaries, for incursion into the territory of another State.
>
> Every State has the duty to refrain from organizing, instigating, assisting or participating in acts of civil strife or terrorist acts in another State or acquiescing in organized activities within its territory directed towards the commission of such acts, when the acts referred to in the present paragraph involve a threat or use of force.[51]

The most pragmatic approach to the problem lies in identifying the parameters of the offence of international terrorism and seeking a solution to the various categories of the offence. To obtain a precise definition would be unwise, if not impossible. Once the offence and its parasitic qualities are clearly identified, it becomes necessary to discuss briefly its harmful effects on the international community. It is only then that a solution can be discussed that would obviate the fear and apprehension we suffer in the face of this threat.

Acts of International Terrorism

It is said that terrorism is the selective use of fear, subjugation and intimidation to disrupt the normal operations of society.[52] Beyond this statement which stands both for national and international terrorism any attempt at a working definition of the words 'international terrorism' would entail complications. However, in seeking a solution which would lead to the control of international terrorism it is imperative that contemporaneous instances of the infliction of terror be identified in order that they may be classified either as acts of international terrorism or as mere innocuous acts of self-defence. Broadly acts of international terrorism may be categorized into two distinct groups. In the first category may be included what are termed as acts of oppression such as the invasion of one state by another. In the second category are acts which are deviously claimed to be acts of defence. While the former is self-explanatory, the latter – by far the more prolific in modern society – can be identified in four separate forms of manifestation. They are:

1 Acts claimed to be committed in self-defence and in pursuance of self-determination to circumvent oppression;
2 Nonviolent acts committed internationally which are calculated to sabotage and destroy an established regime;
3 Random acts of violence committed internationally by an individual or groups of individuals to pressurize a state or a group of individuals to succumb to the demands of terrorists; and,
4 Acts committed internationally which aid and abet national terrorism.

With the exception of the first category of invasion, the others are *prima facie* acts of international terrorism which are essentially extensions of national terrorism. That is to say that most acts of international terrorism are a form of national terrorism.

Acts of Defence

Some states claim that internal oppression either by foreign invasion or by an internal totalitarian regime necessitates guerilla warfare for the achievement of freedom. With more emphasis, it has been claimed that one state must not be allowed to exploit and harass another and that the physical manifestation of desire to attain freedom should not be construed as terrorism.[53] Often, such acts of self-defence prove to take extreme violent forms and manifest themselves overseas, thus giving rise to international terrorism. Acts of defence, as they are called, are common forms of international terrorism and are categorized as political violence. These acts take the form of:

> ... acts of disruption, destruction, injury whose purpose, choice of targets or victims, surrounding circumstances, implementation and/ or effects have political significance ... .[54]

Organized political groups plan strikes and acts of violence internally while extensions of these groups carry out brutal assassinations, kidnappings and cause severe damage to property overseas. The retaliatory process which commences as a token of self-defence transcends itself to terroristic violence which is totally ruthless and devoid of moral scruples.[55] Usually, a cause which originates as dedicated to self-defence and self-determination aligns itself to gaining the support of the people, disarming the military strength of the regime against which it rebels and above all seeks to strengthen itself in order that the terrorist movement attains stability. In this instance terrorist acts seek primarily to carry out a massive propaganda campaign in the international community while at the same time concentrating more on individual instances of terrorism in populated urban areas which attract more attention than those committed in isolated areas.[56] Advertising a cause in the international community becomes an integral part of political terrorism of this nature.

Both the international community and the governments concerned should be mindful that acts of defence can be treated as such only in instances where people defend themselves when they are attacked and not when retaliatory measures are taken in isolation to instil fear in the international community. To that extent, acts of defence can be differentiated from acts of terrorism.

Non-violent Acts

There are instances where terrorism extends to destabilizing an established regime or a group of persons by the use of threats which are often calculated to instil fear in the international community. Typical examples of this kind of terrorism are the spreading of false propaganda and the invocation of threats which unhinge both the nation or a group of persons against whom the threats are carried out and the nations in which such acts are said to be committed. There have been instances in the past where export consumer commodities of a nation such as food items have been claimed to be poisoned in order that foreign trade between nations be precluded. Although such acts are devoid of actual physical violence, they tend to unhinge the economic stability of a nation particularly if such nation depends solely on the export of the item in question. In such instances, international terrorism assumes proportions of great complexity[57] and succeeds at least temporarily to disrupt the infrastructural equilibrium of the nation against which such threat is aimed. The government concerned is immediately placed on the defensive and attempts counter-propaganda.[58] In spreading propaganda of this nature, the media is the terrorist's best friend. The media of television and radio is used as a symbolic weapon to instil fear in the public and to cripple the persons or government against which the attack has been aimed. The effect of publicity on people is truly tangible, whether it pertains to the statement of facts or whether it relates to the issuance of threats. Primarily, media terrorism creates an emotional state of apprehension and fear in threatened groups and secondly, draws world attention to the existence of the terrorists and their cause. In both instances, the terrorist succeeds in creating a credibility gap between his target and the rest of the world. Psychological terrorism of this nature is perhaps the most insidious of its kind. It is certainly the most devious.

Random Acts of Violence

A random act of violence is normally a corollary to a threat though not necessarily so. Often as it happens, the international community is shocked by a despicable act of mass murder and destruction of property which take the world completely by surprise. Responsibility for the act is acknowledged later though in many instances no responsibility is claimed. In the latter instance when no responsibility is claimed, the offended nation and the world at large are rendered destitute of an immediate remedy against the offence. Even if motive is imputed to a particular terrorist group, the exercise of sanction becomes difficult as the international community would not condone sanction in the absence of concrete and cogent evidence.

The difficulty lies largely in the fact that any terrorist act is usually carefully planned and executed. Often one observes that the terrorist cautiously retracts his or her steps obscuring all evidence unless seeking publicity. The average terrorist is a militant who employs tactics aimed at instilling fear in the minds of the international community. Terrorist acts are calculated to instil fright and paralyze the infrastructure of a state by totally exhausting the strength of the target.[59] The terrorist further disarms the target by introducing the element of surprise to the attack. Perhaps the most outstanding element of a random attack is the psychological element where excessive and sporadic acts of violence instill both fear and psychological disorientation in a society. This in turn contributes to undermining and weakening a government's authority and control. The disruptive influence that terrorism of this kind exercises over society often creates disharmony within the political circles of a nation and unhinges the psychological behavioral pattern of an organized society. Most often the gap between the citizen and the established government both in the state in which the act is committed and in the state against which the act is committed is widened as the average citizen tends to regard personal security as the most inviolate of rights that has to be protected by his or her government.

Acts which Aid and Abet National Terrorism

The fourth facet of international terrorism pertains to acts which promote national terrorism and which are committed outside the state against which the terrorist cause exists. These acts manifest themselves in the maintenance of overseas training camps for terrorists where guerilla warfare, techniques of assassination, destruction and sabotage are taught to terrorist groups who, after sustained training, return to their country and practise what they learn overseas. Such training camps are conducted usually by revolutionary groups and mercenaries on the request of terrorist organizations. A natural corollary to this trend is the collection of funds overseas for the financing of such training programmes, the purchase of arms, ammunition and explosives and the collection of monies involved in meeting the costs incurred by foreign propaganda.

Indirect acts of international terrorism such as those which aid and abet national terrorism indicate clearly that although there is no identifiable definition of the word 'terrorism', the word itself can no longer be associated only with violent acts of aggression. In fact, recent studies reflect that any organized campaign of international terrorism involves both direct and indirect acts in equal proportion.[60]

Broadly, international terrorism embitters humanity and antagonizes one nation against another, one human being against another. The eventual consequence of the problem is aggression and even war. The main aim of use of the psychological element by the international terrorist which is by far the most obnoxious and objectionable ambition is to polarize humans and society. However, its immediate manifestation and future development are not without features sufficient to cause grave concern to the world.

Acts of international terrorism, whether in the form of violent or non-violent acts have clear and immediate international consequences. They are numerous in nature and warrant a separate study. However, in effect they obtain for the miscreant the same result of creating disharmony and disruption in society. The concept has grown in recent times to portend more serious problems to the international community. Those problems are worthy of comment.

Terrorism has so far not reached the proportions of being an international conspiracy although one group identifies its objectives and purpose with another. We have not had the misfortune of seeing all terrorist groups band together to work as a composite element. This has not happened for the reason that diverse ideologies and religions have kept each group separate. Nevertheless, there is a strong identity bond between groups and even evidence that one helps the other with training and military aid, even though their causes are quite different. The link between terrorist groups is an important consideration for the world as close association between groups could strengthen a weak force and nurture it to maturity. In addition, strong and established terrorist organizations, under cover of burgeoning groups, could carry out campaigns which would cover their tracks and make identification difficult. In most instances, this was found to be true and investigation reveals that a small group, not too significant at that time to take account of, has been responsible for an act or acts whereas later it is revealed that a much stronger group had masterminded the offences for its benefit. Another important feature of the growing incidence of international terrorism is the assistance the terrorists receive from the advancement of technology in communication, the manufacture of sophisticated weaponry and the proliferation of nuclear armament. In today's context, terrorism has blown up to unmanageable proportions with the use of advanced weapons of destruction. Arms control plays a vital role in the control of aggression and it naturally follows that terrorism also benefits from the availability of new modes of aggression. The vulnerability of the international community has been mainly brought upon by the paucity of adequate security measures to prevent nuclear theft. With the growth of the nuclear power industry, developed nations exposed themselves to the vulnerability of theft by power groups, in whose hands nuclear weapons act as threats of destruction. The most effective counter measure that can be taken in this instance against the threat of nuclear theft is to take such effective measures as are necessary to protect the stored items and to make known to the terrorist the high risk involved in an attempt to steal such material. Ideally, any hope of theft must be obviated. This can be achieved by strengthening governmental security.

Problems of Deterrence

The only deterrence that would be effective against terrorism of any nature is broadly based on the success of convincing the terrorists that the risk they take outweighs the benefits which may accrue to their cause by their acts. The futility of attempting to wipe out terrorism by the use of military force or the threat of general sanction on an international level is apparent. The terrorists have to be shown that any attempt at terrorist activity would cause them and their cause more harm than good.[61] Deterrence in this context attains fruition when effective punitive sanctions are prescribed and carried out whilst simultaneously denying the terrorists their demands. In both instances the measures taken should be imperatively effective. It is not sufficient if such measures are merely entered into the statute books of a state or incorporated into international treaty. The international community has to be convinced that such measures are forceful and capable of being carried out.

However, deterrence does not stop at the mere imposition of effective sanction nor does it complete its task by the denial of terrorist demands. Perhaps the most effective method of countering terrorism is psychological warfare. The terrorists themselves depend heavily on psychology. Their main task is to polarize the people and the establishment. They want popular support and a sympathetic ear, a lot of people listening and watching, not a lot of people dead.[62] Counter measures taken against a terrorist attack, be it hostage taking, kidnapping or a threat of murder, should essentially include an effective campaign to destroy the terrorist's credibility and sincerity in the eyes of the public. Always, the loyalty of the public should be won over by the target and not by the terrorist. It is only then that the terrorists' risk outweighs the benefits obtained. To achieve this objective it must be ensured that the terrorist receives publicity detrimental to them, showing the public that if the threatened person, group of persons or state comes to harm, the terrorists alone are responsible. Therefore, the most practical measures that could be adopted to deter the spread of terrorism can be accommodated in two chronological stages:

1 Measures taken before the commission of an offence such as the effective imposition and carrying out of sanctions and the refusal to readily comply with the demands of the terrorists;
2 Measures taken after the commission of the act such as the skilful use of the media to destroy the credibility of the terrorist cause and to convince the people that the responsibility for the act devolves at all stages solely upon the terrorists.

One difficulty in exercising deterrence against terrorism in general and international terrorism in particular, is that often the measures taken are not effective enough to convince the terrorists that in the end, more harm would be caused to them than good. Negotiation with the terrorists in particular has to be done by professionals specially trained for the task. *A fortiori,* the media has to be handled by specialists with experience. Things would be much more difficult for the terrorists if these were done. The greatest problem of deterrence is the pusillanimity of the international community in the face of terrorism and the feeble response offered by states as a composite body. The reasons for this hesitation on the part of the international community to adopt effective measures against international terrorism is by no means inexplicable. When one state supports a revolutionary cause which is aimed against another, it is quite natural that the terrorists are aware of the support they are capable of obtaining from at least one part of the already polarized world. Therein lies the problem.

The Practical Solution

The primary objective of international peace and security is the endeavour to preserve the right to life and liberty. This right is entrenched in Article 3 of the Universal Declaration of Human Rights of 1948 and is accepted today as constituting an obligation on all member states to recognize the legally and morally binding nature of the Declaration.[63] Therefore the destruction of human life and the restriction of liberty are acts committed against international law and order. International terrorism destroys both life and liberty. Indeed there need be no doubt in our minds that international terrorism is illegal. To begin with, there should be more awareness in the world today that every human being has the inherent right to life[64] and that the right is protected by law.[65] Any act of terrorism being illegal, becomes subject to law and its punitive sanctions. However, in this instance, unlike in a simple instance of murder where sanction itself may act as a deterrent, the two forces of law and sanction are not sufficient to curb terrorism. The international community should realize that the solution to terrorism lies rather in its prevention than in its cure. Therefore the problem has to be approached solely on the basis that the terrorists on the one hand have to be dissuaded that their acts may not succeed while on the other they have to be persuaded that even if they succeeded in committing the act of terrorism, it would not achieve for them the desired results. The philosophy of warfare against terrorism is therefore based on one single fact – that of convincing the terrorists that any attempt at committing a terrorist act would be fruitless and would entail for them unnecessary harm. This simple philosophy should be adopted gradually in stages with the sustained realization that each measure taken is as important as the next and that all measures should be adopted as a composite element and not as those that are mutually exclusive.

A potential terrorist can therefore be attacked in two ways:

1 By the adoption of practical measures to discourage the commission of the act.

2 By the adoption of such effective measures as would impose severe punitive sanctions if the act is committed.

In the first instance measures of self-help are imperative . They should be adopted with careful planning and the terrorists should be made aware that the community at large are afforded the full protection of these measures. They are: [66]

1 The establishment of a system of intelligence which would inform the state concerned of an impending terrorist attack.
2 The establishment of counter-terrorism mechanisms which would effectively preclude such catalysts as the collection of arms, ammunition and weaponry.
3 The adoption of such practical measures of self-help and attack as are necessary in an instance of an attack.
4 The existence of the necessary machinery to retain the confidence and sympathy of the public at all times.[67]
5 The persuasion necessary to convince the public that terrorism of any kind is evil and should not be condoned, whatever its cause is.[68]

The second instance is concerned with measures taken in the event a terrorist act is committed. If strongly enforced with unanimity, such measures as the imposition of laws which bind all nations to view terrorist acts as crimes against humanity can be an effective deterrent. *A fortiori*, sanctions would further discourage the terrorist.

Practical Measures

The first step that should be taken to deter terrorism is to be equipped with the expertise to detect a potential threat beforehand and to be prepared for an attack. The next is to intensify security in all susceptible areas, particularly in such places as airports, subway terminals, etc. Surveillance of all people who are seen in such areas as targets of terrorist acts, is imperative. There should be more awareness of the threat of terrorist activity particularly in international airports and international bus and train terminals where travel documents should be checked and passengers double-checked.[69] Electronic surveillance of passports and other documents have proved to be effective methods of deterrence in this context. Perhaps the most important facet of surveillance is the use of personnel who do not reveal their identity to the public but unobtrusively mingle with the crowds. This category of person can easily detect an irregularity without arousing suspicion and without alarming people. It is recommended that together with the armed personnel there should also be trained personnel who in all informality may work together with the security forces in such instances. Another significant requirement is the support of the people. Maximum use should be made of the media to educate the public as to how to react in an emergency and also to be totally distrustful of the terrorist whose acts are calculated to evoke sympathy. The state or persons against whom the terrorist attack is launched should, at all times, use the media to convince the public that responsibility for any destruction or harm resulting from a terrorist act devolves totally on the terrorist.

Legal Measures

Terrorism is usually a by-product of political discord between nations. The terrorist is well aware of this situation and usually exploits political disharmony among nations. Whatever laws that are enacted are rendered destitute of effect as they cannot be enforced with uniformity. Political asylum is a product of this anomaly and remains by and large the greatest catalyst to the proliferation of terrorism in the world today.

In the past the United Nations General Assembly has made sustained efforts to adopt collective measures to prevent terrorism. Among the various recommendations that have been placed before the United Nations have been those which urge all nations to contribute collectively to the progressive elimination of the causes of terrorism at national and international levels. In its effort, the United Nations has succeeded in focusing the attention of its member nations on the increasing problems of terrorism and its natural corollaries such as the proliferation of arms, the emergence of mercenaries, etc. However, the efforts of the international community in entering into treaties has been rendered nugatory due to two reasons – the first being the aura of ambiguity that shrouds the nature and force of an international agreement and the second being the lack of enthusiasm on the part of most states to label terrorism as an offence against humanity. The latter, if recognized, would immediately entail the mandatory punishment of the terrorist by all states concerned. The question of whether international law upon which international treaties are based has the nature and force of law has aroused much debate. Although 19th century Austinian thinking did not consider international law to be endowed with the attributes of law,[70] there is a strong view to the contrary.[71] The theory that international law is not enforceable law was based on the thinking that laws emanate from a sovereign authority which was politically superior to those on whom such law was imposed. International law, it was claimed, did not emanate from such authority. The contrary view, which is coercive, holds that if international law had mere force of morality, such authorities as precedents and opinions of jurists would not be cited in instances of adjudication.[72] In addition, certain judicial decisions have expressly recognized the fact that international law is enforceable and has all the attributes of law.[73]

Once it is accepted that international law is enforceable, the second question arises whether treaties in general have the necessary obligatory force to demand adherence from their signatories. Although treaties are founded upon the expectancy of the observance of good faith under the principles of the *pacta sunt servanda*, the emergence of competent courts and tribunals and the increasing dependence upon precedent and scholastic opinion in this field are sufficiently compelling factors in support of the enforceability of treaties. Legislative measures, like practical measures, can be effectively adopted. The first step is for all states to recognize that terrorism of any nature is a crime against humanity. The second is for all states to reach agreement either to punish a terrorist or to deport him or her to a country which has sufficient interest in the offence to enforce punishment. The treatment of the offence by all states should be devoid of political ideology and the tendency to offer political asylum to terrorists. It may not be possible for all states to sign one agreement on this issue. However, states could negotiate bilaterally or in groups and enter into treaties, the provisions of which could accrue to other states as well, on the principle of the most-favoured-nation treatment clause.[74] The most important factor is to involve all states one way or another to form a composite force and not to isolate them in the face of terrorism.

The threat of terrorism can be curbed only if terrorism is recognized as an offence against humanity collectively by the international community. The lack of consensus leads to the situation where acts of terrorism can be prosecuted only if they fall within the purview of municipal law and are categorized as crimes within these laws.[75] Once consensus is reached cooperation between individual states could be enforced by treaty. An international institution such as the United Nations should coordinate the liaison between states and initiate the establishment of interest groups which would assist practically any state which faces the threat of terrorism. The setting up of a powerful and vigilant anti-terrorist squad and the establishment of a trust fund to finance anti-terrorist campaigns in less affluent nations are two measures which would be positive steps towards establishing mutual help and understanding in this context. Above all, what is required is a synthesis of practical and legal measures that would help to unite the world against this crime and discourage the terrorist.

Hijacking Identified

Sixty-eight years have lapsed since the first recorded instance of a hijacking in Peru in 1930. Before the occurrence of this incident any idea of crimes pertaining to aircraft was indeed purely imaginary.[76] Since then, hijacking has become the most significant area of international civil aviation law causing the greatest concern and producing sustained research on its possible control.[77] The offence has been identified primarily as the seizure by force, or control of an aircraft in flight by a person on board,[78] and also been called 'aircraft piracy', 'aircraft hijacking', and more recently, as 'skyjacking'[79] – the latter being also called 'aerial hijacking', an act of terror-violence.[80] The offence has been distinguished from the general term 'piracy' – the latter being a universal crime and implying *inter alia* the robbery at sea for personal enrichment.[81]

Although the first effective countermeasures against hijacking were introduced in 1970, it was not until 1973, when airlines introduced passenger and cabin baggage searches, that the incidents of hijacking decreased. Unfortunately, this progressive countermeasure by the airlines only succeeded in spuring the hijacker towards developing more sophisticated methods of smuggling arms and explosives into aircraft. The diligent work of the terrorist was rewarded in 1985 when the world's worst rate of hijackings was recorded. In response to the hijacker's tenacity, the world reacted by tightening aviation security globally, resulting in 1986 in a sharp decrease in the incidents of hijackings.

Infrequently, hijacking has also been recognized as a separate norm thus differentiating it from the broad rubric of political terrorism.[82] A good example of which was seen recently when thieves wrote a new chapter in the annals of aviation by hijacking a helicopter on 11 August 1992 and swooping down on a passenger jet, stealing a shipment of currency and passenger baggage that was in the aircraft's cargo hold, just as the aircraft was attempting to take-off from a Corsican airport.[83]

An internationally acceptable definition of terrorism and hijacking can be attained only if all nations unanimously agree to treat any act of undue influence which takes advantage of and affects the integrity and interests of any nation. Such an act has to be universally recognized as punishable and free from the restrictions imposed by national laws and other jurisdictional fetters. A universal definition of terrorism is not meant to create a universal political ideology. Nor is it realistic to expect such an eventuality. States can, however, effectively control such instances of terrorism as hijacking if it is made known that the offence would be treated on the same basis, with the same punitive measures attached to it throughout the world. To attain this objective, the subjectivity and hypocrisy with which the concept of terrorism is viewed should be totally eschewed. Furthermore, as will be discussed later in this chapter, the meaning, purpose and function of international law should also be seriously reviewed.

Hijacking and International Conventions

The Tokyo Convention of 1963 on Offences and Certain Other Acts Committed on Board Aircraft,[84] referred to any offence committed or act done by a person on board any aircraft registered in a contracting state, while the aircraft is in flight or on the surface of the high seas or of any other area outside the territory of such state.[85] The aircraft is considered to be in flight from the moment power is applied for the purpose of take-off until the moment when the landing run ends.[86] In addition, the Tokyo Convention mentions acts of interference, seizure of or other wrongful exercise of control of an aircraft, implying its concern over hijacking.[87]

The Hague Convention of 1970[88] in Article 1 identifies any person who, on board an aircraft in flight, unlawfully by force or threat or by any other form of intimidation seizes or takes control of such aircraft, or even attempts to perform such an act, as an offender.[89] Anyone who aids such an act is an accomplice, and is included in the category of the former.[90] It is clear that the Hague Convention by this provision has neither deviated from Article 11 of the Tokyo Convention nor offered a clear definition of the offence of hijacking. It merely sets out the ingredients of the offence – the unlawful use of force, threat or any other form of intimidation and taking control of the aircraft. The use of physical force, weapons or firearms or the threat to use such modes of force are imputed to the offence in this provision. The words force, threat or intimidation indicate that the element of fear would be instilled in the victim. It is an interesting question whether these words would cover an instance where the use of fear as an implement to execute the offence of hijacking covers non-coercive measures such as the drugging of food or beverages taken by the passengers or crew. The Hague Convention does not ostensibly cover such instances. In this context, many recommendations have been made to extend the scope of its Article 1.[91] It is also interesting that the Convention does not envisage an instance where the offender is not on board the aircraft but remains on the ground and directs operations from there after planting a dangerous object in the aircraft. According to Article 1, the offence has to be devoid of a lawful basis albeit that the legality or illegality of an act is not clearly defined in the Convention.

It is also a precondition in Article 1 that the offence has to be committed in flight, that is while all external doors of the aircraft are closed after the embarkation of the passengers and crew.[92] The mobility of the aircraft is immaterial. Furthermore, Article 1 is rendered destitute of effect if an offence is committed while the doors of the aircraft are left open.

The Convention for the Suppression of Unlawful Acts Against The Safety of Civil Aviation signed at Montreal on 23 September 1971,[93] also fails to define in specific terms the offence of hijacking, although it circumvents barriers placed by Article 1 of the Hague Convention.[94] For instance, it encircles instances where an offender need not be physically present in an aircraft; includes instances where an aircraft is immobile; its doors open; and even draws into its net any person who disseminates false information which could endanger an aircraft in flight.[95] None of the three conventions have however succeeded in identifying the offence of hijacking or advocating preventive measures against the offence itself.

The failure of all attempts at identifying the offence of hijacking and formulating a cogent system of preventive criteria attains its culmination in a political terrorist act. Such offences underscore the significant fact that not only is political terrorism treated subjectively under different social and political contexts, but also that so far the only attempts at recognizing the threat of terrorism have been made on an intrinsic approach, more to condemn the offence than to find a cure for the deep-seated social and political factors which form the permanent breeding grounds for terrorism. The inevitable continuity of the commission of this offence cannot be stopped if the following are not seriously considered:

- the reasons for the perpetration of terrorist acts;
- the universal definition of such acts;
- the fact that such acts transcend national boundaries and affect the entirety of the civilized world; and,
- the fact that every act of terrorism brings a political advantage to certain nations.

The most obvious and the primary stage at which the offence of hijacking can be controlled is at the time of check-in when a comprehensive search of all passengers and their baggage for concealed weapons would greatly alleviate the problem.[96] The United States of America have adopted this measure by introducing electronic screening of all passengers by statute in 1973. The results of this measure were almost immediately visible with the sudden drop in the incidents of hijackings in the United States in 1973.[97] In addition to these measures, direct criminal sanction on a similar basis, on national level, by each of the states who enter into international agreement on the prevention and control of hijacking has been recommended.[98] It is an enlightened view that:

> Violence, terrorism, assassination, undeclared wars all threaten to destroy the restraint and moderations that must become the dominant characteristic of courage. Unless we establish a code of international behaviour in which the resort to violence becomes increasingly irrelevant to the pursuit of national interests, we will crush the world's dream for human development and full flowering of human freedom.[99] Based on the above thinking, a universal statutory proposal has been recommended.[100] This proposal extends the scope of the three international Conventions only slightly but does not change their structure radically. For instance, Section 2 of the recommended statute covers acts of violence perpetrated on aircraft in flight or those which endanger the safety of an aircraft in service.[101] However, the proposed statute does not envisage all possibilities of hijacking.

On a different note it is strongly felt that the modern age has left us with the almost irrefutable concept that political offenders need not as a rule be extradited, thus making the element of political asylum almost a mandatory doctrine for most of the international community.[102] In this context, an observation on the threat of hijacking was made as early as 1973 which is worthy of note. It said:

> Potential criminals, and hijackers in particular, will be discouraged from committing acts only if there is no country in which they can find refuge. This requires international agreement among States, followed by legislation in each State, providing either for the punishment of persons committing such crimes, or for their extradition to another State where they will be punished.[103]

The above view is consistent with the approach that agreement should be reached by as many states as possible if not all, either to provide for the punishment of a guilty person on a universally agreed basis or to extradite him or her to a country which has sufficient interest to enforce punishment. In this instance, what is known as the freedom of political expression should give way to the blending of international law enforcement and security of the passenger. The crime itself has to be viewed as a common one which erodes all norms of fundamental human rights.[104]

Although the offence of hijacking has shown a decreasing trend, it becomes apparent that, *non obstante*, more cooperation is needed among nations to review the remedial measures that have been adopted to counteract the threat. Such measures should be viewed under four broad areas. They are:

1 A wider definition of the offence itself to cover every possible exigency of the safety of aircraft, passengers and goods;

2 More liberal attitudes towards the extradition of offenders and the total abstinence of states from encouraging the concepts of political asylum and political havens;
3 More world-wide awareness of the need to strengthen internal security and individual checking of passengers and travel documents;
4 Total agreement between states that the offence of hijacking, once identified, be viewed on a singular basis devoid of any political differences which would encourage the commission of the offence. Punitive measures should be similar if not identical in order that a potential offender be precluded from choosing his or her alternatives.

The proliferation of dangerous weapons and the rapidity of scientific advancement, coupled with increasing political discord among nations show that the offence of hijacking should not be viewed subjectively as a sporadic occurrence anymore. It is more a planned inversion of socio-political values and the erosion of human rights.

It can no longer be viewed simply as the illegal diversion of an aircraft to a destination other than that which was envisaged in the original flight plan or more simplistically as the seizure by force of an aircraft in flight.[105] It is even more than the mere seizure or exercise of control by force or violence or threat of force or violence and with wrongful intent, of an aircraft in flight in air commerce.[106] It should be viewed as an extortion-oriented act committed against the international order and world peace which is calculated to take advantage of the most susceptible human quality of the endeavour to protect human life at any cost. This broad attitude would engulf and cover even the rare instance of a demented offender who perpetrates the offence for no apparent reason. In the ultimate analysis, any attempt at hijacking involves more than one nation, thereby immediately transcending all national boundaries and exposing the sensitivities of the nations involved. The offence therefore becomes an immediate threat to world peace and should be treated as such. It is needless to say that any nation which views the offence differently encourages universal discord. It is submitted that in the light of the increasing incidence of hijacking, the offence should be defined and accepted by the world as any wilful act calculated to endanger the safety of an aircraft or any passenger in service or in flight. The words 'in service' in this context should mean any period of time when a serviceable aircraft which is used for air transportation is left standing in a hangar, while the words 'in flight' should cover the period of time when an aircraft is taken out of the hangar until it returns to the hangar. In this event, the offence would not be mere 'aerial piracy' but an offence against the safety of air travel.

As for the need for a more flexible approach to the extradition of offenders, the establishment and recognition of a universal offence against the safety of aircraft would almost automatically nurture mutual cooperation between nations. Often, if a hijacker imputes politics to the offence committed by him, he is granted political asylum by the host nation merely because the latter sympathizes with the alleged motive for the offence as represented by the hijacker. Once this takes place it no longer remains the commission of an offence universally condemned but becomes an altercation between nations on political beliefs and convictions.[107]

International and internal security are also major areas of importance in the prevention and control of hijacking. Quite apart from the growing need for the establishment of a separate international anti-terrorist squad under the auspices of the United Nations, the need is visible on a national basis for more stringent security measures to be adopted against possible offenders. There should be more awareness of the threat at the airport itself with the checking of travel documents, double-checking of passengers once they are at the airport and later just before boarding. In this context, use could be made of computer checking of police records which would include details of suspicious passengers who may be previous offenders, the introduction of magnetic cards on passports and rigid inspection of all travel documents at the airport. Electronic surveillance, wherever it has been carried out has proved an effective measure of prevention of the offence. In addition to the need for a cogent definition of the offence, universal sanction is needed for the prevention of the offence. It is noteworthy that as far back as 1971 an attempt was made by the the United States and Canada to draft a multilateral convention to establish rigid sanctions for the offence of hijacking on a multilateral basis. This was to have been under the auspices of the ICAO. The draft recommended powers of arbitration and intervention by ICAO in instances of dispute with regard to extradition. The draft did not attain fruition and result in the adoption of a convention.

In July 1978, leaders of seven nations[108] met in Bonn and adopted what was later to be called the Bonn Declaration, which in essence, proclaimed that heads of states and governments would ensure the cessation of all flights into a country which refuses the extradition or prosecution of a person or persons who perpetrates the offence of hijacking. The Bonn Declaration attempted to achieve two goals: the first being to implicitly recognize the fact that states are often accomplices after the fact of hijacking; and the second being that it was time for a universal consensus on and action against the offence of hijacking. The rationale of the Declaration is primarily deterrence, and secondarily, consensus against the offence.[109]

Acts of Sabotage

The most recent major incident involving acts of sabotage against civil aviation was the explosion over Lockerbie, Scotland on 21 December 1988 of PAN-AM flight 103. The explosion is believed to have been caused by the detonation of a plastic explosive concealed in a portable radio/cassette player. The substance used was Semtex, a plastic explosive having its origin in Semtin, Pardubice, Czechoslovakia. Earlier in 1986, a TWA Boeing 727 aircraft had been blown up by a plastic explosive just before the aircraft landed in Athens. Professor Michael Milde states:

> The brutal tragedy of PAN-AM 103 focused the attention of ICAO on the need to tighten the preventive security measures in particular in the field of detection of explosive substances.[110]

Accordingly, an *ad hoc* group of specialists on the detection of explosives was established by the ICAO Council. This group met in Montreal in March 1989. The United Nations Security Council, in June 1989 adopted Resolution 635 which *inter alia* urged ICAO to intensify its work aimed at preventing all acts of terrorism against international civil aviation, and in particular its work on devising an international regime for the marking of plastic sheet explosives for the purpose of detection.[111] At the 27th Session of the ICAO Assembly in September/October 1989, the delegations of Czechoslovakia and the United Kingdom presented to the Executive Committee a paper which contained a Draft Resolution on the marking of sheet explosives for the purpose of detection.[112]

The international conference on air law held in Montreal under the aegis of ICAO unanimously adopted a Convention on the Marking of Plastic or Sheet Explosives for the Purpose of Detection.[113] While the scope of the Convention has been extended to other means of transport by the Preamble to the Convention, the definition of explosives has been enlarged to include explosive products commonly known as 'plastic explosives' including explosives in flexible elastic sheet form, as described in the Technical Annex to the Convention.[114] Each state party is obligated to take the necessary measures to prohibit and prevent the movement into and out of its territory of unmarked explosives[115] while exercising strict and efficient control over the possession and transfer of explosives referred to in the Technical Annex to the Convention.[116] While it is popularly felt that the Convention is a spectacular and impressive achievement which was very quickly accomplished,[117] the new Convention is by no means the only and ultimate solution to the problem of sabotage of civil aviation. It is merely one more step in the long line of legal and practical measures.[118]

Surface-to-air Missile Attacks

There have been a few reported incidents of serious damage caused by surface-to-air missiles (SAM) against civil aviation. In late 1978 and early 1979 two Air Rhodesia aircraft were destroyed by SAM missiles. There were heavy casualties. There are also reports of the Mujahedeen of Afghanistan obtaining and using SAM equipment on aircraft over Afghanistan.[119] There have also been many unsuccessful reports of attacks launched by terrorists against aircraft in flight over Europe – particularly over Rome and Paris.[120] Unlike other types of terrorism, this particular species of offence can be controlled to a large extent owing to the difficulty of trans-border transport of surface-to-air missiles.

Armed Attacks against Airports and Persons

Armed terrorist attacks are a common form of terror in the world of aviation. The first recorded armed attack in an airport was in June 1972 when Seikigunha (Japanese Red Army) guerillas opened fire with automatic weapons and threw grenades in the premises of Ben Gurion Airport in Tel Aviv. Since then there have been incidents in Athens Airport in August 1973, and in Rome and Vienna in 1985 and numerous later attacks on airports and aviation-related properties world-wide. Armed terrorist attacks have led to sustained litigation for claims for damages from the airlines on the basis that passengers in an airport are under the control of the air carrier they fly with.[121] In the recent case of *Buanocore* v. *Trans World Airlines Inc.*,[122] where the plaintiffs' son, John Buanocore was killed during a terrorist attack on da Vinci Airport, Rome, on 27 December 1985, the court held that the plaintiffs could not claim damages from the airline for their son's death since the airline did not exercise control over the activities of the deceased. Be that as it may, a sustained *cursus curiae* reflects numerous instances where armed terrorist attacks against persons and property at airports, airline offices, and other aviation-related locations have led to litigation in courts and the subsequent award of compensation to the plaintiff.

Narco-terrorism

The illegal carriage by air of narcotics and other psychotropic substances and its various corollaries of violence or 'narco-terrorism' as it is popularly known as, has become an intractable problem in recent years. Narco-terrorism is considered an offence on two grounds: the fact that the illicit trafficking of drugs is an offence against public health; and, the illicit carriage by air of these substances leads to other crimes against international civil aviation such as the unlawful seizure of aircraft and the causing of damage to persons and property related to international civil aviation.[123] The problem has grown to unmanageable proportions owing to the rapid proliferation of air travel as a means of communication. ICAO records that 9350 turbo jet aircraft were active in commercial air transport in 1990[124] which fact was also borne out by Boeing in its 1992 estimation of the world jet fleet.[125] It is not difficult therefore to figure out the tremendous encouragement given to the drug trafficking trade by the numerous aircraft movements that would be spread out by these aircraft over the now functional 14 488 land airports in the world.[126] It is not surprising therefore that there have been numerous instances where aircraft had been seized by governmental authorities owing to the presence of narcotic drugs.[127]

Narco-terrorism in international civil aviation has its genesis in the illicit trafficking of drugs which has been the focus of attention of the world community in general and the United Nations in particular. Professor Michael Milde, describing the efforts of the United Nations and its specialized agencies to curb the problem of illicit drug trafficking observes:

> An 'international campaign against traffic in drugs' was launched as a matter of 'highest priority' and contemplated the convening of a specialized international conference dealing specifically with illicit drug trafficking, characterized as an 'international criminal activity'. Another resolution directly linked drug abuse and illegal trafficking with 'international criminal activities such as the illegal arms trade and terrorist practices', and considered them to be a 'threat to the well being of peoples, the stability of democratic institutions and the sovereignty of States'.[128]

Narco-terrorism involves two facets: the transportation of drugs and narcotics by aircraft and across national boundaries by air; and the act of loading and unloading them at aerodromes and airports. The two acts are claimed to be integrally linked to one another. As Antonio Francoz Rigalt observes:

> In actual fact, the essential elements of the unlawful act, i.e. 'transport by air' and 'trafficking' are inseparable. Nevertheless, there is a distinction to be made between them. Air transport involves carrying the drugs from one place to another by aircraft, and this may be done either lawfully or unlawfully. It is lawful when carried out for medicinal purposes and with the permission of the appropriate authorities. It is unlawful when these requirements are not fulfilled; and another characteristic here is the element of continuity because the transport, be it by land, sea, or air is carried out with a single criminal intent and

> a plurality of actions which together violate the same legal rule and which, in addition, may be 'continuous' when it takes some time to complete, involving, as it always does, frequent trips by air.[129]

Rigalt also points out that the illegal transportation of drugs and narcotics encompass other criminal acts that come within the purview of offences against public health. He claims further that narco-terrorism could give rise to heinous offences such as the destruction of aircraft, unlawful use of traffic installations, damage to private and public property, theft and robbery.[130]

Taking note of the outcome of the United Nations International Conference on Drug Abuse and Illicit Trafficking, held in Vienna from 17–26 June 1987[131], ICAO, at the 27th Session of its Assembly in September–October 1989 adopted Resolution A 27–12 which recognized the deleterious effects on international civil aviation of the illegal carriage of narcotics and psychotropic substances and urged the ICAO Council to continue its work in order to prevent the illicit transport of narcotic drugs and psychotropic substances by air[132] and to propose necessary action and measures to combat the threat, including the preparation of guidance material on the problem.[133] The Assembly, by the same Resolution, called upon contracting states to continue their efforts to prevent the illicit trafficking of drugs by air.[134]

Pursuant to Resolution A 27–12, the ICAO Secretariat issued a State Letter[135] to the United Nations as well as to other relevant international organizations[136] and to contracting states for their information and seeking their views on possible action to be taken. More than half the replies to the State Letter indicated that states were taking necessary action and measures to enact municipal legislation to curb the threat.[137]

Earlier, the 10th Session of the ICAO Facilitation Division held in September 1988 had recommended numerous amendments to Annex 9 of the Chicago Convention to reflect narcotics control requirements in the Annex. The objective of these amendments was to ensure that a balance is achieved between the interests of facilitation and those of narcotics control.[138]

A Common Threat

Terrorism is a risk that accompanies air travel[139] and may be aimed at achieving several objectives. Acts of terrorism may be aimed at: extracting specific concessions, such as the release of prisoners or payment of ransom; gaining publicity; attracting attention of the international press to the terrorist cause; causing widespread disorder in a society to demoralize and breakdown the existing social order; provoking repression, reprisals and counter-terrorism; enforcing obedience and cooperation; and punishing the victim of the terrorist attack. Often the terrorist does not discriminate between his or her actual target and innocent bystanders.[140]

Although as Dr. Bockstiegel once said, there are no perfect solutions, legal or otherwise, for the problems relating to aviation security,[141] the terrorist is often aided by the lack of supervision and vigilance on the part of the victim. This was found to be so by the committee of inquiry that looked into the security situation relating to the 1985 Air India disaster[142] and the 1988 PAN-AM disaster.[143] *A fortiori* therefore, the aviation industry is a high profile, soft target that remains highly susceptible as an easy prey on account of its weakness in security.[144]

International Law and Action

The Chicago Convention

The Convention on International Civil Aviation[145] signed at Chicago on 7 December 1944 serves as the main repository of principles relating to the development of international civil aviation. The Chicago Convention states in its Preamble that the abuse of international civil aviation can become a threat to the general security, and recognizes the desirability of developing international civil aviation in a safe and orderly manner. ICAO derives its legitimacy and legal sustenance from the Chicago Convention which provides that one of ICAO's objectives is to ensure the safe and orderly growth of international civil aviation throughout the world.[146] The Chicago Convention also stipulates two other objectives of ICAO:

1 That ICAO promotes safety of flight in international aviation[147]; and,
2 That ICAO, through the development of its standards and practices meets the needs of the peoples of the world for safe, regular, efficient and economical air transport.[148]

The latter aim devolves upon ICAO the responsibility of developing standards and recommended practices to ensure both the safety and efficiency of air transport. The two attributes of safety and efficiency are considered complementary and not mutually exclusive. Accordingly, ICAO has drawn attention to the importance of aviation security in Annex 9 to the Chicago Convention[149] while at the same time conversely providing in Annex 17 to the Chicago Convention dealing with aviation security:

> Each contracting State should whenever possible, arrange for the security measures and procedures to cause a minimum of interference with, or delay to the activities of international civil aviation.[150]

This approach makes both security and facilitation equally important to the development of international civil aviation. Annex 17 to the Chicago Convention impels each contracting state to establish a national civil aviation security programme[151] whose objective is to ensure the safety, regularity and efficiency of international civil aviation by providing, through regulations, practices and procedures, safeguards against acts of unlawful interference.[152] The theme of the Annex is international cooperation in aviation security matters in such areas as the prevention of the usage of dangerous weapons, explosives or any other dangerous devices within their territory[153] and the provision of facilities for air services so as to ensure safety of flight of all aircraft.[154]

International Conventions

The Tokyo Convention was perhaps the first major attempt at curtailing the menace of hijacking. Not only did it deal solely with jurisdiction over offences committed in an aircraft in flight, but it also did not exclude any criminal jurisdiction which would have been exercised according to the provisions of any law.[155] The element of nationality underlines the parochial nature of the treatment of the offence and the obstinate refusal of the international community to infuse a universality to the treatment of the offence. Perhaps, as one commentator observed,[156] the international community was not prepared in 1963 to address this problem on a collective basis.

The subsequent Hague Convention emphasized that each contracting state undertakes to impose severe penalties without defining what these penalties should be.[157] Furthermore, the geographic limitations set out in Article 1 curtail the punitive measures recommended in the Convention significantly. The Convention makes a further serious omission in stating that it applies only if the place of take-off and place of landing is outside the state of registration of the aircraft.[158] This gives rise to a serious anomaly in that if an aircraft with a destination outside its territory of nationality is seized in mid-air prior to leaving its airspace and brought back to the place of take-off the Convention would not apply, even to scheduled flight.

The Montreal Convention which followed in 1971, although extending the period in which the offence would be committed to a period beginning at pre-flight preparation which ends 24 hours after landing, does not cover acts of sabotage, destruction or any damage effected before the above period starts 24 hours after landing. The

Montreal Convention however, is the best attempt so far at attempting to control or curb the offence of hijacking on an international level. Even so, the three attempts so far at international accord fail to cover certain gaps which still exist in this area of prevention and control of hijacking. They are:

1 That the Conventions do not provide for and guarantee the trial of an offender and do not specify adequate punitive measures;
2 That no obligation is cast on contracting states for the extradition of an offender.
3 That no provision is made for the universal adoption of standards of precaution and safety.
4 That the initial attempt, albeit somewhat unsophisticated, of the Tokyo Convention at a remedial approach has been thwarted by the repressive attitude of the two subsequent Conventions.

The Bonn Declaration of 1978 was yet another attempt by the international community to combat terrorism related to international civil aviation. The major economic powers – Canada, France, Federal Republic of Germany (as it then was), Italy, Japan, UK and USA – collaborated to intensify efforts to combat terrorism. The seven signatory states pledged to take immediate action to cease all flights to a country which refuses to extradite hijackers or return hijacked aircraft, and to halt all incoming aircraft from that country or from any airlines of that country. The view has however been forwarded that under the principles of the Bonn Declaration, retaliatory action in the nature of self-preservation by third states against an offending state are subjectively assessed, and that action taken should be commensurate with the gravity of the infringement of the provisions of the Declaration.[159] Be that as it may, the Bonn Declaration was a clear demonstration that positive action can be taken against the threat of interference with international civil aviation if there is international cooperation. The signatories to the Bonn Declaration were the largest manufacturers of aircraft and their airlines covered more than half the world's scheduled passenger kilometres. They obviated the insurmountable difficulty of obtaining all the signatures of the ICAO's contracting states while amply demonstrating that agreements of this nature are effective tools against the terrorist.[160]

At a United Nations Conference in Vienna on 25 November 1988, delegates from 100 states adopted a Convention against illicit trafficking in narcotic Drugs and Psychotropic Substances.[161] The new Convention was intended to supplement the two major international drug control treaties[162] in meeting the challenges posed by the upsurge in illicit drug trafficking and associated organized criminal activities. The Convention provides for: sanctions for offences relating to drug trafficking; the tracing, freezing and forfeiture of proceeds derived from drug trafficking; extradition for offences relating to drug trafficking; mutual legal assistance in the investigation and presentation of drug trafficking offences; and measures to eradicate illicitly cultivated narcotic plants.

From a legal standpoint, it would be best to assess the problem fully by collecting data and statistics extensively and reviewing current methodology used in combatting drug trafficking, before establishing an aviation-related legal regime on a conclusive basis. It is also necessary to ensure the implementation of the legal regime that is established by firstly introducing sustained training programmes in the control of narcotics trafficking and monitoring trends of abuse. It would therefore be prudent to establish a global legal regime that would ensure full awareness of the problem on the basis of priority.

Emerging Trends

Dr. H.A. Wassenbergh points out that there is a protective imperative that governs human life in modern society:

> Man's primary concern intellectually speaking, is his safety, then his health and relative position in his society and only then his (relative) freedom in his society, that is, the wish to be master in his own 'territory'.[163]

The primary aim of humanity is to preserve life and liberty.[164] This right, which is entrenched in Article 3 of the Universal Declaration of Human Rights[165] makes the destruction of human life and the restriction of liberty, acts committed against law and order. International terrorism destroys both life and liberty and therefore is incontrovertibly illegal. There should be more awareness in the world today that every human being has the inherent right to life[166] and that the right is protected by law.[167] Any act of terrorism being illegal, becomes subject to law and its punitive sanctions, if any. In this instance however, unlike in a direct instance of murder where sanction itself may act as a deterrent, the two forces of law and sanction are not sufficient to curb terrorism. The international community should realize that the solution to terrorism lies rather in its prevention than its cure.

Therefore, the problem has to be approached solely on the basis that the terrorists on the one hand have to be dissuaded that their act may not succeed, while on the other, they have to be persuaded that even if they succeeded in committing the act of terrorism, it would not achieve the desired results.

The philosophy of warfare against terrorism is therefore based on one single fact – that of convincing the terrorist that any attempt at committing a terrorist act would be fruitless and would entail for them unnecessary harm. The simple philosophy should be adopted gradually in stages with the sustained realization that each measure taken is as important as the next and that all measures should be adopted as a composite element and not as those that are mutually exclusive.

A potential terrorist can therefore be attacked in two ways:

1 By the adoption of practical measures to discourage the commission of the act.
2 By the adoption of such effective measures as would impose severe punitive sanctions if the act is committed.

In the first instance measures of self-help are imperative. They should be adopted with careful planning and the terrorist should be made aware that the community at large are afforded the full protection of these measures. They are:

1 A wider definition of the offence itself to cover every possible exigency of the safety of aircraft, passengers and goods.
2 More liberal attitudes towards the extradition of offenders and the total abstinence of states from encouraging the concepts of political asylum and political havens.
3 More world-wide awareness of the need to strengthen internal security and individual checking of passengers and travel documents.
4 Total agreement between states that the offence of hijacking, once identified, be viewed on a singular basis devoid of any political differences which would encourage the commission of the offence. Punitive measures should be similar if not identical in order that a potential offender be precluded from choosing his or her alternatives.
5 The establishment of a system of intelligence that would inform the state concerned of an impending terrorist attack;
6 The establishment of counter-terrorism mechanisms that would effectively preclude such catalysts as the collection of arms, ammunition and weaponry;
7 The adoption of such practical measures of self-help and attack as are necessary in the instance of an attack;
8 The existence of the necessary machinery to retain the confidence and sympathy of the public at all times;
9 The persuasion necessary to convince the public that terrorism of any kind is evil and should not be condoned, whatever its cause is.

If strongly enforced with unanimity, such measures as the imposition of laws which bind all nations to view terrorist acts as crimes against humanity can be effective deterrents. *A fortiori*, sanctions would further discourage the terrorist.

The Role of Treaty Law

The role of treaty law is perhaps best illustrated by the concept of interference by states in matters of security. An appropriate analogy under this rubric is the issue of humanitarian intervention in states undergoing a security crisis or natural disaster. The Charter of the United Nations, which was signed on 26 June 1945 and came into force on 24 October 1945 lists the achievement of international cooperation in solving international problems of an economic, social, cultural or humanitarian character, as one of the purposes of the United Nations.[168] The problems that the United Nations is mandated by its Charter to solve should therefore be necessarily of an international nature. Article 2 (7) of the Charter expands the scope of this philosophy further when it provides that the United Nations is not authorized to intervene in matters which are essentially within the domestic jurisdiction of any state, without prejudice to the right of the United Nations to intervene in matters which are within the domestic jurisdiction of any state, and apply enforcement measures where there is an occurrence of acts of aggression, a threat to the peace or breach thereof.[169] Therefore *stricto sensu*, the United Nations cannot intervene in instances where natural disasters such as famine, drought or earthquakes render the citizens of a state homeless, destitute and dying of starvation unless invited by the state concerned. The principle however cannot be too strictly interpreted, as natural disasters may usually lead to breaches of the peace. In such instances the United Nations Security Council may take such actions by air, sea or land as may be necessary to maintain or restore international peace and security.[170] For such instances, Article 43 of the Charter provides:

> All members of the United Nations, in order to contribute to the maintenance of international peace and security, undertake to make available to the Security Council, on its call and in accordance with a special agreement or agreements, armed forces assistance and facilities, including rights of passage necessary for the purpose of maintaining international peace and security.

Here again, action can only be taken for the maintenance of international peace, effectively precluding any direct intervention in a domestic issue.

The Resolutions adopted by the United Nations Security Council in 1992 relating to Somalia[171] and Bosnia and Hercegovina[172] clearly demonstrated the parameters of the scope of United Nations' intervention under its Charter.[173] In the case of Somalia, the United Nations Security Council recognized the unique character of the situation in the country, where conflict and violence demanded that all concerned take all necessary measures to facilitate the measures of the United Nations, its specialized agencies and humanitarian organizations to provide humanitarian assistance to the affected population in Somalia. In the case of Bosnia and Hercegovina the Security Council recognized in its Resolution that the situation in the two States constituted a threat to international peace and security. In both Resolutions, the Security Council had to function within its mandate of intervention only in instances of conflict and breaches of the peace.

Since it is clear that the intervention of the United Nations Security Council in a matter lying within the domestic jurisdiction of a state can only be justified in instances where there is a threat to international peace and security, a breach of the peace within a state or an act of aggression, a question which arises when a relief flight is operated as a part of a humanitarian project is whether the operation of such a flight could form a legitimate ground for unilateral action by states. The question would essentially be ground in a legal analysis of the principles of humanitarian law and state sovereignty. On the one hand, everyone has the right to life, liberty and security of person[174] and the right to a standard of living adequate for the health and well being of self and family, including food, clothing, housing and medical care.[175] On the other, there is overall recognition of the fact that every state has complete and exclusive sovereignty over the airspace above its territory.[176] Except for the Paris Convention of 1956,[177] which provides for civil aircraft registered in a member state of the European Civil Aviation Conference (ECAC) to fly freely into member states for the purposes of discharging or taking on traffic where such aircraft are engaged *inter alia* in non-scheduled flights for the purpose of meeting humanitarian or emergency needs,[178] there is no multilateral or bilateral agreement that admits of unilateral intervention of a state in another for humanitarian purposes, where the intervening state does not obtain permission of the recipient state. In fact, the United Nations General Assembly at its 46th Session in December 1991 adopted Resolution 46/182 which explicitly provides in the Annex to the Resolution that the sovereignty, territorial integrity and national unity of states must be fully respected in accordance with the Charter of the United Nations and that in this context, humanitarian assistance should be provided with the consent of the affected country and in principle on the basis of an appeal by the affected country. These conflicting principles, although not bestowing legal authority on the United Nations to intervene in a state with relief flights, at least give some degree of justification to the United Nations' efforts to mediate with states concerned in the promotion of relief operations and to seek the support of other states, with the concurrence of affected states.

Since under general law, no one can intervene unilaterally in a state to provide relief flights to that state, the question is whether there are any special circumstances that the law may construe as an exception to the rule. The answer would seem to lie in what legal commentators call 'humanitarian intervention' which is considered to be a basic moral response of one human being to another, to save the latter's life. One definition identifies:

> Humanitarian intervention as the proportionate transboundary help, including forcible help, provided by governments to individuals in another State who are being denied basic human rights and who themselves would be rationally willing to revolt against their oppressive government.[179]

The general principle of intervention for the provision of relief on moral grounds has been subject to a great degree of intellectual polarization. One view is that if humans are dying, one has got to help at all costs.[180] The other is that the mere act of treating humanitarian intervention as an extant legal doctrine would be to erode the applicable provision of the United Nations Charter on recourse to force.

The latter view, which discourages humanitarian intervention is substantiated by the following arguments:

1 The 'good samaritan' must fight for the right to perform an act of humanitarian intervention and may end up causing more injury than he or she averts;
2 the authorization for forceful and unilateral humanitarian assistance may be abused; and,
3 unilateral recourse to force even for genuinely humanitarian purposes may heighten expectations of violence within the international system and concomitantly erode the psychological constraints on the use of force for other purposes.[181]

The essence of intervention is compulsion. Compulsion could either take place through the use of force, armed or otherwise. The legal question, with regard to the inviolability of the sovereignty of a state is not whether the intervention concerned was an armed or unarmed one, but whether it was effected unilaterally under compulsion or threat by the intervening state.[182] Starke is inclined to stretch the principle of sovereignty to accommodate external involvement by a state in the affairs of another in special circumstances:

> 'Sovereignty' has a much more restricted meaning today than in the eighteenth and nineteenth centuries when, with the emergence of powerful highly nationalised States, few limits on State autonomy were acknowledged. At the present time there is hardly a State which, in the interests of the international community, has not accepted restrictions on its liberty of action. Thus most States are members of the United Nations and the International Labour Organization (ILO), in relation to which they have undertaken obligations limiting their unfettered discretion in matters of international policy. Therefore, it is probably more accurate today to say that the sovereignty of a State means the *residuum* of power which it possesses within the confines laid down by international law. It is of interest to note that this conception resembles the doctrine of early writers on international, law, who treated the State as subordinate to the law of nations, then identified as part of the wider 'law of nature.'[183]

Oppenheim holds a similar view that the 'traditional' law of humanity is incorporated into contemporary international law. He views this attitude as:

> Recognition of the supremacy of the law of humanity over the law of the sovereign State when enacted or applied in violation of human rights in a manner that may justly be held to shock the conscience of mankind.[184]

Some authorities in international law also believe that intervention should, if absolutely necessary, be effected when there is cogent evidence of a breakdown in the minimum guarantees of humanity.[185] Accordingly, it may be argued that any act of intervention aimed at saving the lives of human beings in danger would be legally and morally justifiable. Fernando Teson[186] argues that since the ultimate justification for the existence of states is the protection and enforcement of the natural rights of the citizens, a government that engages in substantial violations of human rights betrays the very purpose for which it exists and so forfeits not only its domestic legitimacy, but also its international legitimacy as well. He goes on to say:

> I suggest that from an ethical standpoint, the rights of States under international law are properly derived from individual rights. I therefore reject the notion that States have any autonomous moral standing – that they hold international rights that are independent from the rights of individuals who populate the State.

Schwarzenberger analyses the concept somewhat clinically and concludes that in the absence of an international *jus cogens* which corresponds to municipal *jus cogens* of advanced communities, where the latter prevents the worst excesses of inequality of power, the supremacy of the rule of force would prevail.[187]

There is also a contrasting view that humanitarian intervention is generally resorted to by states only in instances of serious abuses of human rights by one state upon its people or others. Dr Michael Akehurst argues that if a state intervenes forcibly on the territory of another in order to protect the local population from serious human violations, such an armed intervention could inevitably constitute a temporary violation *de facto* of the territorial integrity of the latter state, and to an extent of its political independence, if carried out against its wishes.[188]

Notes

1 *Charter of the United Nations and Statute of the International Court of Justice*, Department of Public Information, United Nations, New York, *DPI/511- 40108 (3-90), 100M* at 1.

2 United Nations Charter. *Id*. at 3.

3 On 17 November 1989 the United Nations General Assembly adopted Resolution 44/23 which declared that the period 1990–1999 be designated as the United Nations Decade of International Law (the full text of Resolution 44/23 is included as Appendix 1 at the end of this book). The main purposes of the decade have been identified *inter alia* as:

   a the promotion of the acceptance of the principles of international law and respect therefor;
   b the promotion of the means and methods for the peaceful settlement of disputes between States including resort to the International Court of Justice with full respect therefor;
   c the full encouragement of the progressive development of international law and its codification;
   d the encouragement of the teaching, studying, dissemination and wider appreciation of international law.

   The four tasks of the Resolution have been predicated upon the fact that the purpose of the United Nations is to maintain peace and security. See *Resolutions and Decisions Adopted by the General Assembly During its Forty-fourth Session*, Vol. 1, 19 Sept–29 Dec 1989, *General Assembly Official Records: Forty-fourth Session*, Supplement no. 49 (A/44/49), United Nations, New York, 1990, 31. For a detailed discussion on Resolution 44/23 see Abeyratne, R.I.R. (1992), 'The United Nations Decade of International Law', *International Journal of Politics, Culture, and Society*, vol. 5, no. 3, New York, Human Sciences Press, Inc., 511–523.

4 *Supra*. There are, of course, earlier instances where public safety has been considered in the international context. *The Convention Relating to the Regulation of Aerial Navigation* dated 13 October 1919, Alébiéé et Cie-Paris, October 1932, (hereafter referred to as the Paris Convention), prohibited the transportation of certain articles as a measure of public safety. See Paris Convention, Chapter VI, Articles 26 and 28. The Paris Convention was later replaced by the Chicago Convention of 1944 (*infra*) and is no longer in force. The Pan-American Con-

vention on Commercial Aviation, signed at Habana, 15 February 1928, (hereafter referred to as the Habana Convention) also included the above provision of the Paris Convention in its Articles XV and XVII. See 'Sixth International Conference of American States: Final Act: Motions, Agreements, Resolutions and Conventions', at 97–109 (*Habana Imprenta y Paoeleria de Rambla, Bauza y Ca.*); *American J. of Int. Law*, XXII, Supplement p.124, cited in Colegrove, K.W. (1930), *International Control of Aviation*, Boston, Massachusetts, World Peace Foundation at 173.

5 Convention on International Civil Aviation, signed at Chicago on 7 December 1944. See *ICAO Doc 7300/6*, (1980) (6th ed.).

6 Chicago Convention, *ibid.*, the Preamble to which stipulates:
Whereas the future development of international civil aviation can greatly help to create and preserve friendship and understanding among the nations and peoples of the world, yet its abuse can become a threat to the general security; and
Whereas it is desirable to avoid friction and to promote that cooperation between nations and peoples upon which the peace of the world depends;
Therefore, the undersigned governments having agreed on certain principles and arrangements in order that international civil aviation may be developed in a safe and orderly manner and that international air transport services may be established on the basis of equality of opportunity and operated soundly and economically.

7 *Ibid.*

8 ICAO (1946), *What is Picao?*, Montreal, Canada, Provisional International Civil Aviation Organization, at 9.

9 PICAO Doc 2783 C/324, 14/2/47 Minutes, 7th Meeting, 7th Session at 3, Agenda Item 17.

10 PICAO Doc 2824 C/330, 21/2/47, Minutes, 8th Meeting, 7th Session at 5, Nos. 12 and 13.

11 *PICAO Journal* (1985), August–September, at 74.

12 See *Appendix* 2.

13 See ICAO C-WP/6635, 8/11/77 at 1. Also see ICAO Assembly Resolutions A22-16 and A22-17 which have now been consolidated in Resolution A26-7 appearing herein as Appendix 3 and incorporated in ICAO Doc 9509, *Assembly Resolutions in Force* (as of 10 November 1986) at V11–2.

14 ICAO Resolution A 26–7 *infra.*

15 *Halsbury's Laws of England,* (4th ed.), London, Butterworths, 1990, vol. II (1), para 1 at p.16.

16 *DPP* v. *Morgan* (1981) All ER 628, at 639.

17 *R.* v. *Kimber* (1983) 3 All ER 316 at 320.

18 (1987) 3 All ER (CA) 411.

19 *Id.* at 414. See also *R.* v. *Abraham* (1973) 3. All E.R. 694 at 696.

20 *Ibid.*

21 See *Halsbury's Laws of England,* op. cit., vol. II (1) paras 4–9.

22 Allen, C.K. (1931), *Legal Duties,* Oxford, The Clarendon Press, at 230. Also Cecil Turner, J.W. (ed.) (1962), *Kenny's Outlines of Criminal Law* (18 ed.), Cambridge, Cambridge University Press, Section 1. See also (1931), *Proprietary Articles Trade Association* v. *A.G. of Canada* AC 310 at 324, where it was held that the domain of criminal jurisprudence can only be ascertained by examining what acts at any particular period are declared by the state to be crimes. A general definition of a crime is that it is 'a violation or neglect of legal duty of so much public importance that the law, either common or statute, takes notice of and punishes it'. See May, J.W. (1985), *The Law of Crimes,* Littleton Colorado, Fred B. Rothman & Co., at 1. The author goes on

to say that 'intent' to commit a crime should appear either expressly or by implication (supra, at 5). According to this definition and reasoning, the intent has to be unlawful.

23 See generally, Cecil Turner, J.W. (ed.) (1986), *Russell on Crime*, (12th ed.) London, Sweet and Maxwell Limited, Littleton, Colorado, Fred B. Rothman & Co., vol. 1, at 24–36.

24 Milde, M. (1992), 'Law and Aviation Security', *Air and Space Law: De Lege Ferenda, Essays in Honour of Henri A. Wassenbergh*, Dordrecht, The Netherlands, M. Nijhoff, at 93.

25 ICAO was created in 1944 to promote the safety and orderly development of civil aviation in the world. A specialized agency of the United Nations, it sets international standards and regulations necessary for the safety, security, efficiency and regulation of air transport and serves as the medium of cooperation in all fields of civil aviation among its 184 contracting states.

26 ICAO State Letter EC 2/65–91/6 dated 16 January 1991.

27 *Id.*, at 1.

28 The other challenges to civil aviation as identified in the State Letter were: human factors in flight safety; environment; regulatory developments; commercial developments, airport and airspace congestion; legal issues; financial resources; and human resource development.

29 ICAO C-WP/9307, 30/5/91.

30 See *Annual Report of the Council* – 1990, ICAO Doc 9568, Chapter VII, at 96. ICAO records that while acts of unlawful seizure increased from 8 in 1989 to 20 in 1990 (*id.* 97), the number of persons killed by violence against civil aviation actually decreased from 279 persons in 1989 to 137 in 1990 (*id.* at 99), and the number of acts of sabotage against civil aviation amounted to one in 1990 as against two in 1989 (*ibid.*).

31 *Annual Report of the Council* – 1990, ICAO Doc 9568, 96.

32 Kotaite, A., 'ICAO Policy and Programmes in the Field of Aviation Security', Address on the Occasion of the Fourth International Civil Aviation Conference, Philadelphia, Pennsylvania, USA, 15–17 April 1985, published in (1985) *X Annals of Air & Space L.*, 83. See also, Kotaite, A. (1980), 'Security of International Civil Aviation – Role of ICAO', VII *Annals of Air & Space L.*, 95–101.

33 Milde, M. (1990), 'Draft Convention on the Marking of Explosives', *XV Annals of Air & Space L.*, 155.

34 See Appendix.

35 McWhinney, E. (1987), *Aerial, Piracy and International Terrorism: The Illegal Diversion of Aircraft and International Law*, (2nd ed.), Dordrecht, The Netherlands, M. Nijhoff, at 165.

36 Abeyratne, R.I.R. (1990), 'Invasion of the Maldives and International Terrorism – Definitions and Solutions', *The 1988–89 Annual on Terrorism*, (Y. Alexander and H. Faxman eds), Dordrecht, Kluwer, 83 at 93. See also, 'IATA Proposes Five-point Programme to Combat Terrorism', *IATA Current Information Summary* (CIS) No 4277, 20 September 1988, where IATA recommended the use of the legal and organizational structure of the United Nations to create:

1 an international group to advise airports and countries on security;
2 an international group to investigate terrorist incidents after they occur and make recommendations;
3 an international military response team to resolve an incident, if need be, with force;
4 an international court for trial; and,
5 an international detention centre.

37 Partan, D.G. (1987), 'Terrorism, an International Law Offence', *Connecticut Law Review*, (19) at 751. See also generally, Ludwikowski, R.R. (1988), 'Political and Legal Instruments in Supporting and Combatting Terrorism: Current Developments', *Terrorism*, Dordrecht, The Netherlands, Kluwer, (vol. 11), 197–211.
38 Hanoch Tel Oren v. Libyan Arab Republic cited in Alexander, Y. and Nanes, S. (eds) (1986), *Legislative Responses to Terrorism*, Dordrecht, M. Nijhoff, V1.
39 Abeyratne (1990), *op. cit.*, 84.
40 *Dictionnaire*, Supplement, (Paris) an V11 (1798), at 775.
41 Murray's *Oxford English Dictionary* defines terrorism as:

> Government by intimidation as directed and carried out by the party in power in France during the Revolution of 1789–1794; the system of the 'Terror'.

See Murray, J. (1919), *A New Dictionary on Historical Principles*, Oxford.
42 Adams, J. (1989), *The Financing of Terror*, New York, Simon & Schuster, 7.
43 *Id.* at 12.
44 See Abeyratne, R.I.R. (1983), 'Skyjacker gets Life Imprisonment in Sri Lanka', *Lloyds Aviation Law*, vol. 2. no. 24 15 December at 4. See also generally, Abeyratne, R.I.R. (1989), 'The Ekanayake Hijacking Appeal in Sri Lanka – A Critical Appraisal', *Air Law*, 14, 58–68.
45 Silets, H.L. (1987), 'Something Special in the Air and on the Ground: The Potential for Unlimited Liability of International Air Carriers for Terrorist Attacks Under the Warsaw Convention and its Revisions', *JALC*, 53 321 at 358.
46 Nechayev, S. (1971), 'Revolutionary Catechism', cited in Rapoport, D.C. (1971), *Assassination and Terrorism*, Toronto: Canadian Broadcasting Corporation, at 79. Another noteworthy definition was the one adopted at the Conference of the International Law Association in Belgrade, 1980 which states:

> The definition of 'international terrorist offence' presented here is more comprehensive than the definitions which appear in the multilateral convention relating to the control of international terrorism which has been concluded in the past two decades. The term comprehends serious criminal acts, such as murder, assault, arson, kidnapping, extortion, sabotage and the use of explosive devices which are directed towards selected targets. These targets include internationally protected persons, places and international civil aircraft which are already protected under the conventional or customary international law.

See Delaney, R.F. (1979), 'World Terrorism Today', *California Western International Law Journal*, vol. 9 at 454. See also, *The Draft Convention of the International Law Association*, Belgrade Conference (Committee on International Terrorism), August 1980, at 9, for definitions of 'terrorism' proposed by the Haitian and French delegations at the Conference.
47 Levitt, S. (1986), 'Is Terrorism Worth Defining?', *Ohio Northern University Law Review*, 13, 97.
48 See Kittrie, M. (1973), 'Terrorism and Political Crimes in International Law', *American Journal of International Law*, 67, 87. Also Paust, J.J. (1978), 'Some thoughts on Preliminary Thoughts on Terrorism', *American Society of International Law*, 68, 502, 503.
49 See Friedlander, R.A. (1977), 'The Origins of International Terrorism', *Terrorism: Interdisciplinary Perspectives*, (J. Alexander, S.M. Finger eds), McGraw-Hill, London, at 31.

50 See Abeyratne, R.I.R. (1985), 'Hijacking and the Teheran Incident – A World in Crisis?', *Air Law*, vol X, no. 3 120 at 121. See also, Abeyratne, R.I.R. (1984), 'Aerial Piracy and Extended Jurisdiction in Japan', *I.C.L.Q.* 33, 596 at 597. Also McWhinney, E. (1987), *The Illegal Diversion of Aircraft and International Law*, 6. Clutterbuck R. (1975), *Living With Terrorism*, Pergamon Press, New York, 143. Evans, Alona E., 'Aircraft Hijacking, its Cause and Cure' *A.J.I.L.* 63, 701–703. Lissitzyn, O.J. (1973), 'Hijacking, International Law and Human Rights', *Aerial Piracy and International Law* (E. McWhinney ed.) 116, 119.
51 UNGA Res. 2625 (xxv) Part 11, Annex paragraph 1.
52 Horowitz, I.T. (1977), *Terrorism: Interdisciplinary Perspectives*, (J. Alexander, S.M. Finger (eds), McGraw-Hill, London at 283.
53 See UN Papers A/40/445 of 1984, at 15.
54 Nieburg, H.L. (1969), *Political Violence: The Behavioural Process*, Kluwer, Dordrecht, 13.
55 Luttwak, E. (1968), *Coup d'Etat: A Practical Handbook*, 24. Also, Eckstein, H. (1965), 'On the Etiology of Internal Wars', *History and Theory*, vol. 4, no. 2 , 133–134. Galula, D. (1964), *Counterinsurgency Warfare, Theory and Practice*, 4–5., Gurr, T.R. (1970), *Why Men Rebel*, 11.
56 See Moss, R. (1971), *Urban Guerilla Warfare*, International Institute for Strategic Studies 210.
57 UN Papers A/40/445 of 19 July 1985, 10.
58 See Document on Terror, Anon (1952), *News From Behind the Iron Curtain*, (vol. 3) March, 43–47. See also generally, Paust, J.J. (1974), 'Terrorism and the International Law of War', *Military Law Review*, (vol. 64), 1–36, Weisband, E. and Roguly, D. (1975), 'Palestinian Terrorism: Violence, Verbal Strategy and Legitimacy', *International Terrorism* (Y. Alexander ed.) 278–279. Finger, S.M. (1975), *Terrorism*, (L.A. Sobel ed.) 83–106. Sayegh, F.A. (1975), 'The Palestinians Response to Zionism: From Resistance to Liberation', *Arab Journal*, vol. 53, No. 4, July, 684–685.
59 Fromkin, D. (1975), 'The Strategy of Terrorism', *Foreign Affairs*, vol. 53, No. 4, July, 684– 685.
60 See UN Papers A/40/445 of 19 July 1985, at 11.
61 The *George-Smoke* formula introduced in the United States of America in the early 1970s argued that if the cost and risk involved in a terrorist operation outweighed the benefit gained by such operation, deterrence could be successfully gained. George, A. and Smoke, R. (1974), *Deterrence in American Foreign Policy Theory and Practice* 48 at 59–60.
62 See Jenkins, B. (1975), 'International Terrorism – A New Mode of Conflict', *Research Paper No. 48*, California Seminar on Arms Control and Foreign Policy, at 3. See also generally, Marighella, C. (1971), 'The Mini-manual of the Urban Guerilla', *Urban Guerilla Warfare*, (R. Moss ed.) at 40.
63 See Espiell, H.G. (1981), 'The Evolving Concept of Human Rights', *Human Rights, Thirty Years After The Universal Declaration*, Oldham, Penn., 41, at 45.
64 See *United Nations Covenant on Civil and Political Rights*, 1966, Article 6 (1).
65 *European Convention on Human Rights*, (1953), Article 2 (1).
66 The following measures and their implications are dealt with extensively with examples in A.E. Evans and J.F. Murphy (ed.) (1978), *Legal Aspects of International Terrorism* at 541, 546 and 547.
67 *Id.*, 636–637.
68 *Ibid.*
69 See *ibid.*, 539.
70 Morrison, W.L. (1982), *John Austin*, Stanford University Press, California, 78.
71 Starke, J.G. (1984), *Introduction to International Law*, (9th ed.) 18. See also Lloyd,

D. (1970), *The Idea of the Law*,(Revised ed.), Harmondsworth, Middlesex, Penguin, 37–40.

72 *Ibid.*, 18–21.

73 See *The Charming Betsy*, (1804) 2 Cranch 64 at 118, where Marshall, C.J. cited Article V1, para 2 of the United States Constitution which gives constitutional validity to international law. See also *The Paquete Habana* (1900) 175 US 677 at 700 per Gray, J. who went on to say that international law must be ascertained and administered by the courts of justice of appropriate jurisdiction.

74 First introduced in 1947 by the General Agreement on Tariffs and Trade (GATT), the most-favoured-nation-treatment clause ensures that certain benefits accrue to nations other than the signatory states in instances that apply to those non-signatory states.

75 Partan, D.G. (1987), 'Terrorism: An International Law Offence', *Connecticut Law Review*, 19 at 751. See also generally, Ludwikowski, R.R., op. cit., 197–211.

76 Wilberforce, A. (1963), 'Crime in Aircraft' *J.R.Ae.S.* 67, 175. See also, Horlick, G.N. (1971), 'The Developing Law of Air Hijacking', *Harvard International Law Journal* 12, 33.

77 Wilberforce, *ibid.* See also, Evans, A.E. (1969), 'Aircraft Hijacking, its Cause and Cure', *Am J Int. Law* 63, 695. Shubber, S. 'Is Hijacking of Aircraft Piracy in International Law?' (1968–1969), 43, *British Yearbook of International Law*, Vol. 43, 193. Lee, B.A. (1962), 'The Legal Ramification of Hijacking Airplanes', *American Bar Association Journal* 1034. Fitzgerald, G.F. (1969), 'Development of International Legal Rules for the Repression of the Unlawful Seizure of Aircraft', *The Canadian Yearbook of International Law*, VII, 269.

78 Shawcross and Beaumont, (1991), *Air Law*, (4th edn.) (vol. 1), London, Butterworths, Para. 620, p. 521.

79 McClintock, M.C. (1975), 'Skyjacking – Its Domestic, Civil and Criminal Ramifications', *JALC* 39, 31.

80 Friedlander, R.A. (1977–1978), 'Banishing Fear From the Skies – A Statutory Proposal', *Duquesne Law Review* 16, no. 3 at 286. See also, McGrane, R.J. (1972–1975), 'A Search for an International Solution to the Problem of Aircraft Hijacking', *Auckland University Law Review* 2, at 83. Evans, A.E. op. cit., 695. Chaturvedi, S.C. (1971), 'Hijacking and the Law', *Indian Journal of International Law* 11, 89. Abeyratne, R.I.R. (1984), 'Aerial Piracy and Extended Jurisdiction in Japan', *I.C.L.Q.* (July), 33, 596 at 597–600.

81 Hackworth, G. (1941), *Digest of International Law* 681. See also, (1968) *Black's Law Dictionary* (4th ed.), 1306. Also, the Geneva Convention on the high seas (1958), Article 15.

82 Whiteman, A. (1977), '*Jus Cogens* in International Law with a Projected List', *Georgia J. of International and Comparative Law*, 7, 609, at 625. Early definitions of hijacking identified five types of 'hijackers'.

1 the disgruntled national who unlawfully seizes the aircraft and expresses his defiance by directing its flight to a country whose political ideology he shares and admires;
2 the 'flying commando' who has taken his *casus belli* to the air. This type of person is particularly dangerous, as he is liable to cause death or injury to his hostages and destruction of the aircraft and other property so as to focus attention upon his cause;
3 the mentally deranged individual who has chosen hijacking either as a device to gain recognition and notoriety or as a mode of escape from intolerable psychological pressures;
4 the common criminal, who uses the aircraft as a vehicle of escape from pending prosecution or incarceration; and,

5 the extortionist, who uses the hijacking as a gateway to acquiring instant wealth. See Fenello, M.J. (1971), 'Technical Prevention of Air Piracy', *International Conciliation*, November, no. 585, at 30.

83 See *Interavia Air Letter*, No. 12,558, Thursday 13 August 1992, at 3.
84 Hereafter referred to as the Tokyo Convention.
85 Tokyo Convention, Ch.1., Article 1 (2).
86 *Id.*, Chapter 1., Article 1 (3).
87 *Id.*, Chapter 4., Article 11.
88 *Convention for the Suppression of Unlawful Seizure of Aircraft*, The Hague, 16 December 1970, hereafter referred to as the Hague Convention.
89 *Id.*, Article 1(a).
90 *Id.*, Article 1(b).
91 See Shubber, S. (1973), 'Aircraft Hijacking Under the Hague Convention 1970 – A New Regime?', *I.C.L.Q.* 22, 687 at 692. See also, ICAO (1970), *The Report of the Legal Committee*, ICAO 17th Session, ICAO Doc 8877-LC/161, page 1., para 4.
92 Hague Convention, *op. cit.*, Article 3, Para 1.
93 Hereafter referred to as the Montreal Convention.
94 Montreal Convention, Article 1.
95 *Ibid.*
96 Rosenfeld, S.B. (1973–74), 'Air Piracy; Is it time to relax our Security?', *New England Law Review* 9, 81.
97 *Federal Aviation Regulations* (FAR) Section 121.533 as amended on 5 December 1972. See also, *Federal Aviation Administration (FAA) Memorandum* CC-1, 21 March 1969.
98 *Federal Aviation Administration (FAA) Information*, 19 March 1969.
99 US Dept. of State (1977), *US Dept of State Bulletin* No. 547, October.
100 Friedlander, R.A. (1980), *Banishing Fear From the Skies: A Statutory Proposal*, Butterworth, New York, at 288.
101 *Id.*, 290–291.
102 Van Panhuys, H.F. (1970), 'Aircraft Hijacking and International Law', *Columbia Journal of Transnational Law*, 9, 13.
103 A quote from Heller, P.P. (1973) in *New Zealand and South Pacific Aviation Digest*, Otago, Christchurch, 37, 6 cited in McGrane, R.J. (1973), *A Search for an International Solution to the Problem of Aircraft Hijacking*, Law Book Co., Sydney, 91.
104 See Abeyratne, R.I. R. (1984), 'Aerial Piracy and Extended Jurisdiction in Japan', *I.C.L.Q.*, 33, 612.
105 Shawcross and Beaumont, *op. cit.*, para 620, p. 521.
106 Evans, A.E. (1973), 'Aircraft Hijacking, What is Being Done?', *American Journal of International Law*, 641 at 653.
107 See generally, McGrane, R.J., *op. cit.*, 91–95.
108 Canada, France, The Federal Republic of Germany (as it then was), Italy, Japan, The United Kingdom of Great Britain and Northern Ireland, and the United States of America.
109 Mark E. Fingerman states:

> The Declaration focuses on sanctions designed to deter nations from encouraging the commission of the offence. In effect, the spirit of the Declaration is a recognition of the fact that States are frequently *de facto* accomplices to acts of skyjacking ... The rationale of the Declaration would appear to be the foreclosing of the possibility of a skyjacker finding refuge which reduces the attractiveness of the offence. See Fingerman, M.E. (1980),

'Skyjacking and the Bonn Declaration of 1978: Sanctions Applicable to Recalcitrant Nations', *California Western International Law Journal*, vol. 10, at 142.

110 Milde (1992), *op. cit.*, 159.
111 See Appendix A, ICAO Doc LC/27-WP/3, 22/1/90.
112 Executive Committee Paper A 27-WP/115, Ex37. For an elaborate discussion on the chronological sequence of activities in this regard see Milde, *op. cit.*, 4–9.
113 See ICAO Doc. 9571, 1991.
114 *Id.*, Article 1.1.
115 *Id.*, Article 11.
116 *Id.*, Article 1V.5.
117 Milde (1992) *op. cit.* 178. See also van Dam, R.P. (1991), 'A New Convention on the Marking of Plastic Explosives for the Purpose of Detection', *Air Law*, XVI, no 4/5, at 176.
118 See Milde, M. (1992), 'Law and Aviation Security', *Air and Space Law: De Lege Ferenda, Essays in Honour of Henri A. Wassenbergh*, Dordrecht, The Netherlands, M. Nijhoff, where Professor Milde observes on page 96:

> ... the new convention on the marking of plastic explosives will not be a panacea but only a small addition to the general mosaic of the general legal measures. The Convention will become useful, not when all plastics are properly marked for the purpose of detection, but only when affordable and efficient detection equipment will become available at all international airports and other critical areas of the world.

119 Alexander, Y. and Sochor, E. (eds) (1990), *Aerial Piracy and Aviation Security*, Dordrecht, the Netherlands, Kluwer Academic Publishers, M. Nijhoff, 38.
120 *Id.*, 39.
121 *Husserl* v. *Swiss Air Transport Co. Ltd.*, 485 F. 2d. 1240, (2nd cir. 1975), *Day* v. *TransWorld Airlines Inc.*, 528 F. 2d. 31 (2nd cir. 1975), *Evangelinos* v. *TransWorld Airlines Inc.*, 550 F. 2d. 152 (3rd cir. 1976), *Salerno* v. *Pan-American World Airways* 19 Avi 17,705 (SDNY 1985).
122 900 F. 2d. 8 (2d cir., 1990).
123 Rigalt, A.F. (1990), 'Illegal Transport by Air of Drugs and Psychotropic Substances', *Air Law*, vol. XV, no. 1, 17 at 20.
124 *Civil Aviation Statistics of the World 1990*, ICAO Statistical Yearbook, Doc. 9180/16, at 12. See also, ICAO (1990), *Civil Aircraft on Register*, ICAO Digest of Statistics no. 382, at 27.
125 *Boeing World Jet Airplane Inventory 1990* at 31, where the figure given by Boeing is 8936 aircraft – a figure compatible with the ICAO statistics.
126 *Annual Report of the Council*, ICAO Doc. 9568, *op. cit.* at 31.
127 Donald Bunker says:

> The trafficking and illicit use of drugs has affected peoples' lives throughout the world, and the aviation industry has not escaped the disease. Leaving aside the problem of drug use by air crews, the problem of drug trafficking is starting to have a worrisome effect on aviation and the financial community which supports it.

See Bunker, D.H. (1990), 'The Effect of Drug Trafficking on Aircraft Financing', *Air Transport Management*, March/April, vol. 3, no. 1, 4 at 6.

128 Milde, M. (1988), 'The Role of ICAO in the Suppression of Drug Abuse and Illicit Trafficking', *Annals Air & Space L.*, vol. XIII, 133–134.
129 Rigalt, A.F. (1990), 'Illegal Transport by Air of Drugs and Psychotropic Substances', *Air Law*, vol. XV, no. 1, 17 at 18.
130 *Id.*, at 20.
131 The conclusions reached at this conference and other related conferences will be discussed in detail later on.
132 ICAO Assembly Resolution A 27–12, para 3. See *Assembly Resolutions in Force*, ICAO Doc. 9558, 1–31.
133 *Id.*, para 5, at Doc. 9558, *op.cit.* 1–32.
134 *Id.*, para 6.
135 State Letter E 2/2.7–89/109 dated 6 December 1989.
136 C-WP/9235, 6/2/91 at para 9.
137 *Id.*, para 12.
138 See Annex 9 to the Convention on International Civil Aviation, (9th ed.), chapter 1, page 2, and provisions 2.2, 2.2 note 2, 3.2 note 2, 3.30. 3.31, 5.14, 6.1 note 2.
139 *Evangelinos* v. *TransWorld Airlines Inc. op. cit.* 154. See also 14 CCH Avi 17,612 at 17, 616, (Seitz J. Dissenting) (CA3. 1977).
140 For example, the victims of the Lod Airport Massacre in 1972, most of whom were Christians, had used Israeli visas as tourists in Israel and therefore were guilty in the eyes of the terrorists who carried out the massacre.
141 Karl-Heinz Bockstiegel, Concluding Remarks, *Aviation Security Conference Proceedings*, 22–23 January 1987, Hague, International Institute of Air and Space Law, 1987, at 174.
142 *International Herald Tribune*, No. 15, 1985, cited in *IATA Current Information Summary* No. 3583–15 November 1985, where it was revealed that baggage on board the Air India flight was not subject to x-ray inspection prior to departure from Toronto.
143 *International Herald Tribune*, 2 March 1990, cited in *IATA Current Information Summary* No. 4642 – 2 March 1990, which revealed serious security lapses by PAN-AM security divisions in charge of the flight.
144 Alexander, Y. and Sochor, E. (eds) (1990), *Aerial Piracy and Aviation Security, supra.*, Introduction at VIII. Paul Stephen Dempsey says:

> Terrorism is the symptom of the disease. It is the disease of the militarily weak, the politically frustrated, and the religiously fanatic ... Each faces a well armed government where aims are antithetical. All suffer from the same malaise which inspires indiscriminate aggression.

See Dempsey, P.S. (1987), *Law and Foreign Policy in International Aviation*, Dobbs Ferry, New York, Transnational Publishers Inc., 381.
145 Hereafter referred to as the Chicago Convention.
146 Chicago Convention, ICAO Doc. 7300/6, 6th ed., 1980, Article 44 (a).
147 *Id.*, Article 44 (h).
148 *Id.*, Article 44 (d).
149 See Annex 9 to the Convention on International Civil Aviation, Facilitation, 9th ed., July 1990, Standard 5.1, Note 1.
150 Annex 17 to the Convention on International Civil Aviation, Security, 4th ed., 1987, at 2.2.
151 *Id.*, 3.1.1.
152 *Id.*, 3.1.2.
153 *Id.*, 4.1.1.
154 See generally Chapter 5 of Annex 17 to the Chicago Convention.

155 Tokyo Convention, *op. cit.*, Article 3 (3).
156 Lowenfeld, A.F. (1972), *Aviation Law, Cases and Materials*, New York, M. Bender, at 87.
157 Hague Convention, *op. cit.*, Article 2.
158 *Id.*, Articles 1 (4), 3, 4, and 7.
159 Schwenk, W. (1979), 'The Bonn Declaration in Hijacking', *Annals of Air and Space Law*, vol. IV, 307 at 321.
160 Taylor, L. (1990), 'Aerial Piracy – A Pilot Viewpoint' – *Aerial Piracy and Aviation Security*, (Y. Alexander and E. Sochor eds), *op. cit.* 36.
161 See *UN Information Letter*, September–December 1988, Nar/Inf. Lett./1988 at 1.
162 Single Convention on Narcotic Drugs 1961, and Convention on Psychotropic Substances 1971.
163 Wassenbergh, H.A. (1989), 'The "Protectionist" Imperative in International Civil Aviation', *Liber Amicorum–Nicholas Mateesco Matte*, Canada, De Daro Publishers, 301.
164 UN Papers OPI/146, 4 (1963). See also generally, Das, K. (1973), *Proceedings of the Second Annual Conference of the Canadian Council of International Law*, 181.
165 *Op. cit.*
166 See UN Covenant on Civil and Political Rights, 1966, Article 6 (1).
167 European Convention on Human Rights, (1935) Article 2 (1).
168 *Charter of the United Nations and Statute of the International Court of Justice*, United Nations: New York, Article 1.3.
169 *Id.*, Chapter VII Articles 39, 41 and 42.
170 *Id.*, Article 42.
171 S/RES/794 (1992) 3 December 1992.
172 S/RES/770 (1992) 13 August 1992.
173 See also the earlier Security Council Resolution 688 (1991), 5 April 1991 whereby the Security Council expressed grave concern at the repression of the Iraqi civilian population in parts of Iraq and insisted that Iraq allow immediate access by international humanitarian organizations to all parts of Iraq.
174 *Universal Declaration of Human Rights*, United Nations Department of Public Information, Article 3.
175 *Id.*, Article 25.
176 Chicago Convention, *op. cit.* ICAO Doc. 7300/6 (6th ed.) 1980, Article 1.
177 *Multilateral Agreement On Commercial Rights of Non-Scheduled Air Services In Europe*, signed at Paris on 30 April 1956, see *Selected International Agreements Relating to Air Law*, (Gabriel Weishaupt ed.) 1979, at 409.
178 *Multilateral Agreement*, op. cit., Articles 1 (a) and (b) and 2.1.(a).
179 Teson, F.R. (1956), *Humanitarian Intervention: An Inquiry into Law and Morality*, Dobbs Ferry, New York, Transnational Publishers Inc., at 5.
180 See letter to the Editor by Professor Leff, Yale Law School, *New York Times* 4 October 1968 at 46 Column 3, cited in *Humanitarian Intervention and the United Nations*, 1973 (Richard B. Lillich ed.), Charlottesville, University Press of Virginia at 151.
181 The principle of non-intervention has been strongly espoused in order that sovereignty of a state be retained as sacrosanct. See Vattel, N. (1916) *le droit des gens*, Bk II, Chapter V (Scott, ed.) at 135. Also, Hall, E. (1924), *International Law* (Higgins, ed. 8th ed.) at 343. Lawrence, O. (1923), *Principles of International Law* (Winfield, ed. 7th ed.) at 126.
182 de Lima, F.X. (1971), *Intervention in International Law*, The Hague, Vitgeverij Pax Nederland at 16.
183 Starke, J.G. (1977), *An Introduction to International Law*, (7th ed.) London, Butterworths at 106.

184 Oppenheim, (1955), *International Law*, vol. 1 (Lauterpacht, ed. 8th ed.) at 312–320.
185 *Stowell's Intervention at International Law*, 1921 at 126 and 350. Also, Wehberg, R. (1938), *La Guerre Civil et le Droit International* 63, Hague Recueil, at 115.
186 *Op. cit.* at 15.
187 Schwarzenberger, G (1971), *International Law and Order*, London, Stevens and Sons, at 63.
188 Akehurst, M. (1977), 'The Use of Force to Protect Nationals Abroad' 5 *Int. Rel.* 3, at 16.

3 Analysis of the Problem and its Legal Recognition

Issues Involved

The international community is linked together by air transportation and assisted by advanced communications technology. In the global community in which we live, the primary linkages between people are accomplished through communications technology and air transportation. The design technology of larger aircraft has coped well with the demand for larger capacity and increase in air travel which is needed in the future.[1]

New forms of criminal activity is a natural corollary to this advancement in transportation technology and communication. Unlawful interference with aircraft and airline facilities, particularly in the form of violence or the threat of violence, have dealt a crippling blow to the credibility of international air transportation as a means of communication and travel. The primary focus of this analysis is on such types of criminal activity as may affect international civil aviation, including hijacking, carriage of narcotics by air and criminal acts connected thereto, bombing, and assaults on aircraft and airports. Such attacks are performed for varying reasons to further terrorist goals to achieve a traditional criminal gain, such as extortion; to escape from criminal prosecutions in a country or enter a 'safe haven' or as a result of a behaviourial reaction of the deranged mind of the perpetrator. It is therefore necessary to inquire into the need for the development of public policy related to airline security, which involves political, legal and operational initiatives. This analysis would examine political initiatives related to terrorism which have been responsible for the handling of the problem of unlawful interference with international civil aviation. For the purpose of this analysis there will also be an examination of the various international conventions which address the issue of unlawful interference with international civil aviation, and the problems facing the implementation of these conventions. The impact of these conventions will be assessed by a case study analysis later in this chapter.

This chapter also addresses on an empirical basis the effects of the use of metal detectors as a security initiative at airports. Although some may argue that the use of metal detectors at airports helps control hijacking, others claim that this practice has led to the unexpected consequence of encouraging bombings, missile attacks and other crimes that result from the displacement of the possible crime on board the aircraft, which is often achieved by the use of metal detectors. There are two considerations that could be used to determine the validity of the latter claim:

1 increased security at airports reduces incidents of hijacking; and,
2 the relationship between hijacking and other crimes such as bombing, missile attacks and attacks at airports.

The general belief that supports the use of metal detectors at airports is based on the premise that they serve as a deterrent. Therefore, this book will also analyse the deterrent effect of metal detectors on attacks on airports and aircraft and examine the use of criminal prosecution in reducing the threat. Another consideration that will be addressed is whether the decrease of one threat would, on the basis of the displacement theory of crime increase the threats to international civil aviation. In other words, would detectors at airports such as intense body searches and metal detectors encourage the prospective offender to focus attention on other possible crimes such as missile attacks on aircraft and gun attacks at airports? It is therefore compelling to draw the relationship between the various facets of unlawful interference with international civil aviation. For this purpose, descriptions of some hijacking incidents that best illustrate specific characteristics of the offence of unlawful interference and bring to bear the various overtones of criminality this offence portends, will be included. Furthermore, since international agreements and conventions are critical to the promulgation of international guidelines introduced to provide for legal controls related to the offence and the choice of jurisdictions that would apply to a particular offence, the historical development of such treaties also forms an integral part of this book.

Both international agreements and internal laws of states apply to international air transportation. Although domestic laws would generally apply within a country, violations of international law, treaties and conventions may involve universal principles that may perforce affect the interests of the states affected by the offence concerned. The status of international conventions at law raises valid issues of their legitimacy in their role as enforceable law.[2]

Current Trends in International Air Transport

With the major forces of the world's nations moving towards a global economy and the development of international markets, the number of air travellers is expected to increase significantly. Although in the years 1991 to 1993, the demand for air transportation was seen to slacken during the world recession and because of the Gulf war, now that the economy is rebounding, a burgeoning demand for international travel services is a certainty in the future. ICAO has suggested that 3 425 thousand million passengers will be carried in 2003 (as against 1 953 thousand million in 1992). It is estimated that these passengers will be carried by 11 000 aircraft.[3] One of the most significant features of 'damaged assessment' in relation to death or injury caused to innocent persons in that in some instances, states may quantify the value of human life in monetary terms. Many governments use economic formulae to calculate the monetary value of human life. This fiscal theory plays a pivotal role in how governments respond to specific problems such as aircraft hijacking. For example, the Federal Aviation Administration (FAA) in 1989 estimated the value of a statistical life as $826 666. The value of a statistical injury is estimated at $60 000 if it is serious, and 22 666 for a minor injury. The aircraft replacement cost for a Boeing 747 is between 125 and 175 million dollars.

Unlawful acts against international civil aviation may also cause political instability in a country. If a state or state instrumentality appears inept in curbing these acts, or if the state appears over aggressive, the political consequences can prove to be significant. Government, as a rational actor, must determine what policies would be permissible in responding to the offence.

The Need for Policy Analysis

Recent attempts made towards attaining peace in such areas as the Arab–Israeli conflict and the Northern Ireland issue have been thwarted by the proliferation of incendiary acts against the world at large, thus amply demonstrating the inherent difficulties attendant upon such peace processors. In the context, unlawful interference with international civil aviation has become a principle area of concern to the world community both as a recognized threat toward peace and security and as a grave social malady which needs a fast cure. The bombing of a PAN-AM aircraft over Lockerbie in December 1988 and the mortar attacks on London Heathrow Airport in March 1994 are two events which occurred over a period of six years, graphically illustrating the effects of terrorism on international civil aviation and world peace. While the former incident caused diplomatic and legal ripples between Libya and the United States, leading up to its adjudication in the International Court of Justice, the latter caused a further widening of the bridge between the British Government and the Irish Republican Army (IRA).

The applied research approach contained in this chapter addresses primarily, crimes against aircraft and airports. The primary focus is on understanding the offence of unlawful interference with international civil aviation and efforts to combat this phenomenon. This approach explores the various components of the hijacking problem. Since there has been some success in efforts to reduce hijacking the analysis also addresses other problems, such as bombing, missile attacks, and attacks at airports in order to better understand the hijacking issue from a broadened policy perspective. In applying the facts which so far reflect offences in these categories one could apply a policy analysis which is a form of applied research carried out to acquire a deeper understanding of social and technical issues and to bring about better solutions. One could attempt to bring modern science and technology to bear on society's problems, policy analysis searches for feasible courses of action and generate information while marshalling evidence of the benefits and other consequences that would follow their adoption and implementation.

The airline industry is a highly competitive business domestically and internationally which drives airline companies to operate in the most efficient ways possible. Airline companies which try to operate profitably also try to offer comfortable and safe air transportation. Efficiency, comfort and safety are not always complementary components which work in harmony but may tend to be mutually exclusive, particularly in the world of commercial aviation. For policymakers, it is difficult to make a trade-off among those components and to decide which alternative will achieve an acceptable level of security in the most efficient way.

A sound legal policy that is calculated to combat the offence has to be routed in a deep study of the dangers facing international civil aviation. This can be arrived at by studying past incidences in order to analyse the dangers, and by developing a model based on the types of threats which are likely to exist in the future. A review of the procedures which are utilized to combat crimes against aircraft and facilities should then be carried out, using the model so developed.

For consistency this analysis uses a database created to reflect facts pertaining to the offence over a decade (1980–1990) with some monthly figures during that period. Descriptive data and aggregate data relating to these facts have been analysed to form both a descriptive study and an aggregate study.

The data needed to analyse a legal problem or system should be defined quite directly by the model that is designed to handle the prediction problem. Therefore it is useful to specify the model fairly early; it will clearly and unambiguously indicate the sort of data needed and can thus lead to a more efficient organization of what can be an extremely tedious job. In fact, if it turns out that the model as originally specified demands data that cannot be furnished, some reworking of the model to accommodate what is available may be sensible.

Legal policy relating to strategies which are designed to prevent terrorist incidents are likely to be more effective when it takes into account the value of general intelligence estimates of individual groups, their capabilities and strategic approaches. Such legal policy would inevitably have to take into account the need for a high degree of co-operation between airport security officials and criminal intelligence organizations, such as Interpol. An overall legal policy would also have to consider the prescription of 'target hardening' approaches as legal measures that may be adopted by some states such as metal detectors and passenger screening.

Unlawful Seizure of Aircraft (Hijacking)

The first incident of unlawful seizure of an aircraft occurred in 1930 when several Peruvian revolutionaries seized control of an aircraft in order to flee the country[4]. That particular instance of hijacking remained the solitary incident in the otherwise smooth operation of international civil aviation until 1947, when hijacking became frequent.

The first wave of hijacking began in July 1947 when three Rumanians commandeered a state-owned DC-3 aircraft when in flight and ordered it to land in Turkey[5]. During the next three years another 14 successful incidents of hijacking took place in Eastern Europe which were caused by persons trying to flee their countries[6].

In 1958 a second wave of hijacking commenced with the ascension of Fidel Castro to power in Cuba, where officials of the overthrown government hijacked a civil aircraft in order to escape from Cuba.[7] In 1961 the first hijacked US aircraft was diverted to Cuba. Between 1961 and 1968, about 66 aircraft were hijacked, most of them being diverted to Cuba.

In 1973 a Memorandum of Understanding was signed by and between the United States and Cuba on the hijacking of aircraft and vessels, so as to provide for the extradition or punishment of hijackers.[8] After understanding was reached, the number of hijackings involving the USA and Cuba reduced dramatically. Cuba, however, denounced the agreement on the grounds of 'American complicity' in October 1976, after the bombing on 6 October of a Cuban aircraft, in which 73 passengers and crew members were killed.[9]

On 28 June 1976 an Air France aircraft was hijacked[10] on a flight from Tel Aviv to Paris. The hijackers diverted the aircraft to Uganda's Entebbe airport and held the passengers as hostages until the authorities met their demands. On 3 July 1976 an Israeli aircraft entered the airspace of Uganda and landed at Entebbe in a rescue mission. During the operation, seven hijackers, three hostages and several Ugandans and Israelis were killed. As a reprisal to the Israeli act on 9 July 1976, the United Nations Security Council began considering a complaint brought on behalf of Uganda by Mauritius. The complaint referred to the 'act of aggression' committed against Uganda by Israel.[11]

On 12 July 1976, two draft resolutions[12] were introduced, one by the United Kingdom and the United States and the other by Tanzania, Libya and Benin.

The US–UK joint resolution[13] condemned hijacking and called on states to prevent and punish all such terrorist acts, while reaffirming the need to respect the sovereignty and territorial integrity of all states. The tri-state resolution[14] condemned Israel's violation of Ugandan sovereignty and territorial integrity and demanded that Israel meet Uganda's claims for food compensation for damages and destruction.

In October 1977, a Lufthansa aircraft, with 82 passengers and five crew members on board was hijacked on a flight from Majorca to Frankfurt.[15] The hijackers murdered the pilot. On the fifth day following the hijacking, a West German commando unit stormed the aircraft on an airport runway in Mogadishu, Somalia, and ended the hijacking by freeing all of the hostages.

While in the Israeli operations in Entebbe, the commandos entered Uganda without permission, the Government of Somalia carried out the rescue operation by the foreign armed force in its country and actively co-operated with it.

On 2 March 1981, three hijackers seized a Pakistan International airline aircraft and forced it to land in Kabul, Afghanistan.[16] The hijackers demanded the release of 92 political prisoners from Pakistani jails. After the aircraft had sat on a runway in Kabul for a week and the Pakistani Government had refused to meet the hijackers demands, the hijackers shot dead a Pakistani diplomat passenger and dumped his body onto the tarmac. The aircraft then flew to Damascus, where the hijackers released more than 100 hostages and threatened to blow up the aircraft. The hijackers were talked into lengthy extensions of their deadline while negotiations continued by radio with Syrian and Pakistani officials in the Damascus control tower. The hijackers finally agreed that they would settle for the release of just 55 prisoners. The Pakistani government concurred, ordering the prisoners to be flown to Libya. When the aircraft carrying the released prisoners was approaching Tripoli, the Libyan authorities suddenly announced that they had changed their minds about granting asylum to the hijackers and the released prisoners. The aircraft had nowhere to go, and the hostages' lives were again in jeopardy. Syria then announced that it would accept the prisoners, at which time the hijackers surrendered the aircraft and the hostages. All the hijackers were prosecuted in Pakistan and sentenced to death.

On 29 September 1981 an Indian Airlines Boeing 747 with 117 passengers on board were hijacked by seven terrorists who forced the aircraft to land in Lahore, Pakistan.[17] On 30 September 1981 several Pakistani commandos dressed as airline maintenance workers stormed the hijacked aircraft, arrested the hijackers, and without any casualties, freed the hostages. The hijackers were then charged in Pakistan for air piracy and illegal entry. As a result of criminal prosecution in Pakistan, three hijackers were sentenced to death; two to life imprisonment; and two were acquitted.

On 22 June 1983, a Libyan Arab airlines Boeing 707 was hijacked by two armed men during its flight from Athens, Greece, to Tripoli, Libya. The hijackers forced the aircraft to land at Rome airport for refuelling and then requested that the aircraft fly to Larnaca, Cyprus.[18] After several rounds of negotiations the hijackers surrendered to the authorities. Both hijackers were sentenced in Cyprus on 2 August 1983 to prison terms of seven years for hijacking and three years for possession of explosives.

On 28 August 1984 and 8 September 1984 two Iranian aircraft (Airbus 300 and Boeing 737) were unlawfully seized during a domestic flight and after refuelling stops in Bahrain and Cairo, were diverted to Iraq. The hijackers surrendered and they were granted political asylum. On 11 June 1985 an ALIA Boeing 727 aircraft was hijacked at Beirut Airport.[19] After lengthy negotiations, the hijackers finally released all passengers and crew members, destroyed the aircraft with explosives and escaped.

On 25 December 1986, the attempted hijack of an Iraqi Airways Boeing 737 aircraft during a scheduled flight from Baghdad, Iraq, to Amman, Jordan, resulted in the crash of the aircraft near Arar, Saudi Arabia. The crash which was aggravated by a post-impact fire totally destroyed the aircraft killing 65 persons, including three crew members, and seriously injured 35 others.

On 23 December 1987, a KLM Boeing 737 with 91 passengers on board was hijacked and forced to land at Rome airport during a scheduled flight from Amsterdam to Milan.[20] The hijacker was a 15-year-old Italian national, who claimed to have a bomb in his hand luggage and demanded a ransom of US$1 million in exchange for the release of the passengers. He also demanded to be flown first to Kuwait, then to Chad and finally to the United States. He was arrested and taken into custody when he left the aircraft to board another aircraft to New York. There were no casualties during the incident. The offender was sent back to the Netherlands by the Italian authorities and was delivered to the juvenile protection authorities there.

On Monday, 4 December 1984, for the second time in a month, a flight originating in a Gulf country was forced to land in Tehran. This time, it was a Kuwait Airways Airbus A-310 which had taken off from Dubai on its way to Karachi. On board the aircraft were 145 passengers, 11 crew members and 5 hijackers. The object of the hijacking was to secure the release from Kuwaiti jails of perpetrators of a series of bombings carried out against targets in Kuwait in December 1983. The real reason of course was to help perpetuate international terrorism.

Apparently this was no different from the usual incident of hijacking that one reads about so frequently. On 5 December 1984 Tehran's Mehrabad International Airport experienced the drama and suspense that typifies a hijacking. Shots broke out as the Airbus landed. One person was evacuated and another was shot dead and kicked out of the aircraft. Initially, 44 women and children were freed and in Beirut an anonymous representative of a fundamentalist group claimed responsibility for the act. The two governments of Kuwait and Iran immediately set up a dialogue which included an earnest request to the United Nations and other international organizations to help solve the crisis. Syria offered to intervene. Iran, the host country, had its share of the usual innuendoes and invectives alleging its involvement in the act. Finally, after several hostages were killed and injured by the hijackers the aircraft was stormed by Iranian commandos on 11 December 1984. The last nine hostages on board were freed thus ending the fiasco of another devastating terrorist venture.

At the end of it all, the world witnessed the complete sequence of events which constitute the necessary corollaries to a typical hijacking incident – the demands of the hijackers, the deadline set to blow up the aircraft with the hostages, the sustained negotiations and the ensuing stalemate, and above all, the usual demonstration by the nations concerned that we are faced with a world in disunity and total discord. Such disunity is perhaps the single factor which motivates violence of this nature. The total refusal by the Iranian authorities to extradite the captured hijackers to Kuwait as requested by the Government of the United States more than underscores this significant fact.

The startling inevitability of Iran's refusal to extradite the hijackers surfaces the latent feature of this offence – that its beginnings lie in the enormity of the differences in political ideology between nations. The statement issued by the Iranian government that it is an independent nation and that action will be taken against the hijackers only if it thought necessary, according to the beliefs and the laws of its people, clearly shows that the offence is frequently viewed subjectively in an isolated environment. More so, the offence itself is often used by states to assert their stand in international politics.

The Tehran incident of 4 December 1984 more than ever before reiterated certain basic facts pertaining to the offence of hijacking without an awareness of which an effective solution is beyond our reach. They are that:

- Hijacking is really a by-product of the broader spectrum of universal political discord and unfair bargaining power wielded by nations in positions of advantage.
- Such *status quo* as given above is always exploited by the hijackers.
- Whatever their political ideologies, states refuse to unite themselves in combating the offence of hijacking by exploiting the offence to their advantage.

It is eminently clear that the existing international order sustains its guilt by effectively manifesting itself as both the accessory before and after the fact of the hijacking. The former is accomplished by motivating and encouraging the offence of hijacking in an indirect way by not attempting to eradicate disunity among nations on broad political issues. The latter is accomplished by not establishing international accord for the prevention and equal treatment of the offence.

The above clearly indicates that Iran's position of 4 December 1984 is not isolated. It is but a natural consequence of the existing *status quo*. To control the threat of hijacking and to change the *status quo* it is necessary to consider the applicability of a norm that would help build a universal rule of conduct on a multilateral basis. This norm should be constituted of two facts. They are that:

1 Nations identify the offence of hijacking positively, assess its contribution to international terrorism and universal discord; and
2 Notwithstanding diverse political beliefs and practices, nations treat the identification and punitive aspects of the offence on a universally applicable basis so that every nation would behave identically in a single crisis.

Aircraft Sabotage

On 7 May 1949, the first reported incident of sabotage occurred when a Philippines Airline aircraft[21] crashed into the sea during a scheduled flight from Daet to Manila. The crash was allegedly a time bomb, delivered to the aircraft by two ex-convicts, hired by a woman and a man with the intention of killing the woman's husband, a passenger on the aircraft. All 13 passengers and crew members on board were killed.

The second incident occurred on 9 September 1949 when a Quebec airways[22] DC-3 exploded 40 miles from Quebec during a flight from Quebec City to Baie Comeau. The explosion had been caused by a bomb in a forward luggage compartment. All 23 passengers and crew members on board were killed. Three persons were executed for this crime.

On 6 January 1960, a National Airlines[23] DC-6B exploded over Bolivia at 18 000 feet during its flight from New York to Miami. The explosion had occurred as a result of the detonation of dynamite by dry-cell batteries located in the passenger compartment under one of the seats. All 34 passengers and crew members on board were killed.

On 15 June 1972, a Cathay Pacific Airways[24] (Hong Kong) CV-880 crashed over the central highlands of Vietnam during a scheduled commercial flight from Bangkok to Hong Kong. A bomb which was located in a suitcase under a passenger seat was alleged to have been detonated and all 81 passengers and crew members on board were killed. A police officer, whose fiancée and her daughter were on board, was charged with the crime.

On 1 January 1976, a Middle East Airline[25] crashed into the Arabian Desert, as a consequence of a bomb on board which had caused a massive explosion in the forward baggage compartment. The incident had occurred between Saudi Arabia and Kuwait during a scheduled flight between Beirut and Dubai. All 82 passengers and crew members on board the aircraft were killed.

On 23 September 1983, a Gulf Air[26] Boeing 737 crashed 30 miles from Abu Dhabi, United Arab Emirates, after a bomb had exploded in the baggage compartment. The crash occurred in the desert while the aircraft was preparing to land. All 112 people on board were killed.

On 23 June 1985, an Air India Boeing 747[27] crashed into the Atlantic ocean about 100 miles southwest of the Irish coast during a scheduled flight from Montreal to Bombay via London. All 329 passengers and crew members on board were killed. The crash was allegedly caused by the explosion of a bomb in the forward cargo hold of the aircraft.

On 29 November 1987, a Korean Boeing 707[28] crashed into the Andaman Sea near the Thai-Burmese border during a scheduled flight from Abu-Dhabi to Seoul. All 115 passengers and crew members on board were killed. A preliminary report, pursuant to Article 13 of the Montreal Convention of 1971 was submitted by South Korea to ICAO. The authorities who had investigated the crash had concluded that it was caused by the explosion of a time bomb, hidden in a portable radio and liquor bottle. According to the report, the two alleged perpetrators, a 26-year-old woman and a 70-year-old man, had placed the explosive device in the cabin overhead baggage bin above their seat, setting the bomb to explode nine hours later. They had disembarked from the aircraft during a stop-over at Abu-Dhabi and had travelled to Bahrain, where they were detained by the authorities for carrying forged passports. During the investigation, both had attempted to commit suicide by swallowing capsules of potassium cyanide. The man died instantly and the woman survived and subsequently was extradited to South Korea for prosecution. On 7 March 1989, the woman pleaded guilty to mass murder and destruction of the aircraft.

On 21 December 1988, a PAN-AM Boeing 747[29] crashed over the Scottish village of Lockerbie during a scheduled flight from London to New York. All 259 passengers and crew members on board and eleven persons on the ground were killed. An analysis of the debris had positively identified an explosive residue which was consistent with the use of Semtex – a high-performance plastic explosive. No group or individual claimed responsibility for the incident.

Airport Attacks

Attacks at airports serving international civil aviation and at other aviation facilities have also been a major terrorist strategy and for many years this serious problem[30] has caused deaths, injury, and property damages. From 1973 to 1985, more than 36 attacks occurred at international civil airports, in peace time, resulting in more than 117 killings.[31]

On 5 August 1973, two armed men entered the international transit lounge at Athens airport and proceeded to open fire on passengers in the lounge awaiting embarkation. Four people were killed; 55 others were severely wounded.[32]

On 29 December 1975, 25 sticks of dynamite exploded in a baggage claim area at La Guardia Airport[33] in New York City. Several persons were killed; others were wounded. In the same airport, another explosion[34] occurred on 10 September 1976, in which a police officer was killed and three others wounded.

On 11 August 1976, an attack on the international airport in Istanbul[35] resulted in the deaths of four people and injury to four others when armed men set off explosives and fired machine guns at passengers boarding their flight.

On 9 May 1985, a gunman fired several shots at aircraft parked on the ramp of the Buffalo International Airport in the state of New

York[36]. Two Boeing 727 aircraft suffered severe damage. The loss was estimated to be in excess of one million US dollars. The suspect was arrested and taken into custody.

A bomb exploded in a crowded departure lounge at the Frankfurt International Airport[37] on 19 June 1985, killing three people and wounding 42 others. The explosion occurred beyond the security zone where baggage is inspected, destroying several airline ticket counters. The intended target of the attack was never identified.

The new Tokyo International Airport has been a target of attacks and explosions[38] and most of these incidents resulted in deaths, injuries and destruction of airport property. For example, investigators in a June 1985 incident revealed that on 23 June 1985, an explosion ripped through a baggage sorting area at Narita airport killing two cargo handlers and injuring four others. The bomb had been placed on a CP-Air Boeing 747 aircraft in Vancouver, Canada.

Two people had made reservations on the flight but not boarded the aircraft in Vancouver. Reports also indicated that this incident was linked to the Air India crash which occurred on the same day[39].

On 23 December 1985, a bomb in an automobile exploded in the parking lot at the Jorge Chavez International Airport[400] in Lima, Peru. Three persons were wounded and 10 vehicles were damaged. The Shining Path, a Peruvian revolutionary group, claimed responsibility for the explosion.

Two other incidents[41] at international airports, both of which occurred on 27 December 1985 at approximately the same time, had similar overtones suggesting a single plot. In the first incident, at Leonardo da Vinci Airport in Rome, four Palestinians were assaulted with gunfire in the international departures area of the airport. During an exchange of gun fire between the group and airport police, at least 13 persons in the departure area were killed and another 80 wounded. Three members of the group were killed during the exchange; the fourth was captured. A note found in the pocket of the surviving attacker indicated that the attack was in retaliation for an earlier raid on the Palestine Liberation Organization (PLO) headquarters in Tunis[42].

On the same day, at Schwechat Airport in Vienna[43], three Palestinians armed with grenades and automatic weapons carried out an attack on the departures area of the airport. Four persons were killed and approximately 40 others wounded. This incident was almost identical to the attack at Rome Airport. Investigators suspected that El-Al Israeli Airline was the target of both attacks and connected the attacks to the Palestinians. The surviving attackers of both incidents were arrested and taken into custody for prosecution.

In March 1988, a similar incident occurred at Bombay Airport[44] when a gunman shot and wounded the captain of an Alitalia aircraft.

The attack had occurred just as the crew members were climbing aboard an airport bus bound for a city hotel. The perpetrator had fired four shots and tossed two grenades before he was arrested by the police.

Missile Attacks against Aircraft

After the adoption of the Montreal Convention of 1971, which provided aircraft protection against acts of sabotage, missile attacks against aircraft became an acute problem in the 1980s. This prompted legal experts to inquire whether the Convention would encompass missile attacks against aircraft. The answer to this question is in the affirmative, since the word 'violence', used in Article 1, sub-paragraph (a), could be interpreted to include a missile attack. The sub-paragraph (a), could be interpreted to include a missile attack. The sub-paragraph and the opening language of Article 1 could be used to include a person performing an act of violence who is not actually on board the aircraft. Thus the Convention does apply to a person who is outside the aircraft and fires a gun or missile at an aircraft.

The most important general lesson we must all learn from the recent history of aviation terrorism is never again to allow the terrorist to get so far ahead of the world's airport security systems. We should already be anticipating the tactics that the terrorists are likely to use once the method of sabotage bombing has been blocked. For example, we should already be devising ways of preventing terrorists from obtaining and using surface-to-air missiles against civil aviation.

Attacks against Airports

The Tokyo Convention of 1963, the Hague Convention of 1970, and the Montreal Convention of 1971 focused on offences against aircraft. There was, therefore, a need to provide protection to airports. In Montreal on 24 February 1988, the final text of a protocol to provide protection for airports was presented as a supplementary document to the Montreal Convention of 1971. It stated that:

> Any person commits an offence if he unlawfully and intentionally, using any device, substance or weapons:
>
> a) performs an act of violence against a person at an airport serving international civil aviation which causes or is likely to cause serious injury or death; or

b) destroys or seriously damages the facilities of an airport serving international civil aviation or aircraft not in service located thereon or disrupts the services of the airport.[45]

Policies related to Airline Security

Many varying policies and procedures aimed at combating hijacking were developed and implemented as a response to the increase of hijacking as a world-wide problem in the 1960s, and growing public concern. Profiling, identification cards, screening passengers, and body searches were implemented in many airports. The policy of fully 'screening' all passengers seemed to have a dramatic effect in reducing hijacking incidents.

Hijacking became a significant problem arousing public concern in the United States in the 1960s. The United States government in response to these concerns took the lead in establishing public policy to combat aircraft hijacking. The US implemented a major policy which required screening all passengers with metal detectors to prevent weapons finding their way on board an aircraft.

The Montreal Convention of 1971 for the Suppression of Unlawful Acts Against the Safety of Civil Aviation defines certain acts (described previously) as criminal acts. The Convention indicates that each contracting state should undertake to make these offences punishable by severe penalties.

The Montreal Protocol of 1988 for the Suppression of Unlawful Acts of Violence at Airports Serving International Civil Aviation addresses acts of violence which occur at airports.[46]

Deterrence and Crime Prevention Policies

In order that basic strategies are employed for preventing crime and to combat crime when prevention is impossible, crime prevention strategies adopt two methods of combating crime. The first method is to prevent or stop potential criminal acts. The second method is to apprehend and punish anyone who commits a criminal act. These methods follow the philosophy that the prevention of crime can be achieved by increasing the probability of apprehension and applying severe penal sanction to a crime. For example, installation of metal detectors at airports increases the probability of detecting and apprehending potential hijackers or saboteurs. Theoretically the high risk of being apprehended decreases the potential threat and the stringent penal sanction that may apply as a consequence to such apprehension compounds the ominous quality of the prevention means taken.

Empirical Studies of Deterrence

Many studies focus on aspects of the deterrence theory with the application of the deterrent theory to the varied effects of criminology applications on various modes of crimes. These studies relating to the prevention of crime attracted interesting conclusions which went on to reflect that increasing certainty and the severity of punishment reduced the rate of homicide in the United States. It was found by this study that the effect of severity was greater than that of certainty. There were negative correlations between the certainty of imprisonment and total crimes. Another observation was that increasing the certainty of punishment decreased the incidence of homicide, robbery, assault, burglary, larceny and car theft. It was also found that certainty appeared to have an independent effect separate from severity of punishment. In view of the fact that effects of severity decreased as certainty of punishment decreased, it would be reasonable to conclude that it is better for policy to concentrate on increasing certainty in order that such an approach be more effective.

In the application of the above surveys in the US have revealed that increasing the number of police on patrol decreased the number of robberies in New York City subways. Also, increasing the number of police on patrol decreased the number of outdoor crimes in the 20th Precinct of New York. Increasing the certainty and severity of punishment for drink-driving is effective in reducing drink-driving. Increasing the mandatory punishment for carrying a gun illegally in Massachusetts reduced the use of guns in violent crime.

Increased penalties or enhanced enforcement have improved compliance with child-support laws. Enhanced enforcement of law decreased spouse abuse. Improving enforcement and increasing penalties reduced accidents and deaths from drink-driving. Increasing penalties and enhancing enforcement also increased the number of people wearing seat belts.

Severity of the penalty influenced offender decision-making in combination with anticipated gain or perceived risk. Increasing risks of being arrested and severity of penalties reduced burglaries.[47]

Generally, these studies support the hypothesis that two factors lead a criminal to perceive a greater risk of punishment. These factors are: firstly, certainty, or a high probability of being arrested and convicted, secondly, the severity of the punishment. Certainty and severity of punishment each have an individual effect on crime prevention; but there is a greater impact when certainty and severity are combined.

Theoretical Bases

Deterrence, as a theoretical concept that can be applied in most instances of criminology with practical results, is based on the fundamental assumption that individuals are rational beings. Rationality promotes benefit-maximizing behaviour that is perceived by human beings even when set against constraints. This means that individuals as rational beings pursue their maximizing goals by making the best choices they can. The underlying concept of deterrence theory supports the hypothesis that rationalists consider potential criminals as rational decision-makers faced with constraints and uncertainty in their decision-making process. The explanation of governmental actions follows the same pattern of the rational model. Therefore, an analyst could conclude that criminals and government officials are engaged in a 'game' where criminals try to maximize their illegitimate goals through the 'least expensive' (apprehension and punishment) approaches and government policy-makers try to prevent crimes by increasing the probability of apprehension and creating a punishment which will serve as a deterrent.

The model that when other variables are held constant, an increase in the person's probability of conviction would decrease the number of offences he or she commits was first introduced in 1968, where a model was developed based on an individual's participation in criminal activity. This theory holds the view that changing the probability of conviction (certainty) has a greater effect on the number of offences than a change in punishment (severity).

In 1973, a formulation of a more comprehensive model of the decision to engage in unlawful activities, based on available empirical evidence, tested the earlier theory and revealed that the rate of specific crimes was positively related to estimates of relative gains, and negatively related to estimates of costs associated with criminal activity.

In 1978, an interesting modality was introduced by Landes who used ordinary least squares (OLS) regression techniques to assess the effectiveness of metal detectors, sky marshals, stiffer penalties, and intelligence profiles on skyjackings originating in the United States in the late 1960s and early 1970s. The main task that this study undertook was to discover what accounted for the dramatic reduction in US aircraft hijacking after 1972. The study concluded that increases in the probability of apprehension, the conditional probability of incarceration, and the sentence (punishment) were associated with significant reductions in aircraft hijackings from 1961 to 1976. Also, a mandatory screening programme (installation of metal detectors in airports) was highly effective in terms of the number of hijackings prevented.

Landes' findings are supported by utilizing hijacking data from 1960 to 1976. Also, Landes' regression model tests each explanatory factor separately; that method does not include a control test for the effects of punishment in testing the effects of mandatory screening at airports.

Research Design

A recent research design built in the US tested the use of technical implements such as metal detectors in crime deterrence.

Three primary hypotheses were tested which related to the use of metal detectors as a deterrent, the displacement effect of this strategy, (the shifting of the type of crime to avoid a particular deterrent) and the impact of metal detectors and prosecution (conviction) as a deterrent.

The design also tested two diametrically opposed hypotheses:

1 that a use of metal detectors at airports decreases hijackings;
2 that the use of metal detectors produced the unintended consequence of shifting criminal activities from hijacking to bombings and missile attacks. In order to explain this shift a correlation analysis was utilized. This analysis measured the relationship between hijacking and other crimes such as bombing, missile attacks, and attacks at airports.

The first concern of the study was how to assess the impact of metal detectors which were introduced in January 1973 in the US as a means of intervention to prevent hijacking. Time-series were being used to measure the impacts of policy on social exigencies.[48] The impact of metal detectors was measured by looking at trends in hijacking over a period of time.

An interrupted time-series was used to assess the impact of metal detectors on hijacking. The purpose of the interrupted time-series analysis was to infer whether the policy had any impact. If it did, it was concluded that one could expect the hijackings after the introduction of metal detectors to be different from those before it, that is, the hijacking series should show signs of an 'interruption' at the time metal detectors were introduced.

In this model, the data on US hijacking were utilized, to the extent available. While the use of US data limits the generalization of findings, the choice of US statistics for the study was facilitated by the fact that the use of metal detectors was fully implemented through a federal programme in which all US airports were required to adopt. However, a problem caused by the model was that metal detectors were not introduced in all airports around the world at the same time, and there are problems related to the accuracy of the data.

The study also utilized multiple regression analysis to measure the impact of using metal detectors and convictions on hijacking. In the analysis, a time-series model examined data on convicted airline hijackers in the US Data on convictions in the US were used because available records on world-wide convicted hijackers is inadequate, and one is also faced with the problem of different definitional terms.

The measurement of the relationship between hijacking and other crimes against aircraft after introducing metal detectors formed the second component of the study. Zero-orer correlation and partial correlation were used to measure the relationships between hijacking, bombing, missile attacks, and attacks at airports.

The model also used data which supported a detailed analysis of 208 hijacking cases. The analysis aimed at collating a descriptive data related to the characteristics of these incidents. Since threats and measures adopted by the aggressor vary and the countermeasures must be adopted to keep pace with changes in the type or method of the threat, a regression analysis was undertaken to explain the relationship between hijacking, increased security, and other crimes. The descriptive analysis of hijackings provided additional information which impacts on security policies.

The analysis proved that contrary to popular belief, the vast majority of hijackings took place while the plane was on the ground. However, negotiation proved successful much more often in individual hijackings. Not surprisingly, group-related incidents were much more likely to involve more than one hijacker.

In the area of airport and aircraft security, countries have utilized passenger screening, through metal detectors, since 1973. Indications are that these techniques have reduced hijacking and bombing significantly. However, the research also supports a preliminary conclusion that 'target hardening' at airports has increased the probability of missile attacks against aircraft. There is a direct correlation between the decrease in hijacking and an increase in bombing incidents.

The conclusion of the study therefore signals the ominous prospect that the displacement effect would theoretically outrun basic deterrent measures in practicality. Against this backdrop, one way to consider the extent to which international law can be used as an instrument which enforces rights of individuals and states in the aftermath of an attack against civil aviation is to discuss a recent adjudication in the International Court of Justice (ICJ) which brought out the legal nuances of the problems at hand.

Legal Issues Measures – A Case Study

The PAN-AM Case

On 3 March 1992, the Registry of the ICJ received an application by the Socialist Peoples' Libyan Arab Jamahiriya (hereafter referred to as Libya), instituting proceedings against the United States of America. The application referred to a dispute between Libya and the United States, which arose as a result of the destruction of PAN-AM flight 103 on December 1988 over Lockerbie, Scotland. On 14 November 1991, a Grand Jury of the United States District Court for the District of Columbia, indicted two Libyan nationals, charging them *inter alia* with causing a bomb to be placed on board PAN-AM flight 103; the bomb had exploded causing the aeroplane to crash. Consequently, the British and American governments declared that Libya must:

- surrender for trial all three charged with the crime; and accept responsibility for the actions of Libyan officials;
- disclose all it knows of this crime, including the names of all those responsible, and allow access to all witnesses, documents and other material evidence, including all the remaining timers;
- pay appropriate compensation.[49]

The United Nations Security Council considered this declaration and on 21 January 1992 adopted Resolution 731 (1992), strongly deploring the fact that the Libyan government did not effectively respond to the requests contained in the declaration of the British and the American governments, and urging Libya to provide a full and effective response to those requests so as to contribute to the elimination of international terrorism.[50]

In the course of the oral proceedings before the ICJ, reference had been made by both the United Kingdom and the United States to the possibility of sanctions being imminently imposed by the Security Council on Libya in order to require it to extradite the accused to the United States or the United Kingdom. Libya's application before the ICJ was therefore to invoke the jurisdiction of the Court for provisional measures that would *inter alia* preclude the United States and the United Kingdom from taking any initiative within the Security Council for the purpose of impairing Libya's right to exercise its own jurisdiction over the accused.

The Security Council adopted a further Resolution – Resolution 748 of 1992[51] – expressing its deep concern that the Libyan government had not provided a full and effective response to the requests of its earlier Resolution 731 (1992) and deciding that the Libyan government must commit itself to ceasing all forms of terrorist action and by concrete actions, demonstrate its renunciation of terrorism. The Security Council, acting under authority of Chapter VII of the United Nations Charter, which, under Article 39 grants the Security Council powers to determine the existence of any threat to international peace, also decided by Resolution 748 that all states adopt appropriate measures against Libya. The Security Council Resolution also called upon all states, including states that were not members of the United Nations, and all international organizations, to act strictly with the provisions of the Resolution, notwithstanding the existence of any rights or obligations conferred or imposed by any international agreement or any contract entered into or any licence or permit granted prior to 15 April 1992.

The Agent of the United States, by a letter of 2 April 1992, drew the ICJ's attention to the adoption of Security Council Resolution 748 (1992). In his letter, the United States' Agent stated:

> That resolution, adopted pursuant to Chapter VII of the United Nations Charter, decides that the Libyan Government must now comply without any further delay with Paragraph 3 of Resolution 731 (1992) of 21 January 1992 regarding the requests contained in documents S/23306, S/23308 and S/23309. It will be recalled that the reference requests include the request that Libya surrenders the two Libyans suspected of the bombing of PAN-AM flight 103 to the United States or to the United Kingdom. For this additional reason, the United States maintains its submission of 28 March 1992 that the request of the Government of the Great Socialist Peoples' Libyan Arab Jamahiriya for the indication of provisional measures of protection should be denied, and that no such measures should be indicated.[52]

Libya in reply claimed that the risk of contradiction between Resolution 748 (1992) and the provisional measures requested of the Court by Libya did not render the Libyan request inadmissible, since there is in law no competition or hierarchy between the Court and the Security Council, both being equal organs of the United Nations, exercising their own competence.[53] Libya also recorded that it regarded the decision of the Security Council as contrary to international law and one which had been taken to avoid applicable law in the guise of the Security Council's powers under Chapter VII of the United Nations Charter. Libya claimed that the foundation of the Court's jurisdiction lay in the Convention for the Suppression of Unlawful Acts Against the Safety of Civil Aviation, signed in Montreal on 23 September 1971[54] (hereafter referred to as the Montreal Convention).

Article 14 (1) of the Montreal Convention stipulates:

> Any dispute between two or more Contracting States concerning the interpretation or application of this Convention which cannot be settled through negotiation, shall, at the request of one of them, be submitted to arbitration. If within six months from the date of the request for arbitration the parties are unable to agree on the organization of the arbitration, any one of those Parties may refer the dispute to the International Court of Justice by request in conformity with the Statute of the Court.

There is no doubt that this provision had been drafted in imperative terms, and any dispute that required the interpretation or application of the provisions of the Convention could be submitted to the Court for arbitration. Therefore, the contentious issue of the extradition of the Libyan nationals was a matter clearly within the jurisdiction of the Court since Article 7 of the Montreal Convention provides:

> The Contracting State in the territory of which the alleged offender is found shall, if it does not extradite him, be obliged, without exception whatsoever and whether or not the offence was committed in its territory, to submit the case to its competent authorities for the purpose of prosecution ...

It was Libya's claim that according to this provision, it had the right to try its own nationals and was not obligated to extradite them to either the United States or the United Kingdom as was required by the Security Council Resolution. It was also Libya's contention that the ICJ had explicit jurisdiction by virtue of Article 14(1) of the Montreal Convention to interpret Article 7.

The United States claimed that irrespective of the Montreal Convention, Libya was bound as a member of the United Nations to abide by the United Nations Charter which in Chapter VII (Article 39) granted absolute power to the Security Council to decide on the measures to be taken to restore and maintain international peace and security. The United States also invoked Article 25 of the United States Charter which provides that:

> The members of the United Nations agree to accept and carry out the decisions of the Security Council in accordance with the present Charter.

The Court, in its decision agreed with the contention of the United States that both Libya and the United States, as members of the United Nations, are obliged to accept and carry out the decisions of the Security Council in accordance with Article 25 of the United Nations Charter. This obligation, according to the Court, extended to Resolution 748 (1992). The Court also cited Article 103 of the United Nations Charter which stipulates:

> In the event of a conflict between the obligations of the members of the United Nations under the present Charter and their obligations under any other international agreement, their obligations under the present Charter shall prevail.

The Court held therefore that the provisions of the Montreal Convention cited by Libya were subservient to the Security Council Resolution and accordingly denied Libya's application.

The Effect of United Nations Security Council Resolutions on the International Court of Justice

The United States, in its submission to the International Court of Justice in the PAN-AM case, contended that the Security Council was actively in possession of the situation which was the subject of Libya's application and that therefore the Court should not indicate provisional measures as requested.[55] Judge Oda, Acting President of the Court, observing that Libya instituted proceedings against the United States in respect of the interpretation and application of the Montreal Convention, noted that it was a general principle of international law that no state could be compelled to extradite its nationals and that the state concerned held the prerogative of trying the accused of a crime in its own territory. Judge Oda seemed to recognize two principles in his opinion:

1 While any state can request extradition, no state can coerce extradition of nationals of another state.
2 Whether or not a state can compel extradition is a matter for resolution by the general principles of international law and not necessarily those stipulated in the Montreal Convention.

It appears that the question in Judge Oda's mind was therefore whether the Security Council, by its Resolution 748 (1992) which required Libya to extradite its nationals either to the United States or to the United Kingdom, had the authority to override an established principle of international law. The answer to this question was, in Judge Oda's view, in the affirmative when he opined:

> I do not deny that under the positive law of the United Nations Charter a resolution of the Security Council may have binding force,

> irrespective of the question whether it is consonant with international law derived from other sources. There is certainly nothing to oblige the Security Council, acting within its terms of reference, to carry out a full evaluation of the possibly relevant rules and circumstances before proceeding to the decisions it deems necessary. The Council appears, in fact, to have been acting within its competence when it discerned a threat against international peace and security in Libya's refusal to deliver up the two Libyans accused. Since, as I understand the matter, a decision of the Security Council, properly taken in the exercise of its competence, cannot be summarily reopened and since it is apparent that Resolution 748 (1992) embodies such a decision, the Court has at present no choice but to acknowledge the pre-eminence of that resolution.[56]

Judge Oda was emphatic that the Security Council Resolution had overriding effect over any principle of international law. He observed however, that if the Court appeared to have *prima facie* jurisdiction over a legal issue that was the subject of its consideration, the Court was not precluded from indicating provisional measures applied for, merely because of the absolute pre-emptive powers of the Security Council Resolution. The learned judge concluded that, in this case, the application of the Libyan Government would have been rejected by the Court in any case, as the application was based on the Montreal Convention and not on the general customary international law principle *aut dedere aut judicare*. Judge Oda was also unequivocal in his view that the Security Council Resolution would prevail over any established rule of international law.

Judge Ni on the other hand, in his opinion, observed that the Security Council and the International Court of Justice could simultaneously exercise their respective functions without being excluded by each other. Citing the arbitration that came up before the ICJ in respect of the United States diplomatic consular staff in Tehran, Judge Ni quoted from that judgement:

> ... it is for the Court, the principal judicial organ of the United Nations, to resolve any legal questions that may be in issue between parties to a dispute; and the resolution of such legal questions by the Court may be an important, and sometimes decisive factor in promoting the peaceful settlement of the dispute. This is indeed recognized by Article 36 of the Charter, Paragraph 3 of which specifically provides that:
>
> In making recommendations under this Article the Security Council should also take into consideration that legal disputes should as a general rule be referred by the parties to the International Court of Justice in accordance with the provisions of the Statute of the Court.[57]

Judge Ni also analysed Article 24 of the United Nations Charter which provides:

> In order to ensure prompt and effective action by the United Nations, its members confer on the Security Council *primary* responsibility for the maintenance of international peace and security...

The learned judge reasoned the Charter did not confer exclusive responsibility upon the Security Council and observed that the Council has functions of a political nature assigned to it whereas the Court exercised purely judicial functions. According to Judge Ni therefore, both organs could perform their separate but complementary functions with respect to the same events. On the above reasoning, Judge Ni concluded that since the Court held independent jurisdiction, it could interpret the applicable law, which in this case was Article 14(1) of the Montreal Convention.[58] The ICJ could therefore, according to Judge Ni, by no means be pre-empted by a Security Council resolution, in its exercise of jurisdiction and application of the principles of international law.

Judges Evensen, Tarassov, Guillaume, and Aguila Mawdsley expressed their collective opinion that prior to the adoption by the Security Council of Resolution 748 (1992), the United States and the United Kingdom, although having the right to request extradition, could only take measures towards ensuring such extradition that were consistent with the principles of international law. With the Resolution in force however, the judges concluded that the Court was precluded from indicating provisional measures against the United States.

Judge Lachs, although in a separate opinion declared that the ICJ was bound to respect the binding decisions of the Security Council, seems to have recognized the co-existence of the two institutions, and the right of the Court to render its opinion irrespective of the application of Security Council resolutions. Judge Lachs said:

> The framers of the Charter, in providing for the existence of several main organs, did not effect a complete separation of powers, nor indeed is one to suppose that such was their aim. Although each organ has been allotted its own Chapter or Chapters, the functions of two of them, namely the General Assembly and the Security Council, also pervade other Chapters other than their own. Even the International Court of Justice receives, outside its own Chapter, a number of mentions which tend to confirm its role as the general guardian of legality within the system. In fact the Court is the Guardian of legality for the international community as a whole, both within and without the United Nations. One may therefore legitimately suppose that the intention of the founders was not to encourage a blinkered parallelism of functions but a fruitful interaction.

> Two main organs of the United Nations have the delivery of binding decisions explicitly included in their powers under the Charter: the Security Council and the International Court of Justice. There is no doubt that the Court's task is 'to ensure respect for international law...' (*ICJ Reports* 1949, p.35). It is its principal guardian. Now, it has become clear that the dividing line between political and legal disputes is blurred, as law becomes ever more frequently an integral element of international controversies. The Court, for reasons well known, so frequently shunned in the past, is thus called upon to play an even greater role. Hence it is important for the purposes and principles of the United Nations that the two main organs with specific powers of binding decision act in harmony – though not, of course, in concert – and that each should perform its functions with respect to a situation or dispute, different aspects of which appear on the agenda of each, without prejudicing the exercise of the other's powers. In the present case the Court was faced with a new situation which allowed no room for further analysis nor the indication of effective interim measures. The order made should not, therefore, be seen as an abdication of the Court's powers; it is rather a reflection of the system within which the Court is called upon to render justice.[59]

Judge Shahabuddeen, recognizing that there is no superior authority to that of the Security Council, added in his opinion that treaty obligations can be overridden by a decision of the Security Council's sanctions. Addressing the critical question whether a decision of the Security Council may override the legal rights of states, Judge Shahabuddeen did not attempt an answer, but merely concluded that such a decision may stand in the way of the legal rights of a state or its subjects being judicially scrutinized. Judge Bedjaoui in his opinion added to the opinion of Judge Shahabuddeen, saying that as a rule, the International Court of Justice does not exercise appellate jurisdiction over the Security Council.[60] The learned judge however, strongly dissented from the views of his colleagues which recognized that a Security Council resolution completely pre-empted the jurisdiction of the International Court of Justice and effectively precluded the latter from performing its judicial functions. Judge Bedjaoui stringently maintained that there were two aspects to the problem between Libya and the United States on this issue – political and judicial. In his view, although it was not possible for the Court to override the Security Council Resolution, the Court was by no means precluded from declaring provisional measures, as applied for by Libya, even if such a declaration by the Court was rendered destitute of effect by the Security Council Resolution.[61]

Judge Weeramantry, concurring with Judge Bedjaoui, conceded that although Article 25 of the United Nations Charter required member states of the United Nations to accept and carry out decisions of the Security Council, the Court was not deprived of its jurisdiction in issuing provisional measures as applied for by Libya. Adding that the International Court of Justice and the Security Council were created by the same Charter to fulfil the common purposes and principles of the United Nations, Judge Weeramantry concluded that the two agencies are complementary to each other, each performing a special role assigned to it. The Court was however, unlike most courts that were vested with domestic jurisdictions, not enabled to sit in review of the executive (which in this context was the Security Council). The dichotomy arose, in Judge Weeramantry's mind, when the principal judicial organ of the United Nations was restrained by decisions of its executive arm when deciding, according to the principles of international law, disputes that are submitted to it. The conclusions reached by judge Weeramantry were based on the Kelsenian observation that the Security Council and the General Assembly were only quasi-judicial organs of the United Nations and that the Security Council was by no means a judicial organ since its members were not independent;[62] and the Court ought to *collaborate* (emphasis added) with the Security Council if the circumstances so require.[63] Judge Weeramantry therefore emphasized that the Court must at all times preserve its independence, particularly in view of the fact that Article 24(2) of the Charter provides that the Security Council shall act in accordance with the purposes and principles of the United Nations, which are set out in Article 1(1) of the Charter as being those aims to settle international disputes and situations that might lead to breaches of the peace, according to the principles of justice and international law.

Judge Weeramantry further observed:

> A great judge once observed that the laws are not silent amidst the clash of arms. In our age we need also to assert that the laws are not powerless to prevent the clash of arms. The entire law of the United Nations has been built up around the notion of peace and the prevention of conflict. The Court, in an appropriate case, where possible conflict threatens rights that are being litigated before it, is not powerless to issue provisional measures conserving those rights by restraining an escalation of the dispute and the possible resort to force. That would be entirely within its mandate and in total conformity with the Purposes and Principles of the United Nations and international law. Particularly, when situations are tense, with danger signals flashing all around, it seems that this Court should make a positive response with such measures as are within its jurisdiction. If the conservation of rights which are *sub judice* comes within the jurisdiction of the Court, as I have no doubt it does, an order restraining damage to those rights through conflict must also lie within that province. If international law is to grow and serve the cause of peace as it is meant

to do, the Court cannot avoid the responsibility in an appropriate case.

I would indicate provisional measures *proprio motu* against both parties preventing such aggravation or extension of the dispute as might result in the use of force by either or both parties. Such measures do not conflict with any decision the Security Council has made under Chapter VII, nor with any obligation arising under Article 25, nor with the principle underlying Article 103. The way towards a peaceful resolution of the dispute may thus be preserved before the parties find themselves on paths from which there may be no return. This action is based on Article 41 of the Statute of the Court and Articles 73, 74 and 75 of the Rules of Court.[64]

Scholastic Views

The status of the International Court of Justice as an organ of the United Nations that dispenses justice and hence has full capacity to examine and determine legal issues stands clear in the minds of legal scholars. Hans Kelsen, analysing Article 92 of the United Nations Charter which provides that the International Court of Justice shall be the principal judicial organ of the United Nations observes:

If the term judicial organ in Article 92 means 'tribunal' the International Court of Justice is not only the 'principal' but also the only judicial organ of the Organization, at least, the only tribunal established directly by the Charter as an organ of the United Nations.[65]

The word 'tribunal' generally means a 'place of judgement' or decision and specifically means a court of justice[66] when it exercises judicial powers. Therefore, Kelsen's analysis admits no other conclusion than that the International Court of Justice is the only judicial organ of the United Nations, as in Kelsen's words, 'The Security Council is not a judicial organ because its members are not independent'.[67]

Kelsen's claim is further supported by the provisions of the United Nations Charter themselves. According to Article 36(1) of the Charter, the International Court of Justice has jurisdiction to hear all cases referred to it by the states' parties, and according to Article 36(2), that jurisdiction extends to determining questions of international law and interpretation of treaties. The disconcerting dichotomy is that while Article 25 of the Charter obligates member states to adhere to or abide by decisions of the Security Council, Article 36 grants the Court jurisdiction to hear and decide issues *inter alia* on questions of international law or interpretation of treaties and their nature and reparation to be made in cases of breaches of the peace. In addition,

Article 38 of the Charter allows the Court to apply *inter alia*, international convention and international custom in the reaching of its decision. According to these principles, the Court could have decided on the legal issues of the Libyan application by considering the customary rule of international law, *aut dedere aut judicare* and interpreted the Montreal Convention and delivered its opinion on the legal status of Libya and the United States. At least, by doing so, the International Court of Justice could have fulfilled its role as the primary judicial body of the United Nations, irrespective of whether under Article 25 of the Charter, Security Council resolutions were mandatory. What is expected of the International Court of Justice by the Charter includes the performance of its judicial role of interpreting the law, irrespective of its adherence to its findings by member states. In this perspective, the International Court of Justice is truly complementary to the Security Council and need not necessarily give way to Security Council resolutions without making its observations known.

The eleven to five majority decision in the Libyan application which was based almost entirely on Article 25 of the Charter, and its peremptory requirement that states should follow the decisions of the Security Council and Article 103 which pre-empted treaty provisions from creating obligations on member states has therefore made the International Court of Justice disregard its role as the primary, if not the sole judicial body of the United Nations which was empowered to consider questions of law by the Charter.

The PAN-AM case has amply demonstrated that the United Nations Charter is generally considered supreme as the primary source of international law. This recognition, strengthened by the International Court of Justice in unanimity, at least adds some specificity and definitive parameters to the characteristic ambivalence of international law. It also confers an added dimension upon the United Nations as the watchdog of all nations and equips the United Nations better to perform its functions. At least now, one knows where one is headed with international law. It is now up to all concerned to define parameters more unequivocally, on a balanced formula that blends harmoniously the interests of states with international peace and security.

Notes

1 The leading airlines of Asia, Europe and the United States have said that they already need an aircraft bigger than the 747 at peak times. To cope with this demand, Boeing will launch a 600-800 'Super 747' and Airbus is proposing a rival A 3XX. It has been forecast that airlines will buy 1 000 megajets by 2030 if

the design revolutionizes comfort and is in service within five years of the Super 747. The megajet will have a shopping arcade, restaurant and promenade decks, with 'first class' seating for 1 100 and 'military' seating for 2 000. See Ramsden, J.M. (1994), 'The Megajet', *Aerospace*, August 1994 at 16–21.

2 The universality principle gives all countries the right to arrest and prosecute international criminals as pirates on the high seas, outside their territorial boundaries.

3 *Investment Requirements for Aircraft Fleets and for Airport and Route Facility Infrastructure to the Year 2010*. Circular 236-AT/95 at 10.

4 Ghosh, S.K. (1985), *Aircraft Hijacking and the Developing Law*, New Delhi, Ashish Pub. House, at 1.

5 *Ibid.*

6 *Ibid.*

7 *Ibid.*

8 12 *International Legal Materials* (1973) at 370.

9 Statement made by Cuba before the United Nations General Assembly on November 3, 1977, UN Doc *A/32/PV.56* at 8–10.

10 See generally, Stevenson, W. (1976), *90 Minutes at Entebbe* Random House, New York.

11 15 *International Legal Materials* (1976) at 1226–1227. See also, UN Doc S/12126.

12 *Ibid.*

13 *Id.* at 1226. The draft resolution was withdrawn by its sponsors on 14 July 1976.

14 *Id.* at 1227. The tri-state draft was not pressed to a vote, but in the statement by the Tanzanian Delegate on 14 July, the co-sponsors reserved the right to revive consideration of it 'at an appropriate moment'.

15 See Cooper, H.H.A. (1978), 'Hostage Rescue Operations: Denouncement at Algeria and Mogadishu compared'; *Chitty's Law Journal*, vol. 26, at 91.

16 Ghosh (1985), *supra*, at 3.

17 Ghosh (1985), *supra*, at 8.

18 US Department of Transportation, Federal Aviation Administration, Aircraft Hijacking and other Criminal Acts against Civil Aviation: Statistical and Narrative Reports (Washington, DC 1986) at D112 (hereafter referred to as Aircraft Hijacking).

19 ICAO Doc. C-WP/8540, Appendix C at 28.

20 *Id.*, at 30.

21 Ghosh (1985), op. cit., p. F-1.

22 *Ibid.*

23 *Id.*, p. F-2

24 *Id.*, p. F-6

25 *Id.*, p. F-10

26 *Id.*, p. F-12

27 ICAO Doc. C-WP/8540, *supra*, p. 31

28 *Id.*, p. 32.

29 ICAO Doc. UI-WP/205, *supra*, p. 9

30 Faller, E.W. (1987), 'Current Legal Activities in ICAO: Development of a Legal Instrument for the Suppression of Unlawful Acts of Violence at Airports Serving International Civil Aviation', *Zeitschrift fur Luft-Und Weltraumrecht*,(German Journal of Air and Space Law), p. 219.

31 ICAO Doc. LC/SC-VIA-Report, Appendix C, p. 25.

32 Faller, (1987). *Supra*, note 30 at 219.

33 ICAO (1975), *ICAO Chronology of Unlawful Interference with Civil Aviation*, (mimeo.), p. 1.

34 *The New York Times*, 11 Sept. 1976, p.1.

35 *The New York Times*, 12 Aug. 1976, p. 1.

36 Ghosh, (1985) Aircraft Hijacking, op. cit., p. G-8.
37 *Id.*, p. G-10.
38 *Id.*, pp. G-1–25.
39 *Ibid.*
40 *Id.*, p. G-23.
41 *Id.*, p. G-24.
42 *Ibid.*
43 *Ibid.*
44 ICAO Doc. UI-WP/205, op. cit., p. 9.
45 The Montreal Protocol of 1988, Protocol for the Suppression of Unlawful Acts of Violence at Airports Serving International Civil Aviation, Supplementary to the Montreal Convention. Parties: there are 17 parties to the Protocol. The United States has signed the Protocol but it is not yet in effect. (The Presidents' Report of 1989).
46 Montreal Protocol final text was presented on 24 February 1988.
47 Decker, S., Wright, R., Logie, and Robert. (1993), 'Perceptual Deterrence Among Active Residential Burglars: A Research Note', *Criminology*, vol. 31, no. 1.
48 Time-series data is data collected over a period of time. Such data may be collected at regular intervals, such as monthly, quarterly or annually. The data may be quantitative (continued) or qualitative (categorical).
49 Questions of Interpretation and Application of the 1971 Montreal Convention Arising From the Aerial Incident at Lockerbie (*Libyan Arab Jamahiriya* v. *The United States of America*) Provisional Measures, Order of 14 April 1992, *ICJ Reports*, 1992, 114 at 122.
50 *Id.*, 123–124.
51 *Ibid.*
52 *Id.*, 125.
53 *Id.*, 126.
54 *Ibid.*
55 *ICJ Report*, (1992) *op. cit.*, at 122. By letter of 2 April 1992, a copy of which was transmitted to Libya by the Registrar, the Agent of the United States drew the Court's attention to the adoption of Security Council Resolution 748 (1992) the text of which he enclosed. In that letter the Agent for the United States stated: That resolution, adopted pursuant to Chapter VII of the United Nations Charter, 'decides that the Libyan Government must now comply without any further delay with paragraph 3 of Resolution 731 (1992) of 21 January 1992 regarding the requests contained in documents S/23306, S/23308 and S/23309'. It will be recalled that the referenced requests include the request that Libya surrender the two Libyan suspects in the bombing of Pan-Am flight 103 to the United States or to the United Kingdom. For this additional reason, the United States maintains its submission of 28 March 1992 that the request of the Government of the Great Socialist Peoples' Libyan Arab Jamahiriya for the indication of provisional measures for protection should be denied, and that no such measures should be indicated. See *ICJ Report*, (1992) *op. cit.* at 125.
56 *Id.* at 129.
57 *ICJ Report* (1980), at 22, para. 40.
58 *Op. cit.*
59 *ICJ Report* (1992), *op. cit.*, 138–139.
60 *Id.* at 140.
61 *Id.*, 155–156.
62 Kelsen, H. (1951), *The Law of the United Nations*, New York, Praeger, 476–477. See *ICJ Report*, (1992), *op. cit.*, 167.
63 *ICJ Report* (1992), *op. cit.*, 168.
64 *Id.* at 172.

65 Kelsen (1951), *op. cit.*, 476.
66 *Shorter Oxford Dictionary on Historical Principles*, (1980) vol. 11, Oxford, Clarendon Press.
67 *Id.*, 477.

4 Some International Attempts at Ensuring Peace and Security in Aviation

United Nations General Assembly Resolutions

During its 24th Session in December 1969, the United Nations General Assembly discussed the problem of 'forcible diversion of civil aircraft' and adopted Resolution 2551 (XXIV),[1] in which the General Assembly stated its deep concern over acts of unlawful interference with international civil aviation. The General Assembly also called upon states to take every appropriate measure to see that their respective national legislation provides an adequate framework for effective legal measures against all kinds of acts of unlawful seizure of civil aircraft. It furthermore called upon states to ensure that persons on board who perpetrate such acts are prosecuted. The General Assembly urged that states give their fullest support to the International Civil Aviation Organization in its endeavours towards the speedy preparation and adoption of a convention which would provide for appropriate measures which would make the offence of unlawful seizure of aircraft punishable. The commission of the offence would lead to the prosecution of persons who commit it. By this resolution, the General Assembly also invited states to ratify and accede to the Convention on Offences and Certain Other Acts Committed On Board Aircraft, signed in Tokyo on 14 September 1963.[2]

On 25 November 1970 the General Assembly adopted Resolution 2645 (XXV)[3] which condemned without exception whatsoever all aerial hijacking or other interference with civil air travel caused through the threat or use of force. The Resolution also condemned all acts of violence which may be directed against passengers, crew and aircraft engaged in, and air navigation facilities and aeronautical communication used by civil air transport. The Assembly called upon states to take all appropriate measures to deter, prevent or suppress such acts within their jurisdiction, at every stage of the execution of those acts, and to provide for the prosecution and punishment of persons who perpetrate such acts, in a measure commensurate with the gravity of those crimes, or extradite such persons for the purpose of their prosecution and punishment. Furthermore, the Assembly condemned the exploitation of unlawful seizure of aircraft for the purpose of taking hostages, calling upon states to take joint and separate action, in accordance with the United Nations Charter and in cooperation with the United Nations and International Civil Aviation Organization so that passengers, crew and aircraft engaged in civil aviation are not used for purposes of extortion.

The international community thus condemned terrorism against air transport by giving official recognition to such condemnation and called upon all states to contribute to the eradication of the offence by taking effective, preventive and deterrent measures. Notwithstanding the weight of these resolutions the General Assembly has seemingly deprived itself of the opportunity of declaring the offence of hijacking an international crime under international law. The world condemnation of the offence has left the question open to states as to whether the international community would collectively respond in the face of a crisis related to unlawful interference with civil aviation. Another blatant weakness of the resolution is that its provisions regarding extradition are ambivalent. The resolution also does not say whether political motive would be a valid ground against extradition or not. It is submitted that the General Assembly should have considered adopting the principle that political motive will not be a factor affecting the extradition of hijackers.

The resolution, with all its failings, has many advantages, such as its condemnation of the offence of unlawful interference and call for international action against the offence. The persuasive nature of resolutions will facilitate nations in interacting with each other and assisting each other.

The United Nations has, over the past 20 years extended an invitation to nations, to cooperate with each other in eradicating or controlling international terrorism. For instance, Resolution 2645 (XXV) recognized that international civil aviation is a vital link in the promotion and preservation of friendly relations among states, and that the Assembly was gravely concerned over acts of aerial hijacking or other wrongful interference with civil air travel. The resolution condemned without exception, all acts of aerial hijacking or other interference with civil air travel and called upon states to take all appropriate measures to deter, prevent or suppress such acts within their jurisdiction.[4] Earlier, the Security Council had adopted Resolution 286 (1970) which expressed the Council's grave concern at the threat to innocent civilian lives from the hijacking of aircraft and any other interference in international travel. The Security council appealed to all parties concerned for the immediate release of all passengers and crews without exceptions, held as a result of hijackings and other interference in international travel, and called on states to take all possible legal steps to prevent further hijackings or any other interference with international civil air travel.[5]

On 18 December 1972, the United Nations General Assembly, at its 27th Session adopted a resolution[6] expressing the deep concern of the Assembly over acts of international terrorism which are occurring with increasing frequency and recalled the declaration on principles of international law which called for friendly relations and cooperation among states in accordance with the Charter of the United Nations. The resolution urged states to devote their immediate attention to find quick and peaceful solutions to the underlying causes which give rise to such acts of violence.[7]

One of the salutary effects of this resolution was the sense of urgency it reflected in reaffirming the inalienable right to self-determination and independence of all people and the condemnation it issued on the continuation of repressive acts by colonial, racist and alien regimes in denying people their legitimate right to the enforcement of their human rights. The resolution followed up with the invitation to states to become parties to the existing international conventions which relate to various aspects of the problem of international terrorism.[8]

On 21 January 1977, the General Assembly commenced drafting an international convention against the taking of hostages, which was authorized by Resolution A/RES/31/103 which broadly invoked the Universal Declaration of Human Rights; and the International Convention on Civil and Political Rights which provides that everyone has the right to life, liberty and security. The resolution established an *ad hoc* committee on the drafting of an international convention against the taking of hostages. The committee was mandated to draft, as early as possible, an international convention. The President of the General Assembly was requested by the Assembly to appoint the members of the *ad hoc* committee on the basis of equitable geographical distribution and representing the principal legal systems of the world.[9] The resolution was adopted on 15 December 1976.

In December 1979 the General Assembly adopted a resolution[10] which revised the work of the *ad hoc* committee and called for international cooperation dealing with acts of international terrorism. The resolution, while welcoming the results achieved by the committee, called upon states to fulfil their obligations under international law to refrain from organizing, instigating, assisting or participating in civil strife or terrorist acts in another state, or acquiescing in organized activities within their territory directed towards consensus of such acts.[11]

A major contribution of this resolution was its recognition that in order to contribute to the elimination of the causes and the problem of international terrorism, both the General Assembly and the Security Council should pay special attention to all situations, including, *inter alia*, colonialism, racism and situations involving alien occupation, that may give rise to international terrorism and may endanger international peace and security. The application, when feasible and necessary, of the relevant provisions of the Chapter of the United Nations, was also recommended. The resolution also requested the Secretary General of the United Nations to prepare a compilation on the basis of material provided by mentor states of relevant provisions of material legislation dealing with the combating of international terrorism.

In December 1985 the United Nations General Assembly adopted Resolution 40/61 which unequivocally condemned as criminal, all acts, methods and practices of terrorism, whenever committed, including those which jeopardize international peace and security which affect states or their property.[12] The resolution referred to the international conventions that had been adopted in relation to unlawful interference with civil aviation and called upon states to fulfil their obligations under international law to refrain from organizing, instigating, assisting or participating in any terrorist acts against other states, their people or property.

The resolution, while citing the relevant conventions relating to unlawful interference with international civil aviation, once again appealed through the General Assembly to states that had not done so, to become parties to such conventions, including other conventions which related to the suppression of international terrorism. While encouraging ICAO to continue its efforts aimed at promoting universal acceptance of and strict compliance with the international air services conventions, the resolution also called upon all states to adhere to the ICAO conventions that provide for the suppression of terrorist attacks against civil aviation transport and other forms of public transport.[13]

Simultaneously, the Security Council, in December 1985 adopted Resolution S/RES/579 which expressed deep concern at the prevalence of incidents of hostage-taking and abduction following terrorist acts. The resolution appealed to all states to become parties *inter alia* to the ICAO Conventions. This resolution further urged the development of international cooperation among states according to international law, in the facilitation of prevention, prosecution, and punishment of all acts of hostage-taking and abduction which were identified as manifestations of international terrorism.[14]

The General Assembly, in December 1987, adopted another resolution[15] which referred to the recommendations of the *ad hoc* committee which had called for stringent measures of international cooperation in curbing international terrorism, which repeated the appeal of the previous resolutions for more participation by states in controlling the problem and welcomed the efforts of ICAO and IMO (International Maritime Organization) to curb unlawful interference with civil aviation and shipping respectively. The resolution also called upon other specialized agencies and inter-governmental organizations, in particular, the Universal Postal Union, the World Tourism Organization and the International Atomic Energy Agency, within their respective spheres of competence, to consider what further measures could usefully be taken to combat and eliminate terrorism.[16] This resolution was followed by another, in December 1989, which called for a universal policy of firmness and effective measures to be taken in accordance with international law in order that all acts, methods and practices of international terrorism may be brought to an end.[17] The resolution also expressed the grave concern of the United Nations Mentor states at the growing and dangerous link between terrorist groups, condemned traffickers of drugs and paramilitary gangs which had been known to perpetrate all types of violence, and thereby endanger the constitutional order of states and violate basic human rights.[18]

In 1991, the United Nations General Assembly once again unanimously condemned as criminal and unjustifiable all acts, methods and practices of terrorism; called firmly for the immediate and safe release of all hostages and abducted persons; and called upon all states to use their political influence in accordance with the Charter of the United Nations and the principles of international law to secure the safe release of all hostages and abducted persons and do their utmost to prevent the commission of acts of hostage-taking and abduction.[19] The plea for international cooperation was reviewed by the General Assembly in December 1993 where the Assembly urged the international community to enhance cooperation in the fight against the threat of terrorism at national, regional and international levels.[20]

Convention for the Prevention and Punishment of Terrorism (1937)

Prior to the Tokyo Convention of 1963, most of the legal work relating to the security of international civil aviation was undertaken by the League of Nations or thereafter by the United Nations. The League of Nations, which was impelled to act in response to the increase of international terrorist activities following World War I, had already made several multilateral attempts to deal with the problem. Its initial efforts towards multilateral accord were directed towards the establishment of an International Convention for the Prevention and Punishment of Terrorism[21]. In spite of these attempts, governments took determined action against terrorism only after a major terrorist attack on 9 October 1934, which resulted in the assassination at Marseilles of King Alexander I of Yugoslavia, during his visit to France, and the murder of the French Foreign Minister, Mr. Louis Barthou, who was officially receiving the King in Marseilles[22]. The Yugoslav government made a request to the Council of the League of Nations to investigate the incident.[23]

The Council of the League of Nations set up a Committee of Experts on 10 December 1934 to prepare a draft convention for the prevention and punishment of terrorism. The draft was submitted to an international conference in Geneva in November 1937 and was adopted. Subsequent to approval of this convention, it was unfortunately precluded from entering into force owing to the outbreak of World War II.

Convention on International Civil Aviation (Chicago Convention of 1944)

At the time the Chicago Conference was held in 1944, and during the drafting of the Convention on International Civil Aviation[24], although no explicit mention was made of the security of international civil aviation since such acts were unknown at that time, several states made reference to the significance of the Convention to security and safety of air travel. The Preamble to the Convention endorses its role at ensuing security and safety of international civil aviation in creating and preserving international civil aviation friendship and understanding among the nations and peoples of the world, and the necessity, therefore, to develop international civil aviation in a safe and orderly manner and to establish international air transport services on the basis of equal opportunity as well as sound and economic operation. Other provisions of the Convention also indicate clearly that safety of civil aviation is one of its main objectives. Article 25 of the Convention provides that:

> Each Contracting State undertakes to provide such measures of assistance to aircraft in distress in its territory as it may find practicable, and to permit, subject to control by its own authorities, the owners of the aircraft or authorities of the State in which the aircraft is registered to provide such measures of assistance as may be necessitated by the

> circumstances. Each Contracting State, when undertaking searches for missing aircraft, will collaborate in co-ordinated measures which may be recommended from time to time pursuant to this Convention.[25]

This principle gives effect to one of the oldest principles of customary international law,[26] which incorporates principles of humanitarian law, falling under the category of International Humanitarian Law. At the time of its incorporation into the Chicago Convention, however, it was deemed one of the lesser significant aspects of international law.

'Aircraft in distress' is not defined in the Chicago Convention or in other ICAO documents. In its report, the *ad hoc* Group of Experts on unlawful interference agreed that, regardless of the terminology used, the objective of assistance to aircraft in distress provided some sense of security for international civil aviation.[27]

The Convention defines its scope in Article 3:

- this Convention shall be applicable only to civil aircraft, and shall not be applicable to state aircraft;
- aircraft used in military, customs and police services shall be deemed to be state aircraft;
- no state aircraft of a contracting state shall fly over the territory of another state or land thereon without authorization by special agreement or otherwise, and in accordance with the terms thereof;
- the contracting states undertake, when issuing regulations for their state aircraft, that they will have due regard for the safety of navigation of civil aircraft.

The Chicago Convention applies only to civil aircraft, to the exclusion of state aircraft[28]. While the Convention defines state aircraft to include aircraft used in military, custom, or police services[29], it fails to define a civil aircraft. All aircraft not devoted to military, customs and police services may be deemed to be civil aircraft, although it would not be incorrect to apply definitive boundaries to Article 3 in the light of the ambivalence of the provision.

Article 3(d) requires contracting states, when issuing regulations for their state aircraft, to have due regard for the safety of navigation of civil aircraft. It should also be noted that a state cannot use civil aircraft in a manner that is incompatible with the purposes of the Chicago Convention. In other words, according to the Convention, abuse of civil aviation is prohibited.

Article 4 of the Convention states:

> Each Contracting State agrees not to use civil aviation for any purpose inconsistent with the aims of this Convention.

and therefore deals explicitly with the problem of misuse of civil aviation. It can therefore be assumed that the intent of the states' parties to the Chicago Convention was to preclude any threat to the security of nations by adopting this provision.[30]

United Nations Charter

Although the Charter contains no provision which deals directly with the security of civil aviation, it is one of the most salutary international legal documents in the area of civil aviation security. The Preamble to the Charter stipulates that citizens of the member states of the United Nations will practice tolerance and live together in peace with one another as good neighbours. The principle of security is embodied in several articles of the Charter. Article 1 (2) provides that the purpose of the United Nations is to pursue the development of friendly relations among nations based on respect for the principle of equal rights and self-determination of peoples, and to take other appropriate measures to strengthen universal peace.

As civil aircraft are by definition presumed to transport civilians, the principles of the Chicago Convention should ensure the protection of civilians and their property from dangers affecting civil aircraft in flight. The United Nations Charter can therefore be regarded as imputing to the international community a duty to protect human beings and their property in relation to flight:

> There is a mandatory obligation implied in article 55 of the Charter that the United Nations 'shall promote respect for, and observance of, human rights and fundamental freedoms'; or, in terms of Article 13, that the Assembly shall make recommendations for the purpose of assisting in the realization of human rights and freedoms. There is a distinct element of legal duty in the understanding expressed in Article 56 in which all members pledge themselves to take joint and separate action in cooperation with the organization for the achievement of the purpose set forth in Article 55.[31]

A civil aircraft, when identified as such cannot be attacked[32]. The United Nations Charter opposes the use of force against civilian aircraft. Article 2 (4) of the Charter prohibits the use of force in any manner inconsistent with the purposes of the Charter. There is also provision for the settlement of disputes by peaceful means.[33]

An armed attack against an aircraft is a special kind of aggression[34] and is protected by the right of self-defence which is recognized against such an attack, by Article 51 of the Charter. This provision narrows the field of the exercise of self-defence to circumstances involving an armed attack. An unauthorized entry into the airspace of a state by an unarmed aircraft does not constitute an armed attack, even if such entry is effected for the purposes of espionage or provocation.[35] Although no authoritative definition of an armed attack has ever been adopted internationally, it is generally presumed that an armed attack would constitute belligerence endangering the safety of those affected by such attack when it is carried out by offenders wielding weapons.

Other International Conventions

The Geneva Convention on the High Seas (1958)

Transportation systems have often attracted terrorist attacks and the international community has come to terms with the vulnerability of modern aviation, taking sustained steps towards the protection of aviation.

The earliest forms of terrorism against international transportation was piracy. Pirates are considered by international law as common enemies of all mankind. The world has naturally an interest in the punishment of offenders and is justified in adopting international measures for the application of universal rules regarding the control of terrorism. The common understanding between states has been that pirates should be lawfully captured on the high seas by an armed vessel of any particular state, and brought within its territorial jurisdiction for trial and punishment. Lauterpacht recognized that:

> Before international law in the modern sense of the term was in existence, a pirate was already considered an outlaw, a *hostis humani generis*. According to the Law of Nations, the act of piracy makes the pirate lose the protection of his home State, and thereby his national character. Piracy is a so-called international crime, the pirate is considered the enemy of all States and can be brought to justice anywhere.[36]

It is worth noting that under the rules of customary international law the international community had no difficulty in dealing with acts of terrorism which forms the offence of sea piracy. Due to the seriousness of the offence and the serious terroristic acts involved, the offence was met with the most severe punishment available – death. The universal condemnation of the offence is reflected in a statement noting that, in the past, it was apparently a customary rule of international law that, after the seizure of a ship, pirates could immediately be hanged or drowned by the captor.

The laws dealing with the offence of piracy went through a sustained process of evolution. In 1956, while considering legal matters pertaining to the law of the sea, the International Law Association addressed the offence of piracy and recommended that the subject of piracy at sea be incorporated in the Draft Convention of the Law of the Sea. This was followed by the United Nations General Assembly Resolution 1105 (XI) in 1957 which called for the convening of a diplomatic conference to further evaluate the Law of the Sea. Accordingly, the Convention of the High Seas was adopted in Geneva in 1958 and came into force in September 1962.

The Geneva Convention on the High Seas 1958[37] was the first attempt at international accord to harmonize the application of rules to both piracy at sea and in the air. The Convention adopted authoritative legal statements on civil aviation security, as it touched on piracy over the high seas.[38]

Article 5 of the Convention inclusively defines piracy as follows:

Piracy consists of any of the following acts:

1 Any illegal acts of violence, detention or any act of depredation, committed for private ends by the crew or the passenger of a private ship or a private aircraft, and directed:
   - on the high seas, against another ship or aircraft, or against persons or property on board such ship or aircraft;
   - against a ship, aircraft, persons, or property in a place outside the jurisdiction of any state;

2 Any act of voluntary participation in the operation of a ship or of an aircraft with knowledge of facts making it a pirate ship or aircraft;

3 Any act of inciting or of internationally facilitating an act described in sub-paragraph 1 or sub-paragraph 2 of this Article.

As provided for by Article 14 of the Convention, there is incumbent on all states a general duty to 'cooperate' to the fullest extent in the repression of piracy as defined by the Convention. One commentator has observed:

> The International Law Commission in its 1956 report, however, deemed it desirable to enjoin co-operation in the repression of piracy, to define the act to include piracy by aircraft, as set forth in the repressive measures that may justifiably be taken. The United Nations conference on the Law of the Sea in Geneva in 1958 accordingly incorporated these adjustments of the law to modern times in its convention on the High Seas.[39]

Article 14 seemingly makes it a duty incumbent upon every state to take necessary measures to combat piracy by either prosecuting the pirate or extraditing him to the state which might be in a better position to undertake such prosecution. The Convention, in Article 19, gives all states universal jurisdiction under which the person charged with the offence of aerial or sea piracy may be tried and punished by any state into whose jurisdiction he or she may come. This measure is a proactive one in that it eliminates any boundaries that a state may have which would preclude the extradition or trial in that state of an offender. Universal jurisdiction was conferred upon the states by the Convention also to solve the somewhat complex problem of jurisdiction which often arose under municipal law where the crime was committed outside the territorial jurisdiction of the particular state seeking to prosecute an offender. The underlying salutary effects of universal jurisdiction in cases of piracy and hijacking which was emphasized by the Convention, is discussed in the following manner:

> The absence of universal jurisdiction in relation to a given offence, means that, if a particular State has no jurisdiction either on the basis of territoriality or protection, or on the personality principle, whether passive or active, it will not be authorized to put the offender on trial, even if he is to be found within the territorial boundaries of the State.[40]

The inclusion of the offence of 'piracy' in the Convention brings to bear the glaring fact that the crime is international in nature, giving the international community the right to take appropriate measures to combat or at least control the occurrence of the offence. The General Convention by its very nature and adoption has demonstrably conveyed the message that piracy is a heinous crime which requires severe punishment. The Convention also calls for solidarity and collectivity on the part of nations in combating the offence in the interests of all nations concerned.[41]

Notwithstanding the above, it is worth noting that the phenomenon of hijacking as it exists today need not necessarily fall within the definition of piracy as referred to in Article 15 of the High Seas Convention (1958). Although there exists a marked similarity between the offences of unlawful seizure of aircraft and acts of piracy directed against ships on the high seas, in that in both cases, the mode of transportation is threatened and abused and the safety of the passengers, crew members and the craft itself is endangered by the unlawful use of force or threat, there may still be a subtle difference that may exist between the offence as applying to sea transport and to air transport.

While admittedly there are similarities between the acts of piracy against ships and those against aircraft, the legal differences that may exist should have to be determined in order to inquire whether aircraft hijacking amounts to piracy as defined by the Convention.

The essential features of the definition of piracy as incorporated in the Geneva Convention are as follows:

1 the pirate must be motivated by 'private' as opposed to 'public' ends;
2 the act of piracy involves action affecting a ship, an aircraft;
3 the acts of violence, detention, and depredation take place outside the jurisdiction of any state, meaning both territorial jurisdiction and airspace above the state;
4 acts committed on board a ship or aircraft, by the crew or passengers of such ship or aircraft and directed against the ship or aircraft itself, or against persons or property, do not constitute the offence of piracy.

Upon close examination, it appears that the definition of piracy does not apply to the phenomenon of aerial piracy or hijacking. Firstly, it is a fact that most hijackings are not carried out in pursuance of private ends. Interpol[42] reported in 1977 that the percentage of cases in which political motives had impelled the offender was 64.4 per cent. Hijacking of aircraft for political motives would thus not relate to Article 15 (1) of the Convention on the High Seas (1958) since acts solely inspired by political motives are excluded from the notion *piracy jure gentium*. Sami Shubber has observed of the 1958 Convention that its inapplicability to the notion of aerial piracy may lie in the fact that private ends do not necessarily mean that they can affect private groups, acting either in pursuance of their political aims, or gain. The fact that it is not always possible to distinguish between private ends and public ends in defiance of the political regime of the flag state may be said to be covered by Article 15 (1) of the Convention.[43] The reasons given by Shubber were that 'private ends' do not necessarily mean private gain.

Under the definition, the act of illegal violence or detention must be directed on the high seas, against another ship or aircraft. It is obvious therefore that this interpretation does not apply to hijacking since the offence of hijacking is committed by the offender who travels in the aircraft. It is hard to imagine that an offender could enter an aircraft from outside while the aircraft is in flight. The Convention also excludes acts committed on board a ship by the crew or passenger and directed against the ship itself, or against persons or property on the ship, from the scope of piracy,[44] which will also make the definition inconsistent with the exigencies related to the offence of aerial piracy.

Although piracy, according to the Convention, must be committed on the 'high seas', instances of hijacking may occur anywhere. Furthermore, piracy under Article 15 of the Convention must involve acts of violence, detention or depredation. Most hijackings, however, have been carried out simply by the use of threats, and may even be carried out through a variety of means other than those involving violence or force.

It is therefore reasonable to conclude that hijacking does not necessarily and absolutely fall within the 'aircraft piracy' as defined by the Geneva Convention on the High Seas.[45] The hopes of the international community to control the crime of hijacking through the application of the Geneva Convention on the High Seas (1958) may therefore have been frustrated by the exclusivity of the nature of the two offences of aerial piracy and piracy related to the high seas. The Convention remains therefore to be of mere academic interest for those addressing the issue of aerial piracy.

Concerted Action under the Auspices of the International Civil Aviation Organization – The Tokyo Convention (1963)

Shocked by the rising trend of aircraft hijacking in the early 1960s and the failure of the Geneva Convention on the High Seas to offer rules applicable to the offence of hijacking, the international community considered adopting the Tokyo Convention of 1963, which was adopted under the aegis of ICAO. This Convention attempted to provide certain rules that would address the offence.

Prior to 1960, most of the collective action to combat international terrorism was undertaken by the United Nations or its predecessor, the League of Nations. Although the League of Nations made cohesive efforts to create an international criminal court, to deal with, among other things, acts of international terrorism by drafting a Convention to Combat International Terrorism in 1937,[46] it was unfortunate that this Convention was signed by only 13 states and ratified by one state which effectively precluded the Convention from coming in force.

At the end of 1950, a new crusader against international terrorism – particularly when it applied to aerial incidents of terrorism – appeared on the international scene to adopt necessary international measures to combat terrorism against air transport. This new entity was the International Civil Aviation Organization (ICAO). In retrospect, it is noted that although the United Nations was unsuccessful in adopting sufficiently compelling measures of international cooperation to deal with aircraft hijacking, ICAO has made significant strides in the area of adoption of multilateral conventions. The primary aim of these Conventions has been to adopt measures, through international agreement, to control and arrest terrorist activities which are aimed against international air transport. It has been said of ICAO on its regulatory attempts in this field:

> These menacing incidents during the last few years have resulted in intense activities aimed at finding possible solutions on the basis of universally accepted international treaty and/or other technical remedies. The beginning of concerted international effort since the formation of ICAO in relation to the so-called problem of hijacking can be traced back to the formulation of certain provisions in the 'Convention on Offenses and Certain Other Acts Committed on Board Aircraft Commonly Known as the Tokyo Convention 1963.'[47]

The Tokyo Convention was the first substantial effort at dealing with terrorism in the air. It was followed by the Hague and Montreal Conventions.[48]

In 1950, the Legal Committee of ICAO, upon a proposal from the Mexican Representative on the ICAO Council for the study of the legal status of airports, referred the subject to the *ad hoc* Sub-committee established by the Legal Committee.[49] After a survey had been made of all the problems relating to the legal status of aircraft, it was decided by the Committee that the best course would be to confine the work to a detailed examination of some particularly important matters, namely crimes and offences committed on board aircraft, jurisdiction relating to such crimes and the resolution of jurisdictional conflicts. The Sub-committee thought that resolving these problems was of vital importance for the following reasons:[50]

1 One characteristic of aviation is that aircraft fly over the high seas or over seas having no territorial sovereign. While national laws of some states confer jurisdiction on their courts to try offences committed on aircraft during such flights, this was not the case in others, and there was no internationally agreed system which would coordinate the exercise of national jurisdiction in such cases. Further, with the high speed of modern aircraft and the great altitudes at which they fly as well as other factors, such as meteorological conditions, and, in certain parts of the world, the fact that several states may be overflown by aircraft within a small space of time, there could be occasions when it would be impossible to establish the territory which the aircraft was in at the time a crime was committed on board. There was, therefore, the possibility that in such a case, and in the absence of an internationally recognized system to exercise national jurisdiction, the offender may go unpunished.
2 National jurisdictions in respect of criminal acts are based on criteria which are not uniform; for example, the nationality of the offender, or nationality of the victim, the locality where the offence was committed, or the nationality of the aircraft on which the crime occurred. Thus, several states may claim jurisdiction over

the same offence committed on board aircraft, in certain cases. Such conflict of jurisdictions could be avoided only by international agreement.

3 The possibility that the same offence may be tried in different states might result in the offender being punished more than once for the same offence. This undesirable possibility could be avoided by a suitable provision in the Convention.

After sustained deliberation and contradiction, the Sub-committee on the Legal Status of Aircraft produced a draft convention which was submitted to the Legal Committee on 9 September 1958.[51] The Legal Committee in turn considered the draft convention at its 12th Session held in Munich in 1959[52], undertaking a substantial revision of the draft. The revised text was submitted to the ICAO Council subsequently, who in turn submitted the draft to member states and various international organizations for their comments. A new Sub-committee was formed for the purpose of examining the Convention of State Organization in 1961 to examine and prepare a report. This report was studied by the Legal Committee in its 14th Session held in Rome in 1962. A final text of a Convention was drawn up at this meeting and communicated to member states with a view to convening a diplomatic conference in Tokyo with the long-term prospect of adopting a Convention on aerial rights. This Convention was signed in Tokyo on 14 September, 1963 by the representatives of 49 ICAO member states, and entered into force after six years, on 4 December 1969.[53] This slow process of ratification of the Convention was by no means due to the ineptitude of the Convention as has been claimed[54] but was solely due to the fact that the Convention was drafted prior to the series of hijacking in the late 1960s and was not implemented with due dispatch by most states. Another reason for the delayed process was the complicated legal and political issues facing many countries at the time of the adoption of the Convention[55]. A significant feature of the Tokyo Convention is that although at first states were slow in acceding to or ratifying the Convention, 80 states ratified the convention between 1969–70 presumably in response to the spate of hijackings that occurred during that period.

The main purpose of the Tokyo Convention was to secure the collaboration of states in restraining terrorist activity directed at air transport. It has therefore been said that:

> The first action taken by the international community to combat hijacking was the Tokyo Convention 1963. This Convention was originally designed to solve the problem of the commission of crimes on board aircraft while in flight where for any number of reasons the criminal might escape punishment.[56]

The objectives of the Tokyo convention may be subsumed into four principal areas:

1 The Convention makes it clear that the state of registration of the aircraft has the authority to apply its laws. From the standpoint of states such as the United States, this is probably the most important aspect of the Convention, since it accords international recognition to the exercise of extra-territorial jurisdiction under the circumstances contemplated in the Convention.
2 The Convention provides the aircraft commander with the necessary authority to deal with persons who have committed, or are about to commit, a crime or an act jeopardizing safety on board the aircraft through use of reasonable force when required, and without fear of subsequent retaliation through civil suit or otherwise.
3 The convention delineates the duties and responsibilities of the contracting State in which an aircraft lands after the commission of a crime on board, including its authority over, and responsibilities to, any offenders that may be either disembarked within the territory of that state or delivered to its authorities.
4 The crime of 'hijacking' has been addressed in some degree of depth.[57]

The Convention applies to any act that is an offence under the penal laws of a contracting state, as well as to acts which, whether or not they are offences, may jeopardize safety, good order and discipline on board. The Convention thus does not define the offence at the international level nor does it explicitly explain the nature of the offence. Alona E. Evans has observed:

> The offence is not made a crime under international law; its definition is to be determined by the municipal laws of the contracting State.[58]

Admittedly, there are some limitations placed upon the scope of the application of the Convention. Firstly, the Convention excluded from its operations aircraft used in military, customs or police services. It should be noted that reference is not made in the Convention to 'state aircraft' as mentioned in Article 3 of the Chicago Convention, which does not apply to such aircraft. This difference in terminology is explained by the fact that state aircraft provide air transport that is usually provided by civil aircraft and civil transport in some cases. Secondly, offences against penal laws of a political nature or those based on racial or religious discrimination are not covered by the Convention except to the extent that the Convention addressed such acts which jeopardize safety or good order and discipline on board.

The reason for excluding those offences from the scope of the Convention could be attributed to the view:

> Penal laws forbidding various forms of racial and religious discrimination take many and varied forms, and the views of the Courts of the Contracting States may differ on the issue of whether one or the other is within or without the Convention. Even more divergence of view can be expected in decisions which involve the question of whether a particular offence is of a 'political nature'.[59]

Although the Convention does not define the offence of hijacking, Article 11 specifies the circumstances that would constitute the offence as:

> When a person on board has unlawfully committed by force or threat thereof an act of interference, seizure or other wrongful exercise of control of an aircraft in flight or such an act is bound to be committed.

When the offence of hijacking is committed in the above manner, the state in which the aircraft lands has two obligations which it must satisfy according to the terms of the Convention. The first obligation is that the landing state 'shall take all appropriate measures to restore control of the aircraft to its lawful commander or to preserve control of the aircraft and shall return the aircraft and its cargo to the person lawfully entitled to possession.'

R.P. Boyle emphasized the above contention when he stated:

> The obligation assumed by a State under the Tokyo Convention with respect to the disposition of the hijacker ... is to take all appropriate measures to restore control of the aircraft to its lawful commander and to permit the passengers and crew to continue their journey as soon as practicable and to return the aircraft and cargo to persons lawfully entitled.[60]

The powers given to aircraft commanders and others in order to combat hijackings The Convention gives wide powers to the aircraft commander to control the offence of hijacking. Article 6 enables the aircraft commander to use reasonable measures, including restraint, to protect the safety of the aircraft, and maintain good order and discipline, when he or she has a reasonable ground to believe that a person has committed an offence contemplated in Article I (1), namely:

- offences against penal laws;
- acts which, whether or not they are offences, may jeopardize the safety of the aircraft or of persons or property therein or which jeopardize good order and discipline on board.

An interesting observation may be made in respect to first requirement listed above. The aircraft commander will have, according to that paragraph, the power to take measures and restrain a passenger even if the offending act did not amount to jeopardizing the safety of the aircraft or the person or the property therein. This may lead to absurdity. If, for example, two passengers conspire, while on board the aircraft, to commit some illegal act upon landing, or upon termination of the flight, according to the first point above the commander can restrain them on suspicion that the act they are conspiring to commit, is against penal law of a particular jurisdiction. This seems to be illogical when one recalls that the principal objective of the Convention is to assure the maintenance of safety and good order 'on board' the aircraft.

The aircraft commander in discharging his or her duties according to the Convention can require or authorize the assistance of the crew and request the assistance of passengers for that purpose. Even passengers and crew members are authorized under Article 6 (2) to take reasonable preventive measures without any authorization from the aircraft commander whenever they have reasonable grounds to believe that such action is immediately necessary for safety reasons. Although this clause has tried to give powers to other people other than the aircraft commander in order to tighten the measures that lead to the thwarting of acts of unlawful interference against civil aviation, some delegates at the Tokyo Conference attacked this approach on the ground that passengers normally would not be qualified to determine whether a particular act jeopardized the safety of the aircraft or persons and property therein. For this reason, it was unwise to give this authority to passengers.[61] However, this argument was rejected 'on the ground that this provision contemplated an emergency type of situation on which the danger of the aircraft or persons and property on board was clearly present, and in fact no special technical knowledge would be required to recognize the peril'.[62]

The powers entrusted to the commander in order to suppress any unlawful act that threatens the safety of the aircraft go as far as requiring the disembarking of any person (who commits any of the acts referred to in Article 1 (1) and discussed above) in the territory of any state in which the aircraft lands and delivering the offender to its competent authorities.[63] The state is under an obligation to allow the disembarkation and to take delivery of the person so apprehended by the aircraft commander, but such custody may only be continued for such time as is reasonably necessary to enable the criminal extradition proceedings, if any are to be instituted. In the meantime the state of landing should make a preliminary enquiry into the facts and notify the state of registration of the aircraft[64] (Articles 12 and 13).

In any event, the commander as well as the crew members and passengers are given immunity from suits by the alleged offender against whom they acted. Article 10 expressly provides:

> Neither the aircraft commander, any member of the crew, any passenger, the owner or operator of the aircraft, nor the person on whose behalf the flight is performed shall be held responsible in any proceedings on account of the treatment undergone by the person against whom the actions were taken.

This protection was given to the aircraft commander and other persons in order to encourage them to fight the wrongful acts contemplated by the Convention.

Jurisdiction to punish the terrorists The major problem that states often face in the process of combating terrorism is the issue of jurisdiction. This is most evident in cases of hijacking where the crime often takes place outside the jurisdiction of the receiving state, although in most, if not all of the cases it could be argued that the offence is of a continuing nature. Under international law, states' jurisdiction to prosecute is founded upon two traditional concepts. Firstly, there must exist a substantial link between the person or the act and the state claiming sovereign jurisdiction and secondly, this theoretical basis must be actualized through a sovereign act, that is legislation for implementation of this theoretical act. In an act of international nature, such as hijacking, two or more states involved may possess jurisdiction to prosecute. As a result, jurisdictional conflicts are eminent, since two or more of those states can claim the right to prosecute and press claims against each other through diplomatic channels. In order to eliminate these conflicts, the jurisdictional rules incorporated in the Tokyo Convention were preferred. The Tokyo Convention was adopted to grant powers to states to establish jurisdiction which would be uncomplicated by diplomatic claims over criminal acts committed on board aircraft.

Jurisdiction over offences and acts committed on board apply primarily to the state of registration of the aircraft (Article 3 (1)). The adoption of this rule guarantees to the flights over the high seas the assured presence of the criminal law. It provides a sound legal basis for extra-territorial exercise of criminal jurisdiction extending even to cases of flight within foreign airspace. A.I. Mendelssohn has observed:

> As a matter of international law, therefore, any crime aboad an international carrier, no matter where, by or against whom it is committed, can be punished by at least one sovereign – the State of registration of the carrier. All doubts are removed on the question whether the flag

> will henceforth follow the aircraft as it traditionally has followed a vessel.[65]

Article 3 (2) of the Convention provides:

> Each Contracting State shall take measures as may be necessary to establish its jurisdiction as State of registration over offenses committed on board aircraft registered in such State.

It is clear that the fundamental objective of this sub-paragraph was to make the act of combating hijacking an international issue in which all states must take part when the need arises.

Article 3 (3) went further to give more grounds of jurisdiction in order to eliminate the gravity of the obstacles that hinders the prosecution of hijackers. It provides that the Convention does not exclude criminal jurisdiction exercised in accordance with the national law. Mendelssohn has commented on this sub-paragraph:

> Its objectives are (a) to retain all existing jurisdiction presently asserted by the various States; (b) to enable them to enact further legislation providing for even more extensive jurisdiction; and most important, (c) to require the State of registration to extend at least some of its criminal laws to its aircraft and to provide an internationally accepted basis for the application and enforcement of these laws.[66]

The Convention also authorizes a contracting state which is not a state of registration to interfere with an aircraft in flight in five cases in which the offence

1 has an effect on the territory of the state;
2 has been committed by or against a national or permanent resident of the state;
3 is against the security of the state;
4 consists of a breach of any rules or regulations relating to the flight or manoeuvre of aircraft in force in such state;
5 that the exercise of such jurisdiction is necessary in order to ensure the observance of any obligation of such state under a multilateral international agreement.

As regards the geographic scope of the Convention for jurisdictional purposes, Article 1 provides that the Convention applies in respect of acts or offences committed while the aircraft is 'in flight' or on the surface of the high seas or on another area which does not have a territorial sovereign. The term 'in flight' is defined in Article 1 (3) as 'from the moment when the power is applied for the purpose of take-off until the moment when the landing run ends'. Hence, hijacking attempts initiated during the time the aircraft is parked or taxiing are not considered to be within the ambit of the Convention. As a consequence, the provisions of the Tokyo Convention fell short of curbing the crime of sabotage of air transport facilities. This shortcoming of the Tokyo Convention, *inter alia,* led to the adoption of the Montreal Convention (1971).

Powers and duties of states It is a basic obligation of a state to cooperate with other states in order to ensure the safety of international civil aviation. Article 11 of the Tokyo Convention, which is referred to above, provides that contracting states have certain obligations whenever a person on board an aircraft has unlawfully committed by force or threat thereof an act of interference, seizure or other wrongful exercise of control. The question of whether a particular act is lawful or unlawful is to be judged by the law of the state of registration of the aircraft or the law of the state in whose airspace the aircraft may be in flight. Paragraph 1 of Article 11 imposes on all the contracting states the obligation to take appropriate measures to restore or to preserve to the aircraft commander control of the aircraft. The words 'appropriate measures' are intended to mean only those things which it is feasible for a contracting state to do and also only those which it is lawful for a contracting state to do. Thus, a contracting state, which is situated thousands of miles away from the scene of the hijacking, is not under any obligation to take any action, because it would not be feasible for it todo so.

Article 12 imposes another obligation on each contracting state. This Article is a corollary to Articles 6 and 8 of the Convention. The latter two Articles authorize the aircraft commander to disembark any person who has committed, or is about to commit, an act of the type described in Article I of the Convention. Article 12 obliges a contracting state to allow the commander of an aircraft registered in another contracting state to disembark the alleged offender. Article 12 provides:

> Any Contracting State shall allow the commander of an aircraft registered in another contracting state to disembark any person pursuant to Article 8, Paragraph 1.

Thus, it is clear that the obligation of a contracting state to permit disembarkation of a hijacker, at the request of the aircraft commander, is an unqualified obligation.

Article 13 of the Convention deals with the obligation of a contracting state to take delivery of a person from the aircraft commander. This provision should be contrasted with the authority of the aircraft commander to disembark. The obligation of the contracting state under this Article is a corollary to the authority given to the aircraft commander under Articles 6, 7 and 9.

Paragraph 1 of Article 13 states the primary unqualified obligation of each contracting state as to 'take delivery'. Paragraph 2 addresses the obligation of a contracting state, after having taken delivery, to take custody. It provides that the contracting state is under an obligation to take 'custody' only if it is satisfied that the circumstances so warrant such action. Thus, the state is left free to judge for itself whether the act is of such a nature as to warrant such action on its part and whether it would be consistent with its law, since under Paragraph 2 any such custody is to be affected only pursuant to the law of the state taking custody. However, such custody may only be continued for that period of time which is reasonably necessary to enable criminal proceedings to be brought by the state taking custody, or for extradition proceedings to be instituted by another interested or affected state. On the other hand, any person taken into custody must be given assistance in communicating immediately with the nearest appropriate representative of the state where he or she is a national (Article 13 (3)).

Extradition Article 16 of the Convention provides that offences committed on aircraft registered in a contracting state are to be treated, for the purpose of extradition, as if they had been not only in the place where the offence has occurred, but also in the territory of the state of registration of the aircraft. Without prejudice to this provision it is declared that 'nothing in this Convention shall be deemed to create an obligation to grant extradition.' A commentator observes:

> The Tokyo Convention does not oblige the Contracting State to punish an alleged offender upon his disembarkation or delivery. Ironically, the landing State must set him free and let him proceed to the destination of his choice as soon as is practicable if it does not wish to extradite or prosecute him. The Contracting States are obliged to extradite the offenders, if at all, only under provisions of other treaties between them.[67]

The failure to provide for a machinery of mandatory extradition if prosecution was not conducted was considered a major failing of the Tokyo Convention. However, the above loopholes from which the Convention severely suffers are not the only ones:

> Looking for the vantage point today, it is obvious that the Tokyo convention left major gaps in the international legal system in attempting to cope with the scope of aircraft hijacking. There was no undertaking by anyone to make aircraft hijacking a crime under its national law, no undertaking to see to it the crime was one punishable

by severe penalties and most important, no undertaking to either submit the case for prosecution or to extradite the offender to a State which would wish to prosecute.[68]

Responsibilities of states As has been mentioned, all states party to the Convention undertake to permit disembarkation of any person when the commander considers that it is necessary to protect the safety of the flight or for the maintenance of good order and discipline on board. States also commit themselves to take delivery of any person the commander reasonably believes has committed a serious offence on board[69]. In this case, when they have taken delivery, states concerned must make an immediate inquiry into the facts of the matter and report the findings to both the state of registration and to the state where the person is a national[70]. Where the state considers the circumstances to warrant such action, it shall take custodial or other measures, in accordance with its laws, to ensure that the person delivered to it remains available while the inquiry is conducted. Such measures may be continued for a reasonable time to permit criminal or extradition proceedings to be instituted when such proceedings follow from the inquiry[71].

Although the Convention is unequivocal in providing clearly that all contracting states should ensure their legal competence in respect of aircraft on their register, thus addressing jurisdictional issues with regard to crimes on board aircraft, there are a number of lapses in the Convention which make it open for criticism.

Firstly, the Convention does not apply to 'aircraft used in military, customs or police services'[72]. This is a topical issue which requires clarity, as in modern exigencies of airlines there are instances when civilian aircraft are called upon to carry military personnel or supplies, as much as military aircraft are sometimes deployed to execute civilian flights.

Problems concerning registration, particularly when the Convention insists on registration as a pivotal issue may also change the circumstances, although commanders could be totally ignorant of the laws of the state in which the aircraft they are flying is registered. The commander may be required to determine whether a certain action on the aircraft does in fact constitute a crime and more particularly, a serious crime, since at most, a commander may have some familiarity with the laws of the state of the operator. The United Kingdom[73] has elected to incorporate the terms of the Convention into its domestic legislation, thereby widening its scope to cover any aircraft controlled by its own nationals.

The Convention could also be improved in its terms of chronology of the offences, in that its applicability extends to the period from 'the moment when power is applied for the purpose of take-off until the moment when the landing run ends'[74], and in relation to the powers of the commander, who has authority for the purposes of the Convention, only from the time at which the external doors are closed following embarkation to the time when doors open for disembarkation[75].

These parameters are far from satisfactory. In relation to the first, courts have been inconsistent in interpreting similar definitions of flights used in insurance policies. It has been contended that power is first applied 'for the purpose of take-off' when the aircraft first begins to move under its own power to the take-off position[76]. In relation to the second, the terms 'all its external doors' also leaves confusion made worse as it is unclear whether 'all its external doors' includes, for example, cargo or baggage-hold doors, or doors giving access to such areas as the electronic compartment of the aircraft. It is not difficult to envisage circumstances in which these areas could be of significance. The main problem, however, is that the Convention does not provide for the manner in which the offender should be dealt with after he or she has been removed from the aircraft. The somewhat poor and inadequate drafting in Articles 14 and 15 seems to suggest that it is only where the person disembarked or delivered cannot or does not wish to continue his or her journey, that the state of landing can take action[77]. They do not offer a state any guidance as to questions arising from requests for the extradition of an offender or extradition by the state's own initiation.

The Convention also fails to identify the 'offences and certain other acts committed on board' which are its subject matter as extraditable offences, and therefore all requests for extradition arising out of an offence under the Convention must be dealt with under existing extradition arrangements. Even where those agreements are existing between the two states concerned, this could often lead to confusion and delay. Furthermore, in any case, many 'jeopardizing' acts are unlikely to be recognized as forming a basis for extradition. A marked omission from the Convention is that while it creates and defines 'jeopardizing' acts, it does not require states to treat these as 'serious crimes' although the Convention's procedures in respect of delivery and extradition are applicable only to serious crimes.

With respect to extradition, the state of registration of a leased aircraft which is involved in an offence will have little interest in pursuing a matter in which none of its nationals have been involved. A dry lease can further complicate the issue of extradition, since often in these circumstances such a state which is not directly involved in the offence is unlikely to be enthusiastic about incurring the trouble and expense associated with extradition and subsequent trial.

An answer? It was the Roman Emperor Marcus Aurelius who concluded sadly that the choice in most human issues was 'educate, or endure'.

The international community must recognize that the Tokyo Convention is relatively ineffective if states do not make provisions in their own laws to give legal effect to the concerted action that is required at international law to combat terrorism. They must be persuaded to ensure, for example, that their laws of custody permit the immediate inquiry prescribed by the Convention to be properly conducted, an essential requirement if the evidence required for a successful prosecution is to be gathered. For this reason there should also be a requirement that an inquiry should follow any disembarkation.

States must also ensure that their laws in respect of extradition are framed in such a manner as to facilitate the state of registration taking action against the perpetrators of a crime or 'jeopardizing' acts on board its aircraft. These laws should also be at least receptive to the idea of the state of the operator exercising a jurisdiction in respect of events on board aircraft controlled by its nationals.

States must also be persuaded of the need to exercise the criminal jurisdiction they have in respect of their own aircraft in such a manner as to deter potential offenders. Finally, states might embark upon a process of education to make their airport immigration and police authorities aware of the existence of the Tokyo Convention and of its provisions for disembarkation and delivery.

The airlines must also embark on a programme of education within their own ranks. In general there is great uncertainty on the part of captains as to the extent and limits of their authority and they are often in total ignorance of the Tokyo Convention. All airlines should ensure that guidance material on the relevant sections of the Convention is carried on the flight deck, also any assistance material together with a current list of the contracting states. This material can prove invaluable when a commander is confronted by officials whose first reaction is often to refuse to permit a requested disembarkation or delivery.

Airlines do need to inform their pilots on the contents of the Convention and to brief them on how to collect evidence, how to request an investigation and how to file a complete report of the incident. They also need to liaise with their own local authorities to ensure that they are aware of the extent and seriousness of the problem and of the measures which the international community has devised for dealing with it. There is much work to be accomplished by the security, legal and operations departments of the individual airlines. A further incentive is that such a programme of benign propaganda may have the collateral effect of persuading immigration authorities of the folly of insisting on putting potentially violent deportees on board our aircraft.

Finally, the airlines themselves can and must do more to deal with the problem themselves. Alcohol is the underlying cause of the majority of incidents. Yet too often obviously drunk and unruly passengers are boarded – regardless of laws which make it an offence to enter any aircraft when drunk or to become drunk in an aircraft, as in the United Kingdom[78], or for a pilot to allow a person obviously under the influence of drink or drugs to be carried in the aircraft, as in the USA. The airlines should be careful to include in their contract with their passengers a condition which allows the airline to refuse carriage for reasons of safety or if, in the exercise of its reasonable discretion, the carrier determines that:

> ... (b) the conduct, age or mental or physical state of the passenger is such as to ... (ii) cause discomfort or make himself or herself objectionable to other passengers or (iii) involve any hazard or risk to himself or herself or to other persons or property...[79]

Too often airlines fail to exercise reasonable discretion to avoid potential offences from being committed. It is all too common an occurrence that, once airborne, cabin crew members, in the absence of clear instructions from their employer, continue to supply alcohol to passengers even when the signs of impending trouble are obvious.

Airlines are often strangely reluctant to impose the very effective sanction available to them of refusing to carry on the return leg, a passenger who has been troublesome on the outbound leg of his journey. This is a powerful deterrent and each airline should explore the possibility of using it with their own legal adviser.

If potential troublemakers were aware that their disruptive behaviour was likely to be followed not only by effective action by the state authorities but also likely to result in their being blacklisted by airlines, it is probable that the aviation community would advance a considerable distance towards at least preventing the problem of crime and unruliness on our aircraft from spiralling out of control. Therefore, the airline industry must embark on a programme of education and persuasion.

The Hague Convention on Hijacking (1970)

The vast increase in the number of aircraft hijackings and the growth of peril to international civil aviation posed by such incidents, together with the inadequacy of the Tokyo Convention led the ICAO Assembly at its 15th Session held in Buenos Aires from 3–28 September 1968 to adopt Resolution A16-37 on the subject. This resolution reads as follows:

- Whereas unlawful seizure of civil aircraft has a serious adverse effect, on the safety, efficiency and regularity of air navigation.
- Noting that Article 11 of the Tokyo Convention on Offences and Certain Other Acts Committed on Board Aircraft provides certain remedies for the situation envisaged.
- Being however of the opinion that this Article does not provide a complete remedy.
- The Assembly

1 Urges all states to become parties as soon as possible to the Tokyo Convention on Offences and Certain Other Acts Committed on Board Aircraft.
2 Invites states, even before ratification of, or adherence to the Tokyo Convention, to give effect to the principles of Article 11 of that Convention.
3 Requests the Council, at the earliest possible date, to institute the study of other measures to cope with the problem of unlawful seizure.

In connection with clause 3 above, the Council by its resolution of 16 December, 1968, decided to refer the question of unlawful seizure to the Legal Committee of ICAO. Thus, the Legal Committee was once again ordered to draft a new Convention on the subject.

The Legal Committee held its first session from 10–22 February 1969 in Montreal. It considered that the basic objective in its search for a solution to the problem under study should be to deter persons from committing unlawful seizure of aircraft and, more specially, to ensure – as far as practicable – the prosecution and punishment of these persons. The most efficient way of attaining this objective would, in the opinion of the Sub-committee of the Legal Committee entrusted with the subject, be through an international agreement between states (either a protocol to the Tokyo Convention or an independent convention) which would be capable of ratification or adherence independently of the Tokyo Convention.

On 1 December 1970 the draft Convention was submitted to an ICAO Conference at the Hague attended by 77 states, and there the Convention was adopted on 16 December 1970 after considerable debate.

The Hague Convention, unlike the Tokyo Convention, makes hijacking a distinct offence and calls for severe punishment of any person found within the territory of a contracting state who has hijacked an aircraft. As one writer succinctly observes:

> The Hague Convention specifically defined the offence of unlawful seizure of aircraft as a model for individual national legislation, and

> provides ... that each Contracting State undertakes to make the offence punishable by severe penalties.[80]

Whereas Article 1 of the Tokyo Convention applied in respect of acts which, whether or not they are offences, the Hague Convention appeared to answer the first of the problems unsolved by the Tokyo Convention. The offence as defined by the Hague Convention reads as follows:

Any person who on board an aircraft in flight:

- unlawfully, by force, or threat thereof, or by any other form of intimidation, seizes, or exercise control of, that aircraft, or attempts to perform any such act; or
- is an accomplice of a person who performs or attempt to perform any such act, commit an offence.

Article 2 of the Convention provides that each contracting state should make the offence punishable by severe penalties. However, the Convention does not list the exact penalties to be imposed by the contracting state, other than describing them as severe penalties.

The scope of the Convention There are several limitations placed on the application of the Convention as expressed by the articles of the Convention. Under Article 1, the act must be committed by a person on board an aircraft 'in flight' and it thereby excluded offences committed by persons not on board the aircraft such as saboteurs who remain on the ground. Thus, the Hague Convention seems to suffer in the same respect as its predecessor, the Tokyo Convention. D.Y. Chung has observed:

> The question of hijacking has been pretty well covered by the Tokyo and Hague Conventions. However, the type of hijacking these two Conventions dealt with is only 'on board hijacking', while 'non on board hijacking' is not included. It is possible that someone who is not on board but who has placed a bomb or some destructive device on an airliner, may practice extortion on the airline or divert the plane to another destination. In other words, it is possible to hijack the plane by remote seizure or remote control. Another possibility is that of sabotage. Such a situation is also not covered by the above two Conventions, i.e. Hague and Tokyo.[81]

Similarly, according to Article 1, the Hague Convention only applies to accomplices who are on board an aircraft in flight, and not to those who may be on the ground aiding and abetting the unlawful act. The Representative of the Netherlands on the ICAO Legal Committee once said in this respect that 'it is obviously possible to be an accomplice without being on board an aircraft'.[82]

Article 3 of the Convention provides that the aircraft is deemed to be 'in flight' at any time from the moment when all its external doors are closed following embarkation until the moment when any such door is opened for disembarkation. Hence, any hijacking initiated or attempted before the closing of the doors of the aircraft after embarkation or after the opening of the doors for disembarkation is not covered by the Convention. Rene Mankiewicz observes:

> This limitation leaves outside the scope of the Convention any hijacking initiated or attempted before the closing or after the opening of the aircraft doors. As a consequence, such acts are punishable only under the law of the State where committed; the jurisdictional articles of the new Convention do not apply thereto. Furthermore, it follows that such acts are punished merely by the general criminal or air law of the concerned State, unless special legislation is introduced for punishing unlawful seizure committed or attempted on the ground.[83]

A further limitation expressed by the Convention (Article 3 (2)) is that it shall not apply to aircraft used in military, custom or police service, nor in the cases of joint air 'transport' operating organizations or international operating agencies which operate aircrafts which are subject to joint or international registration (Article 5), if the place of take-off or landing of the aircraft on board which the offence is committed is situated in the state of registration of such aircraft (Article 3 (4)). On the other hand, the Convention would apply if the place of take-off or that of actual landing is situated outside the territory of the state of registration of the aircraft, on the understanding that it is immaterial whether the aircraft is engaged in an international or a domestic flight.

Powers and duties imposed upon states in order to combat hijacking Besides the obligation to make the offence of hijacking punishable by severe penalties, the Convention imposed upon the contracting states a series of obligations that are geared towards stamping out hijacking. These obligations are that:

- Each state shall take measures as may be necessary to establish – apart from any existing national criminal jurisdiction (Article 4 (3)) – its jurisdiction over the offence and any act of violence against a passenger or crew when (Article 4 (1)):

  1 the offence is committed on board an aircraft registered in that state;

2 the aircraft on board which the offence is committed lands in the territory with the alleged offender still on board;
3 the offence is committed on board an aircraft leased without a crew to a lessee whose principle place of business or, if there is no such place of business, whose permanent residence is in that state.

In addition, every contracting state must take necessary measures to establish its jurisdiction over the offence in cases where the alleged offender is present in its territory and it does not extradite him (Article 4 (2)). Mankiewicz further observes:

> This provision is necessary in order to increase the effective punishment even if the hijacker is not prosecuted in, or escaped from, the State of landing or is not extradited to the State of registration of the aircraft. Thus, the alleged hijacker can be arrested no matter where the offence took place as long as he is present in a Contracting State. This provision seems to introduce the principle of universal jurisdiction into the Hague Convention.[84]

The jurisdictional powers conferred upon states by Paragraph 1(b) of Article 4 cited above, may be considered as an important factor in the attempts of the international community to stamp out and deter hijacking, in that it gives contracting states a legal instrument, which they may otherwise lack, in view of the absence of any link between them and the state of landing, to act in these situations. This is an acceptable situation, whereby contracting states can extend the basis of jurisdiction under international law.

On the other hand, according to Article 4 (1) three states possess concurrent jurisdiction over an alleged offender: first, the state of registration of the aircraft; second, the state of landing if the offender is on board the aircraft, and third, any party to the Convention within whose boundaries the alleged offender is present, once that state has chosen not to extradite him to the state of registration of the aircraft or to the state in which the aircraft landed while the offender is still on board the hijacked aircraft, or to the state described in sub-division 1 (c). In addition, sub-section (3) sanctions such bases of jurisdiction as 'passive nationality' where the national law so provides. It is interesting to note that the jurisdiction of the state of registration of the aircraft is equal to the other states described in Article 4.

A third instance of concurrent jurisdiction was added to Article 4 of the Hague Convention during the Diplomatic Conference at the Hague. Jurisdiction was granted to the state where the carrier, who operates an aircraft but is not the owner of this aircraft, has his or her principal place of business, or permanent residence. Article 4 (c) of the Convention covers the case of the so-called 'bare hull charter agreements' or 'dry lease', i.e. when an aircraft is hired without crew to an operator. Thus, when an offence is committed on board an aircraft which is registered in a contracting or non-contracting state, and which is 'dry'-leased to an operator having a head office or permanent residence in a contracting state, the latter shall take necessary measures to establish its jurisdiction over the offence. This has been a useful improvement of Article 4 of the Convention in view of the great many leased agreements the air transport industry is using at present.

A very important point worth mentioning is that although Article 4 requires the contracting state to assume jurisdiction over the unlawful seizure of aircraft within the limit of Article 3, it does not provide for obligation on the part of any state to actually prosecute the alleged offender. However, a provision which may be of some relevance is found in Article 7 which reads:

> The Contracting State in whose territory the alleged offender is found shall, if it does not extradite him, be obliged, without exception whatsoever, and whether or not the offence is committed in the territory, to submit the case to its competent authorities, for the purpose of prosecution. Those authorities shall make their decision in the same manner as in the case of any ordinary offence of a serious nature under the law of that State.

Thus, Article 7 states that authorities having jurisdiction under Article 4 are at liberty not to prosecute the hijacker, or an accomplice if it is determined that the offenders would not be prosecuted. R.P. Boyle has observed that the Diplomatic Conference which discussed the draft of the Hague Convention rejected the contention to apply compulsory prosecution or alternatively extradition because:

> ... this obligation is only to submit the offender for prosecution. There is no obligation to prosecute. Many careful distinctions have been adduced. One obvious one is that in case of universal jurisdiction, the State having the hijacker may not have available to it proof of the crime since conceivably it was committed in a distant State and thus the witnesses and other necessary evidence to the State having custody of the hijacker... .
>
> However, the reason for rejection of adopting compulsory prosecution appears to me to be a political one for some which States do not want any interference in their sovereign right to permit political asylum in some form for whatever purpose, despite the gravity of the offence. It is interesting to note that both U.S.A. and the Soviet Union have urged that States should be compelled to prosecute the alleged offender if

> extradition was not granted. It is submitted that this lack of either compulsory jurisdiction or extradition is a serious weakness in the Convention, and stands in the way of an effective international solution to hijacking.[85]

Another obligation which is imposed upon contracting states is that each state is required to include the offence referred to in the Convention as an extraditable one in every new extradition treaty. Existing treaties are deemed to include it already. The Convention may in case of a request for extradition, and in absence of an extradition treaty, be given consideration by the states which make extradition conditional on the existence of an extradition treaty, as the necessary legal basis for extradition. For the purpose of extradition, the offence is treated as if it had been committed not in the place in which it occurred, but in the territory of the states required to establish their jurisdiction in accordance with Article 4 above. Article 8 of the Convention states:

1 The offence shall be deemed to be included as an extraditable offence in any extradition treaty existing between contracting states. Contracting states undertake to include the offence as an extraditable offence in every extradition treaty to be concluded between them.
2 If a contracting state which makes extradition conditional on the existence of a treaty receives a request for extradition from another contracting state with which it has no extradition treaty, it may as its option consider this Convention as the legal basis for extradition in respect of the offence. Extradition shall be subject to the other conditions provided by the law of the requested state.
3 Contracting states which do not make extradition conditional on the existence of a treaty shall recognize the offence between themselves subject to the conditions provided by the law of the requested state.
4 The offence shall be treated, for the purpose of extradition between contracting states, as if it had been committed not only in the place in which it occurred, but also in the territories of the states required to establish their jurisdiction in accordance with Article 4, Paragraph 1.

Thus according to Article 8, if a contracting state receives a request for extradition from a state with which it has no extradition treaty, the Convention shall be considered as the legal basis for extradition. The effect of this provision is to enlarge the scope of existing international treaties on extradition to include hijacking. Where a state is usually prohibited by domestic law from extraditing a hijacker in the absence of a treaty, the state must extradite the offender under the provisions of the Convention.

The obligation to extradite an airline hijacker is subject to all other customary and conventional rules of law governing extraditable offences. As a general rule, extradition is denied where an individual is accused of committing a political offence. Most states recognize the granting of political asylum as a right to be determined by the state from which it is requested. As the laws of a state may preclude extradition of an airline hijacker if the offence is regarded as political, the existence of hijacking in an extradition treaty may not result in mandatory extradition. However, if a state does not extradite the offender, according to Article 7, the case must be submitted to the proper authorities for prosecution. I.D. Johnston has stated the following in relation to Article 8:

> The Convention obliges the parties to include hijacking in extradition treaties to be concluded between them and insert it retrospectively into existing extradition treaties. Parties which have not concluded extradition treaties but which make extradition conditional on a treaty can regard the Convention itself as a legal basis for extradition. These provisions increase the possibility of extradition but by no means make it a certainty. The Russian Proposal, supported by the U.S.A., that hijackers be returned in all cases was rejected at the Conference. Automatic extradition, though probably the best deterrent, was considered too drastic a commitment by most of the negotiating States. What they are prepared to accept however, was the duty to prosecute offenders whom they did not extradite as provided for by Article 7.[86]

Be that as it may, so far as the extradition of nationals is concerned, there is no indication in the Convention as to what the position is. Sami Shubber is of the view that even though there is no mention of the extradition of the states' own national according to the Convention or to the term 'offender' in Article 8, still such extradition is possible.

> There is no reason to suppose that hijackers who happened to be nationals of the State requested to extradite him should be excluded from the scope of extradition under the Convention, provided that course of action is compatible with the national law of the State concerned. This interpretation is not incompatible with the intention of the drafters and the purpose for which the Convention has been created.[87]

Other provisions The Hague Convention imposed further obligations on the contracting state to preserve the security and efficiency of air transport. States are obliged to take reasonable measures to restore control of aircraft to its lawful commander or to preserve his or her control over it and to facilitate the continuation of the journey of the passengers and the crew. In addition, states are obliged to return the aircraft and its cargo to those entitled without delay (Article 9) and report promptly as possible to the Council of ICAO any relevant information (Article 11). Article 10 imposes an obligation on the contracting states to give one another the greatest measure of assistance in connection with the criminal proceedings.

When comparing the contents of the Hague Convention with that of the Tokyo Convention, one observes that the two Conventions overlap and are even contradictory on some issues and their interrelation is far from clear.

The Hague Convention may be considered as a significant step forward in the endeavour of the international community to suppress the hijacking of aircraft and remove the threat caused by it to international civil aviation. The Convention has enlarged the number of the states competent to exercise jurisdiction over a hijacker and included the introduction of a new basis for the exercise of jurisdiction of the state where the charterer of an aircraft has his or her principal place of business or permanent residence.

Another encouraging fact is that the Hague Convention grants every contracting state the power to exercise jurisdiction over a hijacker if such states are affected by an offence committed under the Convention, thus making it impossible for a hijacker to escape the normal process of the law.

The Hague Convention, despite its efficiency in some areas, is not without its weaknesses. Mankiewicz[88] comments:

> The Hague Convention deals only with 'unlawful seizure committed on board aircraft' and does not apply to sabotage committed on the ground, nor does it cover unlawful interference with air navigation, facilities and services such as airports, air control towers or radio communications. Attempts made further to extend the scope of the Convention were unsuccessful. Nevertheless, the Seventeenth session of the Assembly of ICAO, held in Montreal in June, 1970, adopted a Resolution directing the Council of ICAO to convene the Legal Committee, if possible not later than November, 1970, in order to prepare ... a draft Convention on Acts of Unlawful Interference Against Civil Aviation with the view to its adoption ... as soon as practicable'. Consequently, the draft Convention was prepared and was opened for signature at Montreal on September 23, 1971.

The Montreal Convention (1971)

Since both the Tokyo and the Hague Conventions dealt only with unlawful seizure committed on board aircraft, they did not cover sabotage committed on the ground, nor unlawful interference with air navigation facilities and services. The Montreal Convention was drafted *inter alia*, to remedy those lapses. The objectives of the Montreal Convention are best summed up as follows:

> The primary aim of the Montreal Convention was to arrive at a generally acceptable method of dealing with alleged perpetrators of acts of unlawful interference with aircraft. In general, the nations represented at the Montreal Conference agreed that acts of sabotage, or violence and related offences interfering with the safety and development of international civil aviation constituted a global problem which had to be combated collectively by concerned nations of the international community. A multilateral international convention had to be adopted which extended both the scope and efficacy of national legislation and provided the legal framework for international cooperation in the apprehension, prosecution and punishment of alleged offenders.[89]

Definition of in service To achieve the above objectives, the Montreal Convention first sought to expand the scope of the activity covered by the Convention in order to include a new series of offences which can be committed without the offender being on board the aircraft. The same definition for an aircraft in flight as given in Article 3 (1) of the Hague Convention applies but the Montreal Convention introduces a new term, 'aircraft in service', which is defined as follows:

> Aircraft is considered to be in service from the beginning of the preflight preparation of the aircraft by ground personnel or by the crew for a specific period until twenty-four hours after the landing. The period of the service shall, in any event, extend for the entire period during which the aircraft is in flight[90].

The expression was deemed important as it covered a more extended period of time than the expression 'in flight' as defined in Article 3 (1) in the preceding Hague Convention. The term 'in service' would cover such acts as the bombing of and discharge of weapons against aircraft on the ground, as well as similar acts against aircraft in flight, whether or not the acts were performed by a person on board or outside the aircraft. Another significance of the term 'in service' is that it serves to specify the physical position in which the aircraft must be if the offences covered by the subparagraph of Article 2 are to come under the Convention. An extensive definition of the expression could encompass attacks against an aircraft while in the hangar or at a parking area. But the states at the Montreal Conference were not willing to go that far. This is because an extensive definition would mean that the states would, under another provision of the

Convention, be bound either to extradite the suspected perpetrator of such attack, or if it did not extradite him or her, submit the case to its competent authorities for the purpose of prosecution. States are notoriously reluctant to enter into international arrangements on criminal matters if those arrangements markedly reduce domestic jurisdiction. Yet, too narrow a definition of the expression 'aircraft in service' would compromise the utility of the Convention.[91]

The definition of the term 'in service' posed a difficult problem during the deliberations of the Montreal Conference. Although the beginning of the in-service period afforded few problems, the main difficulty was in the definition of the end of the 'in service' period, when applied to lengthy stopovers or night stops in a country, and awaiting turnaround before commencement of the homeward-bound journey. It was decided that the aircraft should be protected by the Convention, that is, it should be deemed to be 'in service' when it makes a stopover or night stop in another country. The present wording of the term 'in service' attempts to solve the problem by specifying that an aircraft shall be considered in service 24 hours after any landing. The expression 'in service' as it stands includes the term 'in flight' under Article 2 (a). Therefore, in the event of a forced landing occasioned by hijacking, the period 'in service' is deemed to continue until the competent authorities take over the responsibility for the aircraft and for persons and property on board.

Definition of the offence Another approach adopted by the Montreal Convention in its endeavours to curb hostile acts against civil aviation is to define the offence broadly in order to embrace all the possible acts that might occur. The first issue which faced the drafters of the Convention in this respect related to the provision of substantial coverage of serious offences, at the same time avoiding the difficulties that may arise in connection with the listing of specific crimes in a convention intended for adoption by a great many states. After much debate and deliberation, this issue was settled and the final conclusion of the meeting is reflected in Article 1. G.F. Fitzgerald described the method of enumerating the offences in the Convention as being 'novel':

> Article I is novel in that it describes a number of penal offences within the framework of a multilateral convention.[92]

Article 1 of the Convention defines and enumerates the offences of unlawful interference with aircraft as follows:

1 Any person commits an offence if he or she unlawfully and intentionally:

a Performs an act of violence against a person on board an aircraft in flight if that act is likely to endanger the safety of that aircraft in flight; or
b destroys an aircraft in service or causes damage to such an aircraft in flight if that act is likely to endanger its safety in flight; or
c places or causes to be placed on board an aircraft in service, by any means whatsoever, a device or substance which is likely to destroy that aircraft, or to cause damage to it which renders it incapable of flight, or to cause damage to it which is likely to endanger its safety in flight; or
d destroys or damages air navigation facilities or interferes with their operation, if any such act is likely to endanger the safety or aircraft in flight; or
e communicates information known to be false, thereby endangering the safety of an aircraft in flight.

2 Any person also commits an offence if he or she:

a Attempts to commit any of the offences mentioned in Paragraph 1 of this Article;
b is an accomplice of a person who commits or attempts to commit any such offence.

It should be noted that while Article 1 delineates several different offences, the dual requisites of unlawfulness and intent apply to the acts of the offences enumerated. G.F. Fitzgerald observes:

> The introductory language of paragraph 1 makes it clear that the dual element of unlawfulness and intention must be present in all of the acts covered by subparagraphs (a) to (e); otherwise those acts will not be offences. The dual element would also apply to attempts and complicity covered by subparagraph 2.[93]

Subparagraph (a) of Article 1 is designed to deter and punish acts of violence committed against persons on board aircraft in flight. It should be noted that not all acts of violence come within the scope of the offence, but only those likely to endanger the safety of the aircraft. The notion of an act of violence referred to in this subparagraph includes armed attack and also attack against the lives of persons and the aircraft by other means, such as by blows, strangling, poisoning or lethal injection.

The word 'violence' used in subparagraph 1 (a) can be interpreted as including not only an armed attack or physical assault, but also administration of poison through, for example, its introduction into the food or drink served on board aircraft.[94]

The act of violence perpetrated upon a person on board an aircraft according to subparagraph 1 (b) may come from within or without the aircraft.

The manner in which subparagraph 1 (a) is worded, when it is read with the opening language of Article 1, would lead one to conclude that the person performing the act of violence does not have to be on board the aircraft in order to come under the Convention. This means that the convention would apply to a person who, being outside the aircraft (for example, a low-flying and slow-moving helicopter or light aircraft) in flight or who, while on the ground has poisoned food which is later consumed by a person on board such aircraft.[95]

According to this subparagraph, the act of violence is not restricted to those acts which imperil the life of the victim. Any act of violence perpetrated against a person on board which is likely to interfere with the safety of the aircraft falls within the scope of the offence. Hence, the standard for determining whether the Convention is applicable in a given situation does not hinge on the gravity or the heinousness of the act but rather on its effect on the safety of the aircraft in flight. It is to be noted that the same definition as given in Article 3 of the Hague Convention for an 'aircraft in flight' applies in Article 2 (a) of the Montreal Convention.

The two offences which can be committed on board an aircraft in service are enclosed in subparagraphs 1 (b) and 1 (c) of Article 1 of the Montreal Convention.

Subparagraph 1 (b) is designed to deter and penalize acts of sabotage perpetrated against the aircraft itself. The subparagraph encompasses attacks both from within and without the aircraft. The destruction and damage referred to in the subparagraph must occur while the aircraft is 'in service' as the particular act, the consequence of which is the destruction of the aircraft, may be performed before the aircraft is 'in service'. Destruction includes substantial destruction of the aircraft beyond the possibility of rendering it airworthy through repair while the concept 'causing damage' is intended to cover 'the damaging of a vital but inexpensive piece of wiring, which would render the aircraft incapable of flight. It could also cover any damage, whether caused to an aircraft on the ground or in the air, where there is a likelihood that the safety of the aircraft in flight would be endangered.[96]

Subparagraph 1 (c) is an attempt by the Convention to encompass, through using the term 'by any means whatsoever', all situations in which explosives or other devices are placed on board an aircraft.

> The word 'by any means whatsoever' cover the placing of explosives on board an aircraft whether carried on board by the author of the act

> or any unwitting accomplice, sent on board in air cargo or by mail, or even attached to the outside of the aircraft before it undertakes its journey.[97]

Subparagraph 1 (d) is intended to address hostile acts against 'air navigation facilities' which may include airports, towers, radio services and meteorological services used in international flights.

Subparagraph 1 (e) is concerned with making it an offence for anyone to pass, or cause to pass false information relating to an offence, for example, the presence of an explosive device or would-be hijacker on board the aircraft. Although most national legislation may have already enacted legislation concerning this subject, it was felt that measures to restrain such acts could especially be included in this Convention, as it was intended to cover a type of offence which very definitely interferes with the orderly conduct of commercial air services. It must be noted that in order for the act to fall within the Convention, the offender who communicates the information must know that the information is false.

Article 1 (2) covers the case of an attempt to commit an offence and the case of being an accomplice to committing one of the offences listed in the subparagraphs of the Article. During the debate on the Montreal Convention, there was an attempt to include conspiracy in the definition, but some delegations, including France, were of the view that since conspiracy was not an offence under their national systems of penal law, it should not be included in the Convention. After long deliberations, it was decided by a vote that reference to conspiracy would not be made in the Convention.

Penalties and the scope of the Convention Like the Hague Convention, the Montreal Convention provides for the undertaking by each contracting state to make the offences covered by the Convention punishable by 'severe penalties'. Article 3 of the Montreal Convention states that each contracting state undertakes to make the offences mentioned in Article 1 punishable with severe penalties. Unlawful acts against the safety of civil aviation are thus considered to be serious crimes which the contracting states must punish by severe penalties. The term 'severe penalties' is, however, not defined.

The French delegate explained at the discussions leading to the adoption of the Hague Convention that in connection with Article 2 the Sub-committee and the Committee at the Hague deliberations had been faced with the question as to whether or not the severity of the punishment to be imposed upon the offender should be stated. The Sub-committee had come to the conclusion that this could not be done, considering the diversity of criminal codes in different countries. A more general wording, that is, 'severe penalties', was therefore considered more appropriate. It was not customary for international conventions of this type to stipulate minimum penalties, and a number of states did not have any provisions for them in their national legislation.[98] This omission has been criticized as one of the weaknesses of the convention.[99]

Article 4 of the Convention stipulates which flights are to be covered by the Convention. Paragraph 1 excludes from the operation of the Convention aircrafts used in military, customs, or police services.

According to Paragraph 2 of Article 4, the scope of the Convention is determined primarily in terms of the international element of aviation. In the case of the offences contemplated in clauses (a), (b), (c) and (e) of Article 1 (1), the Convention applies irrespective of whether the aircraft is engaged in an international or domestic flight, only if, as stated in Article 4 (2):

- The place of take-off or landing, actual or intended, of the aircraft is situated outside the territory of the state of registration of that aircraft; or
- the offence is committed in the territory of a state other than the state of registration of the aircraft.

The Convention also applies in cases of international flights if the offender or the alleged offender is found in the territory of the state other than the state of registration of the aircraft.

Paragraph 5 of Article 4 provided:

> In the case contemplated in subparagraph (d) of paragraph 1 of Article 1, this convention shall apply only if the air navigation facilities are used in international air navigation.

Hence, the Convention will apply only if the air navigation facilities are used in international air navigation, that is, the sabotage of domestic air navigation facilities is outside the scope of the Convention, notwithstanding the fact that the saboteur of domestic facilities may be found in another state. G.F. Fitzgerald observes:

> In the case of air navigation facilities mentioned in subparagraph (d) of Article 1(1), the Convention applies only if the facilities destroyed, damaged, or interfered with are used in international navigation.[100]

Jurisdictional powers given to states under the Montreal Convention (1971) Article 5 of the Convention, which concerns jurisdiction, provides that each contracting state shall take such measures as may be necessary to establish its jurisdiction over offences in the same three instances as those contained in the Hague Convention, and a fourth instance when the offence is committed in the territory of that State. This Convention, along with its predecessor[101] does not exclude any criminal jurisdiction exercised in accordance with national law. Fitzgerald states:

> A controversial topic in the Montreal Convention is that of jurisdiction, since, like the Hague Convention, this Convention attempts to establish a form of universal jurisdiction over the alleged offender.[102]

Article 5 of the Montreal Convention provides that each contracting state shall take such measures as may be necessary to establish its jurisdiction over the offenders in the following cases:

1 a When the offence is committed in the territory of that state.
  b When the offence is committed against or on board an aircraft registered in that state.
  c When the aircraft on board which the offence is committed lands in its territory with the alleged offender still on board.
  d When the offence is committed against or on board an aircraft leased without crew to a lessee whose principal place of business or, if the lessee has no such place of business, whose permanent residence is in that state.
2 Each contracting state shall likewise take such measures as may be necessary to establish its jurisdiction over the offences mentioned in Article 1, Paragraphs 1(a), (b) and (c) and in Article 1, Paragraph 2, in so far as that paragraph relates to those offences, in the case where the alleged offender is present in its territory and it does not extradite him or her pursuant to Article 8 to any of the states mentioned in Paragraph 1 of this Article, that is, Article 5.
3 This Convention does not exclude any criminal jurisdiction exercised in accordance with the national law.

An analysis of Article 5 would lead to the conclusion that at least four states are specifically empowered to exercise concurrent jurisdiction over an alleged offender. These states are:

1 The state within whose territorial boundaries the offence is committed (whether the offence takes place on its territory or within its airspace) this reaffirming and codifying the traditional basis of territoriality.
2 The state of registration of the aircraft (hence, such state is empowered to exercise its jurisdiction over offenders who commit their crimes on board aircraft registered in those states).
3 The state of landing, if the offender is on board the aircraft.

4 Any party to the Convention within whose boundaries the alleged offender is present, if that state refuses to extradite the offender to any of the states having jurisdiction under Article 5 (1).

Article 5 (2) adopts the interpretation of universal jurisdiction as contained in the Hague Convention. Furthermore, Article 5, Paragraph 3, provides that the jurisdictional basis delineated by the Convention do not supersede any criminal jurisdiction that has derived from national laws of the parties to the Convention. Consequently, the jurisdictional relation to nationality may be asserted by the state of nationality of the alleged offender, and the states which are the targets of the offence or whose nationals are threatened, maimed or killed by the offender may invoke the protective principle or the lesser recognized jurisdictional basis of passive nationality. These additional bases of jurisdiction are expected to further increase the possibility of suppressing the offenders.

In his concluding remarks, Professor Fitzgerald has observed:

> Thus, the Montreal Convention breaks new ground and goes beyond codification in providing for the international legal action to be taken by states in respect of many acts ...[103]

By adopting the Montreal convention, concerned states attempted to provide a framework which would substantially widen the scope and application of national legislation and thereby both penalize and deter unlawful interference with aircraft.

Extradition or prosecution? Article 7 of the Montreal Convention, like its predecessor, embodies the principle of *aut dedere aut judicare*, which is the basis of the whole draft. It reads as follows:

> The State party in whose territory the alleged offender is present shall, if it does not extradite him, submit without exception whatsoever and without undue delay, the case to its competent authorities for the purpose of prosecution, through proceeding in accordance with the laws of that State.

According to this provision, a contracting state has an obligation either to extradite the alleged offender found in its territory or submit his case to the competent authorities for the purpose of prosecution. It appears from the overall reading of 'without exception whatsoever' that the Convention makes prosecution mandatory. However, a deeper analysis of the Article brings to bear the fact that it does not mandate the actual prosecution of the offender but merely the submission of the case to the competent domestic prosecuting authorities. This contention is supported by the fact that during the

Montreal Conference the Israeli delegation proposed that the Convention include a mandatory prosecution provision, although this proposal was defeated by a vote of 35 to 2 with 6 abstentions.

The failure of the Montreal Convention to provide an objection to prosecute when the offender is not extradited was considered a weakness regarding the system of sanctions *aut dedere aut punire*. A commentator observes:

> The lack of mandatory system of prosecution with respect to aerial terrorism must be emphasized. Despite the repeated efforts of some delegations during the Hague and Montreal Conferences, the existing texts on aerial terrorism do not recognize the system of mandatory prosecution in case of denial of extradition requests. On the contrary, the State authorities in charge of the handling of prosecution may well decide that according to their domestic law, the alleged offender should not be prosecuted at all.[104]

Extradition and other principles As far as extradition is concerned, the Montreal Convention repeats verbatim the Hague provision regarding extradition. The Convention also repeats the Hague Convention provision, discussed previously, relating to: the taking of the alleged offender into custody; joint air transport operating organizations or international operating agencies, which operate aircraft that are subject to joint international registration; continuation of the journey of the passengers, crew, and aircraft; assistance between states in connection with criminal proceeding; and, the reporting of the process to the ICAO Council.

Although the Montreal Convention was considered a breakthrough in combating terrorism against air transport, it remains, like its predecessors, tenuous and destitute of real effect. It would be a platitude to state that the effectiveness of any convention, however well drafted and universally accepted, would depend on the willingness and ability of states to enforce within their own territory the rule of law.

> Even if it is widely ratified, a small number of States can undermine its (a treaty's) effectiveness by actively supporting or condoning acts of unlawful interference and by providing havens for the perpetrators of such acts. Because of conflicting ideologies and political exegesis, such events have in fact occurred.[105]

Another problem is that although all three conventions have entered into force, barely half of the world community subscribes to either one or all of these agreements, and therefore their total impact has been less than inhibiting. At the time of writing, 153 states have ratified the Tokyo Convention, 153 have ratified the Hague Convention and 155 have ratified the Montreal Convention.[106] This low rate of ratification, when compared to the 183 member states of ICAO has drastically reduced the Conventions' effectiveness:

> Whether the Convention will fulfil its aims is dependent upon the breadth of support it obtains, indicated in part by the number of ramifications it receives. For the Convention to be effective, it must be acceded to by almost all nations.[107]

Some states have not only failed to ratify the conventions, but have also undermined the Conventions' effectiveness by providing sanctuaries for alleged offenders. Motivated by political and economic interests, other states have granted tacit support, and occasionally even active aid to the perpetrators.

As a direct effect of the failure of the international community to provide an effective machinery for combating terrorism against air transport, threats to international civil aviation have consistently become more alarming and grave. New facets, and more spectacular types of offences have evolved as a result.

In an effort to redress the situation, concerned actions, under the auspices of ICAO, have attempted to formulate and adopt multilateral international accord which would compel recalcitrant states into adherence to both customary and international law and with the provisions of the Tokyo, Hague and Montreal Conventions.

The Bonn Declaration

At the close of a two-day economic meeting held at Bonn, Germany, July 16–17, 1978, leaders of the governments of Canada, France, the then Federal Republic of Germany, Italy, Japan, the United Kingdom of Great Britain and Northern Ireland, and the United States of America agreed to act jointly in a common undertaking against countries failing to act swiftly against hijacking. The declaration on cooperative action reads:

> The heads of States and governments concerned about terrorism and the taking of hostages, declare that their governments will intensify their joint efforts to combat international terrorism.
>
> To this end, in cases where a country refuses extradition or prosecution of those who have hijacked an aircraft and/or do not return such aircraft, the heads of States and governments are jointly resolved that their governments should take immediate action to cease all flights to that country.
>
> At the same time, their governments will initiate action to halt all incoming flights from that country or from any country by the airlines of the country concerned. The heads of States and governments urge other governments to join in this commitment.

It is evident that the declaration was intended to create an international regime for preventing and deterring acts of unlawful interference with civil aviation by the imposition of stringent sanctions that would adversely affect the economic and political interests of a delinquent State. Mark E. Fingerman observes:

> The Declaration focuses on sanctions designed to deter nations from encouraging the commission of the offence. In effect, the spirit of the Declaration is a recognition of the fact that States are frequently *de facto* accomplices to acts of skyjacking ... The rationale of the Declaration would appear to be the foreclosing of the possibility of a skyjacker finding refuge and thereby reducing the attractiveness of the offence.[108]

The object of the Bonn Declaration as is indicated in its preamble is to intensify the joint effort of states to combat international terrorism. In order to achieve this objective, the Declaration has set out respective obligations on a third state in the event a hijacked aircraft ended in the territory of such state. If the third state failed to meet the obligations specified in the Declaration, the Declaration envisages that a definite sanction will be inflicted upon the state as a sort of punishment.

The Declaration refers to an act of hijacking, without actually defining the offence. It can be assumed that the act referred to would be interpreted in accordance with the definition in Article 1 of the Hague Convention. The Declaration seemingly refers to an act that has been completed, which means that the hijackers should have reached their final destination. Thus, a state in whose territory a hijacked aircraft lands only for the purpose of refuelling would not act contrary to the Declaration if it allowed the landing without taking action against the hijacker.

The Declaration applies in instances where a state refuses to prosecute or extradite the hijackers and/or return the hijacked aircraft. The words 'prosecution and extradition' as contained in the Declaration have the same meaning as used in Articles 8 and 7 of the Hague and Montreal Conventions respectively. Of course, for this provision to be applicable a state must be in a position to prosecute or extradite, that is, the hijacker must stay in the country and be available for prosecution by the competent authorities. However, once a state is able to take appropriate action but does not act and the hijacker disappears, such omission would be regarded as defaulting according to the spirit of the Declaration.

The sanctions which the contracting states would impose are: (*a*) taking immediate action to cease all flights to that country, and (*b*) initiating suspension all incoming flights which arrive from the defaulting state or are operated by airlines of a defaulting state. These sanctions are in essence an economic boycott or a 'reprisal' in international law and are meant as a deterrent. The Declaration recognizes in spirit that some states may act as *de facto* accomplices to acts of hijacking and may give refuge and safe haven to an offender.

The Legal Status of the Bonn Declaration

The suspension of aerial communication as envisaged in the Bonn Declaration has been considered a serious measure in the context of international relations.

> Naturally, the suspension of aerial communications was not an economic step... This was a political sanction, because the suspension of aerial communications meant in practice a deterioration in relations between States. It meant stoppage of the carriage of cargo and passengers, it would interfere with diplomatic communications, etc.[109]

Another contentious aspect of the Bonn sanction machinery is that the boycotting of a delinquent state would not only affect the interests of the specific state violating the obligations specified in the Declaration, but also of those states which applied or agreed to apply such sanctions and third-party states.

There is strong feeling among some jurists who consider that the imposition of sanctions against offending states falls exclusively within the domain of the Security Council of the United Nations, and thus, any independent convention or declaration permitting the use of sanctions by party states themselves would violate the United Nations Charter. In support of this argument, Articles 39 and 41 of the Charter of the United Nations have been cited.

Article 39 of the Charter states:

> The Security Council shall determine the existence of any threat to peace, breach of peace, or act of aggression and shall make recommendations, or decide what measures shall be taken in accordance with Articles 41 and 42 to maintain or restore international peace and security.

Article 41 states:

> The Security Council may decide what measures not involving the use of armed force are to be employed to give effect to its decisions, and it may call upon the members of the United Nations to apply such measures. These may include complete or partial interruption of economic relations and of rail, sea, air, postal, telegraphic, radio and other means of communications and the severance of diplomatic relations.

It is usually accepted therefore that states cannot take joint sanctions against another state unless such action was authorized by the Security Council of the United Nations.

The above view had also been voiced in the ICAO Legal Committee where delegates of France and the then USSR expressed the opinion that to apply sanctions against states in the form of interruption of full or partial air services was within the exclusive jurisdiction of the Security Council. The French delegate observed:

> The sanctions approach had been very thoroughly discussed in the Special Sub-committee and some rather serious objections to it had been raised. The first was whether the machinery for consideration of sanctions was compatible with Article 41 of the United Nations Charter, which empowered the Security Council to decide upon measures in the nature of sanctions, including the complete or partial interruption of air services, and called upon members of the United Nations to apply them.[110]

A similar opinion is voiced by the Soviet Union delegate who argued that joint action in a form of suspension of flight, if implemented, would be in contradiction to the competence of the Security Council:

> Indeed, according to Article 41 of the United Nations Charter, one of the measures that the Security Council of the United Nations was empowered to apply included the suspension of air communications. The imposition of collective sanctions against States, outside the framework of the United Nations, would be precluded by U.N. Charter.[111]

Another approach which indicates the incompatibility of the measures adopted by the Bonn Declaration with international law is reflected in Article 2 (3) and Chapter VII of the United Nations Charter. Under Article 2 (3), all members of the United Nations pledge themselves to settle their international disputes by peaceful means in such manner that international peace and security and justice are not endangered. Article 33 then enumerates various procedures for the settlement of such disputes, notably 'negotiation, inquiry, mediation, arbitration, judicial settlement, resort to regional agencies or arrangements or other peaceful means (chosen by parties to the dispute).

It has been observed by Brosche that:

> Even if this list is not considered to be exhaustive, it is quite clear that embargo, boycott, blockade, reprisal or other kinds of economic pressure do not constitute procedures of pacific settlement. They are not peaceful means and not appropriate for the solution of disputes.

> The use or imposition of such measures would constitute a violation of the obligation to settle international disputes by peaceful means. Due to these facts, it becomes evident that the use of any kind of [economic] pressure is contrary to the [Charter] principles of peaceful settlement of disputes.[112]

It is clear from the above that the aerial boycott adopted by the Bonn Declaration is not permissible according to international law as incorporated in the Charter of the United Nations. It is clear that states will be held responsible for a boycott instituted directly by their governments if such measure is found by the international community to be *ultra vires* the established norms of international law.

Furthermore, it may also be relevant to view the Bonn Declaration by reference to the doctrine of non-intervention, as elaborated in various international instruments in recent years. Thus, in Paragraph 2 of its Declaration on the Inadmissibility of Intervention in Domestic Affairs of States and the Protection of their Independence and Sovereignty of 21 December 1965 [(Resolution 2131 (XX)], the United Nations Assembly decreed that:

> No State may use or encourage the use of economic, political or any other type of measures to coerce another State in order to obtain from it the subordination of the exercise of its sovereign rights and to secure from it an advantage of any kind.

The Incompatibility of the Bonn Declaration with the Vienna Convention on the Law of Treaties

The Bonn Declaration was designed to be invoked by seven states against an allegedly defaulting state, whether or not the latter is a party to the Declaration. Mark E. Fingerman feels:

> The legal force of the Bonn Declaration upon non-parties is of critical importance; it is against these nations that the Declaration's sanctions were most intended to apply. The Declaration calls for the imposition of its sanctions upon any State that violates its provisions, whether or not the State in question is a party to the Declaration or any civil aviation convention.[113]

Articles 33 and 34 of the Vienna Convention on the Law of Treaties specifically state that states which do not become party to a treaty would not be bound by that treaty unless they expressly agree in writing to be bound by it. Only the state parties to a treaty (including a declaration) could be considered as being bound by the provisions of that treaty. While it may be conceded that a treaty could create rights for third states which those states could accept, it cannot impose obligations on third states in terms of requiring them to commit acts such as prosecuting or extraditing offenders against civil aviation or returning the aircraft against which such offence is committed. International law does not envisage the imposition of obligations on states which are not parties to a treaty. Therefore, the scope of application of the Declaration should be limited to states which are parties to it. The Note presented by the French Government on the Resolution adopted by the Council of ICAO on 19 June 1972 on the question of joint sanction stated:

> The Convention can establish obligations only for states party to it and would permit imposing sanctions only on those parties, pursuant to Articles 34 and 35 of the Vienna Convention on the Law of Treaties. Therefore, the Convention could be effective only if it was universally accepted.[114]

Therefore, the Declaration will be ineffective as far as it intended to impose an obligation upon third parties to prosecute or extradite the hijacker and to release the aircraft.

The Incompatibility of the Bonn Declaration with the Chicago Convention and the International Air Services Transit Agreement

Another difficulty emerging from the Bonn Declaration was the relationship of the Declaration to other international conventions. The problem of suspension of air transport services as a sanction under the Bonn Declaration becomes particularly relevant in this context. Article 5 of the Chicago Convention confers certain rights upon contracting states:

> Each Contracting State agrees that all aircraft of the other Contracting States, being aircraft not engaged in scheduled international air services shall have the right subject to the observation of this Convention to make flights into or in transit non-stop across its territory and to make stops for non-traffic purposes without the necessity of obtaining prior permission and subject to the right of the States flown over to require landing.

The Transit Agreement or the so-called 'Two Freedoms Agreement' also contains a reciprocal concession among ICAO members relating to their scheduled air services whereby their carriers could fly across the territory of a state without landing or land in its territory for non-traffic purposes.

Therefore, it appears that the imposition of a restriction upon the airline of a defaulting state to fly over or to land in the states subscribing to the Bonn Declaration is incompatible with the provisions of the Chicago Convention and the Transit Agreement. The rights to fly over or land belong to states party to the Chicago Convention, and those rights could not be derogated by a contrary provision in another treaty, such as the Bonn Declaration. The Spanish delegate to the ICAO Legal Committee observed about sanctions against air services:

> One of the problems ... was the compatibility of the air services with the right of the States party to the Chicago Convention and Air Transit Agreement.[115]

The French Government stated the following in regard to the question of suspension of air services as a sanction:

> Decisions on the suspension of air services could not be taken without amending the bilateral agreement which grants traffic rights, and, perhaps, even the Chicago Convention itself.[116]

In negotiating air transport agreements, both parties will endeavour to promote safe commercial operations of the type contemplated by the Chicago Convention and seek the grant of rights for their carriers. Bilateral agreements on air traffic rights are usually not intended to cover the continuation of operation into and from victim states by aircraft of the states which are seen to promote the disruption of safe commercial aviation, in a manner specified in the Declaration. Failure by states to take practical measures necessary to prevent the disruption of international aviation – which is caused by such acts of detention and seizure of aircraft as specified by the Declaration – would therefore not be consistent with the granting by peace-loving states, of rights necessary for the conduct of air traffic by another state. Therefore, it is not logical to say that bilateral air transport agreements can properly be interpreted as granting rights to airlines of states to continue air services to and from a delinquent state if such state detains passengers, crew or aircraft or fails to prosecute or extradite the perpetrators. Walter Schwenk has the following view:

> In interpreting the bilateral, the conclusion may be reached, however, that there seems to be sufficient justification for the suspension of air traffic rights under the bilateral itself without the need to resort to general principles of international law.[117]

The Chicago Convention established principles and arrangements designed to assure that international civil aviation would develop in safe and orderly manner. It imposed obligations upon each contracting state 'not to use civil aviation for any purpose inconsistent with' such aims.[118] More directly, the Convention specifically requires each contracting state 'to adopt all practicable measures ... to facilitate and expedite navigation by aircraft between the territories of contracting states, and to prevent unnecessary delays to aircraft crews, passengers and cargo.'[119] Refusal by a state to adopt generally agreed procedures to eliminate the threat to international civil aviation posed by such acts of detention and unlawful seizure as specified in the Bonn Declaration, would constitute a failure by that state to carry out its obligation under Articles 2 and/or 44 of the Chicago Convention. Therefore, suspension of flights in the circumstances referred to in the Declaration would not be incompatible with the Chicago Convention or the Transit Agreement, contrary to the views of some scholars.

Moreover, the sanction adopted by the Bonn Declaration involving suspension of air services in no way deprives a state of a fair opportunity to operate an international airline pursuant to Article 44 (f). On the contrary, a state found to be in default would not be giving a fair opportunity to other states. The US Representative in the Legal Committee held in Montreal in 1973 said:

> Defaulting States no longer had the privilege of Article 44 (f) until such time as it provided a fair opportunity to the rest of the community. Article 44 (f) would have to be read in context with Articles 44 (d) and (h), and with the directive as stated in Article 44 (a) that the Organization shall ensure safe and orderly growth of international civil aviation throughout the world.[120]

The US Representative said that the power to suspend air services as a sanction is not only compatible with the Chicago Convention but also with international law.

> If a party to the Chicago Convention committed a material breach of the obligation to ensure the safety of civil aviation, then other parties individually had the right to suspend the operation of the Convention in whole or in part with respect to the defaulting State in accordance with customary international law, as specified in Article 60 of the Vienna Convention on the Law of Treaties.[121]

When states ratify or adhere to the Chicago Convention, they not only become members of ICAO, but also, they undertake to take appropriate steps to ensure the safety and security of international civil aviation. Hence, the harbouring of perpetrators by way of failure to prosecute or extradite may be said to constitute a violation of the basic rationale of the Chicago Convention. To breach the obligation set forth by the Chicago Convention is to implicitly denounce the Convention. Therefore, the defaulting state in such an instance cannot claim the rights conferred upon it by the Convention.

The Problem of Prosecution or Extradition

The fourth problem of the Bonn Declaration is the issue of prosecution or extradition. Sanctions under the Declaration are expected to follow the failure of the delinquent state to prosecute, extradite and/or return the aircraft. However, public international law provides no rule which imposes a duty to extradite or prosecute. Hence extradition or prosecution becomes either a matter of comity or treaty between states. Even when a treaty exists, extradition may be refused in certain circumstances. Therefore, surrender of an alleged criminal cannot be demanded as a right in the absence of a binding treaty between the respective parties. Any attempt to bind states to extradite or prosecute offenders in the absence of a treaty to that effect would definitely be an encroachment on state sovereignty, making such an act a violation of customary international law.

Besides the above problems surfacing from the Bonn Declaration, there exists also certain gaps with respect to the application of the Declaration:

1 How would the decision to suspend air services be taken by the members of the Declaration, would it be by majority or unanimously?
2 Who will judge that a state is no longer in default, and when will the services be resumed? Should there be disagreement among the seven states' parties on these points and should a procedure be laid down in order to regulate these matters?
3 Did the Declaration take into account the diversity of violations attributable to the defaulting state and whether there would be the same penalty automatically applicable to every case?

The Bonn Declaration, unlike the three conventions discussed above, represents a fragmented attempt on the part of the international community to control terrorism or unlawful interference with international civil aviation. This, however, by no means confirms the fact that the three international conventions were comprehensive attempts by the entirety of the international community. While the conventions lacked a certain compulsion in their requirements, the Bonn Declaration, which seemingly had a punitive flavour, lacked respectable representation by the international community. It is time to view both these approaches with a view to combining them to form a synthesis of action. The element of sanction as introduced by the Bonn Declaration should be fused with the international flavour of the three conventions. The international community may be able to create a workable, effective and enforceable instrument on this basis.

A New Convention on the Marking of Plastic Explosives for the Purpose of Detection

Following the Resolution of the ICAO Council and the adoption of a United Nations General Assembly Resolution, the International Conference on Air Law was held under the auspices of the ICAO in Montreal from 12 February to 1 March 1991, where a Convention on the Marking of Plastic Explosives for the Purpose of Detection was unanimously adopted. The Convention was opened for signature on 1 March 1991 and on that day was signed by 41 states.[122] The events which led to the Conference are well known.[123]

The tragedy of Pan-Am flight 103 over Lockerbie, Scotland on 21 December 1988 deepened when the world learned that it was caused by the explosion of a lethal charge of Semtex, a high-performance plastic explosive manufactured commercially in Czechoslovakia, which was placed aboard the PAN-AM flight hidden in a radio cassette player.

The adoption of a new Convention on the marking of explosives was further encouraged by a unanimously adopted United Nations Security Council Resolution on 14 June 1989, which expressed concern 'at the ease with which plastic and sheet explosives can be used in acts of terrorism with little risk of detection' and urged ICAO 'to intensify its work aimed at preventing all acts of terrorism against international civil aviation, and in particular, its work on devising an international regime for the marking of plastic or sheet explosives for the purpose of detection.'[124]

At the 27th Session of the ICAO Assembly in September–October 1989, the delegations of the United Kingdom and Czechoslovakia presented a draft resolution which was unanimously adopted as Resolution A27-8. In it the Assembly called upon the Council:

> To convene a meeting of the Legal Committee, if possible in the first half of 1990, to prepare a draft international instrument [on the marking of plastic and sheet explosives for the purpose of detection], with a view to its adoption at a diplomatic conference as soon as practicable thereafter in accordance with the ICAO procedures set out in Assembly Resolution A7-6.[125]

At the broadest international level, the 44th Session of the United Nations General Assembly urged ICAO 'to intensify its work on devising an international regime for the marking of plastic or sheet explosives for the purpose of detection.'[126]

In June 1989, the ICAO Council considering the overall preference of the international community decided to include in the General Work Programme of the ICAO Legal Committee, with the highest and overriding priority, the subject 'Preparation of a new legal instrument regarding the marking of explosives for detectability.'[127]

Work started quickly after the completion of the 27th Session of the ICAO Assembly. The preparations for the new instrument passed through the following stages:

- A Rapporteur (Mr. A.W.G. Kean, CBE, United Kingdom) was invited to study and prepare the subject; he presented his report in September 1989. The report was considered by a Special Sub-committee of the Legal Committee which met at Montreal from 9 to 19 January 1990 and prepared its report for the 27th Session of the Legal Committee which met at Montreal from 27 March to 12 April 1990.
- The Legal Committee devoted almost all of its time to the new instrument and presented its report which contained the text of a 'Draft Convention on the Marking of Plastic (and Sheet) Explosives for the Purpose of Detection' which the Committee considered to be 'a final draft' under the terms of Assembly Resolution A7-6, to the Council. Consequently, a report was drafted by the Rapporteur appointed to study and prepare the issue with regard to the adoption of a Convention.
- The Council considered the report of the Legal Committee together with the report of the third meeting of the *ad hoc* Group of Specialists on 4 July 1990 and decided to circulate the draft text of the Convention to states and international organizations for comments.
- At the same time the Council convened an International Conference on Air Law to meet at Montreal from 12 February to 1 March 1991.

The major issues to be resolved by the Conference related to:

a The scope of the Convention – in particular whether it should be confined to plastic explosives.

b The obligations of states, especially those related to the prohibition and effective prevention of the manufacture in their territories of such explosives and of the movement in and out of their territories of unmarked explosives.

c The exceptions that should be created and the extent to which they should be created in relation to activities by military or police authorities that were not inconsistent with the purposes and objectives of the convention.

d The manner of and the timing for the disposal of existing stocks.

e The function of the Annex to the Convention as a flexible instrument to address further development of technology, its amendment and the role of the Explosives Technical Commission.

Scope of the Convention

The Convention, which is titled 'Convention on the Marking of Plastic Explosives for the Purpose of Detection'. It has been drawn up in English, French, Russian, Spanish and Arabic.

From the beginning, there has been some confusion with respect to the proper reference to 'plastic explosives'. The relevant UN resolutions as well as Assembly Resolutions A27-8 refer to 'plastic or sheet explosives', the Legal Committee put in its definition of explosives the wording 'and sheet' between square brackets and referred the matter to the *Ad Hoc* Group of Specialists and suggested in its report[127] that the problem was more of a linguistic than of a technical nature.

The Conference deleted the words 'or sheet' in the understanding that they are superfluous and confusing in most languages, except for the French language. Hence, in the French version the words '*et en feuille*' when referring to plastic explosives have been retained.

In the opening clauses reference is made to other means of transport and targets other than aircraft, indicating that the scope of this Convention is clearly wider than the civil aviation sector. However, as aviation has been so far the major victim of the criminal use of plastic explosives, the Conference upheld the tasks entrusted to ICAO and its Council in the draft Convention by both the Legal Sub-committee and the Legal Committee.[128]

Both in the preparatory stage and during the Conference, ICAO's 'sister organization' the International Maritime Organization, participated actively in the deliberations.

The Legal Committee draft in Article 1 defined 'explosives', 'detection agent' and the verb 'mark', while referring to the Annex for further description or clarification of these terms.

The Conference chose to broaden the definition of explosives which now refers to '... explosive products, commonly known as "plastic explosives", including explosives in flexible or elastic sheet form, as described in the Technical Annex to this Convention.'

Thus an elegant if somewhat superfluous solution for the 'plastic and sheet' problem was found.[130]

Furthermore, definitions of the verb 'manufacture', of 'duly authorized military devices' and 'producer state' were added. The Conference discussed at some length the desirability of expanding the scope of the Convention to explosives other than plastic explosives. Supporters of such an approach argued that, by simply deleting any reference to 'plastic or sheet' in the definition, the Convention would cover more than plastic explosives alone. By leaving out the description of the explosives, it could be amended easily in the future to cover other explosives as well. As the Annex would have its own procedure of amendment, no new Convention or Protocol to the Convention would be needed.

The Conference ultimately decided against this suggestion. The 'don't-rock-the-boat' approach prevailed, while many delegations also felt, that such action would be outside their mandate and not in accordance with the relevant UN and ICAO Council decisions which mentioned all plastic and/or sheet explosives. As a compromise, the Conference included in its Final Act a Resolution which, among other things, 'Requests the Council of the International Civil Aviation Organization to initiate, as a matter of high priority, studies into methods of detecting explosives or explosive materials, especially into the marking of those explosives of concern, other than plastic explosives, whose detection would be aided by the use of marking agents, with a view of the evolution, if needed, of an appropriate comprehensive legal regime'.

Obligations of States

At an early stage of the preparations for the new Convention a majority in both the Legal Sub-committee and the Legal Committee opposed initiatives to create an international offence, for example, the act of manufacture or movement of unmarked explosives. Most delegations felt that the 1971 Montreal Convention and the additional 1988 Montreal Protocol adequately covered the offences that needed to be universally punishable in this context and that the new Convention should concentrate on the prevention of the use of plastic explosives by the perpetrators of those offences.

Article II expresses the obligation of states to take the necessary and effective measures to prohibit and prevent the manufacture in their territories of unmarked explosives, while Article III formulates the same obligation towards the movement into or out of the territory of a state party of unmarked explosives.

It is worth noting that Article II and III simply refer to 'necessary and effective measures' to be taken by states as a fulfilment of their obligations. It will be left to the individual states and their national legislation to provide for the necessary prohibitions and sanctions. While these provisions may facilitate the ratification of the Convention, they probably will not contribute greatly to a uniform and strict approach to the problem of containment and destruction of unmarked explosives.

Article IV, which contains provisions for strict control by states over unmarked plastic explosives within their territory and their eventual destruction, was the subject of extensive discussions during the Conference. In the Legal Committee draft, states were under the obligation to consume or destroy their military and commercial stocks of unmarked explosives within fifteen and three years respectively.

The Conference agreed on the three-year period for destroying commercial stocks proposed in the Legal Committee draft, but modified the regime applicable to military explosives. It was felt that it was not realistic to require unmarked explosives, that had already been incorporated into duly authorized military devices,[131] to be destroyed within any time frame. The chances of illegal use of the plastic explosives incorporated into those devices were judged to be remote as they were likely to be under tight control. Moreover, the destruction of these devices would pose grave technical, economical and environmental problems. Consequently, Paragraph 3 of Article IV has been redrafted and now contains the obligation for states to consume, destroy, mark or render permanently ineffective within a period of 15 years only those military or police stocks which are not permanently incorporated in duly authorized military devices. In other words, the bulk, raw stock of unmarked plastic explosives.

Another modification included the addition of three new paragraphs to Article IV as a result of a change in the Technical Annex. During its fourth meeting, from 26 to 30 November in Montreal, the *ad hoc* Group of Specialists concluded that it was necessary in certain cases to exclude unmarked plastic explosives needed to be manufactured or held for research and development, testing and training and forensic science purposes. This has been effected, in the Annex, by excluding them from the definition of explosives referred to in Article 1, Paragraph 1 of the Convention.

As a consequence and in order not to create a possible loophole in the Convention, the obligation for states to exercise strict and effective control over these exempted explosives and to destroy them when they are no longer used for those purposes has been added in Article IV.

Technical Annex

One of the difficulties facing the Conference (and the other preparatory bodies) was the fact that the issue at hand was a complicated one. Not only the 'visual' legal and political problems associated with international instruments aimed at preventing certain criminal activities arose, but parties were also confronted by new, highly technical problems such as the development of detection techniques, chemical additives and marking methods.

It may be assumed that the ICAO Council and the 27th Assembly envisaged in the new Convention an instrument with two major components:

1 strict obligations for states with regard to unmarked plastic explosives pending the eventual extinction of those forms of plastic explosives, and
2 strict technical rules on the detectability of plastic explosives through obligatory marking techniques.

From the beginning, these conditions led to a two-fold, almost completely separated approach. On the one hand the customary ICOA sequence of Rapporteur, Sub-committee, Legal Committee prepared essentially the legal part of the desired international instrument, solving questions and finding solutions on issues like transport and possession of legal and illegal unmarked explosives, depletion of existing military and civil stocks, states' obligations, enforcement and international penal aspects, etc.

On the other hand, the *Ad Hoc* Group of Specialists already established by the Council on 30 January 1989, set out to find one or more acceptable methods of marking plastic explosives for the purpose of detection. This was not an easy task, as 'aceptable' has many connotations in the field of safe handling and production, effectiveness of the proper explosive and of course effectiveness and reliable detection. As a result of its work, culminating in four meetings in Montreal, the *Ad Hoc* Group presented the Council on 3 December 1990 with its results,[32] which contained a proposal for the Annex to the Conventions.

When the two products were joined together by the Conference, there were some anxious moments. Due to amendments proposed by a number of delegations, the annex appeared to be developing into something with the appearance of a 'mini-convention', where, for example, directives and obligations towards state parties were formulated. This process was unacceptable to other delegations, who stressed the need for a straightforward technical annex. After some frantic redrafting a compromise was reached and parts of the proposed draft annex were relocated in Article IV.

The Conference further decided to refer to the annex as the 'Technical Annex' so as to underline its essentially technical nature. A new Article X was added to the Convention, stipulating that the Annex shall form an integral part of the Convention. The legal status of the Annex to the Convention had already been the subject of lengthy discussions in the Legal Sub-committee, Legal Committee and Council. It had been conceived as an integral part of the Convention. Because of its nature and purpose, the Convention would be meaningless and indeed could not exist without the Annex. Therefore it must be subject to the same consensus as the Convention itself at the time of its adoption. On the other hand, the Annex had been given a special status in Article VII with respect to its amendment. The Legal

Sub-committee and Legal Committee had realized that the Annex would contain strictly technical provisions which were subject to evolution and which might require adjustments to be made promptly and with greater flexibility than would be possible under the traditional procedure of amending the Convention through a diplomatic conference.

The Annex consists of two parts.

- *Part 1* provides a technical description of plastic explosives. This part also contains reference to the aforementioned explosives used for training and laboratory purposes.
- *Part* 2 contains, *inter alia,* the chemical and molecular formulas of four[133] different detection agents as determined earlier by the *Ad Hoc* Group of Specialists on the Detection of Explosives.

The four selected compounds are:

- Ethylene glycol dinitrate (EGDN)
- 2,3-Dimethyl-2,3-dinitrobutane (DMNB)
- para-Mononitrotoluene (p-MNT), and
- ortho-Mononitrotoluene (o-MNT).

International Explosives Technical Commission

The Convention provides in Article V for the establishment of an International Explosives Technical Commission (IETC), which is to evaluate the technical developments relating to the manufacture, marking and detection of explosives. The Commission shall also make recommendations to the Council for amendments to the Technical Annex (Article VI).

The Conference decided to put the membership of the Commission at no less than 15 and no more than 19 members, who will be appointed by the ICAO Council from among persons nominated by states party to the Convention.[134]

In the discussions on this subject it was reaffirmed that the Council in its appointment policy would be guided by the need for the presence of experts from both producer and user countries, while the long-standing ICAO principle of equitable geographical representation would also be applied. Paragraph 5 of Article V stipulates that the Commission shall adopt its rules of procedure, subject to the approval of the Council.

The amending procedure of the Annex in the Legal Committee draft was upheld by the Conference.[135] Consequently, Article VII provides for an exhaustive consultation procedure on proposed amendments of the Technical Annex. State parties would be notified of a proposed amendment and invited to communicate their views; after consideration of the comments the Council would formally propose the amendment to all states within 90 days, the amendment would be deemed to have been adopted and would enter into force after 180 days or after such period as specified in the proposed amendment.

If five or more state parties have objected to the proposed amendment, the proposal will be referred back to the IETC for further consideration. In such a situation the Council may also decide to convene a conference of all state parties.

A new Article VIII invited state parties to provide the Council with information that would assist the IETC in its work and to keep the Council informed of measures they have taken to implement the provisions of the Convention. The Council in its turn is to communicate such information to all state parties and international organizations concerned.

The Conference took the decision to insert a new Article IX which is directed at facilitating the implementation of the Convention. The Council of ICAO shall, in cooperation with state parties and international organizations concerned, take appropriate measures to facilitate the implementation of the Convention, including the provision of technical assistance and measures for the exchange of information relating to technical developments in the marking and detection of explosives.[136]

Final Clauses and Final Act

ICAO has been designated the Depositary of the Convention. The Convention is subject to ratification, acceptance, approval or accession by states and shall enter into force 60 days after the deposit of the thirty-fifth such instrument with ICAO, provided that at least five of the ratifying or acceding states are producer states.

Thus a qualifier for enforcement of this Convention has been added. As a result, Article XIII Paragraph 2 of the Convention requires states when depositing their instrument of ratification, acceptance, approval or accession, to declare whether or not they are a producer state.

Article I, Paragraph 6 defines producer state as 'any state in whose territory explosives are manufactured'. No further qualifications have been added, so ultimately it is left to states' parties to decide whether they wish to be considered a producer state.

In the Final Act[137] of the Conference the text of a Resolution is included which was adopted by consensus by the Conference. The Resolution addresses the importance of the marking of explosives to prevent unlawful acts against, *inter alia*, civil aviation, maritime navigation and other modes of transportation and urges states to become party to the Convention as soon as possible.

The Resolution also urges the international community to consider increasing technical, financial and material assistance to states in need of such assistance in order to benefit from the achievement of the objectives of the Convention.

In Resolving Clause 5 it invites the Council to assume the functions assigned to it in the Convention and to maintain, pending the entry into force of the Convention, the existence of the *Ad Hoc* Group of Specialists and to respect the principle of equitable geographical representation in the appointment of the members of the IETC. Finally, the Resolution requests the Council to initiate, as a matter of high priority, studies regarding the marking of explosives other than those referred to in the Convention.

In itself the new Convention represents an impressive achievement of states. The speed of its conception is truly remarkable and reflects positively on the capabilities of ICAO in these matters, as it may be considered due to its scope and purpose a genuine multilateral instrument.

Although the Conference went through several critical phases, the determination of its participants to get results never wavered and that led to the unanimous adoption of a new instrument of international law. Again, as in the case of the additional 1988 Protocol to the Montreal Convention, this result has been achieved in record time.

It is too early to judge the practical value of the Convention, but it is suggested that the possibilities of the Convention are unnecessarily limited by its strict adherence to the term 'plastic' in its definition of explosives. This restriction may impede further possible developments aimed at broadening its impact.

Much will depend on the concrete implementation of the measures proposed in the Convention through a hopefully quick and widespread ratification and the further work of the *Ad Hoc* Group of Specialists and its successor, the International Explosives Technical Commission.

Comment

Interference with civil aviation should be viewed as an extortion-oriented act committed against the international order and world peace which is calculated to take advantage of the most susceptible human quality of seeking personal security as a priority. The offence is an immediate threat to world peace and should be treated with the utmost care. Needless to say any nation which views the offence differently encourages world discord. Any wilful act calculated to endanger the safety of an aircraft, its passengers or any aviation-related property should be collectively regarded as an offence against the safety of air travel.

As for the need for a more flexible approach to the extradition of offenders, the establishment and recognition of a universal offence against the safety of aircraft would almost automatically nurture mutual cooperation between nations. Often, if offenders impute politics to the offence committed by them, they are granted political asylum by the host nation merely because the latter sympathizes with the alleged motive for the offence as represented by the offenders. Once this takes place it no longer remains the commission of an offence universally condemned but becomes an altercation between nations on political beliefs and convictions.

Notes

1 Resolution 2551 (XXIV). The Resolution was adopted by a vote of 77 in favour, 2 against with 17 abstentions.
2 The Tokyo Convention will be discussed in the following subsection.
3 Resolution 2645 was adopted by 105 in favour, none against and 8 abstentions.
4 A/RES/2645 (XXV) 30 November 1970. The Resolution was approved by the United Nations General Assembly on 25 November 1970 by a vote of 105 in favour, none against, and 8 abstentions.
5 S/RES/286 (1976) 9 September 1970.
6 A/RES/3034 (XXVII), 18 December 1972.
7 *Ibid.*
8 *Ibid.*
9 A/RES/31/103, 21 January 1977.
10 A/RES/34/145, 22 January 1980.
11 *Ibid.*
12 A/RES/40/61, 14 January 1986. United Nations Resolutions, (Dusan. J. Djonovich ed., 7th Series), volume XXIV, 1985–1986 at 507.
13 *Ibid.*
14 S/RES/579 (1985), 18 December 1985.
15 A/RES/42/159, 7 December 1987.
16 *Ibid.*
17 A/RES/44/29, 4 December 1989.
18 *Id.* Clause 9.
19 A/RES/46/51, 9 December 1991, Clauses 1 and 8.
20 A/RES/48/122, 20 December 1993, Clause 2.
21 Opened for signature at Geneva on 16 November 1937. For the test see Hudson (1941), *International Legislation*, U.N., New York, vol. VII, p. 862; UN Doc A/C.6/418 Annex 1, p. 1 [hereinafter 1937 UN Convention].
22 McWhinney, E. (1987), *Aerial Piracy and International Terrorism, The Illegal Diversion of Aircraft and International Law*, (2nd revised ed.), p. 128; Dobbs Ferry, NY, Oceana Publications, see also, *American Journal of International Law*, vol. 68, (1974), p. 69.
23 McWhinney (1987), *ibid.*, at p. 129.
24 *Convention on International Civil Aviation*, opened for signature at Chicago on 7

December 1944, entered into force on 4 April 1947. ICAO Doc, 7300/6, [hereinafter Chicago Convention of 1944].

25 *Ibid.*

26 McWhinney (1987), *supra* note 22, at 131.

27 Report of the *Ad Hoc* Group of Experts – Unlawful Interference, Montreal, ICAO Doc. AH-UI/2, 14–18 July, 1986.

28 Art. 3(a) of Chicago Convention of 1944, *supra*.

29 *Ibid.*, Art. 3(a).

30 Milde, M. (1986), 'Interception of Civil Aviation vs. Misuse of Civil Aviation (Background of Amendment 27 to Annex 2)', *Annals Air and Space Law*, vol. XI, p. 122.

31 Lauterpacht, H. (1950), *International Law and Human Rights*, Cambridge University Press, p. 149.

32 Vlasic, I.A. (1982), *Casebook on International Air Law*, McGill, Montreal, p. 161.

33 Art. 33 of the UN Charter.

34 Kunz, J.L. (1948), 'The Inter-American Treaty of Reciprocal Assistance', *American Journal of International Law*, vol. 42, pp. 111, 115.

35 Vlasic (1982), *supra*, note 32, at 275.

36 Cited in Oppenheim (1955), *International Law*, (8th ed.), vol. 1, Cambridge University Press at 609.

37 The Geneva Convention was opened for signature at Geneva on 16 November 1937. See Hudson, *op. cit.*, vol. VII at 862, U.N. Doc. A/C.6/418, Annex 1, at 1.

38 League of Nations (1934), *Official Journal*, at 1839.

39 Reiff, H. (1959), *The United States and the Treaty Law of the Sea*, University of Minnesota Press, at 86.

40 Feller, S.Z. (1972), 'Comment on Criminal Jurisdiction over Aircraft Hijacking', *Israel Law Review*, vol. 7, at 212.

41 *Ibid.*

42 Interpol had submitted to the Legal Committee of ICAO in 1977 that out of recorded hijackings up to that year, the percentage of instances of hijackings which were motivated politically was 6.2 at a ratio of 64:4. See ICAO Doc. 8877-LC/161 at 132.

43 Shubber, S. (1973), *Jurisdiction Over Crimes on Board Aircraft*, Dordrecht, M. Nijhoff, at 226.

44 'Aircraft Hijacking', *Harvard International Law Journal*, vol. 12, 1971, at 65.

45 Van Panhuys, H.F. (1970), 'Aircraft Hijacking and International Law', *Columbia Journal of Transnational Law*, vol. 9, at 13.

46 This Convention was opened for signature at Geneva on 16 November 1937. See Hudson, *op. cit.*, vol. VII at 862. See also U.N Doc, A/C.6/418, Annex 1 at 1.

47 See Sarkar, A.K. (1972), 'International Air Law and Safety of Civil Aviation', *Indian Journal of International Law* vol. 12, at 200.

48 See *International Legal Materials* 1963, (II) at 1042.

49 See Boyle, R.P. (1964), 'The Tokyo Convention on Offenses and Certain Other Acts Committed on Board Aircraft', *Journal of Air Law & Comm.* vol. 30 at 305–328, for a detailed analysis of the Tokyo Convention.

50 Report of the Sub-Committee, LC/SC 'Legal Status', WD No. 23, 10 October 1956.

51 Boyle (1969), *supra*, note 49 at 320.

52 *Id.*, at 321.

53 Boyle, R.P. (1969), 'International Action to Combat Aircraft Hijacking', *Lawyers of the Americas*, Denver, Colorado, at 463.

54 *Id.*, at 463.

55 Abramovsky, A. (1974), 'The Hague Convention', *Columbia Journal of Transnational Law*, vol. 3(3), at 389.
56 Boyle (1964), *supra*, note 49, *loq. cit*.
57 Ibid., at 329.
58 Evans, A.E. (1969), 'Hijacking: Its Cause and Cure', *The American Journal of International Law*, vol. 63, at 708.
59 Boyle (1964), *supra*, note 49 at 333.
60 Ibid., at 331.
61 *Id.* at 340.
62 *Ibid.*
63 See Articles 8 and 9 of the Tokyo Convention.
64 See Articles 12 and 13 of the Tokyo Convention.
65 Mendelsohn, A.I. (1968), 'In-Flight Crime, The International and Domestic Picture under the Tokyo Convention', *Virginia Law Review*, vol. 53 at 515.
66 *Id.*, 514.
67 Chung, D.Y. (1976), *Some Legal Aspects of Aircraft Hijacking in International Law*, Frost, V.A., at 150.
68 Boyle, *supra*, note 49, at 320.
69 Tokyo Convention, Article 13 (1).
70 Ibid., Article 13 (5).
71 Ibid., Article 13 (2).
72 Ibid., Article 1 (4).
73 Ibid., Civil Aviation Act 1982, Section 92.
74 Ibid., Article 1 (3).
75 Ibid., Article 6 (2).
76 For a discussion of this issue see Margo, R.D. (1987) *Aviation Insurance*, (2nd. ed.), London, Butterworths, at p. 154 and McNair, at p. 367. The editors of the fourth edition of *Shawcross and Beaumont* (1991), London, Butterworths, *Air Law*, consider that there is now no doubt that the 'meaning, as suggested by the natural and ordinary meaning of the words used', that is, 'the period between starting to accelerate down the runway and turning off it after landing is the correct one' (although on many occasions pilots would consider that their landing run had been completed long before taxiing to the turning off point). See Shawcross and Beaumont (1991), para. VIII (2), note (3).
77 Tokyo Convention, Article 16 (2).
78 Air Navigation Order 1989, SI 1989 No. 2004 – Article 52.
79 IATA General Conditions of Carriage/passenger and baggage/March 1988 – Article VIII.
80 Feller, S.Z. (1972), 'Comment on Criminal Jurisdiction over Aircraft hijacking', *Israel Law Review*, vol. 7, at 214.
81 Chung *supra*, note 67 at 643.
82 ICAO Doc. 9050 LC/169-2 at 72.
83 Mankiewicz, R.H. (1971), 'The 1970 Hague Convention', *Journal Air Law and Comm.* vol. 37, No. 2, at 201.
84 Ibid., at 203.
85 Boyle, *supra*, note 49, at 473.
86 'Legislation', *New Zealand Law Review*, vol. 5, April 1973 at 307.
87 Shubber, S. (1973), 'Aircraft Hijacking Under the Hague Convention', *ICLQ*, vol. 22, at 725.
88 See Mankiewicz, *supra*, note 83 at 206.
89 Abramovsky, A. (1975), 'The Montreal Convention', *Columbia Journal of International Law*, vol. 14 (2), at 278.
90 Montreal Convention, Article 2(b).

91 Fitzgerald, G.F. (1971), 'Toward Legal Suppression of Acts Against Civil Aviation', *International Conciliation*, November 1971, no. 585 at 71.
92 *Id.*, at 67.
93 *Id.*, 68.
94 *Ibid.*
95 *Ibid.*
96 *Ibid.*
97 *Id.*, at 70.
98 Legal Committee, 18th Session, London 29 September–22 October, vol. 1, Minutes, See ICAO Doc 8936 LC/164-1 at 39.
99 See Horlick, G.N. (1973), *International Response*, Martins Nijhoff, Dordrecht, at 176.
100 Fitzgerald, G.F. (1974), *International Terrorism and Civil Aviation*, Unpublished Speech given to the Third Annual Conference of the Canadian Council of International Law, 2 October 1974.
101 Hague Convention of 1970.
102 Fitzgerald *supra* note 100, at 73.
103 *Id.*, at 75.
104 Costello, D. (1975), 'International Terrorism and the Development of the Principle Aut Dedere Aut Judicare', *Journal Int. Law & Comm.* 11-11, at 488.
105 Abramovsky, A. (1975), 'Multilateral Convention for the Suppression of Unlawful Seizure and Interference with Aircraft, Part II of the Montreal Convention', *Columbia J. of Tr. L.*, vol. 14, at 300.
106 See ICAO Doc. A31-WP/26, LE/2, 4/7/95, at 11.
107 *Ibid.*
108 Fingerman, M.E. (1980), 'Skyjacking and the Bonn Declaration of 1978: Sanctions Applicable to Recalcitrant Nations', *California Western International Law Journal*, vol. 10, at 142.
109 ICAO Doc. 9050-LC/169-1 at 41.
110 ICAO Doc. 9050-LC/169-1 at 10.
111 *Id.*, at 41.
112 Brosche (1974), 'The Arab Oil Embargo and the United States Pressures Against Chile', 7 Case West. Res. *Journal of International Law*, vol. 3 at 2.
113 Fingerman (1980), *op. cit.*, at 144.
114 ICAO Doc. 9050-LC/169-2 at 42.
115 ICAO Doc. 8936-LC/164-1 at 216.
116 ICAO Doc. 9050-LC/169-2, *loc. cit.*
117 Schwenk, W. (1980) *The Bonn Declaration on Hijacking*, Kluwer, Dordrecht, at 317.
118 Chicago Convention, Article 4.
119 Id., Article 22.
120 ICAO Doc. 8936-LC/164-1 at 228.
121 ICAO Doc. 9050-LC/169-1 at 39.
122 ICAO Doc. 9571.
123 For the thorough analysis of the history of the Convention see: Milde, M. (1990), 'Draft Convention on the Marking of Explosives', *Annals of Air and Space Law*, vol. XV, pp. 155–179.
124 United Nations, Security Council, SC/RES/635 (1989).
125 Doc. 9551, A27-RES.
126 Resolution 44/29 of 13 December 1989.
127 C-DEC 127/20.
128 AH-DE/3, Report, Restricted.
129 The last preambular clause to the Convention explicitly confirms this by stating: 'Noting with satisfaction the role played by the Council of the

International Civil Aviation Organization in the preparation of the Convention as well as its willingness to assume functions related to its implementation' – See ICAO Doc. 9571.

130 Superfluous, because the Technical Annex to the Convention provides in: PART 1: DESCRIPTION OF EXPLOSIVES, a detailed definition of Plastic Explosives.

131 Duly authorized military devices refers to: devices such as shells, bombs, projectiles, mines, missiles, rockets, shaped charges, grenades etc.

132 C-WP/9209, Restricted.

133 The *Ad Hoc* Group of Specialists concluded after its 4th meeting, that all four additives which had been selected earlier, should be included in the Technical Annex. As the compounds meet the same criteria in respect of detectability and usability, their mutual inclusion may offer producer states some flexibility in selecting a particular additive.

134 The Conference found an analogy with Article 56 of the Chicago Convention which deals with the composition of the Air Navigation Commission – the most important advisory body to the ICAO Council. Its present membership is limited to 15, but a decision was taken by the 27th ICAO Assembly to amend Article 56 in order to increase its membership to 19. The amendment will require 108 ratifications for its entry into force.

135 Proposals by several delegations to introduce in the Convention, *expressis verbis*, the possibility to amend the Convention itself were decided against by the Conference in the understanding that the main body of the Convention could be amended in the manner provided for and codified in the Vienna Convention on the Law of Treaties.

136 An important decision. The effective detection of marked plastic explosives is of course as important as the marking itself, as the one would be completely useless without the other. As civil aviation security is by definition a global concept, mutual assistance and cooperation is a must.

137 Final Act of the International Conference on Air Law held under the auspices of the International Civil Aviation Organization in February–March 1991. Adopted by the Conference on 1 March 1991.

5 The Illicit Transport of Narcotic Drugs by Air and Narco-terrorism

Introduction

Throughout known history, human society has used substances to alter moods and alleviate physical and mental suffering. These substances, although proving indispensable for the alleviation of pain and suffering, also proved to be addictive and destructive when misused or abused. As a result, early society made rules which allocate the use of these substances for medicinal or religious purposes and entrusted them to priests, leaders and doctors.[1]

The abuse of drugs has been proliferating as a corrosion of social intercourse from the mid-19th century due to the increased availability of products, the expansion of connections, the necessities brought about by changing socio-economic factors, rapid urbanization and changes in attitudes and values. These factors have contributed to a rapid increase in criminality in human society, leading to the exploitation of human society by insidious criminal elements.

As a response to this problem, global control mechanisms have been introduced by the international community – one of which is a regulatory system for the control of illicit transport of narcotic drugs by air. Not only does illicit transportation of narcotics by air *per se* constitute an offence, but it also leads to other criminal acts related to terrorism such as the destruction of airports by those involved in the carriage of narcotic drugs by air, destruction of property and aircraft resulting from attempts to transport narcotic drugs and the threats posed to traffic installations. This chapter will discuss the enormity of the problem, analyse the evolution of the regulatory process related thereto, and evaluate its success.

Historical Facts

The need for an international drug control system was first felt in 1909 when representatives of 13 states met in Shanghai to discuss the proliferation of instances relating to the transportation of narcotics for non-medical consumption. Furthermore, the conference was considered necessary, as by the end of the 19th century, opium smoking had become rampant in China, affecting a third of the adult male population. As early as 1729, Emperor Yong Cheng forbade opium smoking in China, which resulted in a decrease in trafficking. However, this attempt was to little avail, as opium was being smuggled at that time to China through India by the Portuguese and later by the English. The amount of opium that had been smuggled into China had increased from 13 metric tonnes in 1729 to 64 metric tonnes in 1767. During the decade 1820–1830 the quantity of drugs brought into China had taken an upward turn to 2 500 metric tonnes. As a result, China had 20 million opium smokers in 1838. By 1773 the East India Company of England had established a monopoly in the drug trade, thus inaugurating the first recorded enterprise involved in legal drug trafficking on a large scale.[2]

The Opium Wars

With the failure of all diplomatic efforts to curb the flow of opium into China, the Chinese authorities decided to act swiftly. They ordered all foreign merchants to surrender their stocks of opium for destruction. As a result, in excess of 1 400 metric tonnes belonging to the British were seized and thrown into the river at Canton. The Chinese act was considered to be nothing short of treason by the British Mission and on 4 April 1840 England declared war against China. This war is now known as the First Opium War. The Chinese were defeated and so were their efforts to control the abuse and trafficking of opium. As a result of the (peace) Treaty of Nanking signed on 29 August 1842, the British received, *inter alia*, Hong Kong, which they developed as a commercial centre and made the best use of its location in importing opium from India and Iran and exporting it not only to China, but also to Japan, Macao, the Philippines, Indonesia, Australia, Peru, Chile, USA, Canada, England and France.

The First Opium War gave further impetus to the opium trade. Over 3 300 metric tonnes were imported from India into China in 1850 and nearly 5 000 metric tonnes in 1855. The Chinese efforts to stem the tide once again ended in failure. The British and the French defeated them in the Second Opium War (1856–1858) and forced them to sign the Treaty of Tientsin which legalized the opium trade on payment of customs duty (30 teals per picul);[3] the Chefoo Convention (1876) further liberalized the trade. Arguably, this attempt at liberalization was probably the first example of a country actually legalizing drug trafficking, and earning revenue by way of import duties. However, legalization did not stabilize the quantity of opium imported into China let alone reduce it, as, by 1880, the amount of opium imported into China had risen to over 6 000 metic tonnes. In addition, the political and administrative situation within China had deteriorated. The hold of central authority had weakened and the feudal and military lords became powerful in different regions. Within their strongholds they promoted the cultivation of the opium poppy as a means of amassing wealth. Their policy made China the biggest opium producing country in the world. In the four years 1905 to 1908, they produced in excess of 100 000 metric tonnes of opium (23 500 000 kg were produced in 1905, 35 497 360 kg in 1906, 20 685 500 kg in 1907 and 22 953 125 kg in 1908).

This amount, combined with the quantities imported from India and Iran (about 3 000 metric tonnes a year) virtually converted China into a country of opium smokers. Villagers, the bourgeois of the cities, coolies, shopkeepers, businessmen, civil servants, soldiers, palace eunuchs, imperial mistresses, men, women and children of all ages and segments of society fell to the fatal charm of the bamboo pipe.

The Shanghai Commission

The period which followed can now be recognized as one in which a conscious effort was made towards the regulation of opium trafficking. What the governments had failed to accomplish was achieved by a public-spirited group of doctors, intellectuals, churchmen and parliamentarians. In England these professionals belonged to the Anti-Opium League and through its organ 'The Friend of China', they raised their voices against the 'immoral nature of the opium trade' and drew public attention to the ravages caused by opium smoking in China and elsewhere. The anti-opium movement influenced, to some extent, the Liberal Party Government which came to power in England in 1906 and a year later, arranged with China some measures aimed at the gradual reduction of the opium trade from India to China.

China was not the only country with a drug addiction problem. The United States also felt considerably concerned since in its colony of the Philippines, annexed in 1898, opium smoking was rampant. There were also 118 000 Americans of Chinese origin living in the United States at that time, almost half of whom were allegedly opium smokers. Accordingly, a committee was set up to study, in depth, the problem of opium smoking in the Philippines. In pursuit of its work this committee visited some other countries of the Far East and made useful observations.

One of its members, the Reverend Charles H. Brent, American Episcopal Bishop of the Philippines, was particularly touched by the extensive misery caused by opium smoking. He was also one of the first who recognized the international nature of this problem. In July 1906, he addressed a letter to President Theodore Roosevelt, urging him to convene a diplomatic international meeting to discuss measures towards solving the problem of opium smoking and trade. This idea was well received and President Roosevelt proposed a meeting which was finally held at the Palace Hotel in Shanghai in February 1909. This meeting was attended by the representatives of 13 countries: Germany, Austria-Hungary, China, the United States, France, the United Kingdom, Italy, Japan, the Netherlands, Iran, Portugal, Russia and Siam. Turkey, an important opium-producing country at the time, was invited but did not attend the meeting.

The meeting became known as the Shanghai Opium Commission. Its president observed that, it devolved upon him to pronounce with emphasis that the meeting was in fact a commission. Although the idea of a conference had been suggested, it had seemed wise to choose this particular form of action since, for that time at any rate, the members of the commission had not been sufficiently well informed, and not sufficiently unanimous in their attitude, to have a conference with any great hope of immediate success. It is interesting to speculate whether the comment of the president of the commission, that its members were not well enough informed, is applicable in the present day context as well.

The commission passed nine resolutions. Although these resolutions today may seem to be nothing more than pious wishes, in 1909 they represented a monumental achievement. Through them, the Opium Commission, comprising representatives of the 13 countries, recognized the right of China to eradicate the abuse and production of opium. They also recommended the immediate closure of smoking dens, and the adoption of draconian measures for controlling production, sale and distribution of opium and its derivatives at national level. In addition, the commission identified the need for adopting reasonable measures in order to prevent the shipping of opium to the countries which had prohibited its importation.

The Reverend Brent represented the United States and also chaired the commission. Although he, along with the Chinese delegate, sought a more definite and drastic action against the abuse and trafficking of opium, the economic interests of some of the participating countries came into conflict with these sentiments and the final resolutions emerged in a rather diluted form.

Although prior to this, China had been badly affected by drug problems, the founding of the People's Republic of China in 1949 marked the beginning of efforts to eliminate drugs completely. The government adopted a radical policy and issued a series of laws and provisions to combat drug abuse. The 'Order on the Restriction of Opium Addiction', adopted by the State Council in 1950, stipulated that cultivation of the opium poppy was forbidden, and that activities such as smuggling, producing and trafficking in drugs would thenceforth be sanctioned by law. Offenders were to be severely punished; anyone in possession of opium-derived drugs had to surrender them to the authorities within a certain time and cease smoking immediately. Soon after the publication of that order, an operation was launched to counter the cultivation of opium poppies and the sale and consumption of opium; by 1952 the scourge had been eradicated. These decisions, which have been applied to the letter ever since, are widely supported by the Chinese people and have been hailed by the international mass media. However, since the adoption of China's 'open-door' policy, traffickers infiltrated China and used the country as a base for drugs in transit to other countries and other regions. To deal with this situation, the Chinese police adopted stringent measures against trafficking activities in the border regions. Careful and thorough investigations enabled the Chinese to clear up cases of trafficking from outside China, and a significant quantity of opium had been seized at the border by 1985.

Between 1981 and 1986, 92 kg of heroin and 223 kg of opium were seized in China; 20 cases involving heroin smuggled into mainland China were solved; and 43 foreign traffickers were arrested. In 1986, two foreign nationals and a resident of Hong Kong were sentenced to death for drug trafficking.

China has shared information with South-East Asian countries and has improved its surveillance and detection equipment at customs and police posts along its frontiers. It has also sent drug law enforcement officers from the Chinese NCB to the United States for training at the Drug Enforcement Administration. In April 1986, two drugs seminars, attended by over 200 police officers, were organized in Beijing with the help of the French police. Representatives were also sent to international meetings on drug law enforcement, and experts from the United Nations Narcotics Control Board and Division of Narcotic Drugs were invited to China to talk on international drug trafficking trends and the countermeasures to be taken. China proposed several guidelines on arrests of unlawful drug trafficking; based on China's long-standing experience of drug prohibition, and in view of the different tactics used in China and throughout at that time.

It was submitted that drug problems would never be finally solved merely by controlling drug trafficking. The real solution was a three-pronged attack aimed at production, traffic and consumption. The existence of a demand for drugs naturally gives rise to traffic which, in turn, stimulates production, thus creating a vicious circle. It was felt that drug problems could not be eradicated simply by breaking one of the links in the chain. Different countries would be confronted with different aspects of the problem (production, consumption, trafficking) while some countries had to deal with all three aspects. Therefore, the measures applied must be appropriate to each country's particular situation. Also, producing countries should concentrate mainly on finding alternatives to drug cultivation, endeavouring to limit production to within legal requirements. In the opium poppy-producing regions, growers should be encouraged to turn to other substitute crops, while being guaranteed an income high enough for their daily needs. In countries where drug addiction is the main problem it was felt that the emphasis should be placed on treatment and awareness programmes for young addicts, and on the adoption of penal countermeasures aimed at the total suppression of drug consumption. Particular importance should be attached to examining the reasons for the increased addiction among young people and, once the causes have been determined, to finding appropriate solutions. One of the most important proposals was that countries affected by drugs being taken through in transit should adopt strict legal measures. Moreover, it was felt that there should also be more stringent control, detection and interception at ports and at border posts.

One of the significant observations was that the drug problem had such vast social ramifications and is so complex that it could not be dealt with by the police alone. Governments had to establish and mobilize the appropriate judicial and administrative departments and health and information services, each of which had its own part to play in waging a major campaign against drug traffic, abuse, production and cultivation. It was scarcely possible to solve the problem in any other way.

Also, since drug problems affect so many countries, far-reaching international cooperation was essential, and the following international guidelines were recommended:

- Interpol should cooperate closely with other international organizations, such as the United Nations Division of Narcotic Drugs and Commission on Narcotic Drugs, on the preparation and implementation of joint projects;
- Interpol member states should unite in their efforts. In particular, neighbouring countries should share information, assist one another and fight together against the common enemy. As far as China was concerned, cooperation with Interpol Bangkok, Hong Kong and other NCBs was considered to be excellent;

- The General Secretariat's Drugs' Sub-division should serve as the link between member countries. It should carefully study the characteristics and trends of international drug-related crime and disseminate information to members immediately. The Sub-division should also organize the sharing of information concerning specific investigations and provide any necessary assistance with coordination. Finally, it should ensure that different countries' experiences of drug detection methods are available to all.

Recent World Trends in Domestic Drug Traffic

During the 1994–1995 period, the production of heroin, cocaine, cannabis and psychotropic substances was at a record high. The drug trade continued to be a profitable international business in which traffickers aggressively developed new markets for their products.

Increased shipments of morphine and heroin were transported to Europe from source countries in South-West Asia via land and sea routes, while South-East Asian heroin continued to dominate the North American airports. Increased availability of cocaine was evident throughout 1994, with record seizures being effected by drug law enforcement agencies against efforts by South, Central, and North American cartels to transit cocaine into the West European market, and West African nationals emerged as cocaine couriers from South America to Europe via West African airports. Cannabis supplies were in abundance in numerous countries. Multi-tonne shipments of cannabis products were transported between continents in merchant vessels and inside container trucks intermingled with legitimate cargo. The popularity of cannabis coupled with enormous profits has encouraged entrepreneurs to embark on new techniques of cultivation, especially in the United States and the Netherlands.

In recent times, large quantities of amphetamine have been seized in several countries. Europe, the Netherlands and Poland continue to be source countries for the European market. As in the past, methamphetamine continues to be manufactured in clandestine laboratories in the United States. In African countries the abuse of stimulants continues to be a major problem. There is large-scale smuggling of methaqualone from India to African countries and Indian law enforcement agencies have made record seizures at exit ports. In the Asia/Pacific region, methamphetamine abuse is a major concern to the Japanese authorities. In other countries – South Korea, Thailand, the Philippines and Australia – there are regular seizures of various psychotropic substances, indicating increasing abuse in the entire region.

During 1995, the Near-East, South-West Asia, South-East Asia, Mexico and Colombia remained the principal regions of illicit poppy cultivation. In spite of eradication and crop substitution programmes carried out in these regions, the total illegal production of opium is estimated to exceed 4 000 tonnes . There was a regular transnational opium trade between Afghanistan and Iran in South-West Asia and between China and Myanmar in the South-East Asian region. There were increasing reports of the conversion of opium into morphine and heroin in clandestine laboratories in and around the production areas. The principal source and transit countries reporting significant opium seizures were: Iran (38 tons), Pakistan (3.4 tonnes), India (2 tonnes), China (3 tonnes), Myanmar (2.2 tonnes), Thailand (1.1 tonne) and Vietnam (1 tonne). In the western hemisphere, Mexico and Colombia were the principal producers of opium. The Mexican authorities estimate the annual production at 40 tonnes. Colombia's opium production for 1992 was estimated at 200 tonnes.

Illicit traffic in morphine base escalated during 1994–1995. Information received by Interpol indicates that enormous quantities of morphine base, produced in clandestine laboratories in the Afghanistan/Pakistan border region, were transported overland through Iran/Turkey and by sea from the Pakistan coast via the Suez Canal to Europe. The Iranian authorities intercepted over 7 tonnes of morphine base along the country's eastern borders with Afghanistan/Pakistan and on its western border with Turkey. The Turkish authorities made two major seizures of morphine base totalling 3.5 tonnes. They seized 1.5 tonnes of morphine base on the Turkish/Georgian border, an indication that drug traffickers are using this route through the Central Asian Republics to transport morphine base to Europe. In addition, the Turkish authorities intercepted a merchant vessel in the Mediterranean Sea transporting 2 tonnes of morphine base which originated in Pakistan. These seizures are evidence that increased quantities of morphine base are being transported to Europe, presumably for conversion into heroin in clandestine laboratories.

Also during this period there was a significant increase in heroin production and its transnational transportation in spite of improved international law enforcement cooperation. South-West Asian heroin production and traffic were more prevalent than in previous years. This was ostensibly to meet the great demand by consumers in South-West Asia as well as in Europe and North America.

The heroin trail from South-West Asia to the Western European market starts at the Afghanistan/Pakistan border and transits through Iran, entering collection centres in South-East Turkey for onward shipment to Istanbul. It is estimated that during 1994, between 70 per cent and 80 per cent of the 7 tonnes of heroin seized in Europe was transported along the Balkan Route via Turkey. The heroin was mostly hidden in secret compartments in TIR (international road transport) trucks, buses or private cars from Turkey to seven main recipient countries: Germany, Italy, the Netherlands, Belgium, Spain, France and the United Kingdom. The war in Bosnia disrupted the traditional Balkan route, and drug trafficking groups are now transporting the drug in vehicles north through Hungary and the Czech Republic to Germany for onward shipment to other parts of Europe, and via Greek ports where the drug, concealed inside TIR trucks, is ferried across to Italian ports.

The 'opening up' of Central and Eastern European countries has proved advantageous to drug trafficking organizations who are utilizing the countries in the region for storage and transit. Turkish crime syndicates continue to be active transporting heroin and working in close collaboration with organized crime groups based in several European countries.

With the bulk of the heroin from South-West Asia transiting along the Balkan route to Europe, there were fewer heroin seizures at European airports. Asian and African nationals were among the main groups arrested at European airports when seizures did occur.

In the Near-East, Lebanon remained a major source country for illicit narcotics despite efforts in the spring of 1992 by the Lebanese and Syrian security forces to eradicate poppy and cannabis cultivation at some sites in the Bekaa Valley. Harsh winter weather probably destroyed much of the 1992 crop and the eradication campaign destroyed what remained. Intelligence received indicates that the Bekaa Valley continued to be the site of many operational hashish- and heroin-processing laboratories. Lebanese trafficking groups have also forced alliances with South American traffickers, resulting in heroin–cocaine exchanges and a proliferation of cocaine-processing laboratories in Lebanon. Much of the cocaine appears to be destined for the Middle East and European markets. During 1992, officials seized heroin, cocaine and hashish at Beirut International Airport as well as at sites in the Bekaa Valley.

In South-East Asia, the heroin scene has not undergone any dramatic change over the past few years. Heroin processing has continued unabated in the border areas of Thailand, Myanmar and Laos, popularly known as the Golden Triangle. Thailand, with its geographical location, modern transportation, developed coastline and well-connected air and sea ports at Bangkok, remains the principal transit country for these operations. Thailand also continues to be the main conduit for heroin shipments from the region to the international market. During 1994, the Thai authorities seized a total of 379 kg of heroin at Bangkok Airport, mainly found in the possession of East Asian and African nationals, travelling to Africa, Europe and North America.

In a developing trend, China emerged as an alternative route for opium and heroin smuggled from Myanmar to Hong Kong. China's Yunnan Province is at the heart of the trafficking route. During 1994, the Chinese authorities seized 4 tonnes of heroin, the bulk of it in Yunnan Province. Because of its strategically located border in close proximity to mainland China, Hong Kong continues to be a staging area in the Far East region. China–Taiwan emerged as a major transit area for heroin shipments bound for North America. Based on reports received from US drug law enforcement agencies, approximately 56 per cent of the heroin seized in the United States originated from South-East Asia. Countries such as Malaysia, Singapore, the Philippines and Indonesia, where there is domestic heroin consumption, are also utilized as transit countries. Australia is also a major recipient of South-East Asian heroin where organized criminal groups (of Chinese descent) play a major role in the heroin trade.

North America remains the principal heroin market in the world. As noted above, heroin in the United States arrives mainly from South-East Asian countries which have close-knit networks in the United States. Mexican heroin traffic to the United States continues to be controlled by Mexican criminal groups. Colombian heroin is increasingly transported by Colombian nationals using commercial airlines that fly to New York and Miami. Intelligence reports also suggest that South American cocaine cartels may be using existing cocaine-smuggling networks to facilitate the shipment of Colombian heroin to North America and Europe.

According to drug seizure information reported to Interpol, four times as much cocaine as heroin was seized world-wide during 1992. While much of this increased activity can be attributed to aggressive anti-drug efforts, it is also the result of record high levels of cocaine production. Although there is no adequate means to measure the magnitude of the drug problem, a few figures may illustrate the possible seriousness of the threat. According to international sources, during 1994 400 metric tonnes of cocaine were seized globally whereas the potential maximum coca yield was 1 000–2 000 metric tonnes.

Nearly two-thirds of the world's supply of cocaine comes from coca grown in Peru. Estimates of Peru's coca cultivation in 1992 are reported to range from 129 000 hectares to as high as 350 000 hectares. Although there is no consensus on the amount of coca grown in Peru, officials agree that coca cultivation is rising. While the government of Peru pursued a comprehensive programme to eliminate cocaine production and provide alternative development, its efforts are limited by insurgent activity in coca-producing regions.

Colombia is the world's leading supplier of cocaine HCL. Most of the cocaine base is imported from Peru and Bolivia and processed into cocaine by Colombian traffickers. Official Colombian statistics indicate that cocaine HCL seizures dropped to 32 metric tonnes from approximately 77 metric tonnes last year. This was largely the result of shifting enforcement resources to the destruction of the country's rapidly expanding opium poppy crop.

Bolivia is a major producer of coca leaf and coca derivatives. It is the world's second largest producer of coca leaf and the second largest producer of cocaine HCL. The Chaparer is Bolivia's primary coca leaf production region. With the success of a number of interdiction operations, most notably the 'Ghost Zone', traffickers have increased their activities in the Yungas region of Bolivia.

Brazil and Venezuela are major hubs for cocaine trafficking activities. Brazil is a significant transit country for cocaine destined for the United States and Europe and a major producer of precursor and essential chemicals. Venezuela is a transit country for Colombian cocaine. Information received by Interpol indicates that seizures abroad of drugs transhipped through Venezuela totalled more than 30 metric tonnes.

North America, specifically the United States, remains the principal market for cocaine. United States agencies seized approximately 120 tonnes of cocaine during 1992. Successful law enforcement operations against Cali Cartel bases, combined with the capture or surrender of several cartel leaders, disrupted the flow of cocaine which led to a sharp price increase in the United States during the second quarter of 1994. Colombian groups continued to dominate the traffic and are expected to further consolidate their control. Cocaine is transported to the United States primarily by vessel along the south-eastern seaboard, by aircraft using international air corridors over Cuba, and land routes through Mexico. During 1992, the Mexican authorities seized almost 40 tonnes of South American cocaine destined for the United States.

Canada reported record seizures of cocaine in 1992. South American cocaine cartels view Canada both as a transit point for cocaine bound for the United States and as a new market. One of the most striking features in the area of Canadian-related cocaine seizures is the increase in the number of seizures effected by foreign countries of cocaine destined for the Canadian market.

Central America and the Caribbean observed an increase in cocaine trafficking by private aircraft and private and commercial vessels. While sizeable quantities of cocaine are airdropped in the Caribbean to waiting vessels, drug traffickers are making greater use of commercial maritime vessels to transport cocaine concealed within containerized cargo. Pleasure yachts and fishing boats in the Atlantic and Caribbean seas are also attractive to drug traffickers as they provide excellent cover for their illicit activities.

Europe is being flooded with cocaine in an effort to develop a market to compensate for lower profits derived from the United States. During 1994 European law enforcement agencies seized 19 tonnes of cocaine, with record seizures reported in France, Portugal, Spain and the United Kingdom. The importation of cocaine to Europe is predominantly controlled by the Cali Cartel. While smaller in size than the more notorious Medellin Cartel, the Cali-based group has benefited from maintaining a low profile. South American cocaine cartels have forged alliances with organized crime groups in Europe, such as Galician smugglers in Spain and the Mafia in Italy, to transport cocaine to Europe.

Large shipments of cocaine, smuggled by sea from Colombia or Venezuela, often transit via the Canary Islands, the Azores, Cape Verde or Madeira, all situated in strategic locations on the North Atlantic route from South America to Western Europe. Large ports such as Rotterdam and Rostock are being used by drug traffickers to convey shipments of drugs inside legitimate cargo being sent to Europe.

An alarming trend is the increase in the number of cocaine-processing laboratories in Europe. Germany, Italy and Spain reported dismantling illicit laboratories in 1992. Both France and the United Kingdom reported seizing cocaine base transhipped through Brazil for conversion in cocaine-processing laboratories in Europe. Drug traffickers are taking full advantage of the revolutionary changes that are taking place throughout Europe from the collapse of communism to the emergence of a single European Market. South American cocaine cartels are specifically targeting Eastern Europe as a transhipment point.

Africa is a major transit region for cocaine intended for Europe. Africa's strategic location, coupled with the desperately low standards of living over much of the continent, create an ideal climate for drug trafficking. Nigeria is the focal point for cocaine trafficking in Africa. Cocaine comes to Nigeria from South America, primarily by commercial air routes from Rio de Janeiro, Brazil, to Lagos, Nigeria, for re-export to Europe. Nigerian and Ghanaian groups control drug trafficking activities. These groups continue to find new routes, methods and couriers to evade arrest and detection.

The Middle East is emerging as a transhipment point for cocaine destined for Europe and the United States. Lebanese traffickers are collaborating with South American traffickers resulting in heroin–cocaine exchanges and the proliferation of cocaine-processing laboratories in Lebanon. During 1994, the French authorities reported to Interpol the existence of a Lebanese-Brazilian cocaine connection based on several significant seizures involving Lebanese nationals and cocaine shipments confiscated in France.

Cocaine trafficking and consumption are growing problems in Australia. Information indicates that Australia is being targeted by South American cocaine trafficking organizations as a transit point for cocaine intended for the Asian market and also as a new market in itself. Japanese prosperity is attracting traffickers looking to expand their markets. The increase in recent years of travel by South American nationals to Japan, including known members of Colombian cartels, as well as the number of Japanese nationals arrested for cocaine trafficking, support this premise. With enormous profits to be accrued from the cocaine trade in Japan, the involvement of Japanese organized crime (Yakuza) in domestic cocaine trafficking is expected to increase.

Increased trafficking in crack cocaine is a growing concern to drug law enforcement agencies, with nearly every continent reporting seizures. During 1992, Côte d'Ivoire reported its first seizure of crack. Crack is readily available in large metropolitan areas throughout the United Kingdom, Canada and the United States. Distribution networks are believed to be supplied and controlled by Jamaican gangs.

During 1994, cannabis in its various forms was extensively cultivated and traded in various parts of the world. Cannabis reaps tremendous profits for the grower and trafficker, especially the indoor hydroponic operations which are gaining popularity in the West, notably the United States and the Netherlands. These operations reportedly produce four full growing cycles per year, quadrupling the potential of production by other traditional methods. These indoor operations can range from several plants grown in a closet to hundreds or thousands of plants grown in specially constructed subterranean sites capable of producing sinsemilla worth millions. A pound of sinsemilla is sold for US$3 000 to US$9 000.

Because of its weight, the bulk of cannabis is smuggled by land or by ship across continents and within them. Of the total seizures of this drug concerning Europe for the period under review, transport accounted for 65 per cent and freight for 28 per cent. In 1992, 15 African countries seized 112 tonnes (53 tonnes in 1991) of cannabis, including 50 tonnes in Morocco. In Europe, 402 tonnes were seized in 1992 compared to 221 tonnes last year. Spain seized 122 tonnes, the Netherlands 94 tonnes, the United Kingdom 49 tonnes and France 42 tonnes of cannabis. All these seizure figures are substantially higher than those for 1991. Other significant world-wide seizures were in Sri Lanka: 49 tonnes (10 tonnes in 1991); Pakistan: 188 tonnes; India: 60 tonnes (52 tonnes in 1991); Thailand: 126 tonnes (55 tonnes in 1991); Mexico: 19 tonnes; Lebanon: 20 tonnes; United States: 346 tonnes. In two other important producer countries, 11 601 412 million cannabis seedlings were eradicated in the Philippines, and over 800 hectares of cannabis were eradicated in Jamaica.

Some of the more significant world-wide seizures have included:

- 7 740 kg of cannabis in Barcelona, Spain, in March 1992. The drug had arrived by sea from Lebanon for Spain, hidden inside rubber wheels packed in sacks.
- 6 400 kg of cannabis in Istanbul in August 1992. It was concealed in a TIR truck using the Balkan Route for reaching various destinations in Western Europe including the Netherlands.
- 3 000 kg of cannabis resin originating from Afghanistan, in Sydney in August 1992. One yacht and a light private aircraft used in the smuggling were also seized.
- 4 040 kg of cannabis resin at the port of Casablanca, Morocco, in March 1992. It was hidden in a Volvo truck on its way to the Netherlands.
- 2 300 kg of cannabis in Maghria/Akid Lotfi, Algeria, in November 1992. It was hidden in a camping van and had been obtained in Morocco.
- 10 000 kg of cannabis resin in Dunkirk, France, in September 1992 from the ship 'Rossinant' loaded at the port of Jiwani, Pakistan.

According to data available at the Interpol General Secretariat for 1994, the largest quantities of cannabis seized in Europe in various forms originated in Morocco, Pakistan and Lebanon.

A total of 11 tonnes of cannabis was seized in Russia for the period between 1992–1994. Cannabis also grows wild in the five newly independent central Asian countries, which formerly made up part of the USSR. The strategic importance of this area in the context of cannabis traffic lies in its proximity to the well-recognized cannabis sources in South-West Asia on the one hand, and its geopolitical and ethnic proximity to countries such as Turkey, China, Afghanistan, Pakistan, etc. on the other hand. Trafficking organizations are already exploiting the location of these countries to move hashish in sizeable quantities to Russia and other Western destinations. This is confirmed by a record seizure of 14 tonnes of Afghan hashish destined for the Netherlands in February 1993, and another seizure of 13 tonnes in 1992 in Uzbekistan.

Unlike other drugs, psychotropic substances have no 'minimal criteria' concerning quantities when seizures are reported to the General Secretariat. Logically, it should follow that the General Secretariat's database for psychotropic substances should be an accurate reflection of what has occurred around the world as far as these substances are concerned. However, when the drug seizure report (DRST) database is compared with national statistics on illicit drug production, traffic and use, it is evident that the DRST database contains only a fraction of the total seizures made by individual states.

The overall picture shows that there were increases in the amounts of illicitly produced amphetamine and methamphetamine, LSD, MDA and its analogue MDMA. 1994 also saw the proliferation of a new MDA analogue, methylene dioxyethylamphetamine (MDEA) which was introduced in 1992. With the exception of methaqualone, the picture was much the same in 1992 for other stimulants, depressants and hallucinogens as it was in 1991. A greatly increased number of clandestine laboratories – 876 – were reportedly dismantled, the increase being caused largely as a result of the Polish authorities seizing 518 laboratories producing compote, a narcotic drug brewed from poppy straw.

Although no seizures of buprenorphine were reported during 1992 by the DRST, it is known that some European countries – the United Kingdom for example – have made some seizures. The same is true of South-East Asia. In its annual statistical return, New Zealand reported seizing 69 tablets of buprenorphine (Termgesic), together with small quantities of Paradeine and Doloxene. Thirteen countries reported seizing preparations containing codeine, morphine and pethidine during the 1992–1994 period.

Thirteen countries representing all regions of the world reported seizing 19 500 dosage units, 152 grams and 2 078 ml of methadone. The individual seizures were all of very small quantities, involving a very large number of offenders. European sources of the drug seemed to be mainly the Netherlands and Switzerland and, in South-East Asia, Thailand and Vietnam. The majority of seizures took place in Germany, Switzerland, Greece and Singapore.

According to information so far received, butalbital, a Schedule III barbiturate which can be used as both a hypnotic and a sedative, was seized in only one country: Jordan. In 1992 the authorities there removed over 35 000 dosage units from circulation in seven cases, all of which were said to be sourced to Syria. Four other countries reported seizing 77 400 other unidentified barbiturates, 5 434 of which were located in Greece and 71 290 in the United States. The United States authorities also seized 589 97 unidentified tranquillizers.

The large family of benzodiazepines was introduced as a 'safer' alternative to, for example, the barbiturates, as they have less potential for creating dependence. However, these drugs soon became popular on the illicit markets, particularly in West African countries. Diazepam, known most commonly as valium, was seized in 14 countries. Again in 1992, 710 422 dosage units were seized, including 575 910 in the United States, 62 641 in Côte d'Ivoire and 31 306 in Spain. Flunitrazepam (Rohypnol) proved to be the next most popular with 189 690 dosage units being seized, 170 317 of them in Lebanon.

Norway also made a large single seizure of 17 445 dosage units smuggled from Thailand in champagne bottles and cosmetic boxes.

There were also seizures of smaller quantities of alprazolam, clonazepam, flurazepam, cloraepam, midazolam, nitrazepam (70 188 dosage units in Indonesia), oxazepam, temazepam (12 238 dosage units in the United Kingdom) and triazolam, in addition to another 54 300 dosage units of unidentified benzodiazepines. Once again, no geographical location was left untouched by these drugs.

Secobarbital, another drug once very popular among the West African drug abuse population and replaced largely by the benzodiazepines, was seized in only three countries: Côte d'Ivoire (91 400), Sudan (1 038) and Saudi Arabia (1 361 776 dosage units). The tightening of controls by producing countries seems to have had a considerable effect on the availability of the drug.

During 1992 there were two reported seizures of phenobarbital made by the United Arab Emirates. One was an unknown quantity found with heroin smuggled from Pakistan, and the other was 100 kg sent by a British national working in a United Kingdom laboratory. The final destination of the two barrels in which it was concealed was given as Pakistan.

In December 1992, an international conference on the trafficking of methaqualone, a Schedule II central nervous system depressant, was jointly organized by the Indian authorities and the General Secretariat and held in New Delhi. A 'Methaqualone Overview' based on information gained from this meeting was published in 1993. During that year, India alone seized over 7.5 tonnes of methaqualone, the illicit production of which has had such a devastating effect on Eastern and Southern Africa that in some areas it has replaced local currencies.

During 1992 six African countries – Botswana, Kenya, Swaziland, Uganda, Zambia and Zimbabwe – seized approximately 1.66 million dosage units of methaqualone. Another 15 384 and 149 238 were seized respectively by Greece and the United States. South Africa, which had observer status at the New Delhi Meeting, informed delegates that authorities there had seized 2.8 million dosage units in 1992. The increase in the amount being produced, as indicated by seizure figures, has continued into 1993 and 1994 with Indian authorities removing 3 tonnes of methaqualone from the illicit trade in one single case. The drug is mostly produced illicitly in India, although there is also production in South Africa and its neighbouring countries.

Laboratories dismantled included 518 producing compote in Poland where 1 761 200 ml of compote were also seized. A methaqualone-producing laboratory was seized in Luxembourg, together with 35 kg of the finished drug, 50 kg of anthranilic acid and 90 litres of acetic anhydride. Interestingly, it was reported that the laboratory had been operating in an hotel room. The operator had been sending the drug to South Africa concealed in tins of 5 or 10 litre capacity.

World-wide seizures of illicitly produced amphetamine increased considerably in 1992 with 24 countries seizing a total of 1 571 kg. Judging by the large quantities seized in a number of countries, amphetamine abuse is a rapidly developing problem. The following 10 countries seized the amounts shown in brackets: the United Kingdom (601 kg), the Netherlands (267 kg), Sweden (119 kg), Germany (105 kg), Belgium (96 kg), Australia (90 kg), Denmark (73 kg), Hungary (54 kg), Spain (922 kg) and Nigeria (18 kg).

Nigeria was not the only African country to seize amphetamine. Six other African countries reported seizing a total of 304 387 dosage units, 250 313 of which were seized in Côte d'Ivoire. Eight other countries reported seizing 794 422 dosage units of amphetamine of which the United States and Lebanon seized 507 240 and 170 317 respectively. The source countries for amphetamine are the Netherlands, which is the major producer for European countries, together with Poland and the United Kingdom, Belgium, Denmark, Germany, Spain, Sweden, Australia and the United States, all of which in the main produce the drug for consumption within their own respective countries. In all, there were 36 amphetamine-producing laboratories dismantled world-wide.

The total picture for methamphetamine seizures is not as clear, as some of the reports have included ephedrine as part of the overall seizure figure, for example, China Taiwan with a total of 1 ton given as the combined figure. Japan seized 163 kg, China 576 kg, plus 10 laboratories and 2 779 kg of ephedrine, and the Philippines 129 kg, 12 kg of which was 'ice', the crystallized, more potent form of methamphetamine. The United States also reported one seizure of 12 kg of 'ice', together with 47.5 million dosage units of methamphetamine and the dismantling of 287 laboratories.

Norway seized 280 g of methamphetamine and while this figure may not seem important when compared with world-wide figures, what is significant is that 200 g of this drug was sourced to Russia and is the first of its kind recorded in Norway. Russia reported having seized only 12 kg 435 of methamphetamine; however, it is possible that with the availability of precursor chemicals in that country, the Norwegian experience may prove to be an insight into what other European countries may expect in the future.

Sweden dismantled one methamphetamine laboratory and the United Kingdom dismantled three laboratories. Taiwan and China are the two biggest sources for illicit methamphetamine in South-East Asia. Korea, formerly another major source, is now no longer considered to be a major producer due to the intensified efforts of law enforcement in that country.

Fenetylline, a Schedule II substance, is still proving to be a problem for Middle Eastern countries. In 1994, Qatar seized 84 dosage units, Jordan 33 553, and Turkey 560 000, all of which were destined for Saudi Arabia, where an additional 2.3 million tablets were seized. The only other Schedule II stimulant to be seized was 2 kg of phenmetrazine reported by Sweden. One Schedule IV substance was seized by Austria: phendimetrazine, as the principal active agent of 25 000 tablets of antapentan.

Almost 2 tonnes of khat leaves, a mild stimulant classified under 'other natural drugs', were seized in Europe. In the main, the traffickers included Danish, German, Dutch, Norwegian, Swedish and United Kingdom nationals engaged by Somali and Ethiopian users of this substance. The majority of seizures took place in Sweden (1 699 kg), with Switzerland, Italy and Finland accounting for the remainder.

Lysergic acid diethylamide (LSD) is currently enjoying a new wave of popularity, particularly in Europe, with the United Kingdom the centre of activity. In 1992, the latter seized 312 114 dosage units, followed by France with 128 359 and the Netherlands, the principal source country for Europe, with 50 002. The other major source is of course the United States which seized 3.9 million dosage units. Despite the world seizure total of 4.5 million dosage units, only one laboratory was reportedly dismantled, this was in Germany where 295 000 units were seized. LSD is trafficked in much the same way as all other drugs, with similar methods of concealment being used. However, the postal services remain a favourite method of distribution due to the light weight of the product and the reduced risk of detection. In Europe, the 'Strawberry' and 'Om' designs are among those most often seized. In Oceania, the drug's popularity has increased dramatically. During the same period, Australia seized 30 173 dosage units, (four times as many as in 1991), and New Zealand 22 284 units. The drug is cheap and has a 'cleaner' image than it had in the 1960s. It is also less potent, with each dosage unit containing about 40–50 micrograms of LSD.

MDA (methylenedioxyamphetamine) and its analogues MDMA and MDEA (methylenedioxymethylamphetamine) and the relatively new (methylenedioxyethyamphetamine) have all been marketed to young people as 'clean' drugs, in contrast to other 'hard' drugs. Given the common street name of 'ecstasy', they do not have a 'dirty needle' image and are extremely popular with young people attending 'acid' or 'rave' parties. If the quantities being seized are used as an indicator of the amounts available, then this should be a cause for alarm.

Most of the seizures in 1992 took place in Europe and were recorded both by weight and by dosage units. Ten European countries reported seizing 406 000 units of MDMA, 512 000 units of MDEA and 2 700 000 units of MDA. In terms of weight, Germany reported the seizure of 3 097 kg of MDA in a single operation, where the drugs had been produced in Latvia. The Netherlands also seized 776 kg of MDA. Gramme quantities were seized by Finland (MDMA), Germany (MDMA and MDEA), Sweden (MDMA) and Australia (MDMA and MDA). MDA laboratories were dismantled by the United States (2), Germany (1), the Netherlands (1); MDMA laboratories by the USA (9), The Netherlands (1) and the United Kingdom (2); and MDEA laboratories by Hungary (2) and the Netherlands (2). The Netherlands is the principal source country for Europe and 2.7 million dosage units were seized there. These, combined with the kilo seizures previously mentioned, prove that law enforcement in that country is working hard to eliminate this problem. The United Kingdom is the second largest ecstasy centre in Europe and a combined total of just over 825 000 dosage units were seized there.

Small quantities of the Schedule I hallucinogenic drug psilocybin were seized in Germany and the Netherlands. Two countries only mentioned phencyclidine (PCP), a Schedule II substance: Germany in connection with the dismantling of an amphetamine/MDA laboratory, and the United States where four laboratories were dismantled and 47 807 dosage units of PCP seized.

Anabolic steroids are a growing problem in a number of countries and will continue to be so as long as people in sporting circles see them as a way of achieving fame and fortune. Reports of seizures of these substances have been received from Austria, Canada, Finland and, in particular, Sweden where many seizures were made during 1994. The source for European countries seems to be Russia and other Eastern European countries. The United States also reported seizing 244 207 dosage units in the same period. The current dangers with these substances are firstly that they are often injected, thereby increasing the risk of spreading disease, and secondly that they are being counterfeited in a number of South-East Asian centres. Consequently, the users are totally unaware of what it is they are taking.

There were very few reports of precursors and essential chemicals having been seized in 1992. In Europe, there were reports of small quantities of chemicals seized in connection with the dismantling of laboratories in Denmark, Germany, Spain and the United Kingdom. There were only six reports of chemicals seizures from countries in production or transit areas. These were made by Argentina and Colombia (cocaine laboratory chemicals), Pakistan, Thailand and Turkey (heroin-producing chemicals), and China Taiwan (ephedrine for methamphetamine production).

United Nations Initiatives

In December 1985, the General Assembly of the United Nations requested the Economic and Social Council, in accordance with General Assembly Resolution 39/141 and Resolution 1 (XXXI) of the Commission on Narcotic Drugs, to instruct the Commission to decide on the elements that could be included in a Convention against illicit traffic in narcotic drugs and psychotropic substances and to request the Secretary General to prepare a draft on the basis of those elements, and to submit a progress report, including completed elements of the draft, to the Commission for consideration at its 32nd session.

The Assembly also requested the Secretary General to submit to the International Conference on Drug Abuse and Illicit Trafficking, which was held in 1987, a report on progress made towards completing a new convention against drug trafficking. The Assembly emphasized the importance of Resolution 2 adopted by the 7th United Nations Congress on the Prevention of Crime and the Treatment of Offenders, approved by the General Assembly in its Resolution 40/32 of 29 November 1985, in which the Congress recommended *inter alia* that absolute priority should be accorded to the preparation of a new international instrument against illicit drug traffic.

It was also recommended that the new convention should take into account the interests of all countries in order that it may be an effective, operative instrument in the struggle against illicit drug trafficking. The General Assembly further requested the Commission on Narcotic Drugs to report to the Economic and Social Council at its first regular session of 1986 on the results achieved in this respect during its 9th special session.

In its Resolution 40/121 of 13 December 1985, the United Nation's General Assembly[4] reaffirmed that maximum priority must be given to the fight against the illicit production of, demand for and traffic in drugs and related international criminal activities, such as the illegal arms trade and terrorist practices, which also have an adverse effect not only on the wellbeing of people but also on the stability of institutions, as well as posing a threat to the sovereignty of states. The Assembly acknowledged the work of bodies in the United Nations system, in particular the drug control bodies, in assisting efforts and initiatives designed to increase international cooperation, and recommended that this work be intensified; and encouraged member states and the relevant bodies of the United Nations system to provide technical assistance to the developing countries most affected by the illicit production of and traffic in abuse of drugs and psychotropic substances, in order to combat the problem.

The Assembly took note with satisfaction of the decision of the Secretary General to hold an interregional meeting of heads of national drug law enforcement agencies at Vienna from 28 July to 1 August 1986, in accordance with paragraph 10 of General Assembly resolution 39/143; and recommended to the Commission on Narcotic Drugs that it advise the interregional meeting to examine in depth the most important aspects of the problem, especially those that would enhance ongoing bilateral and multilateral efforts, in particular the preparation of a draft convention against illicit traffic in narcotic drugs and psychotropic substances and the proposed International Conference on Drug Abuse and Illicit Trafficking, to be convened by the Secretary General at the ministerial level, and to recommend action on, *inter alia*:

- extradition;
- mechanisms that would enhance interregional coordination and cooperation on a permanent basis;
- modalities of ensuring rapid and secure means of communication between law enforcement agencies at the national, regional and international levels;
- techniques of controlled delivery; and,
- measures to reduce the vulnerability of states affected by the transit of illicit drugs;

It also encouraged member states to be represented at the interregional meeting by officials at the decision-making level of national organizations concerned with the suppression of illicit traffic in drugs and psychotropic substances.

The Assembly made special mention of its invitation to the competent bodies within the United Nations system, as well as the International Criminal Police Organization and the Customs Cooperation Council, to provide technical expertise and to participate actively in the interregional meeting; and requested the Secretary General to submit to the General Assembly at its 41st Session an interim report containing the recommendations of the interregional meeting of heads of national drug law enforcement agencies and to submit a final report to the Economic and Social Council, through the Commission on Narcotic Drugs at its next session.

The Assembly also reiterated its request to the Secretary General to continue to make the necessary arrangements for holding within the framework of advisory services, interregional seminars on the experience gained within the United Nations system in integrated rural development programmes that include the substitution of illegal crops in affected areas, particularly in the Andean region. Furthermore, the Assembly acknowledged the vital role played by the United Nations Fund for Drug Abuse Control and calls upon member states to contribute or to continue contributing to the Fund; and called upon the specialized agencies and all relevant bodies of the United Nations system actively to implement the present resolution and requested the Secretary General to report thereon to the General Assembly at its 41st Session. Included in this resolution was the conviction to include in the provisional agenda of its 41st Session the item entitled 'International campaign against traffic in drugs'.

In its Resolution 40/122 dated 13 December 1985, related to the International Conference on Drug Abuse and Illicit Trafficking, the General Assembly expressed its grave concern and that of nations of the world regarding the awesome and vicious effects of drug abuse and illicit trafficking, which threaten the stability of nations and the well-being of mankind and which therefore constitute a grave threat to the security and development of many countries, focused on the dangers posed for producer, consumer and transit countries alike by the illegal cultivation, production and manufacture of and demand for drugs and by their illicit traffic.

Recalling its earlier resolutions and relevant resolutions and decisions of the Economic and Social Council and the Commission on Narcotic Drugs in the international campaign against traffic in and abuse of narcotic drugs and psychotropic substances, the Assembly recognized special responsibilities of the United Nations and the international community to seek viable solutions to the growing scourge of drug abuse and illicit trafficking. It also noted the work of the Commission on Narcotic Drugs towards the preparation of a draft convention against illicit traffic in narcotic drugs and psychotropic substances.

The Assembly also noted with appreciation the statement made by the Secretary General before the Economic and Social Council on 24 May 1985,[5] referred to in Council decision 1985/131 of 28 May 1985, which drew attention to the gravity, magnitude and complexities of the international drug problem and in response proposed a worldwide conference at the ministerial level in 1987 to consider all aspects of the problem. The Assembly recognized that the interregional meeting of heads of national drug law enforcement agencies, which was convened at Vienna in 1986, could make a significant contribution to the deliberations of the conference at the ministerial level proposed by the Secretary General. They also considered the various reviews of the activities of the United Nations agencies in the narcotics field already undertaken and noted with satisfaction the Secretary General's's designation of the Under-Secretary General for Political and General Assembly Affairs as the overall coordinator of all United Nations activities related to drug control. In view of all this the Assembly strongly urged[6] all states to summon the utmost political will to combat drug abuse and illicit trafficking by generating increased political, cultural and social awareness, and it called upon the United Nations, the specialized agencies and other organizations of the United Nations system to give the highest attention and priority possible to international measures to combat illicit production of, trafficking in and demand for drugs.

Further, the Assembly called upon all states that have not already done so to become parties to the Single Convention of Narcotic Drugs of 1961[7] and the 1972 Protocol Amending the Single Convention on Narcotic Drugs of 1961[8] and to the Convention on Psychotropic Substances of 1971, and, in the meantime, to make serious efforts to comply with the provisions of these instruments.

In 1987 the Assembly decided to convene an International Conference on Drug Abuse and Illicit Trafficking at the ministerial level at the Vienna International Centre as an expression of the political will of nations to combat the drug menace, with the mandate to generate universal action to combat the drug problem in all its forms at the national, regional and international levels and to adopt a comprehensive multidisciplinary outline of future activities which focuses on concrete and substantive issues directly relevant to the problems of drug abuse and illicit trafficking, *inter alia*:

1 To consider whether existing mechanisms, whereby experiences, methodologies and other information in law enforcement, preventive education, treatment and rehabilitation, research and development of manpower relating to the prevention and control of drug abuse can be exchanged, should be improved or, if necessary, complemented by new mechanisms.
2 To intensify concerted efforts by governmental, inter-governmental and non-governmental organizations to combat all forms of drug abuse, illicit trafficking and related criminal activities leading to the further development of national strategies that could be a basis for international action.
3 To create heightened national and international awareness and sensitivity concerning the pernicious effects of the abuse of narcotic drugs and psychotropic substances, paying due attention to the demand dimension of the drug problem and to the role of the mass media, non-governmental organizations and other channels of dissemination of information about all aspects of the drug problem, especially in the prevention of drug abuse.
4 To achieve as much harmonization as possible and to reinforce national legislation, bilateral treaties, regional arrangements and other international legal instruments, especially as they relate to enforcement and penalties against those involved in all aspects of illicit trafficking, including forfeiture of illegally acquired assets and extradition, and to develop cooperation in dealing with drug abusers, including their treatment and rehabilitation.

5 To make further progress towards eradicating the sources of raw material for illicit drugs through a comprehensive programme of integrated rural development, the development of alternative means of livelihood and retraining, law enforcement and, where appropriate, crop substitution.
6 To control more effectively the production, distribution and consumption of narcotic drugs and psychotropic substances with a view to limiting their use exclusively to medical and scientific purposes, in accordance with existing conventions, and, in this connection, to underline the central role of the International Narcotics Control Board.
7 To strengthen the United Nations coordination of drug abuse control activities by, *inter alia,* increasing support for the United Nations Fund for Drug Abuse Control and to reinforce regional and other cooperation between member states.
8 To strongly support current high-priority initiatives and programmes of the United Nations, including the elaboration of a convention against illicit traffic in narcotic drugs and psychotropic substances which considers, in particular, those aspects of the problem not envisaged in existing international instruments.

To this end the Assembly requested the Secretary General to facilitate coordination and interaction between member states and the specialized agencies and other organizations of the United Nations system and, in this regard, to report back to the Secretary General of the International Conference on Drug Abuse and Illicit Trafficking at the earliest possible time. It also requested the Economic and Social Council, at its organizational session for 1986, to invite the Commission on Narcotic Drugs to act as the preparatory body for the Conference, open to the participation of states, and, for this purpose, extended by one week the 9th Special Session of the Commission at Vienna in February 1986 in order to consider the agenda and the organizational arrangements for the Conference and, further, to submit its report on these matters to the Council at its first regular session of 1986.

The Assembly reaffirmed the central role of the specialized expert input of the Commission on Narcotic Drugs and called upon all United Nations bodies to cooperate fully with the Commission and with the Secretary General of the Conference in order to ensure effective preparations for the Conference. The final requirement in the resolution was that the Secretary General, without prejudice to ongoing initiatives, programmes and work of the United Nations in the field of drugs, covered as much as possible the cost of holding the Conference though absorption within the regular budget for the biennium 1986–1987 and to facilitate consideration of the financial implications of the present resolution through established procedures, and further requested the Secretary General to submit progress reports on the financial arrangements and implementation of the present resolution, through the Commission on Narcotic Drugs, to the Economic and Social Council at its first regular session of 1986.

The General Assembly also took the step of addressing strategy and policies for drug control in its Resolution 40/129. The Assembly recalled *in limine* its Resolution 32/124 of 16 December 1977, in which it requested the Commission on Narcotic Drugs to study the possibility of launching a meaningful programme of international drug abuse control strategy and policies. It also recalled its Resolution 36/168 of 16 December 1981, by which it adopted the International Drug Abuse Control Strategy and the basic five-year programme of action[9] proposed by the Commission on Narcotic Drugs in its Resolution 1 (XXIX) of 11 February 1981[10] as well as its Resolution 38/98 of 16 December 1983, in which it decided that, beginning with its 8th Special Session, the Commission on Narcotic Drugs, meeting in plenary during its sessions and in the presence of all interested observers, would constitute the task force envisaged in General Assembly Resolution 36/168 to review, monitor and coordinate the implementation of the International Drug Abuse Control Strategy and the basic five-year programme of action.

Taking note of Resolution 2 (XXXI) of 21 February 1985 of the Commission on Narcotic Drugs[11] and Economic and Social Council decision 1985/130 of 28 May 1985, the Assembly approved the programme of action for 1986, the fifth year of the United Nations basic five-year programme of the International Drug Abuse Control Strategy, reviewed by the Commission on Narcotic Drugs at its 31st session.[12]

In a separate exercise, the Assembly taking into consideration that in response to the threat posed by the drug problem the international community had adopted numerous declarations and initiatives, interregional and regional, multilateral and bilateral, in order to condemn and combat the problem and to achieve its total eradication,[13] commended the valuable contributions of the Secretary General of the United Nations and the Secretary General of the International Conference on Drug Abuse and Illicit Trafficking to the preparatory work for the Conference and noting the continuing efforts of the Commission on Narcotic Drugs, the United Nations Fund for Drug Abuse Control, the International Narcotics Control Board, the Division of Narcotic Drugs of the Secretariat, inter-governmental and non-governmental organizations and the regional commissions in this regard.

The Assembly also welcomed the commitment of the Secretary General to cover the cost of holding the Conference through absorption within the regular budget for the biennium 1986–1987, without prejudice to ongoing initiatives, programmes and work of the United Nations in the field of drug control.

The Assembly therefore, having considered the report of the Secretary General on the status of preparations for the Conference:[14]

1 Requested all states, in reaffirmation of the commitment of the international community and as an expression of their political will to combat the threat posed by drug abuse and illicit trafficking, to give the highest priority to the holding of the International Conference on Drug Abuse and Illicit Trafficking at Vienna in 1987 and to participate actively in the Conference in order to stimulate comprehensive world-wide cooperative action to combat the drug problem in all its forms at the national, regional and international levels.
2 Took note with nations of the report of the Commission on Narcotic Drugs acting as the preparatory body for the International Conference on Drug Abuse and Illicit Trafficking in its 1st Session,[15] and of the recommendations contained in that report, adopted by the Economic and Social Council in its decision 1986/128, in which it decided, *inter alia*, that the preparatory body for the Conference should convene for its 2nd Session immediately following the 32nd Regular Session of the Commission on Narcotic Drugs.
3 Requested the preparatory body for the Conference to complete its work when it next met at Vienna, in February 1987, particularly the drafting of the comprehensive multidisciplinary outline of future activities relevant to the problems of drug abuse and illicit trafficking, based on comments and modifications proposed by governments, so that the Conference may consider it for adoption.
4 Further requested the preparatory body for the Conference to report on its work to the Economic and Social Council at its 1st Regular Session of 1987.
5 Reaffirmed the importance of the contribution of the Commission on Narcotic Drugs and requested all states and all United Nations organs and organizations, as well as non-governmental organizations, to cooperate fully with the Commission and with the Secretary General of the Conference in order to ensure effective preparations for the Conference and its success.
6 Requested the Secretary General to report to the General Assembly at its 42nd Session on the implementation of the present resolution, particularly with regard to the results of the International Conference on Drug Abuse and Illicit Trafficking, for consideration under the relevant agenda item.

In its preparation of a draft convention against illicit traffic in narcotic drugs and psychotropic substances, the General Assembly at its

97th Plenary meeting in December 1986, adopted Resolution 41/126 which expressed its appreciation to and commended the Secretary General for this effective response to the request made in paragraph 4 of Commission on Narcotic Drugs resolution 1 (S-IX), entitled 'Guidance on the Drafting of an International Convention', prepared containing the elements specified in paragraph 3 of that resolution and that the draft be circulated to members of the Commission and other interested Governments. The Assembly also expressed its appreciation to the member states that responded to the request contained in paragraph 5 of the Commission on Narcotic Drugs Resolution 1 (S-IX), in which they were invited to submit their comments on and/or proposed textual changes to the draft, and urged all member states that had not yet done so to comply with this request as soon as possible. One of the requests made by the Assembly in this regard was to the Commission on Narcotic Drugs, through the Economic and Social Council, to continue at its 32nd Regular Session its work on the preparation of a draft convention against illicit traffic in narcotic drugs and psychotropic substances in the most expeditious manner, so that it might be effective, and widely acceptable, and enter into force at the earliest possible time.

There was also the request of the Secretary General to submit to the International Conference on Drug Abuse and Illicit Drug Trafficking, to be held in 1987, a report on progress achieved in the preparation of a new convention against illicit drug trafficking.

The Assembly once again urged all states that had not yet done so to ratify and to accede to the Single Convention on Narcotic Drugs of 1961, the 1972 Protocol Amending the Single Convention on Narcotic Drugs of 1961 and the Convention on Psychotropic Substances of 1971; and requested the Secretary General to report to the General Assembly at its 42nd Session on the implementation of the present resolution.

Simultaneously, the General Assembly inaugurated its international campaign against traffic in drugs in Resolution 41/127 by noting the common concern that exists among people of the world regarding the devastating effects of drug abuse and illicit trafficking, which jeopardize the stability of democratic institutions and the well-being of mankind and which therefore constitute a grave threat to the security and an obstacle to the development of many countries. The Assembly took into consideration that the problem of illicit drug traffic negatively affects all producer, consumer and transit countries, and that there is an urgent need to take joint measures to combat it, including all aspects relating to illicit supply of, demand for and traffic in drugs.

In this context, the Assembly recalled its Resolutions 39/142 of 14 December 1984 and 40/121 of 13 December 1985 and other relevant

Resolutions and decisions of the Economic and Social Council and of the Commission on Narcotic Drugs adopted to advance the international campaign against traffic in and abuse of narcotic drugs and psychotropic substances. The Assembly was disturbed to note that, despite the efforts made, the situation continues to deteriorate, owing, *inter alia*, to the growing interrelationship between drug trafficking and transnational criminal organizations that were responsible for much of the drug traffic and abuse of narcotic drugs and psychotropic substances and for the increase in violence, corruption and injury to society.

It acknowledged once more that the eradication of this scourge called for acknowledgement of shared responsibility in combating simultaneously the problems of illicit demand, production, distribution and marketing, and that action designed to eliminate illicit drug cultivation, trafficking and consumption should be accompanied, where appropriate, by economic and social development programmes. The Assembly recognized that transit routes used by international drug traffickers are constantly shifting, and that an increasing number of countries in all regions of the world, and even entire areas because of their strategic geographical location and other considerations, are particularly vulnerable to the illicit transit traffic.

Considering that cooperative regional and international action is required to reduce the vulnerability of states and regions to the illicit transit traffic and to provide necessary support and assistance, particularly to countries hitherto unaffected, the Assembly commended the work of the Commission on Narcotic Drugs, the International Narcotics Control Board and the Division of Narcotic Drugs of the Secretariat, as well as the positive action of the United Nations Fund for Drug Abuse Control in allocating funds to integrated rural development programmes, including substitution of illegal crops in the most severely affected areas.

The Assembly thereupon focused on the recommendations adopted at the first Interregional Meeting of Heads of National Drug Law Enforcement Agencies,[16] held at Vienna from 28 July to 1 August 1986, which was convened pursuant to General Assembly Resolution 39/143 of 14 December 1984 to examine in depth the most important aspects of the problem, including proposals that might be considered in the preparation of a draft convention against illicit traffic in narcotic drugs and psychotropic substances, and acknowledged the need for states to take these recommendations into consideration. Once again, the Assembly recognized the importance of adherence to existing international legal instruments, including the Single Convention on Narcotic Drugs of 1961,[17] as amended by the 1972 Protocol Amending the Single Convention on Narcotic Drugs of 1961 and the Convention on Psychotropic Substances of 1971,[18] and the urgent need to encourage member states that have not yet done so to ratify these instruments and the need for states that have already ratified them to implement fully their obligations under these instruments.

Taking note with appreciation of the efforts undertaken by states to implement its Resolution 40/122 of 13 December 1985 on the convening in 1987 of an International Conference on Drug Abuse and Illicit Trafficking, at the ministerial level, the Assembly also condemned unequivocally drug trafficking in all its illicit forms – production, processing, marketing and consumption – as a criminal activity and requested all states to pledge their political will in a concerted and universal struggle to achieve its complete and final elimination. It urged states to acknowledge that they share responsibility for combating the problem of illicit consumption, production and transit and therefore to encourage mutual collaboration in the struggle against drug trafficking, in accordance with the relevant international and national norms. Another measure adopted by the Assembly was to call upon all states to adopt appropriate preventive and/or punitive measures of a political, legal, economic and cultural nature so as to bring about social awareness of the pernicious effects of illicit drug use, and individual and collective rejection of all kinds of practices that facilitate such illegal use. The Assembly invited states to use all possible means to discourage practices and domestic and foreign interests that promote the increased illicit production and consumption of drugs; and urged the governments of countries facing problems of drug abuse, particularly those most seriously affected, as part of their national strategy, to give priority to funding programmes that aim to create in society a deep respect for its own health, fitness and well-being and take into account cultural and social factors, to provide appropriate information and advice for all sectors of their communities with regard to drug abuse, its harmful effects and the ways in which appropriate community action can be promoted.

It also recommended that concerted efforts be made to promote cooperation and coordination among states, particularly in the areas of communications and training, with a view to alleviating the problems associated with illicit transit traffic in narcotic drugs and psychotropic substances. Another recommendation was that the Economic and Social Council request the Commission on Narcotic Drugs to consider convening, within available resources, a sessional working group to facilitate the exchange of information on experience gained by states in combating the illicit transit traffic in narcotic drugs and psychotropic substances. The Assembly encouraged member states and the relevant bodies of the United Nations system, subject to observance of the principles of national sovereignty and jurisdiction, to provide economic assistance and technical cooperation to the developing countries most affected by the illicit production of, traffic in and use of narcotic drugs and psychotropic substances, in order to combat this problem; and expressed its appreciation to the Secretary General of the United Nations and to the Secretary General of the International Conference on Drug Abuse and Illicit Trafficking for their valuable efforts in implementing General Assembly Resolution 40/122.

As a further measure taken to ensure the success of the International Conference on Drug Abuse and Illicit Trafficking, the General Assembly adopted Resolution 48/122 in December 1985.

The Assembly recalled its Resolution 40/122 of 13 December 1985, by which it decided to convene in 1987 (in response to the initiative of the Secretary General), an International Conference on Drug Abuse and Illicit Trafficking at the ministerial level at Vienna, with the mandate to generate universal action, and as an expression of the political will of nations to combat the drug menace and as a means of tackling the serious and complex international drug problem in all its forms. It also recalled its Resolution 41/125 of 4 December 1986, referring to the Economic and Social Council decision 1987/127 of 26 May 1987, and the report of the Secretary General on the International Conference on Drug Abuse and Illicit Trafficking,[24] and expressed its determination to strengthen action and cooperation at the national, regional and international levels towards the goal of an international society free of drug abuse.

Noting the need for a review and assessment of the follow-up activities to the Conference, and noting with appreciation the offer of the Government of Bolivia to act as host to a second international conference, the Assembly:

1 Took note of the report of the International Conference on Drug Abuse and Illicit Trafficking,[19] and welcomed the successful conclusion of the Conference, in particular the adoption of the Declaration[20] and the Comprehensive Multidisciplinary Outline of Future Activities in Drug Abuse Control.[21]
2 Affirmed their commitment to the Declaration of the International Conference on Drug Abuse and Illicit Trafficking as an expression of the political will of nations to combat the drug menace.
3 Urged governments and organizations, in formulating programmes, to take due account of the framework provided by the Comprehensive Multidisciplinary Outline of Future Activities in Drug Abuse Control as a repertory of recommendations setting forth practical measures that can contribute to the fight against drug abuse and illicit trafficking.
4 Requested the Secretary General to make available, within existing resources, an adequate number of copies of the Declaration and

the Comprehensive Multidisciplinary Outline of Future Activities in Drug Abuse Control.

5 Decided to observe 26 June each year as the International Day against Drug abuse and Illicit Trafficking.
6 Appealed to member states to provide additional resources to the United Nations Fund for Drug Abuse Control as a priority goal in the follow-up activities to the Conference to enable it to strengthen its cooperation with the developing countries in their efforts to implement drug control programmes.
7 Requested the Commission on Narcotic Drugs, as the principal United Nations policy-making body on drug control, to identify suitable measures for follow-up to the International Conference on Drug Abuse and Illicit Trafficking and, in this context, to give appropriate consideration to the report of the Secretary General on the Conference.
8 The Assembly also requested the Secretary General to report to the General Assembly at its 43rd Session on the implementation of the present resolution.

At this stage, the General Assembly was acutely conscious of the adverse effects of the global problem of drug abuse, illicit production of and trafficking in drugs and psychotropic substances, both on individuals, in that it has pernicious physical and psychological effects and limits creativity and the full development of human potential, and in relation to states, as it is a threat to their security and is prejudicial to their democratic institutions and their economic, social, legal and cultural structures. It considered that the situation continues to deteriorate, owing, *inter alia,* to the growing interrelationship between drug trafficking and transnational criminal organizations that are responsible for much of the drug traffic and abuse of narcotic drugs and psychotropic substances and for the increase in violence and corruption, which injure society.

The Assembly recognized the following factors:

1 The collective responsibility of states for providing appropriate resources for the elimination of illicit production and trafficking and of the abuse of drugs and psychotropic substances.
2 Measures to prevent and control supply and to combat illicit trafficking can be effective only if they take into consideration the close link between illicit production, transit and the abuse of drugs and the social, economic and cultural conditions in the states affected, and that they must be formulated and implemented in the context of the social and economic policies of states, taking due account of community traditions, harmonious development and conservation of the environment.

3 Transit routes used by drug traffickers are constantly shifting and that an increasing number of countries in all regions of the world and even entire areas, because of their geographical location and other considerations, are particularly vulnerable to the illicit transit traffic.
4 Regional and international cooperation is required in order to reduce the vulnerability of states and regions to the illicit transit traffic and to provide necessary support and assistance, particularly to countries hitherto unaffected.
5 The need to reaffirm the effectiveness of human, moral and spiritual values for preventing the consumption of narcotic drugs, at the national and international levels, through information, guidance and educational activities is recognized.
6 The importance of the United Nations Fund for Drug Abuse Control as a catalyst in the United Nations system is recognized, that it has become one of the major sources of multilateral financing for technical cooperation programmes in the context of the international campaign against the abuse of and illicit trafficking in drugs and psychotropic substances.
7 The policy adopted by the Fund for the formulation of master plans takes into account the principal social, economic and cultural factors of countries, as well as their national and regional programmes, and that in those plans both donor countries and recipients of technical assistance are actively involved in concerted action with a view to combating the problem at all stages.

Taking note of the close link existing between governments, public institutions and the Fund and the United Nations Development Programme, in coordination with other organizations of the United Nations system concerned with controlling abuse of drugs and psychotropic substances, the Assembly recalled its Resolution 41/127 of 4 December 1986 and the relevant resolutions of the Commission on Narcotic Drugs and of the Economic and Social Council adopted to advance the international campaign against abuse of and illicit traffic in drugs and psychotropic substances. The following measures were taken by the Assembly:

1 Condemned unequivocally once again drug trafficking in all its forms – illicit production, processing, marketing and consumption – as a criminal activity, and requested all states to pledge their political will in a concerted and universal struggle to achieve its complete and final elimination.
2 Urged states to acknowledge that they share responsibility for combating the problem of illicit consumption, production, transit and trafficking and therefore to encourage international

cooperation in the struggle to eliminate illicit production and trafficking and the abuse of drugs and psychotropic substances, in accordance with the relevant international and national norms.

3 Acknowledged the constant and determined efforts of governments at the national, regional and international levels to cope with the increase in drug abuse and illicit drug trafficking and its increasingly close links with other forms of organized international criminal activities.

4 Noted with appreciation the unanimous adoption of the Declaration[22] and the adoption by consensus of the Comprehensive Multidisciplinary Outline of Future Activities in Drug Abuse Control[23] by the International Conference on Drug Abuse and Illicit Trafficking, and urged states to carry out the recommendations contained in those documents in a determined and sustained manner.

5 Took note of the First Meeting of Heads of National Drug Law Enforcement Agencies, African Region, held at Addis Ababa from 30 March to 3 April 1987, the First Meeting of Heads of National Drug Law Enforcement Agencies, Latin American and Caribbean Region, held at Santiago from 28 September to 2 October 1987, and the Meeting of the Heads of National Drug Law Enforcement Agencies, Asia and the Pacific Region, held at Tokyo from 30 November to 4 December 1987, and requested the Commission on Narcotic Drugs to consider their recommendations at its 10th Special Session, in order to determine the specific measures required for implementation thereof, for possible adoption by the Economic and Social Council at its next session.

6 Encouraged states to use the meetings of the working group of the Commission on Narcotic Drugs for the purpose of exchanging experiences in their struggle against the illicit transit of drugs and psychotropic substances and to increase regional and interregional cooperation in this matter.

7 Reiterated once again their request to the Secretary General to continue to make the necessary arrangements for holding, within the framework of advisory services, interregional seminars on the experience gained within the United Nations system in integrated rural development programmes that include the substitution of illegal crops in affected areas, including the Andean region.

8 Commended the United Nations Fund for Drug Abuse Control for the productive work that it had done as one of the main bodies of the United Nations system providing technical cooperation in the field of drug abuse control, and encouraged it to continue its activities, paying particular attention to requests from developing countries.

9 Called upon all states to continue and increase their political support of and financial contributions to the Fund, and encouraged its Executive Director to continue systematically and consistently strengthening the activities of the Fund in affected countries and regions, so as to enable them to combat all aspects of the problem effectively.
10 Endorsed the Economic and Social Council Resolution 1987/32 of 26 May 1987.
11 Requested the Secretary General to take steps to ensure that the Department of Public Information of the Secretariat includes in its publications information designed to prevent the abuse of narcotic drugs, especially by young people.
12 Called upon the governments of countries facing problems of drug abuse, particularly those most seriously affected, as part of their national strategy to take the necessary measures to reduce significantly the illicit demand for drugs and psychotropic substances with the aim of creating in society a deep respect for its own health, fitness and well-being and to provide appropriate information and advice for all sectors of their communities with regard to drug abuse, its harmful effects and the way in which appropriate community action can be promoted.
13 Requested the Secretary General to take steps to provide, within existing resources, appropriate support for strengthening the Division of Narcotic Drugs and the International Narcotics Control Board, including through redeployment.
14 Requested the Secretary General to report to the General Assembly at its 43rd Session on the implementation of the present resolution and decided to include in the provisional agenda of that session the item entitled 'International campaign against traffic in drugs'.

The Assembly further appealed to member states, on the basis of their national experience, and to specialized agencies and other competent bodies of the United Nations system to respond as constructively and as factually as possible to the invitation in its Resolution 41/132 to communicate to the Secretary General their views on the subject of his report; and renewed its request to the Secretary General to report his findings to the General Assembly at its 43rd Session.

It also decided to consider this question at its 43rd Session under the item entitled 'Alternative approaches and ways and means within the United Nations system for improving the effective enjoyment of human rights and fundamental freedoms'.

In December 1988 the General Assembly, as a further measure towards developing its preparation of a draft convention against illicit traffic in narcotics drugs and psychotropic substances considered the report of the Secretary General[24] on the progress achieved in the preparation of the draft convention, and welcomed with appreciation Economic and Social Council Resolution 1988/8, in which it decided to convene the Review Group in mid-June 1988 at Vienna, with the mandate of continuing the preparation of the draft convention and preparing the organizational aspects of the Conference of plenipotentiaries for the adoption of a convention against illicit traffic in narcotic drugs and psychotropic substances. It noted with satisfaction the report of the Secretary General, and the report of the Commission on Narcotic Drugs on its 10th Special Session[25] and the recommendations therein, approved by the Economic and Social Council in its Resolution 1988/8 and decisions 1988/118 and 1988/120 of 25 May 1988 and 1988/159 of 26 July 1988, in which it decided, *inter alia*, to convene the conference of plenipotentiaries to adopt the convention, and to extend to ten working days the 33rd Session of the Commission on Narcotic Drugs in order to allow it to consider suitable measures to be taken prior to the entry into force of the convention; and requested the Commission on Narcotic Drugs, as the principal United Nations policy-making body on drug abuse control, to identify suitable measures to be taken prior to the entry into force of the convention. The Assembly also urged all states to adopt a constructive approach with a view to resolving any outstanding differences over the text of the convention; and requested all states, while reaffirming their commitment to the Declaration of the International Conference on Drug Abuse and Illicit Trafficking[26] as an expression of the political will of nations to combat the drug problem, to assign the highest priority to the conference of plenipotentiaries and to participate actively in it, at the highest possible level, for the adoption of the Convention.

While expressing its appreciation to the Secretary General, the Commission on Narcotic Drugs and all related organs established by the Commission, for their effectiveness in responding to its request to prepare the draft Convention, the Assembly once again urged all states that had not yet done so to ratify or to accede to the Single Convention on Narcotic Drugs of 1961, as amended by the 1972 Protocol Amending the Single Convention on Narcotic Drugs of 1961, and the Convention on Psychotropic Substances of 1971; and requested the Secretary General to report to the General Assembly at its 44th Session on the implementation of the present resolution, particularly on the conclusions of the conference of plenipotentiaries for the adoption of a convention against illicit traffic in narcotic drugs and psychotropic substances.

The Use of Children in Narcotic Drug Trafficking

The international regulatory regime on narcotic drug trafficking took an interesting turn with Resolution 43/121 on the use of children in the illicit traffic in narcotic drugs and rehabilitation of drug-addicted minors. Here the General Assembly, while recalling its Resolutions 41/127 of 4 December 1986 and 42/113 of 7 December 1987, as well as the relevant resolutions of the Commission on Narcotic Drugs and of the Economic and Social Council adopted to implement the international campaign against drug abuse and illicit trafficking, focused on the provisions of the Declaration of the International Conference on Drug Abuse and Illicit Trafficking[27] and the guidelines contained in the Comprehensive Multidisciplinary Outline of Future Activities in Drug Abuse Control,[28] and expressed its alarm by the fact that drug dealers' organizations are making use of children in their illicit production of and trafficking in drugs, and by the increase in the number of drug-addicted children.

Conscious of the physical and psychological damage inflicted on children by the illicit use of narcotic drugs and of its serious effects both on their potential for development and on their relationships with their families and society, and having in mind the provisions of the Declaration of the Rights of the Child, the Assembly reaffirmed the provisions of its Resolution 42/101 of 7 December 1987 on the question of a convention on the rights of the child, which affirm that children's rights require special protection and call for continuous improvement of the situation of children all over the world, as well as their development and education. While articulating this premise the Assembly:

1 strongly condemned drug trafficking in all its forms, particularly those criminal activities which involve children in the use, production and illicit sale of narcotic drugs and psychotropic substances;
2 urged all states to join together in order to establish national and international programmes to protect children from the illicit consumption of drugs and psychotropic substances and from involvement in illicit production and trafficking;
3 invited the governments of those member states which are most affected by drug use among their child population to adopt urgent additional measures, as part of their national strategies, to prevent, reduce and eliminate drug use by children, with the aim of ensuring for children a social and family environment that will preserve their health, physical fitness and well-being;
4 called upon all states to promote the adoption, by their competent legislative organs, of measures providing for suitably severe punishment of drug-trafficking crimes that involve children;

5 urged all governments, competent international organizations and non-governmental organizations to give high priority in their campaigns to prevent drug addiction among children, and to rehabilitate children so addicted to the dissemination of necessary information and the provision of appropriate advice for all sectors of their communities with regard to the serious effects of the illicit use of drugs among children, as well as to the promotion of appropriate community action;
6 appealed to the competent international agencies and the United Nations Fund for Drug Abuse Control to assign high priority to financial support for prevention campaigns and programmes to rehabilitate drug-addicted minors conducted by government bodies dealing with such matters, and also appealed to all competent international and national agencies to provide all possible support to the non-governmental organizations engaged in such action; and,
7 requested the Secretary General to ensure that the Department of Public Information of the Secretariat includes in its publications, as a matter of priority, information designed to prevent the use of narcotic drugs and psychotropic substances among children.

International Campaign against Drug Abuse and Illicit Trafficking

The General Assembly followed the above work with some recommendations. Recalling its Resolutions 40/122 of 13 December 1985, 41/125 of 4 December 1986, 42/112 and 42/113 of 7 December 1986, and the relevant resolutions of the Commission on Narcotic Drugs and the Economic and Social Council adopted to implement the international campaign against drug abuse and illicit trafficking, the Assembly noted with satisfaction the successful conclusion of the International Conference on Drug Abuse and Illicit Trafficking, in particular the adoption of the Declaration,[29] as an expression of the political will of nations to combat the drug menace, and the Comprehensive Multidisciplinary Outline of Future Activities in Drug Abuse Control,[30] a compendium of recommendations for implementation. Further recognition was given to the fact that the global problem of illicit trafficking in and illicit production and abuse of narcotic drugs and psychotropic substances continues to have a devastating effect on individuals and on states, and the Assembly emphasized that the connections between drug trafficking and international criminal organizations and the violence and corruption associated with them are highly detrimental to the democratic institutions, national security and economic, social and cultural structures of states.

There was, in the view of the Assembly, a compelling need to ensure the implementation of the courses of action recommended in the Comprehensive Multidisciplinary Outline, particularly in the areas of education and public information with regard to the abuse of narcotic drugs and psychotropic substances. In this context noting that the collective responsibility of all states for the international campaign against drug abuse and illicit trafficking was highlighted in the Declaration, the Assembly recognized that measures to prevent and control supply and to combat illicit trafficking can be effective only if they take into consideration the close link between illicit traffic in narcotic drugs and psychotropic substances, including illicit production and abuse, and the social, economic and cultural conditions in the states affected, and are formulated and implemented in the context of the social and economic policies of states, taking due account of community traditions and the harmonious development and conservation of the environment. It also reiterated that the transit routes used by drug traffickers are constantly changing and that an increasing number of countries in all regions of the world, and even entire areas, are particularly vulnerable to the illicit transit traffic because of their geographical location and other considerations, and emphasized that, in order to stop the illicit transit traffic in narcotic drugs and psychotropic substances, regional and interregional cooperation and action and necessary support and assistance are required to strengthen the capability of states and regions, including those hitherto unaffected. The Assembly further noted that the new convention against illicit traffic in narcotic drugs and psychotropic substances, when adopted, should, together with the existing international instruments, greatly enhance the international campaign against drug abuse and illicit trafficking, and took note of the Commission on Narcotic Drugs Resolution 4 (S-X) of 12 February 1988 concerning the financial and human resources available to the Division of Narcotic Drugs of the Secretariat and the Secretariat of the International Narcotics Control Board. Further consideration was given to the importance of the United Nations Fund for Drug Abuse Control as a major source of multilateral funding and expertise for drug abuse control efforts of the developing countries and the Fund's success in fund raising and its improved operations. Recalling its decision to observe 26 June each year as the International Day Against Drug Abuse and Illicit Trafficking, the Assembly:

1 took note of the report of the Secretary General;[31]
2 reiterated its condemnation of international drug trafficking as a criminal activity, and encouraged all states to continue to demonstrate the political will to enhance international cooperation to stop illicit trafficking in narcotic drugs and psychotropic substances, including illicit production and consumption;
3 urged all states to take appropriate action in regard to drug

abuse control, in accordance with international drug control instruments, recognizing the collective responsibility of states, to provide appropriate resources for the elimination of illicit production, trafficking and drug abuse, as set forth in the Declaration of the International Conference on Drug Abuse and Illicit Trafficking;

4 acknowledged that, despite serious economic constraints, particularly in developing countries, governments continue to make determined efforts to cope with the increasing abuse of and illicit traffic in narcotic drugs and psychotropic substances, especially with the destructive activities of international criminal organization;

5 noted with satisfaction the valuable work of the meetings of Heads of National Drug Law Enforcement Agencies, in particular the Second Meeting of Heads of National Drug Law Enforcement Agencies, African Region, held at Dakar from 18 to 22 April 1988, the Second Meeting of Heads of National Drug Law Enforcement Agencies, Latin American and Caribbean Region, held at Lima from 12 to 16 September 1988, and the Fourteenth Meeting of Heads of National Drug Law Enforcement Agencies, Asia and the Pacific Region, held at Bangkok from 3 to 7 October 1988;

6 requested that consideration be given to the convening of regional meetings of heads of national drug law enforcement agencies in regions where they have not yet been held;

7 noted with satisfaction the Second Interregional Meeting of Heads of National Drug Law Enforcement Agencies to be held in 1989 and encouraged it to consider the reports and achievements of all the regional meetings;

8 urged the Interregional Meeting to discuss ways and means of enhancing law enforcement training, especially in those areas that would require new knowledge and skills for the implementation of the provisions of the new convention against illicit traffic in narcotic drugs and psychotropic substances;

9 encouraged states to use the meetings of the working group of the Commission on Narcotic Drugs and other forums for the purpose of exchanging experiences in the fight against the illicit transit of drugs and psychotropic substances and to increase regional and interregional cooperation on this aspect of the drug problem;

10 reiterated once again its request to the Secretary General to continue to make the necessary arrangements for holding, within the framework of advisory services, interregional seminars on the experience gained within the United Nations system in integrated rural development programmes that include the

substitution of illegal crops in affected areas, including the Andean region;

11 endorsed the Commission on Narcotic Drugs Resolution 4 (S-X), the implementation of which is essential for the adequate functioning of the Division of Narcotic Drugs and the Secretariat of the International Narcotics Control Board;

12 commended the United Nations Fund for Drug Abuse Control for the productive work that it has done as one of the main bodies of the United Nations system providing technical cooperation and funding in the field of drug abuse control;

13 appealed to member states to continue to provide additional resources to the Fund to enable it to continue its activities, giving particular attention to requests for assistance from developing countries;

14 once again called upon the governments of countries facing problems of drug abuse, particularly those most seriously affected, as part of their national strategies, to take the necessary measures to reduce significantly the illicit demand for narcotic drugs and psychotropic substances with the aim of creating societies that deeply respect health, fitness and well-being, and to provide appropriate information and advice on the harmful effects of drug abuse, through adequate community action, to all sectors of their communities; and,

15 requested the Secretary General to take steps to ensure that the Department of Public Information of the Secretariat includes in its publications information designed to prevent the abuse of narcotic drugs and psychotropic substances, especially by young people.

The Assembly also took note of the report of the Secretary General;[32] and urged governments and organizations to adhere to the principles set forth in the Declaration of the International Conference on Drug Abuse and Illicit Trafficking[33] and to utilize the recommendations of the Comprehensive Multidisciplinary Outline of Future Activities in Drug Abuse Control[34] in developing national and regional strategies, particularly to promote bilateral, regional and international cooperative arrangements. The Assembly also recommended that, in developing activities to implement the guiding principles contained in the Declaration and the targets of the Comprehensive Multidisciplinary Outline, the United Nations drug control bodies, specialized agencies and other intergovernmental organizations should give particular emphasis to activities identified in the annex to Economic and Social Council Resolution 1988/9 of 25 May 1988. A request was also made that the Secretary General, within the available resources, review current information systems in the United Nations drug control units and to develop an information strategy and submit it, with its financial implications, to the Commission on Narcotic Drugs at its 33rd Session. The Commission was requested to consider the review by the Secretary General and to advise on the creation, within existing United Nations structures, of an information system to integrate inputs from national, regional and international sources, so as to facilitate the linkage, retrieval and dissemination of information on all aspects of narcotic drugs, psychotropic substances and the chemicals used in their illicit processing and manufacturing.

The Assembly called upon the Secretary General to support, within the available resources, the activities of non-governmental organizations concerned and, in recognition of the latter's experience and expertise, to coordinate United Nations activities in this field with this organizations concerned; and requested the Secretary General to ensure continued inter-agency coordination in drug abuse control activities, in particular by rotating the venue of inter-agency meetings on coordination, which will enhance efforts by the Commission to implement follow-up activities to the Conference. As for the work of the Commission, the Assembly called upon the Commission to keep under review action taken with respect to the Declaration and the Comprehensive Multidisciplinary Outline. Finally, the Assembly requested the Secretary General to report to the General Assembly at its 44th session on the implementation of the present resolution and decided to include in the provisional agenda of that session an item entitled 'International campaign against traffic in drugs'.

At its 43rd plenary meeting, in November 1989, the United Nations summoned a special session of the General Assembly to consider the question of international cooperation against illicit production, supply, demand, trafficking and distribution of narcotic drugs, with a view to expanding the scope and increasing the effectiveness of such cooperation. At this session, the General Assembly reiterated its concern about the serious problem of the illicit production, supply, demand, trafficking and distribution of narcotic drugs and about the devastating effect of drug abuse on individuals and society. Noting statements delivered before the Assembly in plenary meeting during its 44th Session, including the address given by the President of the Republic of Colombia on 29 September 1989[35] and, in particular, his call for a special session of the General Assembly, the Assembly decided to hold a special session, at a high political level, to consider as a matter of urgency the question of international cooperation against illicit production, supply, demand, trafficking and distribution of narcotic drugs, with a view to expanding the scope and increasing the effectiveness of such cooperation. It requested the Secretary General to make the necessary administrative arrangements for the convening of the special session.

In December 1989 at its 82nd plenary meeting, the General Assembly, on the subject of implementation of the United Nations Convention against Illicit Traffic in Narcotic Drugs and Psychotropic Substances, expressed its appreciation to the Secretary General for the report on the conclusions of the conference of plenipotentiaries that adopted the United Nations Convention against Illicit Traffic in Narcotic Drugs and Psychotropic Substances at Vienna. It also expressed its appreciation to the states that participated in the preparation and adoption of the Convention; and urged states that have not yet done so to proceed rapidly to sign and to ratify the Convention, so that it may enter into force as early as possible. The Assembly also urged states to establish the necessary legislative and administrative measures so that their internal juridical regulations may be compatible with the spirit and scope of the Convention; and invited states, to the extent that they are able to do so, to apply provisionally the measures set forth in the Convention, pending its entry into force for each of them.

The Secretary General was requested to modify the section of the annual reports questionnaire regarding the implementation of international treaties so that the Commission on Narcotic Drugs, at its regular and special sessions, may review that steps that states have taken to ratify, accept, approve or formally confirm the Convention. The Assembly invited the Commission on Narcotic Drugs, as the principal United Nations policy-making body on the subject, to identify suitable measures to be taken prior to the entry into force of the Convention. It also requested the Secretary General to assign the appropriate priority to providing the Division of Narcotic Drugs of the Secretariat and the Secretariat of the International Narcotics Control Board with the necessary financial, technical and human resources that would enable them to carry out the additional responsibilities under the Convention for the biennium 1990–1991.

The Secretary General was further urged to provide assistance to states, at their request, to enable them to establish the legislative and administrative measures necessary for the implementation of the Convention. All states that had not yet done so were requested to ratify or to accede to the Single Convention on Narcotic Drugs of 1961, as amended by the 1972 Protocol Amending the Single Convention on Narcotic Drugs of 1961, and the Convention on Psychotropic Substances of 1971.

The Assembly also requested the Secretary General, within existing resources and drawing, in particular, on funds available to the Department of Public Information of the Secretariat, to provide for, facilitate and encourage public information activities relating to the Convention and also to disseminate the text of the Convention in the official languages of the United Nations. The Secretary General was requested to report to the General Assembly at its 45th Session on the implementation of the present resolution.

At the same time, the General Assembly considered further its global programme of action against illicit narcotic drugs and expressed its alarm by the dramatic increase in drug abuse and illicit production and trafficking in narcotics, which is threatening the health and well-being of millions of people, in particular young people, in the majority of countries of the world. The deep concern of the Assembly that the evolving drug problem is assuming new dimensions and is threatening the economic, social and political structures of affected countries, through acts of violence perpetrated against their democratic institutions and the extensive economic power of illicit drug organizations, was expressed.

Commending the determined efforts of the Government of Colombia to stop drug trafficking and recognizing the importance of support for such efforts by the international community, and welcoming the increasing international attention to these issues and the unflinching commitment demonstrated at the highest levels by heads of government and state to increase their efforts and resources to achieve coordinated action in the international fight against production, trafficking and abuse of narcotic drugs, the Assembly recognized that the collective responsibility of states for the campaign against the demand for, production of and trafficking in illicit drugs requires intensified international cooperation and joint action, including the capability to provide, in appropriate forms, necessary support and assistance, if requested by affected states, in order to strengthen their capacity to deal with the problem in all its aspects. It noted with appreciation the work carried out within the United Nations in the field of drug abuse control and the valuable knowledge and experience represented there, and recognized the important contributions made to the international campaign against drug abuse and illicit trafficking by the International Conference on Drug Abuse and Illicit Trafficking, held at Vienna from 17 to 26 June 1987, and, in particular, by its adoption of the Declaration[36] and the Comprehensive Multidisciplinary Outline of Future Activities in Drug Abuse Control,[37] as well as by the conference of plenipotentiaries, held at Vienna from 25 November to 20 December 1988, which adopted the United Nations Convention against Illicit Traffic in Narcotic Drugs and Psychotropic Substances.[38] The Assembly also expressed its deep concern that, owing to a lack of resources, it has not been possible for the United Nations organs concerned to execute several of the important steps and measures that were mandated for the biennium 1988–1989.

The Assembly acknowledged the recommendations made by the Administrative Committee on Coordination and the Committee for

Programme and Coordination at their 24th Series of Joint Meetings,[39] at which they concluded, *inter alia*, that the Administrative Committee on Coordination should prepare a system-wide action plan leading to specific activities to be undertaken by organizations of the United Nations system, individually and collectively, and that consideration could be given to the need for the establishment of additional mechanisms to enhance the effectiveness of the United Nations system in the field of drug abuse control, while recognizing that the new dimensions taken on by the drug menace will necessitate a more comprehensive approach to international drug control and a more efficient and coordinated structure in this field in order to enable the United Nations to play the central and greatly increased role necessary for countering this threat.

Bearing in mind its decision, in Resolution 44/16 of 1 November 1989, to hold a special session to consider the question of international cooperation against illicit production, supply, demand, trafficking and distribution of narcotic drugs, with a view to expanding the scope and increasing the effectiveness of such cooperation, and stressing the importance of this special session and of the need for member states to make the fullest possible contributions to its preparatory work, the Assembly:

1 Resolved that action against drug abuse and illicit production and trafficking in narcotics should, as a collective responsibility, be accorded the highest possible priority by the international community and that the United Nations should be the main focus for concerted action against illicit drugs;
2 Agreed to strengthen the capability of the United Nations in order to achieve more efficient and coordinated cooperation at the international, regional and national levels against the threats posed by illicit narcotic drugs and psychotropic substances;
3 Requested the Secretary General, in his capacity as Chairman of the Administrative Committee on Coordination, to coordinate at the inter-agency level, the development of a United Nations system-wide action programme on drug abuse control aimed at the full implementation of all existing mandates and subsequent decisions of inter-governmental bodies throughout the United Nations system, using as a guide the Declaration of the International Conference on Drug Abuse and Illicit Trafficking and recommendations in the Comprehensive Multidisciplinary Outline of Future Activities in Drug Abuse Control and for the attainment of this purpose:

  a Called upon the Division of Narcotic Drugs of the Secretariat, the International Narcotics Control Board and its secretariat, as well as the United Nations Fund of Drug Abuse Control, to consult closely with and contribute their expertise to the other agencies represented on the Administrative Committee on Coordination in developing the action plan:

b Requested the Administrative Committee on Coordination to include in the action plan, *inter alia*:

- a statement of purposes that defines the overall goal and denotes specific objectives;
- an outline of concrete activities that each agency should undertake, within its mandate, ensuring that there is no duplication or overlap;
- a reasonable time-frame for implementation of each portion of the action plan;
- a realistic cost estimate for implementing the action plan, being mindful that resources are limited and that it would be necessary for agencies to focus priorities, review deployment of resources or obtain, if necessary, from their governing bodies the authority needed to fulfil their part of the plan;

c Requested the Administrative Committee on Coordination to present the action plan to all member states no later than 31 March 1990, in order to permit discussions by the Committee for Programme and Coordination at its 30th Session and by the Economic and Social Council at its next regular session of 1990;

d Requested that the executive heads of United Nations bodies report annually to the Administrative Committee on Coordination on the pros made in implementing the action plan and that the Administrative Committee include the same information in its annual report, so as to enable the Committee for Programme and Coordination and the Economic and Social Council to consider it, within their respective mandates, and to make appropriate recommendations to the General Assembly;

e Requested the Administrative Committee on Coordination to make the necessary adjustments to the action plan annually and to ensure that each agency bring up-to-date and revise its related activities annually in order to meet changing circumstances;

4 Requested the Secretary General to select a limited number of experts from developed and developing countries to advise and assist him for a maximum period of one year, in full cooperation

with United Nations officials, in order to enhance the efficiency of the United Nations structure for drug abuse control, taking into account the tasks in the light of existing mandates and of decisions adopted by the General Assembly at its special session, and to report to the Assembly at its 45th session;

5 Requested states, without prejudice to the basic criteria that the General Assembly shall adopt at its special session, to consider in the preparatory work for that session, *inter alia,* the following areas, with the purpose of ensuring that all aspects of the problem are adequately addressed in the elaboration of a global programme of action against illicit narcotic drugs for adoption at the special session.

In the context of Point 5 above, the Assembly further recommended:

- Giving increased attention to curbing the rising demand for narcotic drugs by intensified rehabilitative, legal and preventive measures, including public information and education;
- The possibility of declaring a United Nations decade against drug abuse, with the purpose of raising public awareness through a world-wide campaign against drug abuse;
- The expansion of the scope of international cooperation in support of rural development programmes and other economic development and technical assistance programmes aimed at reducing illicit production and drug trafficking through the strengthening of economic, judicial and legal systems;
- The full involvement of international, regional and national financial institutions within their respective areas of competence in the elaboration of measures to counteract the negative economic and social consequences of the drug problem in all its aspects, paying special attention to the characteristics and magnitude of the conversion and transference of drug-related monies in the economic systems of countries;
- The development of mechanisms to prevent the use of the banking system and other financial institutions for the processing or laundering of drug-related money;
- An examination of recommendations to enhance the efficiency of the United Nations structure for drug abuse control in the most appropriate way to enable the United Nations to perform its increasing tasks in the most effective and coordinated manner;
- The development of recommendations for generating increased financial resources to the United Nations drug effort and for ensuring sufficient regular budget resources for the United Nations drug bodies to carry out their mandates;

- The coordination of an expanded programme of training for national narcotics agents in investigative methods, interdiction and narcotics intelligence;
- The feasibility of establishing a reserve pool of experienced narcotics agents and experts pledged by other states, whose services states may request for specified periods of time;
- The establishment under the United Nations of a facility to gather and collate information on the financial flow from drug-related funds, to be made available to states at their request;
- The feasibility of a United Nations capability that, at the request of states, would provide training and equipment for the anti-drug operations of the states to inhibit the use, interdict the supply and eliminate the illicit trafficking of drugs;
- The elaboration of any other appropriate measures whereby the United Nations can contribute further to concerted international action against illicit narcotic drugs.

The Assembly invited states, at the special session of the General Assembly, to consider requesting the Secretary General to appoint a limited number of experts, representing the various aspects of the drug problem with regard to both developed and developing countries, to further the global programme of action as adopted at the special session. It also requested the Secretary General to give priority to narcotics control activities in his proposals for the medium-term plan for the period beginning in 1992.

The Assembly also urged states to contribute to the United Nations Fund for Drug Abuse Control and to consider giving financial or other support to enhance the efficiency of the United Nations structure for drug abuse control and to assist and promote a truly comprehensive global programme of action. Finally, it requested the Secretary General to transmit the present resolution to the Preparatory Committee of the Whole for the 17th Special Session of the General Assembly, which the Assembly established by its decision 44/410 of 14 November 1989.

Further International Action to Combat Drug Abuse and Illicit Trafficking

The General Assembly's deep concern that the illicit demand for, production of, traffic in and use of narcotic drugs and psychotropic substances has become one of the most serious dangers to the health and welfare of populations, adversely affecting the political, economic, social and cultural structure of all societies, and its recognition that the criminal activities of drug trafficking and its marketing network destabilize economies, adversely affect the development of many countries and pose a threat to the stability, national security and sovereignty of states, is evident in its many reiterations of cooperation by states to crush the problem. The alarm of the international community has led to the Assembly's reaffirmation of the growing connection between drug trafficking and terrorism, reaffirming the principle of collective responsibility of the international community in combating drug abuse and illicit trafficking. The Assembly has on numerous occasions recognized the serious efforts being made by the governments of some countries in their programmes for crop substitution, integrated rural development and interdiction, and that international economic and technical cooperation has so far proved inadequate to the task at hand and therefore should be substantially stepped up, and considered that the necessary steps must be taken to preclude the illicit cultivation of plants containing narcotic drugs and psychotropic substances, such as the opium poppy, coca bush and cannabis plant, together with the manufacture of psychotropic substances not used for industrial, scientific or traditional purposes.

The Assembly has also emphasized the importance of the International Conference on Drug Abuse and Illicit Trafficking adopting unanimously the Declaration[40] and the comprehensive Multidisciplinary Outline of Future Activities in Drug Abuse Control,[41] which represent the proper framework for international cooperation in drug control, and welcomed the efforts made by those countries that produce narcotic drugs for scientific, medicinal and therapeutic uses to prevent the channelling of such substances to illicit markets and to maintain production at a level consistent with illicit demand. One of the most important factors of drug trafficking has been recognized as the constantly changing transit routes used by drug traffickers and that an ever-growing number of countries in all regions of the world, even entire regions, are particularly vulnerable to illicit transit traffic on account, *inter alia,* of their geographical location. The Assembly also recognized the need for greater international cooperation which would facilitate the marketing of crop substitution products and the control of chemical substances used to process illicit drugs and psychotropic substances, as well as the impact of the social and economic consequences of drug-money transfers and conversion, which have an adverse effect on national economic systems. It has also recognized the commendable work carried out by the United Nations in controlling narcotic drugs and psychotropic substances, which is being seriously impeded by a lack of human and financial resources. The Assembly in December 1989 recalled its Resolution 43/122 of 8 December 1988 and Resolution 3 of the United Nations conference for the Adoption of a Convention against Illicit Traffic in Narcotic Drugs and Psychotropic Substances,[42] held at Vienna from 25 November to 20 December 1988, which, *inter alia,* recognized the urgent need for additional resources, both human and financial, for the Division of Narcotic Drugs of the Secretariat and the Secretariat of the International Narcotics Control Board, and reiterated that significant contribution towards curbing the problem of narcotic drug traffickers. The Assembly has also recognized the importance of its Resolution 43/121 of 8 December 1988, which, *inter alia,* strongly condemned the criminal activities that involved children in the use, production and illicit sale of narcotic drugs and psychotropic substances and appealed to the competent international agencies and the United Nations Fund for Drug Abuse Control to assign high priority to the study of proposals designed to tackle the problem.

Having regard to its Resolution 44/16 of 1 November 1989, by which it decided to convene a special session to consider the question of closer international cooperation to combat drug abuse and illicit trafficking, the Assembly voted to:

1 Strongly condemn the crime of drug trafficking in all its forms and urged all states to remain steadfast in their political commitment to the concerted international struggle to put an end to it;
2 Endorse Economic and Social Council Resolution 1989/20 of 22 May 1989 and urged governments and organizations to adhere to the principles set forth in the Declaration of the International Conference on Drug Abuse and Illicit Trafficking and to apply, as appropriate, the recommendations of the Comprehensive Multidisciplinary Outline of Future Activities in Drug Abuse Control;
3 Emphasize that the international struggle against drug trafficking and the abuse and sale of, and illicit traffic in, narcotic drugs and psychotropic substances is a collective responsibility and that the eradication of the problem requires efficient and coordinated international cooperation, in keeping with the principle of respect for national sovereignty and the cultural identity of states;
4 Emphasize the connection between the illicit production and supply of, demand for, sale of and traffic in narcotic drugs and psychotropic substances, and the economic, social and cultural conditions of the countries affected;
5 Recognize that the international community, in seeking solutions to the problem of illicit production of, demand for and trade, transit or traffic in narcotic drugs and psychotropic substances, must take into account the differences and diversity of the problem in each country;
6 Call upon the international community to provide increased international economic and technical cooperation to governments, at their request, in support of programmes for the substitution of illicit crops by means of integrated rural development

programmes that respect fully the jurisdiction and sovereignty of countries and the cultural traditions of peoples;

7 Recognize the importance of international cooperation in facilitating trade flows in support of integrated rural development programmes leading to economically viable alternatives to illicit cultivation, taking into account factors such as access to markets for crop substitution products;

8 Request countries that produce the chemical substances necessary for the manufacture of narcotic drugs and psychotropic substances to take the initiative in adopting measures which ensure effective control of the export of such substances;

9 Request the Secretary General to undertake as soon as possible, with the assistance of a group of inter-governmental experts, a study on the economic and social consequences of illicit traffic in drugs, with a view to analysing, *inter alia*, the following elements:

a the magnitude and characteristics of economic transactions related to drug trafficking in all its stages, including production of, traffic in and distribution of illicit drugs, in order to determine the impact of drug-related money transfers and conversion on national economic systems; and,

b mechanisms which would prevent the use of the banking system and the international financial system in this activity;

10 Request the Secretary General to ask member states for their views on the scope and context of such a study, taking into account the elements set forth in paragraph 9 of the present resolution, and to transmit such views to the group of experts;

11 Consider that a system should be established to identify the methods and routes used for the illicit transit traffic in narcotic drugs and psychotropic substances, to enhance the interdiction capability of those states along such routes;

12 Strongly condemn the illicit arms trade that is arming drug traffickers, causing political destabilization and loss of human lives;

13 Call upon all states, particularly those with high rates of use of narcotic drugs and psychotropic substances, to take prevention and rehabilitation measures and also increasingly stringent political and legal measures to eliminate the demand for narcotic drugs and psychotropic substances, and calls upon the United Nations and other relevant international organizations to devote greater attention to this aspect of the problem;

14 Take note with satisfaction of the proposal by the Government of the United Kingdom of Great Britain and Northern Ireland to convene an international conference on drug demand reduction;[43]

15 Recognize that the publication and dissemination of materials which encourage or stimulate the production of and demand for narcotic drugs and psychotropic substances do not contribute positively to the international action to combat drug abuse and illicit trafficking.
16 Request the Secretary General to report to the General Assembly at its 45th Session on the implementation of its Resolution 43/121 and of Economic and Social Council decision 1989/123 of 22 May 1989;
17 Call upon member states to substantially increase their contributions to the United Nations Fund for Drug Abuse Control, so that it can expand its programmes;
18 Endorse Economic and Social Council Resolution 1989/18 of 22 May 1989;
19 Express its serious concern at the considerable reduction in the budget and staff of the Division of Narcotic Drugs of the Secretariat and the Secretariat of the International Narcotics Control Board, which threatens their ability to carry out adequately any additional responsibilities deriving from the activities which the United Nations must undertake to tackle the new dimension of the problem of drug abuse and illicit trafficking;
20 Recommend that the Secretary General take urgent steps to ensure the increase of allocations to the Division of Narcotic Drugs and the Secretariat of the International Narcotics Control Board;
21 Take note with satisfaction of the results of the Second Interregional Meetings of Heads of National Drug Law Enforcement Agencies;[44]
22 Take note of the reports of the Secretary General[45] and requested him to report to the General Assembly at its 45th Session on the implementation of the present resolution and also to prepare on a yearly basis a detailed report on international drug-control activities reflecting the work done by the United Nations system to implement the recommendations of the comprehensive Multidisciplinary Outline of Future Activities in Drug Abuse Control; and,
23 Decide to include in the provisional agenda of its 45th Session an item entitled 'International action to combat drug abuse and illicit trafficking'.

Also, in December 1989, the Assembly considered measures to prevent international terrorism which endangers or takes innocent human lives or jeopardizes fundamental freedoms and study of the underlying causes of those forms of terrorism and acts of violence which lie in misery, frustration, grievance and despair and which cause some people to sacrifice human lives, including their own, in an attempt to effect radical changes.

The General Assembly expressed the view that it was convinced that a policy of firmness and effective measures should be taken in accordance with international law in order that all acts, methods and practices of international terrorism may be brought to an end. In this context, the Assembly noted the ongoing work within ICAO regarding research as to the detection of plastic or sheet explosives and the devising of an international regime for the marking of such explosives for the purposes of detection, and taking note of Security Council Resolution 635 (1989) of 14 June 1989 relating thereto, expressed its confidence that the ICAO work would contribute significantly towards curbing acts of unlawful interference with civil aviation.

The Assembly also expressed deep concern at the world-wide persistence of acts of international terrorism in all its forms, including those in which states are directly or indirectly involved, which endanger or take innocent lives, have a deleterious effect on international relations and may jeopardize the territorial integrity and security of states. The Assembly called attention to the growing connection between terrorist groups and drug traffickers. It was also convinced of the importance of the observance by states of their obligations under the relevant international conventions to ensure that appropriate law-enforcement measures are taken in connection with the offences addressed in those conventions, and the importance of expanding and improving international cooperation among states, on a bilateral, regional and multilateral basis.

The Assembly was convinced further that international cooperation in combating and preventing terrorism will contribute to the strengthening of confidence among states, reduce tensions and create a better climate among them, and was mindful of the need to enhance the role of the United Nations and the relevant specialized agencies in combating international terrorism.

The necessity of maintaining and protecting the basic rights of, and guarantees for, the individual in accordance with the relevant international human rights instruments and generally accepted international standards was recognized to the extent that the Assembly reaffirmed the principle of self-determination of people as enshrined in the Charter of the United Nations.

The Assembly noted the efforts and important achievements of the International Civil Aviation Organization and the International Maritime Organization in promoting the security of international air and sea transport against acts of terrorism, and recognized that the effectiveness of the struggle against terrorism could be enhanced by the establishment of a generally agreed definition of international terrorism. The Assembly, while condemning unequivocally as criminal and unjustifiable, all acts, methods and practices of terrorism wherever and by whomever committed, including those which jeopardize friendly relations among states and their security, deeply deplored the loss of human life which results from such acts of terrorism, as well as the pernicious impact of these acts on relations of cooperation among states. It called upon all states to fulfil their obligations under international law to refrain from organizing, instigating, assisting or participating in terrorist acts in other states, or acquiescing in or encouraging activities within their territory directed towards the commission of such acts. States were also urged to fulfil their obligations under international law and take effective and resolute measures for the speedy and final elimination of international terrorism and to that end, in particular, to prevent the preparation and organization in their respective territories, for commission within or outside their territories, of terrorist and subversive acts directed against other states and their citizens.

The Assembly also called upon states to ensure the apprehension and prosecution or extradition of perpetrators of terrorist acts; and to endeavour to conclude special agreements to that effect on a bilateral, regional and multilateral basis.

Cooperation of states with one another in exchanging relevant information concerning the prevention and combating of terrorism was considered vital, together with the adoption of steps necessary to implement the existing international conventions on this subject to which they are party, including the harmonization of their domestic legislation with those conventions. The Assembly appealed to all states that have not yet done so to consider becoming party to the international conventions relating to various aspects of international terrorism referred to in the preamble to the present resolution; and urged all states, unilaterally and in cooperation with other states, as well as relevant United Nations organs, to contribute to the progressive elimination of the causes underlying international terrorism and to pay special attention to all situations, including colonialism, racism and situations involving mass and flagrant violation of human rights and fundamental freedoms and those involving alien domination and foreign occupation, that may give rise to international terrorism and may endanger international peace and security. Finally, it firmly called for the immediate and safe release of hostages and abducted persons, wherever and by whomever they are being held.

In December 1984, the United Nations suggested a draft convention against Traffic in Narcotic Drugs and Psychotropic Substances and Related Activities. The Preamble to the Convention reflects the concern of all the states party to the Convention that illicit traffic in and use of narcotic drugs and psychotropic substances transcend the sphere of the physical and moral well-being of mankind and are detrimental to the identity and integration of people, since they constitute a factor of dependence and corruption which undermines their spiritual, cultural, social and economic values. The awareness of parties that such problems must be dealt with within the framework of international cooperation and global geopolitics, since drugs are goods used to weaken the legitimate economies of the countries and to undermine their sovereignty, and that such practices are impeding development, especially in the countries of the Andean region, was also emphasized. States agreed to declare illicit traffic in narcotic drugs and psychotropic substances, the fundamental means of promoting illicit use of such substances, which use is inflicting serious harm on the youth of the world, to be a grave crime against humanity under international law, having regard to the following considerations:

1 Illicit traffic in and use of such substances are detrimental to the integrity and identity of our peoples since they undermine their spiritual, historical and social values, and, as a result of technical advances in the communications media, unprecedented expansion in untoward cross-cultural influences, increase in organized crime and other factors, have reached proportions too great to be dealt with through the isolated demands and actions of states,
2 There is clear evidence that illicit trafficking is closely linked to the designs and actions of some aimed at subverting the legal order and social peace in our countries in pursuit of their despicable commercial aims, and that it constitutes a factor of dependence for developing peoples and impedes economic integration in keeping with their common interests,
3 It is clearly established that illicit trafficking operates by corrupting the political and administrative structures of producing and consuming countries and undermines the security and defence of peoples by sapping their military strength and affecting their sovereignty,
4 There is a need for international legislation that would provide a basis for effective action to combat illicit trafficking in and use of and for punishing those responsible wherever they may be,
5 The volume, magnitude and extent of illicit trafficking and use represent a challenge to society as a whole and constitute activities threatening the very existence and future development of human beings and especially affect youth, a key factor for the development of the people of the world,
6 Drug addiction is detrimental to health, one of the basic assets and inalienable rights of every human being, and without individual health there is no public health, a fact which in turn bears upon and determines the economic development of people,

7 Bearing in mind that the repeated use of narcotic drugs and psychotropic substances affects the individual and through its biological, psychological and social effects, damages the personality and creates problems for the family, society and the State,

8 The illicit use of narcotic drugs and psychotropic substances is taking a very serious and often irreversible toll on youth, which is the noblest part of the human resources of the world's people, and weakens their capacity for cultural and material progress.

The parties have agreed that trafficking in narcotic drugs or psychotropic substances is a grave international crime against humanity. The states party to the Convention undertake to prevent and suppress it.[46] Illicit activities are defined in the Convention as trafficking, distribution, supply, manufacture, elaboration, refining, processing, extraction, preparation, production, cultivation, preservation, transport and storage and the management, organization, financing or facilitating of the traffic in any of the substances or their raw materials referred to in the present Convention.[47] It is deemed an aggravating circumstance if an individual responsible for such activities performs a public function of any kind. Article 5 of the Convention stipulates that the illicit activities enumerated in the Convention shall not be considered as political crimes for the purpose of extradition.

The crimes enumerated in the Convention are imprescriptible. Irrespective of the date on which they were committed, they shall be investigated, and individuals against whom there exists sufficient evidence of having committed such crimes shall be sought, arrested, charged and, if found guilty, punished. Article 6 of the Convention stipulates that the states parties undertake to adopt, in accordance with their respective laws, any legislative or other measures as may be necessary to ensure that statutory or other limitations shall not apply to the prosecution or punishment, as determined by law or otherwise, of the crimes referred to in Article 3 and part A, paragraph 2, of article 10 of the Convention, and that, where they exist, such statutory limitations shall be abolished.

Article 7 provides that the state parties undertake to adopt the legislative measures necessary to ensure implementation of the provisions of the present Convention and, in particular, to provide for stringent criminal penalties against individuals responsible for the activities referred to herein.

Duties of international organizations are specified in Article 8 which requires any state party or competent international organization to seek to have the relevant bodies of the United Nations or of other regional organizations take such action as they deem appropriate, in accordance with the international instruments governing them to prevent and suppress the illicit activities enumerated in the present Convention.

International cooperation is a critical element of implementation in the Convention. State parties are required to cooperate on a bilateral and multilateral basis to prevent and suppress the illicit activities enumerated in the present Convention and shall take all necessary measures towards that end. Accordingly, they are required to affect the following:

1 Ensure that, at the national level, there is coordination of preventive and repressive action against illicit trafficking in narcotic drugs and psychotropic substances. They may assign responsibility for such coordination to an appropriate agency.
2 Provide mutual assistance in combating illicit trafficking and cooperate with each other in identifying, arresting and taking legal action against those suspected of engaging in such illicit activities and their accomplices or abetters and also in seizing and destroying such substances.
3 Cooperate closely with each other and with competent international organizations of which they are members in a coordinated effort to combat illicit trafficking, particularly by collecting information and documents relevant to investigation with the aim of facilitating the prosecution of the persons referred to in the preceding paragraph, and exchange such information.
4 See to it that international cooperation between the relevant agencies is expeditiously carried out.
5 Ensure that writs for judicial action are transmitted between countries directly and expeditiously to the organs designated by the states' parties. This provision shall not prevent any state party from exercising its right to require that such writs be transmitted to it through the diplomatic channel or from government to government.
6 Provide information on illicit activities within their territories that involve narcotic drugs and psychotropic substances, including information on the cultivation, production and manufacture of, trafficking in and use of such substances.
7 Refrain from enacting legislative provisions or taking measures of any other kind which might be prejudicial to the international obligations which they have assumed with respect to the identification, arrest, extradition and punishment of individuals guilty of the crimes enumerated in the present Convention.

Penal provisions are addressed in Article 10 which provides that each of the crimes enumerated in the present Convention, whether committed by the individual or by several acting in collusion in different countries, are considered a distinct offence.[48] Participation or association in the commission of any such crime, conspiracy, instigation or the attempt to commit any such crime, and preparatory actions for such crimes, shall be considered offences.[49] Convictions obtained abroad in respect of such crimes are taken into account in determining whether the accused is a habitual offender.[50] Crimes committed by both nationals and aliens will be tried by the state party in whose territory the crime was committed, or by the state party in whose territory the offender is present if extradition is not authorized under the law of the state party to which a request for extradition is made and if the offender has not yet been tried and sentenced for one of the crimes enumerated in the present Convention.[51]

Each of the crimes enumerated in Article 3 and Article 10 (A 2), are deemed to be included among the extraditable offences covered by any extradition treaty which has been or may hereafter be concluded between the state parties. If a state party which makes extradition contingent on the existence of a treaty receives a request for extradition from another state party with which it has no treaty, it may, should it so choose, consider the present Convention as the necessary legal basis for extradition in respect of the crimes enumerated in Article 3 and in part A, paragraph 2, of the present article. Extradition shall be subject to any other conditions laid down by the law of the state party to which the application is made.[52] State parties which do not make extradition contingent on the existence of a treaty shall recognize the crimes enumerated in Article 3 and in part A, paragraph 2, of the present article as extraditable offences between them, subject to any conditions laid down by the law of the state party to which the application for extradition is made.[53] The provisions of Article 10 do not affect the principle that the crimes in question must be prosecuted and punished in accordance with the national law of each state party.

Anyone involved in any of the activities enumerated in the present Convention may be tried by a competent tribunal in any of the states in whose territory an act or acts to which the Convention applies was or were committed or by such international criminal tribunal as may have jurisdiction under the applicable legal rules.[54] The Convention calls for a fund to be established to assist developing countries affected by the illicit traffic in narcotic drugs and psychotropic substances with a view to combating and overcoming the causes of those phenomena and providing them with adequate means of combating such illicit activities. The fund shall be constituted by contributions from states which are party to the Convention on the basis of the method of assessment used by the United Nations and by voluntary contributions.[55] The Fund shall be administered by a governing board composed of an equal number of representatives from each of the state parties.[56]

The state parties agree to entrust the task of overseeing the activities and obligations set out in the present Convention to the Commission on Narcotic Drugs and the International Narcotics Control Board of the Economic and Social Council of the United Nations.[57]

Article 15 of the Convention requires disputes relating to the interpretation, application or fulfilment of the present Convention to be submitted to the International Court of Justice at the request of one of the state party to the dispute.

The Convention is open for signature or accession by all states, whether they are members or non-members of the United Nations, without limitation as to time; it shall be subject to ratification and the respective instruments shall be deposited with the Secretary General of the United Nations[58] and shall enter into force on the 10th day following the date on which the 20th instrument of ratification or accession is deposited.[59]

The Convention remains in effect for a period of 50 years following its entry into force. The Annex to the Convention contains a Declaration on the Control of Drug Trafficking and Drug Abuse where the General Assembly focuses on the purposes and principles of the Charter of the United Nations reaffirming faith in the dignity and worth of the human person and promoting social progress and better standards of life in larger freedom and international cooperation in solving problems of an economic, social, cultural or humanitarian character, and takes note that member states have undertaken in the Universal Declaration of Human Rights[60] to promote social progress and better standards of life for the people of the world.

In view of the fact that the international community has expressed grave concern at the fact that trafficking in narcotics and drug abuse constitutes an obstacle to the physical and moral well-being of people and of youth in particular, in part all its collective pronouncements against illicit drug trafficking, thus reflecting the awareness of the international community of the urgency of preventing and punishing the illicit demand for, abuse of and illicit production of and traffic in drugs, the Assembly drew the attention of the international community to the work of the Commission on Narcotic Drugs, the International Narcotics Control Board and the United Nations Fund for Drug Abuse Control who have made valuable contributions to the control and elimination of drug trafficking and drug abuse, and urged state parties to adhere to the recommendation of these bodies.

The Assembly also declares in the Annex that:

1 Drug trafficking and drug abuse are extremely serious problems which, owing to their magnitude, scope and widespread

pernicious effects, have become an international criminal activity demanding urgent attention and maximum priority.

2 The illegal production of, illicit demand for, abuse of and illicit trafficking in drugs impede economic and social progress, constitute a grave threat to the security and development of many countries and people and should be combated by all moral, legal and institutional means, at national, regional and international levels.

3 The eradication of trafficking in narcotic drugs is the collective responsibility of all states, especially those affected by problems relating to illicit production, trafficking or abuse.

4 State members shall utilize the legal instruments against the illicit production of and demand for, abuse of and illicit traffic in drugs and adopt additional measures to counter new manifestations of this shameful and heinous crime.

5 State members undertake to intensify efforts and to coordinate strategies aimed at the control and eradication of the complex problem of drug trafficking and drug abuse through programmes including economic, social and cultural alternatives.

The United Nations Convention Against Illicit Traffic in Narcotic Drugs and Psychotropic Substances

On 19 December 1988 the United Nations adopted its Convention Against Illicit Traffic in Narcotic Drugs and Psychotropic Substances. The Convention brought to bear the deep concern of the United Nations regarding the magnitude of and rising trend in the illicit production of, demand for and traffic in narcotic drugs and psychotropic substances, which pose a serious threat to the health and welfare of human beings and adversely affect the economic, cultural and political foundations of society. Concern was also raised at the steadily increasing inroads into various social groups made by illicit traffic in narcotic drugs and psychotropic substances, and particularly by the fact that children are used in many parts of the world as an illicit drug consumers' market and for purposes of illicit production, distribution and trade in narcotic drugs and psychotropic substances, which entails a danger of incalculable gravity.

The Convention recognized the links between illicit traffic and other related organized criminal activities which undermine the legitimate economies and threaten the stability, security and sovereignty of states and that illicit traffic is an international criminal activity, the suppression of which demands urgent attention and the highest priority.

Article I of the Convention provides that the purpose of the Convention is to promote cooperation among the states so that they may address more effectively the various aspects of illicit traffic in narcotic drugs and psychotropic substances having an international dimension. In carrying out their obligations under the Convention, the state parties are required to take necessary measures, including legislative and administrative measures, in conformity with the fundamental provisions of their respective domestic legislative systems.

Article 3 sets out offences and sanctions and provides that each party shall adopt such measures as may be necessary to establish as criminal offences under its domestic law, when committed intentionally:

a (i) the production, manufacture, extraction, preparation, offering, offering for sale, distribution, sale, delivery on any terms whatsoever, brokerage, dispatch, dispatch in transit, transport importation or exportation of any narcotic drug or any psychotropic substance contrary to the provisions of the 1961 Convention, the 1961 Convention as amended or the 1971 Convention;
(ii) the cultivation of opium poppy, coca bush or cannabis plant for the purpose of the production of narcotic drugs contrary to the provisions of the 1961 Convention and the 1961 Convention as amended;
(iii) the possession or purchase of any narcotic drug or psychotropic substance for the purpose of any of the activities enumerated in (i) above;
(iv) the manufacture, transport or distribution of equipment, materials or of substances listed in Table I and Table II,[61] knowing that they are to be used in or for the illicit cultivation, production or manufacture of narcotic drugs or psychotropic substances;
(v) the organization, management or financing of any of the offences enumerated in (i), (ii), (iii) or (iv) above;

b (i) the conversion or transfer of property, knowing that such property is derived from any offence or offences established in accordance with subparagraph (a) of this paragraph, or from an act, of participation in such offence or offences, for the purpose of concealing or disguising the illicit origin of the property or of assisting any person who is involved in the commission of such an offence or offences to evade the legal consequences of the actions;
(ii) the concealment or disguise of the true nature, source, location, disposition, movement, rights with respect to, or ownership of property, knowing that such property is derived from an offence or offences established in accordance

with subparagraph (a) of this paragraph or from an act of participation in such an offence or offences.

The Convention also provides that subject to its constitutional principles and the basic concepts of its legal system, the acquisition, possession or use of property, knowing, at the time of receipt, that such property was derived from an offence or offences, the possession of equipment or materials or substances listed in the Convention, knowing that they are being or are to be used in or for the illicit cultivation, production or manufacture of narcotic drugs or psychotropic substances, are offences. Also, those who publicly incite or induce others, by any means, to commit any of the offences established in accordance with the Convention or use narcotic drugs or psychotropic substances illicitly and participate in, associate or conspire to commit, attempts to commit and aid, abet, facilitate and counsel the commission of any of the offences established in accordance with its definitive provisions shall be guilty of an offence under the Convention.

Subject to its constitutional principles and the basic concepts of its legal system, each party is required to adopt such measures as may be necessary to establish as a criminal offence under its domestic law, when committed intentionally, the possession, purchase or cultivation of narcotic drugs or psychotropic substances for personal consumption. Knowledge, intent or purpose required as an element of an offence set forth in paragraph 1 of this article may be inferred from objective factual circumstances.

Each party is further required to make the commission of the offences established in accordance with paragraph 1 of this article liable to sanctions which take into account the grave nature of these offences, such as imprisonment or other forms of deprivation of liberty, pecuniary sanctions and confiscation.

The parties may also provide, in addition to conviction or punishment, for an offence established by the Convention, that the offender shall undergo measures such as treatment, education, aftercare, rehabilitation or social reintegration. It is also provided that, in appropriate cases of a minor nature, the parties may provide, as alternatives to conviction or punishment, measures such as education, rehabilitation or social reintegration, as well as, when the offender is a drug abuser, treatment and aftercare. The parties may provide, either as an alternative to conviction or punishment, or in addition to conviction or punishment of an offence established in accordance with paragraph 2 of this article, measures for the treatment, education, aftercare, rehabilitation or social reintegration of the offender.

On the subject of jurisdiction, state parties are required to ensure that their courts and other competent authorities having jurisdiction can take into account factual circumstances which make the commission of the offences established in accordance with paragraph 1 of this article particularly serious, such as:

- the involvement in the offence of an organized criminal group to which the offender belongs;
- the involvement of the offender in other international organized criminal activities;
- the involvement of the offender in other illegal activities facilitated by commission of the offence;
- the use of violence of arms by the offender;
- the fact that the offender holds a public office and that the offence is connected with the office in question;
- the victimization or use of minors;
- the fact that the offence is committed in a penal institution or in an educational institution or social service facility or in their immediate vicinity or in other places to which school children and students resort for educational, sports and social activities;
- prior conviction, particularly for similar offences, whether foreign or domestic, to the extent permitted under the domestic law of a party.

The Convention further stipulates that parties shall endeavour to ensure that any discretionary legal powers under their domestic law relating to the prosecution of persons for offences established in accordance with this article are exercised to maximize the effectiveness of law enforcement measures in respect of those offences and with due regard to the need to deter the commission of such offences.

The courts or other competent authorities of the parties are required to bear in mind the serious nature of the offences enumerated above and the circumstances enumerated in the Convention when considering the eventuality of early release or parole of persons convicted of such offences.

Each party shall, where appropriate, establish under its domestic law a long statute of limitations period in which to commence proceedings for any offence established in accordance with the Convention, and a longer period where the alleged offender has evaded the administration of justice.

Each party shall take appropriate measures, consistent with its legal system, to ensure that a person charged with or convicted of an offence established in accordance with paragraph 1 of this article, who is found within its territory, is present at the necessary criminal proceedings.

For the purpose of cooperation among the parties under this Convention, offences established in accordance with the Convention are not considered as fiscal offences or as political offences or regarded as politically motivated, without prejudice to the constitutional limitations and the fundamental domestic law of the parties. The Convention does not encroach on domestic law and provides that nothing contained in it shall affect the principle that the description of the offences to which it refers and of legal defences thereto is reserved to the domestic law of a party and that such offences shall be prosecuted and punished in conformity with that law.

Article 4 of the Convention introduces issues of jurisdiction and provides that each party shall take measures as may be necessary to establish its jurisdiction over the offences it has established in accordance with the Convention when:

- the offence is committed in its territory;
- the offence is committed on board a vessel flying its flag or an aircraft which is registered under its laws at the time the offence is committed;

Also, state parties may take such measures as may be necessary to establish its jurisdiction over the offences it has established when:

- the offence is committed by one of its nationals or by a person who has habitual residence it its territory;
- the offence is committed on board a vessel concerning which that party has been authorized to take appropriate action provided that such jurisdiction shall be exercised only on the basis of agreements or arrangements referred to in the Convention;
- the offence is one committed outside its territory with a view to the commission, within its territory, of an offence established in accordance with the Convention.

Each party is also required to take such measures as may be necessary to establish its jurisdiction over the offences it has established, when the alleged offender is present in its territory and it does not extradite him or her to another party on the grounds:

- that the offence has been committed in its territory or on board a vessel flying its flag or an aircraft which was registered under its law at the time the offence was committed; or
- that the offence has been committed by one of its nationals.

It may also take such measures as may be necessary to establish its jurisdiction over the offences it has established when the alleged offender is present in its territory and it does not extradite him or her to another party. The Convention does not exclude the exercise of any criminal jurisdiction established by a party in accordance with its domestic law.

Article 5 addresses the issue of confiscation, where it provides that each party shall adopt such measures as may be necessary to enable confiscation of proceeds derived from offences established in accordance with the Convention or property the value of which corresponds to that of such proceeds; and narcotic drugs and psychotropic substances, materials and equipment or other instrumentalities used in or intended for use in any manner in offences established in accordance with the Convention.

Article 5 further provides that each party shall also adopt such measures as may be necessary to enable its competent authorities to identify, trace, and freeze or seize proceeds, property, instrumentalities or any other things, for the purpose of eventual confiscation. In order to carry out the measures referred to in this article, each party is required to empower its courts or other competent authorities to order that bank, financial or commercial records be made available or be seized. A party shall not decline to act under the provisions of this paragraph on the grounds of bank secrecy.

Article 6, which refers to extradition, applies to the offences established by the parties in accordance with the Convention. Each of the offences to which this article applies is deemed to be included as an extraditable offence in any extradition treaty existing between parties. The parties undertake to include such offences as extraditable offences in every extradition treaty to be concluded between them. If a party which makes extradition conditional on the existence of a treaty receives a request for extradition from another party with which it has no extradition treaty, it may consider the Convention as the legal basis for extradition in respect of any offence to which this article applies. The parties which require detailed legislation in order to use this Convention as a legal basis for extradition shall consider enacting such legislation as may be necessary.

The parties which do not make extradition conditional on the existence of a treaty are required to recognize offences to which Article 6 applies as extraditable offences between themselves. Extradition is subject to the conditions provided for by the law of the requested party or by applicable extradition treaties, including the grounds upon which the requested party may refuse extradition. In considering requests received pursuant to this article, the requested state may refuse to comply with such requests where there are substantial grounds leading its judicial or other competent authorities to believe that compliance would facilitate the prosecution or punishment of any person on account of race, religion, nationality or political opinions, or would cause prejudice for any of those reasons to any person affected by the request.

The parties are further required to expedite extradition procedures and to simplify evidentiary requirements relating thereto in respect of any offence to which Article 6 applies.

Subject to the provisions of its domestic law and its extradition treaties, the requested party may, upon being satisfied that the circumstances so warrant and are urgent, and at the behest of the requesting party, take a person whose extradition is sought and who is present in its territory into custody or take other appropriate measures to ensure his or her presence at extradition proceedings. Also, without prejudice to the exercise of any criminal jurisdiction established in accordance with its domestic law, a party in whose territory an alleged offender is found shall, if it does not extradite him in respect of an offence established in accordance with the provisions of the Convention, submit the case to its competent authorities for the purpose of prosecution, unless otherwise agreed with the requesting party.

If the state party does not extradite him or her in respect of such an offence and has established its jurisdiction in relation to that offence, it has to submit the case to its competent authorities for the purpose of prosecution, unless otherwise requested by the requesting party for the purposes of preserving its legitimate jurisdiction.

If extradition, sought for the purposes of enforcing a sentence, is refused because the person sought is a national of the requested party, the requested party shall, if its law so permits and in conformity with the requirements of such law, upon application of the requesting party, consider the enforcement of the sentence which has been imposed under the law of the requesting party, or the remainder thereof.

The parties are able to seek to conclude bilateral and multilateral agreements to carry out or to enhance the effectiveness of extradition. They may also consider entering into bilateral or multilateral agreements, whether *ad hoc* or general, on the transfer to their country of persons sentenced to imprisonment and other forms of deprivation of liberty for offences to which this article applies, in order that they may complete their sentences there.

ICAO Initiatives

The Air Navigation Commission at the 11th Meeting of its 24th Session on 25 February 1957 considered a request of ICAO of inviting comments on the carriage of opiates and derivatives in first-aid kits on board aircraft on international flights.[67] Special reference in this letter had been made on the following points:

- Is it believed necessary to carry opiates or drugs containing opiates and their respective derivatives in the first-aid kits of aircraft for use in case of emergency or in the kits carried by airlines for the relief of passengers suffering from certain diseases?
- Do the regulations in a country prohibit the carriage of drugs containing opiates or their derivatives in limited quantities in first-aid kits on board aircraft on international flights? If so, under what safeguards would you allow such drugs to be carried?
- Do the regulations of that country prohibit a qualified crew member from administering subcutaneous or intravenous injections in case of emergency on international flights?

Substantive replies were received from 28 contracting states, the Belgian Congo and Netherlands Antilles. In addition three states (Burma, Guatemala, Mexico) acknowledged receipt or had no comment to offer on the State Letter. Comments were also received from the United Nations European Office, Division on Narcotic Drugs, IFALPA, the Aero Medical Association and the ATA (through the United States government).

Basic Principles of International Narcotic Control

The Commission noted in 1957 that any use or carriage of narcotics was subject to control under international laws on narcotic drugs. The ECOSOC Division of Narcotic Drugs, referring to the ICAO State Letter, had indicated that any discussions ICAO had on the subject or any decisions or regulations they adopted would be of great importance for the work of its Commission on Narcotic Drugs in connection with their preparation of a new Single Convention intended to codify all international treaties relating to narcotic drugs.

The Commission also noted that the international regulations on narcotic drugs consist of a complex system of several conventions under the supervision of ECOSOC and its Committee on Narcotic Drugs. They were directed at establishing international control of all drugs causing addiction and the application of certain principles as regards the manufacture, prescription, sale and traffic of narcotic drugs. These had generally been introduced into national regulations to prevent any abuse and illicit traffic. There was nevertheless some lack of uniformity in the detailed application as not all states are parties to all conventions. It was believed that the codification of all existing treaties into a single convention, planned by ECOSOC, in the near future, would promote uniformity. In principle, there was no intent in the international regulations to restrict the legitimate use of opiates or narcotic drugs for medical purposes and in case of emergencies. A number of states had adopted specific legal provisions for the carriage of such drugs in aircraft first-aid kits. Other states believed that effective control of their contents was difficult so as to prevent any possibility of abuse.

The Commission was of the view that opiates or other restricted substances carried on board were generally subject to control and the laws applicable in the state of registry. For instance, the supplies could only be obtained for legitimate, medical or scientific purposes in limited quantities under control, by medical prescription and from an authorized source. A record had to be kept and any use and replacement of such drugs must be accounted for. It is therefore desirable that first-aid kits be protected against misuse by being kept under lock and key or sealed. Preferably opiates or similar drugs might be kept in a sealed container within the first-aid kit. It was also necessary that a record be kept of the quantity, name of product and manufacturer, date of prescription, dispensing agency and signature of person responsible for the control and its use.

One of the significant achievements of the Commission was its conclusion that the terms 'opiates and derivatives', 'narcotics' and 'narcotic drug' should be considered to include opium, coca leaves, their alkaloids and preparations or derivatives therefrom, whether prepared from substances of vegetable origin or by means of synthesis, or their combinations, and other synthetic drugs liable to produce addiction and controlled by international narcotic regulation.

The Commission concurred with the conclusion that the difficulties reported by some countries might have been caused by a lack of uniformity of national laws and practices developed under a complex system of international narcotic conventions and the detailed conditions under which opiates and similar drugs had been carried on board. It appeared possible to eliminate existing differences – and potential difficulties – if certain principles for effective control and safeguards against abuse, such as quantity limitations, could be more generally agreed upon by all contracting states.

As recommended by the Air Navigation Commission in its 545th Report,[63] the Council decided:

1 that states should be informed of the Commission's study on the carriage of opiates and derivatives in first-aid kits on board aircraft on international flights and of its conclusion that the recommendation of Annex 6 continues to be satisfactory and that the carriage of opiates and derivatives in aircraft first-aid kits is considered desirable;
2 that states should be invited to note the implication in this recommendation that foreign carriers should be permitted to carry

> first-aid kits with contents as described in Annex 6 on international flights, under control, according to international narcotic laws and subject to satisfactory safeguards against abuse, and to notify ICAO when they do not permit this.[64]

It agreed that ECOSOC and the World Health Organization (WHO) should be invited to study the related medical and legal problems, in particular the application of efficient safeguards against abuse and of uniform principles under which opiates or other drugs might be used and carried in first-aid kits on board aircraft, in an effort to promote uniformity under existing laws and to avoid difficulties. It was also agreed that such studies should take into account any factors affecting international civil aviation, such as the safety of persons on board and relief in the case of emergencies in flight or of aircraft accidents, and the ICAO Secretariat should call the attention of the bodies making the studies to these factors.

At its 30th Session in April 1957, the Council considered further the question of the carriage of opiates in aircraft first-aid kits and recognized that there were three points for decision. The first was: 'Is the carriage of opiates in aircraft first-aid kits desirable?' The Commission's conclusion was that it was desirable – there was a Recommended Practice in paragraph 6.2 a) of Annex 6 which listed narcotics and analgesics among the contents of first-aid kits, and the Commission believed that it should stand. The second point was: 'Should their carriage be permitted?' From the ICAO standpoint the answer was obviously 'Yes' – if the carriage of opiates and derivatives was desirable it should be permitted – but the issue was complicated by the fact that the international movement of drugs was subject to international narcotics control. The Commission was of the view that all that could be done in the circumstances was to inform contracting states of the present study, to ask them to note the implication in Annex 6 that foreign operators should be permitted to carry first-aid kits with the contents described in that paragraph, and to request them to notify the organization of differences between their national regulations or practices and this provision. It recommended that the Council decide accordingly. States, ECOSOC and WHO might also be invited to study the related legal and medical problems, in particular the application of efficient safeguards against abuse and of uniform principles under which opiates or other drugs might be used and carried in first-aid kits on board aircraft, in an effort to promote uniformity in existing laws and avoid difficulty. The third point was whether qualified crew members should be permitted to administer narcotic drugs in cases of emergency. On this again national regulations and practices differed, and the Commission's conclusion was that states might be asked to accept the practice of the state of registry of the aircraft.

The Council in its Annual Report to the Assembly for 1957[65] advised that in the light of the replies received from states to the letter inviting comments on the carriage of opiates and derivatives in first-aid kits on board aircraft on international flights, the Air Navigation Commission had concluded that the recommendation in Annex 6 (that first-aid kits should contain analgesics and narcotics) was adequate but that there was a need for more uniformity in its practical application.

Consideration was also given to what action ICAO might take on a number of other medical and health problems in aviation such as the carriage of sick persons, pregnant women, live animals and dead bodies, pollution of food and drinking water on board and removal of refuse from aircraft. A majority of Council members felt that these problems were of much more concern to other organizations (particularly WHO and IATA) than to ICAO and that ICAO could not take any useful action on them. The Secretary General was instructed to keep in touch with developments in connection with them to ensure that any action taken by other organizations would not unnecessarily interfere with ICAO's Facilitation Programme.

The Economic and Social Council, acting on the request of the ICAO Council, considering the problem of the carriage of narcotic drugs in first-aid kits of aircraft engaged in international flight, noted that the Council of the International Civil Aviation Organization at the 8th meeting of its 30th Session, on 1 April 1957, invited the World Health Organization to study the medical aspects of this question.

The Air Navigation Commission of ICAO later noted that in 1958, the United Nations had recommended to governments[66] to take all necessary measures to prevent the misuse and diversion for illicit purposes of narcotic drugs carried in first-aid kits of aircraft engaged in international flight, in particular by ensuring that such drugs are kept in sealed or locked containers to which only authorized persons have access, that adequate records of supply and use, and of stocks, of narcotic drugs are maintained by the airline companies concerned, and that such records and stocks are subject to regular inspection.

In this context, the Economic and Social Council (ECOSOC) had also requested the Secretary General to invite the views of the International Criminal Police Organization (ICPO or Interpol) on the safeguards which should be taken to prevent the diversion of such drugs for illicit purpose and invited the Commission on Narcotic Drugs to consider the report referred to in the preceding paragraph, at its 14th Session if possible, and to advise the Economic and Social Council whether further measures should be recommended to governments for application.

In an overview of action taken by ICAO on the carriage of opiates in first-aid kits in aircraft it was observed that the Air Navigation

Commission first dealt with the subject when considering how to overcome the difficulties experienced by states in the application of Annex 6, dealing with the carriage of narcotic drugs in aircraft first-aid kits.[67] These discussions when reported to the Council resulted in council's invitation to ECOSOC and to the WHO to study various aspects of the problem .

The Air Navigation Commission was then informed on progress on this subject and at that time the Commission had noted that the problem of the carriage of opiates in aircraft first-aid kits on international flights was being studied further by the World Health Organization and the United Nations' Commission on Narcotic Drugs. The Secretary was requested to keep the Commission informed of later developments as appropriate.

It was also observed that the Economic and Social Council in Resolution 689F adopted at its 26th Session in July 1958, had requested the Secretary General of the United Nations to invite the views of the International Criminal Police Organization, on the safeguards which should be taken to prevent diversion of such drugs for illicit purposes[68] and to prepare, if the World Health Organization study supports the carriage of narcotic drugs in first-aid kits of aircraft engaged in international flight, a report on the legal problems, in particular concerning the application of efficient safeguards against abuse and of uniform principles under which opiates or similar drugs might be used and carried in first-aid kits on board aircraft in an effort to promote uniformity under existing laws. This report was to be prepared in consultation with the Secretariats of the International Civil Aviation Organization and the World Health Organization.

Pursuant to this request, the World Health Organization, with the assistance of a consultant with wide experience in aviation medicine and air carrier problems had prepared a study which concluded that it was desirable to carry a limited amount of narcotics in aircraft first-aid kits and commented on a number of medical aspects which might be taken into consideration to prevent abuse. The United Nations Legal Office concluded that while drugs carried in first-aid kits are not exempted from other relevant provisions of the narcotic treaties, the import certificate and export authorization system then prevalent did not apply to drugs carried under appropriate safeguards in first-aid kits for emergency cases as long as they did not cross the customs lines at points of transit or destination.

The World Health Organization report, the United Nations Secretariat legal opinion and the administrative measures proposed by the International Criminal Police Organization to prevent diversion of drugs for illicit purposes were considered by the United Nations Commission on Narcotic Drugs at its 14th Session in April/May 1959. On the basis of the Narcotic Commission's recommendation, the ECOSOC at its 28th Session in July 1959 unanimously adopted Resolution 730C (XXVIII). In this resolution the UN Secretary General had been invited 'in cooperation with ICAO and WHO, and in consultation with ICPO, to prepare and to distribute to governments in sufficient time for consideration at the 15th Session of the Commission on Narcotic Drugs, a set of requirements essential to ensure proper use of narcotic drugs and to prevent their abuse and diversion for illicit purposes, such requirements to be recommended to governments as a basis for the control of the carriage of narcotic drugs in first-aid kits on board aircraft engaged in international flight'. Accordingly a joint Secretariat Working Group of the UN Division of Narcotic Drugs, WHO, ICAO and Interpol had met in Geneva in January 1960 and prepared the set of requirements referred to above under which opiates or similar drugs may be carried in aircraft first-aid kits on international flights and used in an emergency.

The UN Commission on Narcotic Drugs had later discussed and approved the Inter-Secretariat report at its 15th Session in May 1960. Pursuant to this, the ECOSOC at its 30th Session in July 1960, unanimously adopted the Resolution 770E (XXX) prepared by the Commission on Narcotic Drugs which included recommendations to states on the carriage of narcotic drugs in first-aid kits of aircraft engaged in international flights, and safeguards to prevent abuse.

In view of the ECOSOC recommendations aimed at eliminating the difficulties experienced by states, the Air Navigation Commission of ICAO considered whether any further action by ICAO was necessary or whether the subject should be deleted from the work programme.[69]

At its 39th Session the General Assembly of the United Nations adopted Resolution 39/143 on 'International campaign against traffic in drugs' which, *inter alia*, called upon the specialized agencies to participate actively in its implementation. In December 1984, the Secretary General of the United Nations also addressed a letter to the executive heads of the specialized agencies requesting their cooperation in the efforts directed to control the abuse and illicit trafficking of narcotic drugs. Believing that a very large percentage of illicit narcotic drugs and psychotropic substances was carried by air, the United Nations Division of Narcotic Drugs requested the cooperation of ICAO in this field.

ICAO's activities in narcotics control became significant in 1984 when, in November of that year, ICAO was represented at the 11th meeting of Operational Heads of National Narcotics Law Enforcement Agencies, Far East Region (HONLEA). An ICAO observer also attended the 3rd and 4th Sessions of the Enforcement Committee of the Customs Cooperation Council in February and September 1985 respectively, where matters of narcotics law enforcement were discussed. On the same two occasions, the ICAO observer attended the United Nations *Ad Hoc* Inter-agency meetings on coordination in matters of international drug abuse control.

At the informal meeting of the Council on 11 June 1985, a preliminary consideration was given to the constitutional mandate of ICAO in the field of suppression of illicit transport of narcotic drugs and psychotropic substances by air. In this connection it should be noted that:

a Under the agreement between the United Nations and the International Civil Aviation Organization,[70] the Organization is obliged to cooperate in establishing effective coordination of the activities of specialized agencies and those of the UN; in particular, ICAO is obliged to consider formal recommendations made by the United Nations and to furnish to the United Nations required information. In this context, it was therefore noted that UN General Assembly Resolution 39/143 called upon the specialized agencies of the United Nations system to participate actively in the implementation of that resolution, entitled 'International campaign against traffic in drugs'. Consequently, the Organization had a responsibility to undertake a study of the problem of suppression of illicit transport on narcotic drugs and psychotropic substances.
b The Chicago Convention contains several provisions referring to elements of international air law which may be relevant for the control and suppression of drug trafficking.

 1 **Article 10** If all aircraft coming from abroad lands only at designated customs airports and departs only from such airports, the control of illicit transport would be greatly facilitated.
 2 **Article 13** Clearance and departure of cargo are subject to the regulations of the contracting states whose territories are involved; the movement of any specific cargo is subject to the legal regulations and effective control of the states concerned.
 3 **Article 16** Contracting states have the right to search aircraft of other contracting states on landing or departure; obviously, the same right is applicable for the search of aircraft of their own registry.
 4 **Article 23** Customs and immigration procedures affecting international air navigation should be in accordance with the practices established or recommended from time to time pursuant to the Convention; that is clearly reflected in the procedures established in Annex 9 to the Convention; however, the predominant provisions in this field are enacted by states through their immigration and customs legislation, the latter

being coordinated internationally through the Customs Cooperation Council. Annex 9 deals with customs and immigration procedures but mainly in order to ensure that the procedures used are efficient and do not interfere with the speedy clearance of aircraft and their loads.

5 **Article 35 b)** Each contracting state has the right, for reasons of public order and safety, to prohibit the carriage in or above its territory of certain articles; it is within the legislative power of the contracting states to adopt an unconditional interdiction on the carriage of narcotic drugs and psychotropic substances into or over their territory and to establish measures for enforcing such legislation.

6 **Article 37 j)** It is within the legislative function of the ICAO Council to adopt standards, recommended practices and procedures dealing with customs and immigration, import and export of specific articles.

These articles of the Chicago Convention should be read in conjunction with Article 22 of the Convention under the terms of which each contracting state agrees to adopt all practical measures to facilitate and expedite air navigation and to prevent unnecessary delays to aircraft, crews, passengers and cargo. These requirements are further specified in Annex 9.

Although it might perhaps be suggested that Annex 9 could contain provisions urging aeronautical authorities to extend every possible assistance in the suppression of drug trafficking, more detailed instructions or guidance material would seem out of context with the character of Annex 9, which is essentially aimed at overcoming obstacles to the rapid clearance of aircraft and their loads. This objective should be preserved and not diluted by inclusion in the annex of provisions which would appear to run counter to the prime objective. On the other hand, recognition of ICAO's cooperation in drug trafficking control could be made by inclusion of text in the annex, to provide for the following:

1 That any special inspection procedures required in the control of narcotics traffic be accomplished speedily, with efficient equipment, without inconvenience to passengers and in such a way as to ensure the timely clearance of aircraft and their loads on arrival and departure.

2 Most seizures of narcotics and related substances in illicit traffic result from police and drug enforcement intelligence rather than from routine inspection and consequently that sampling rather than exhaustive methods of inspection are to be preferred.[71]

Another ICAO programme which has a bearing on or which would be affected by any ICAO activities related to the campaign against illicit trafficking in narcotic drugs and psychotropic substances is Aviation Security (Annex 17 and the Security Manual (Doc 8973); however the protected interest in the aviation security programme is aviation itself.

Two other international organizations, that is, ICPO-Interpol and the World Customs Organization (WCO), have a direct responsibility in the suppression of illicit traffic in narcotic drugs. Interpol's role has been involved with influencing national legislation and coordinating the work of police services world-wide to eradicate the sources of raw material, processing and refining facilities and the apprehension and prosecution of offenders.

The WCO has for many years been concerned with the suppression of smuggling narcotics and psychotropic substances within its general competence to deal with customs matters. Its main instrument in this field is an international convention on mutual administrative assistance for the prevention, investigation and repression of customs offences, signed in Nairobi in 1977. The Nairobi Convention, as it is called, contains specific references to illicit traffic and an Annex (Annex X) dealing with assistance in action against the smuggling of narcotic drugs and psychotropic substances. These provisions are designed to complement those of prevailing treaties on narcotic drugs. The WCO is also developing with the International Air Transport Association a Memorandum of Understanding between the two organizations containing guidelines for both customs authorities and airlines to follow to help prevent illicit traffic of drugs on board aircraft.

The definition of 'smuggling' contained in the Nairobi Convention applies to all modes of transport. Pertinent exchanges of information undertaken by customs administrations pursuant to the Convention extend to all means of transport used or suspected of being used for the smuggling of narcotic drugs or psychotropic substances or that seem likely to give rise to such operations. Assistance, on request, relating to surveillance extends over 'particular vehicles, ships, aircraft or other means of transport reasonably believed to be used for smuggling narcotic drugs or psychotropic substances into the territory of the requesting contracting party'.

The WCO's main deliberative organ in these matters is its Committee on Customs Enforcement. The current work programme of this Committee in the area of narcotics smuggling includes exchanges of information on couriers, their routes and pertinent traffic trends, development of catalogues of enforcement aids and places of concealment (in cooperation with Interpol and the UN Division of Narcotic Drugs), investigative techniques (undercover work), seminars and training programmes and action to monitor and pre-empt financial transactions relating to narcotics smuggling. A recommendation of the Customs Cooperation Council on 17 June 1985 adopted on the proposal of its Enforcement Committee seeks 'to secure the fullest cooperation of airline and shipping companies and others involved in the international transport and travel industries to assist the international customs community in the suppression of the illicit traffic in narcotic drugs and psychotropic substances'.

In the light of the above, it appears that in this field and in accordance with its constitutional responsibilities, ICAO can play the following role:

1 monitor the adherence of states of the Convention Against the Illicit Traffic in Narcotic Drugs and Psychotropic Substances in order to ensure *inter alia* that international civil aviation interests are not penalized by objective liability or responsibility unless there is a specific criminal involvement of the carrier or its staff;
2 formulate and adopt as required technical specifications related to civil flight operations;
3 develop as required guidance materials;
4 cooperate with the United Nations Division of Narcotic Drugs and other international organizations through consultation and attendance at meetings;
5 ensure that facilitation measures and measures directed to control the illicit traffic of drugs do not have an unnecessarily negative impact on each other so as to maintain the separate thrusts of these programmes.

Facilitation Aspects of Narcotics Control

The Council, at its 18th Meeting of the 116th Session in 1986, considered the role of ICAO in the suppression of illicit transport of narcotic drugs by air.[72] It requested the Air Transport Committee to study the need for guidance material in this field, in order to ensure that facilitation measures and measures directed to control the illicit traffic of drugs do not have an unnecessarily negative impact on each other which could hamper progress in the implementation of those two programmes, also bearing in mind Recommendation 9 of the Third Air Transport Conference.

ICAO's facilitation programme is essentially aimed at the rapid and efficient clearance of aircraft and their loads and the simplification, standardization and improvement of all formalities and paperwork required in effecting border control. The question is whether the measures directed to control the illicit traffic of drugs might conflict with the provisions of Annex 9 and hamper facilitation progress; and conversely, whether the provisions of Annex 9 might unnecessarily interfere with measures directed to control the illicit traffic of narcotics.

From ICAO's perspective, the main international instruments developed for the control of narcotics and the suppression of trafficking are the Single Convention on Narcotic Drugs, New York 1961, as amended by the 1972 Protocol, the Convention on Psychotropic Substances, Vienna 1971, and Annex X to the Nairobi Convention.[73] The first two conventions and the amending protocol recognize the competence of the United Nations in the international control of drugs, with specific functions entrusted to the Commission on Narcotic Drugs of the Economic and Social Council, and the International Narcotics Control Board.

The conventions prohibit the production, manufacture, export, import, trade, possession or use of listed drugs, except in quantities necessary for medical use and scientific research purposes. The drugs concerned are those listed in a series of schedules which may be amended from time to time by the Commission on Narcotic Drugs, subject to review by ECOSOC, at the request of a contracting state, or on the advice of the World Health Organization. The International Narcotics Control Board monitors the production, movement and use of narcotic drugs, using a system of licensing, associated with estimates and statistical reports, which enables it to determine rapidly and effectively the existence of leaks from the legitimate to the illicit trade. Signatory states undertake to adopt appropriate penal provisions, to make arrangements for the seizure and confiscation of drugs in illicit traffic, and to cooperate with one another and with the competent international organizations in the campaign against illicit traffic in narcotic drugs.

State authorities concerned with the suppression of narcotics trafficking in general recognize the impracticability of effecting exhaustive searches and controls of all movements of passengers and cargo. Their strategy is based on random checks of passengers, baggage and cargo, as a deterrent, associated with thorough examinations and searches directed at specific targets on the basis of intelligence reports and the observation of anomalies. This is considered to be the most cost-effective approach, with the very large majority of seizures invariably resulting from intelligence reports rather than from routine inspections. This procedure was emphasized by the World Customs Organization (Customs Cooperation Council as it then was) in 1985, in a recommendation stating 'that the proper balance between the needs of customs enforcement and the facilitation of legitimate trade and travel can best be achieved if customs enforcement is selective and intelligence-based and that it is therefore essential that every effort be made to develop and exploit the best possible intelligence.'

The practice of effecting random and exceptional checks rarely gives rise to facilitation problems. This practice is recommended in a number of provisions of Annex 9 dealing with passengers (paragraphs 3.17, 3.17.1, 3.29, 3.30, 6.27); cargo (paragraphs 4.12, 4.13, 4.22, 4.28, 4.46); and transit traffic (paragraphs 5.1, 5.5, 5.8). Other pertinent provisions of Annex 9 deal with the use of effective search and screening equipment for passengers and their baggage (paragraphs 6.15 and 6.16).

Several of the above Annex 9 provisions are supported and confirmed in similar provisions of the WCO Kyoto Convention[74] and the WCO has supported the development of procedures which demonstrate its concern for facilitation requirements, notably the dual-channel baggage clearance system (paragraph 3.17.1 and Appendix 5 of Annex 9; Recommended Practice 10 and Appendix I to Annex F.3 to the Kyoto Convention). The Kyoto Convention's Annex F.3 also specifies that customs authorities shall normally apply customs control of travellers only on a selective or sampling basis (Standard 7); that personal searches 'shall be carried out only in exceptional cases and when there are reasonable grounds to suspect smuggling or other offences' (Standard 8); that unaccompanied baggage 'shall be cleared under the procedure applicable to accompanied baggage or under another simplified customs procedure' (Standard 16); that the customs formalities for departing travellers 'shall be as simple as possible and eliminated when this is feasible' (Standard 40); and that 'transit passengers who do not leave the transit area shall not be required to pass through any customs control,' except when a customs offence is suspected (Standard 46).

The question that arises is whether the actions of customs and other authorities concerned with the suppression of narcotics trafficking could interfere with facilitation requirements when they are based on intelligence rather than on routine sample inspections. As regards passengers, such methods involve the maintenance of lists of names of persons closely or remotely connected with narcotics trafficking; the determination and recognition of personality profiles, origins, destinations, itineraries, routes and carriers often used by smugglers, places of concealment and methods of smuggling.

The need for drug enforcement authorities to match the names of travellers with lists of suspected persons may in some cases lead to a demand for passenger manifests, which have been eliminated as a requirement for aircraft clearance (Annex 9, Standards 2.6, 2.6.1, 2.3 and 2.4.2). Efforts by various clearance authorities to require the passenger manifest as a control document have, in the past, been successfully countered by pointing out the limitations of this document: only family names are shown on passenger manifests, which may result in a number of unrelated people with the same family name travelling on the same aircraft. Inaccuracies may also result from spelling, last-minute changes (and last-minute boardings, which are often practised by smugglers) and the fact that suspect passengers seldom travel under their real names. These limitations have been recognized by the WCO in Recommended Practice 13 of Annex F.3 to the Kyoto Convention which provides that 'regardless of the mode of transport used, a list of travellers or a list of their accompanying baggage should not be required for customs purposes.' Accordingly, requirements of drug enforcement authorities for passenger lists will be more satisfactorily met by the examination instead of Embarkation/Disembarkation (E/D) cards and passports, and wherever possible, by the use of machine-readable passports. The latter offer strong discouragement against passport alteration, forgery or counterfeiting and will allow efficient and rapid matching of passenger data with lists of suspects, particularly where the reading equipment is linked to a portable or central computer file.

As regards cargo, the control methods used involve the cataloguing of suspect shippers and consignees, the identification of controlled or prohibited substances, the detection of unusual or improbable trade relationships (such as the shipment of chemical substances by industrial equipment or parts manufacturers); and the detection of evidence of tampering with aircraft or shipments.

Methods used by customs and other drug enforcement authorities to control cargo movements may lead to a demand for cargo manifests, baggage lists, stores lists and detailed mail lists, the use of which has either been eliminated or discouraged in various provisions of Annex 9 (paragraphs 2.7, 2.8, 2.8.1, 2.9, 2.10 and 2.11). Again, the requirements of the authorities concerned will be much more satisfactorily met by an examination of commercial invoices, export declarations and air waybills, which contain all the information required in original and accurate form (see for example Annex 9, paragraphs 4.8, 4.9, 4.11, 4.15, 4.16, 4.17, 4.18, 4.19, 4.23 and 4.24). The question of mail is covered in Annex F.4 to the Kyoto Convention and possible amendments would have to be agreed between the customs authorities and the Universal Postal Union world-wide.

Control has been made more difficult by the diversion of listed drugs, precursors and essential chemicals from international commerce.[75] Most of these substances have various industrial applications for which there is a legitimate trade (the pharmaceutical industry, manufacture of pigments, lubricants and plastics, and processing of waxes, oils, scents, gums and alkaloids). However, they can also be used for the clandestine manufacture of narcotic drugs. They tend to have complex names which are not readily meaningful to customs officers and as a rule, they have no obvious identifying characteristics, often taking the form of a powder or a colourless, odourless liquid. A reasonably comprehensive list of the substances concerned contains up to 100 complex scientific names, in addition to more than 100 substances that are listed in the Schedules to the New York and the Vienna Conventions.

Another problem for the control authorities are the so-called 'designer drugs' which may require only slight manipulations of the chemical structure of listed narcotics. The formulae can be varied at will, and since these substances are not formally listed or described in the applicable conventions, this complicates the task of prosecuting traffickers.

These new preoccupations are increasing the pressure on enforcement authorities to require carriers to produce advance documentation giving detailed information on the particulars of all shipments. The United Nations Expert Group on Countermeasures against Drug Smuggling by Air and Sea, which met in Vienna in December 1985 recommended, *inter alia*, that 'governments be encouraged to ensure the provision of cargo manifests as far in advance as possible of the arrival of any aircraft or vessel at its port of destination, especially in respect of container traffic.'

In surface transport, particularly in shipping, this does not present a particular problem because the shipping documents usually arrive well ahead of the consignments. However, because of the speed of air transport, advance shipment documentation can only be arranged through the use of electronic data processing, and provision has been made to this effect in paragraphs 4.4, 4.5, 4.5.1, 4.6 and 4.7 of Annex 9.

To cope efficiently with growing volumes of freight traffic the airlines have developed improved methods of handling, processing and customs clearance. These methods involve the use of computers and communication networks linking freight forwarders and brokers with airlines and customs offices, ensuring immediate transmission of essential information and replacing obsolete documents with machine-readable evidence.[76]

The WCO is presently engaged in a joint project with IATA involving the development of an interface between airline and customs computers. The objective is to establish a communications system with instantaneous notification to the customs office of the destination airport, of the particulars of all shipments destined to that airport, at the time of departure. The customs office of the destination airport will then be able to plan and arrange for rapid and efficient clearance of the cargo following its arrival.

A related development, which assisted drug enforcement authorities to meet their objectives without hindering the clearance of aircraft and their loads, was the completion of the Customs Cooperation Council's (CCC) work on classification. A new commodity description and coding system was developed by the CCC which harmonized the Brussels Nomenclature (1950) with the Standard International Trade Classification (SITC) and other less utilized but important nomenclatures. An International Convention on the Harmonized Commodity Description and Coding System developed by the CCC came into force on 1 January 1987. This considerably facilitated the proposed interface between airline and customs computers, and in order to accelerate the process, IATA undertook to merge its own Commodity Classification System (used for rate-making purposes) with the harmonized system.

The question that remains is what the drug enforcement authorities are expected to do in circumstances of high-volume operations, where the amount of suspected smuggling is such that random or sampling checks cannot be relied upon and exhaustive inspections are required. A related problem is the inspection of cargo in containers, as recent evidence points to the increasing use of regular and volume cargo shipments as a vehicle for the smuggling of narcotics, as well as the use of perishable and refrigerated goods as a decoy (flowers, vegetables, frozen meat and fish which are given priority for customs clearance with the minimum of formalities). In the case of container loads, the selection of one or more containers for inspection may cause major clearance delays; and the selection of particular consignments or unit loads within containers presents similar problems.

The only effective methods for the systematic inspection of high-volume passenger and cargo operations (apart from the use of trained dogs, which is effective in certain cases), require the use of modern, sophisticated and recently developed techniques. These include the machine-readable passport, x-ray baggage scanner, barcode baggage tag scanner (for matching passengers with their baggage), and advanced methods of detecting weapons and narcotics such as mass spectroscopy, chemiluminescence and low-energy neutron bombardment. Some of these methods are very expensive and will tax the resources of even the most advanced states. For instance, a cargo container examination system based on mass spectroscopy has been developed which can rapidly determine the presence of weapons or narcotics in a container, from a sample of the air within the container which the machine can examine from a sealable window. Other methods (for example, digital x-ray images, dual-energy radiography, nuclear magnetic resonance, various tuned-frequency laser beams and advanced biotechnology techniques) are still in the experimental stage.

ICAO Assembly Resolution A27-12

At its 27th Session, held in September/October 1989, the ICAO Assembly adopted Resolution A27-12 which recognized the enormity of drug abuse and illicit trafficking in drugs and psychotropic substances and urged the ICAO Council to give the highest priority to adopt concrete measures in order to prevent and to eliminate the possible use of illicit drugs by crew members, air traffic controllers and other staff of international civil aviation. The resolution also urged the Council to continue its work in order to prevent illicit transport of narcotic drugs and psychotropic substances. *A fortiori,* the Assembly called upon contracting states to continue their efforts to prevent the illicit trafficking of drugs by air, to take appropriate legislative measures to ensure that the crime of illicit transport of narcotic drugs and other psychotropic substances by air is punishable by severe penalties. Contracting states were also urged by this resolution to become parties, as soon as possible, to the United Nations Convention of 1988.

Recent Efforts of the United Nations

One of the significant steps in the international campaign against traffic in drugs of the General Assembly was its pronouncement in December 1994 where, at its 101st Plenary Meeting, the Assembly recalled *inter alia,* its Resolution 36/132 of 14 December 1981 and Resolution 38/93 of 16 December 1983, in which it specifically acknowledged the economic and technical constraints impeding many developing countries from combating the illegal production of and illicit traffic in drugs and drug abuse. The Assembly noted the concern expressed by the Secretary General in his report on the work of the Organization,[77] in which he recognized the need for greater efforts to reduce the traffic in and illicit use of drugs. The Assembly also considered the activities of the Commission on Narcotic Drugs and the International Narcotic Control Board, and appreciated the action being taken by the United Nations Fund for Drug Abuse Control in providing financial resources and support or integrated development programmes, including the replacement of illicit crops in affected areas. It reaffirmed the need to improve and maintain regional and interregional cooperation and coordination, particularly in law enforcement, in order to eliminate drug trafficking and drug abuse, and noted the growing interest in regional and interregional coordination.

Concern was expressed that, despite the significant national efforts deployed for this purpose, including those of a number of Latin

American and Caribbean and Asian countries, the illicit traffic in narcotic drugs and psychotropic substances had increased noticeably. The Assembly was aware of the serious impact on the life and health of peoples and on the stability of democratic institutions resulting from the illicit production, marketing, distribution and use of drugs, and recognized that, to root out this evil, integrated action was required for simultaneously reducing and controlling illicit demand production, distribution and marketing.

It was considered that action to eliminate the illegal cultivation of and traffic in drugs must be accompanied by economic and social development programmes for the affected areas, programming activities for replacing illegal crops in such a manner as to conserve the environment and improve the quality of life of the social sectors concerned.

The Assembly recognized the dilemma of transit states which are seriously affected, both domestically and internationally, by drug trafficking, which was stimulated by demand for and production and use of illicit drugs and psychotropic substances in other countries. The Assembly expressed its awareness of the need to mobilize a coordinated strategy at the national, regional, and international levels, which would cover countries with illegal users and producers and countries used for transit in the world-wide distribution and marketing circuit, in order to eliminate drug trafficking and drug abuse.

Recognizing the importance of ratifying and acceding to the international drug control treaties, the Assembly:

1 took note of the report of the Secretary General;[78]
2 reiterated that urgent attention and highest priority should be given to the struggle against the illicit production of, demand for, use of and traffic in drugs;
3 called upon member states that have not yet done so to ratify the international drug control treaties and, in the meantime, to make serious efforts to comply with the provisions thereof;
4 reiterated the importance of integrated action, coordinated at the regional and international levels, and, for this purpose, requested the Secretary General and the Commission on Narcotic Drugs to step up efforts and initiatives designed to establish, on a continuing basis, coordinating machinery for law enforcement in regions where this does not yet exist;
5 recommended that the highest priority be given to the preparation of specific technical and economic cooperation programmes for the countries most affected by the illicit production of and traffic in drugs and drug abuse;
6 also recommended that appropriate priority be given to the adop-

tion of measures designed to solve the specific problems of transit states through joint regional and interregional efforts;
7 urged member states with available resources and experience to increase their contributions for combating the illegal production of and illicit traffic in drugs and drug abuse, in particular in the countries most affected and where the problem is most serious;
8 encouraged member states to contribute or to continue contributing to the United Nations Fund for Drug Abuse Control so as to enable it to increase its support of drug abuse control programmes;
9 requested the Economic and Social Council, through the Commission on Narcotic Drugs, to consider the legal, institutional and social elements relevant to all aspects of combating drug trafficking, including the possibility of convening a specialized conference.
10 requested the Secretary General to ensure that appropriate steps are taken to implement paragraph 5 (c) of Resolution 37/198 and that a meeting of the heads of national drug law enforcement agencies be convened in 1986;
11 also requested the Secretary General to make the necessary arrangements for holding, within the framework of advisory services, interregional seminars to study the experience gained by the United Nations system, in particular by the United Nations Fund for Drug Abuse Control, and by member states in integrated rural development programmes for replacing illegal crops;
12 called upon the specialized agencies and all other relevant bodies of the United Nations system to participate actively in the implementation of the present resolution;
13 requested the Secretary General to report to the General Assembly at its 40th Session on the implementation of the present resolution;
14 decided to include in the provisional agenda of its 40th Session the item entitled 'International campaign against traffic in drugs'.

In December 1993, at its 85th Plenary Meeting, the Assembly presented a global programme of action on international action to combat drug abuse and illicit production and trafficking. The General Assembly commenced its presentation by reiterating its grave concern that the illicit demand for, production of and traffic in narcotic drugs and psychotropic substances continued to threaten seriously the socio-economic and political systems and the stability, national security and sovereignty of an increasing number of states.

The Assembly was fully aware that the international community was confronted with the dramatic problem of drug abuse and the illicit cultivation, production, demand, processing, distribution and trafficking of narcotic drugs and psychotropic substances and that states needed to work at international and national levels to deal with this scourge, which has a strong potential to undermine development, economic and political stability and democratic institutions. The Assembly emphasized that the problem of drug abuse and illicit trafficking has to be considered within the broader economic and social context, and also the need for an analysis of transit routes used by drug traffickers, which are constantly changing and expanding to include a growing number of countries and regions in all parts of the world. It was alarmed by the growing connection between drug trafficking and terrorism in various parts of the world, and recognized the efforts of countries that produce narcotic drugs for scientific, medicinal and therapeutic uses to prevent the channelling of such substances to illicit markets and to maintain production at a level consistent with illicit demand. It stressed the important role of the United Nations and its specialized agencies in supporting concerted action in the fight against drug abuse at national, regional and international levels, and recognized the role of the Commission on Narcotic Drugs, as the principal United Nations policy-making body on drug control issues, as a positive one.

Reaffirming the importance of the role of the United Nations International Drug Control Programme as the main focus for concerted international action for drug abuse control and commending its performance of the functions entrusted to it, the Assembly affirmed the importance of the role of the United Nations International Drug Control Programme as the main focus for concerted international action for drug abuse control and commended its performance of the functions entrusted to it. It also affirmed the proposals set out in the United Nations System-wide Action Plan on Drug Abuse Control and recognized that further efforts were needed to implement and update it, and invited the relevant agencies of the United Nations system to make greater progress in incorporating within their programmes and activities action aimed at dealing with drug-related problems. On the subject of respect for the principles enshrined in the Charter of the United Nations and international law in the fight against drug abuse and illicit trafficking, the Assembly:

1 Reaffirmed that the fight against drug abuse and illicit trafficking should continue to be based on strict respect for the principles enshrined in the Charter of the United Nations and international law, particularly respect for the sovereignty and territorial integrity of states and non-use of force or the threat of force in international relations.
2 Called upon all states to intensify their actions to promote effective cooperation in the efforts to combat drug abuse and illicit

trafficking, so as to contribute to a climate conducive to achieving this end, and to refrain from using the issue for political purposes.
3 Reaffirmed that the international fight against drug trafficking should not in any way justify violation of the principles enshrined in the Charter of the United Nations and international law.

With regard to international action to combat drug abuse and illicit trafficking, the Assembly:

1 Reiterated its condemnation of the crime of drug trafficking in all its forms, and urged continued and effective international action to combat it, in keeping with the principle of shared responsibility.
2 Supported the focus on national and regional strategies for drug abuse control, particularly the master-plan approach, and urged the United Nations International Drug Control Programme to keep in mind that these should be complemented with effective interregional strategies.
3 Requested the Secretary General to report on the arrangements made by the Programme to promote and monitor the United Nations Decade against Drug Abuse, 1991–2000, under the theme, 'A global response to a global challenge', and on the progress made in attaining the objectives of the decade by member states, the programme and the United Nations system.
4 Welcomed the trend towards ratification and implementation of the Single Convention on Narcotic Drugs of 1961,[79] as amended by the 1972 Protocol,[80] the Convention on Psychotropic Substances of 1971[81] and the United Nations Convention against Illicit Traffic in Narcotic Drugs and Psychotropic Substances of 1988.[82]
5 Requested the programme to include in its report to the Commission on Narcotic Drugs on the Implementation of the United Nations Convention against Illicit Traffic in Narcotic Drugs and Psychotropic Substances, a section on experience gained to date in implementing the Convention, which should contain recommendations and strategies for its further implementation, and invited member states to cooperate with the programme in this regard.
6 Encouraged all countries to take action to prevent the illicit arms trade by which weapons are provided to drug traffickers.
7 Expressed its satisfaction with the efforts of the Commission on Narcotic Drugs to improve the functioning and impact of the meetings of the heads of national drug law enforcement agencies.
8 Requested the programme in its report on illicit traffic in drugs to analyse world-wide trends in illicit traffic and transit in narcotic drugs and psychotropic substances, including methods and routes

used, and to recommend ways and means for improving the capacity of states along those routes to deal with all aspects of the drug problem.

9 Emphasized the link between the illicit production of, demand for and traffic in narcotic drugs and psychotropic substances and the economic and social conditions in the affected countries and the differences and diversity of the problems in each country.

10 Called upon the international community to provide increased economic and technical support to governments that request it in support of programmes of alternative development that take fully into account the cultural traditions of peoples.

11 Took note of the initiative of the programme to study the concept of swapping debt for alternative development in the area of international drug abuse control, and requested the Executive Director of the programme to inform the Commission on Narcotic Drugs of any progress made in this area.

12 Encouraged governments to nominate experts for the roster maintained by the programme, to ensure that the programme and the Commission on Narcotic Drugs may draw from the widest pool of expertise and experience in implementing its policies and programmes.

13 Stressed the need for effective action to prevent the diversion for illicit purposes of precursors and essential chemicals, materials and equipment frequently used in the illicit manufacture of narcotic drugs and psychotropic substances.

14 Commended the International Narcotics Control Board for its valuable work in monitoring production and distribution of narcotic drugs and psychotropic substances so as to limit their use to medical and scientific purposes, and for the effective manner in which it has implemented its additional responsibilities, under Article 12 of the United Nations Convention against Illicit Traffic in Narcotic Drugs and Psychotropic Substances,[83] concerning the control of precursors and essential chemicals.

15 Expressed its satisfaction with efforts being made by the programme and other United Nations bodies to obtain reliable data on drug abuse and illicit trafficking, including the development of the International Drug Abuse Assessment System.

16 Recommended to the Commission on Narcotic Drugs that it consider, at its 37th Session, the world-wide research study on the economic and social consequences of drug abuse and illicit trafficking prepared by the United Nations Research Institute for Social Development in conjunction with the report of the Executive Director of the programme on the economic and social consequences of drug abuse and illicit trafficking, and that it consider including this issue as an item on its agenda.

In its global programme of action, the Assembly:

1 Reaffirmed the importance of the Global Programme of Action as a framework for national, regional and international action to combat the illicit production of, demand for and trafficking in narcotic drugs and psychotropic substances, and its commitment to implementing the mandates and recommendations contained therein.
2 Called upon states individually and in cooperation with other states to promote the Global Programme of Action and to implement its mandates and recommendations with a view to translating it into practical action for drug abuse control.
3 Called upon the relevant bodies of the United Nations, the specialized agencies, the international financial institutions and other concerned inter-governmental and non-governmental organizations to cooperate with and assist states in their efforts to promote and implement the Global Programme of Action.
4 Requested the Commission on Narcotic Drugs, in discharging its mandate to monitor the Global Programme of Action, to take into account the recommendations contained in the report of the Secretary General on the implementation by member states of the Global Programme of Action.[84]
5 Requested the Commission on Narcotic Drugs and the United Nations International Drug Control Programme to consider ways and means to facilitate reporting by governments on the implementation of the Global Programme of Action, so as to increase the level of responses.

The Assembly called upon states to cooperate in the implementation of the United Nations System-wide Action Plan on Drug Abuse Control and stated the following:

1 The role of the Executive Director of the United Nations International Drug Control Programme was to coordinate and provide effective leadership for all United Nations Drug control activities, in order to ensure coherence of actions within the programme as well as coordination, complementarity and non-duplication of such activities across the United Nations system.
2 The updated United Nations System-wide Action Plan on Drug Abuse Control, as was requested in its resolutions, in full cooperation with the Administrative Committee on Coordination, should be completed in time for the review and recommendation of the Commission on Narcotic Drugs at its 37th Session and for the consideration of the Economic and Social Council at its substantive session of 1994 and of the General Assembly at its 49th Session.

3 The following should be included in the updated System-wide Action Plan:

a an annex containing agency-specific implementing plans;
b a reference to the important role of the international financial institutions, as noted in Chapter II of the Comprehensive Multidisciplinary Outline of Future Activities in Drug Abuse Control,[85] and the ability of such institutions to promote economic stability and undermine the drug industry.

4 All relevant United Nations agencies should complete their agency-specific implementation plans for inclusion in the updated System-wide Action Plan and to incorporate fully into their programmes all the mandates and activities contained in the Action Plan and its annex.
5 The Commission on Narcotic Drugs should pay particular attention to reviewing the agency-specific implementation plans of the System-wide Action Plan for consideration by the Economic and Social Council at its coordination segment in 1994.
6 The Economic and Social Council, at its coordination segment, should pay due attention to the role of the international financial institutions in supporting international drug control efforts, particularly in the field of alternative development.
7 The governing bodies of all United Nations agencies associated with the System-wide Action Plan should include the issue of drug control in their agendas with a view to examining the need for a mandate on drug control, assessing the activities taken to comply with the Action Plan and, as appropriate, reporting on how the issue of drug control is taken into account in the relevant programmes.
8 The United Nations International Drug Control Programme, in cooperation with the relevant agencies, particularly the United Nations Children's Fund, should report on the efforts to study the impact of drug abuse and related crime on children and to recommend measures that may be taken to address this problem.
9 That the United Nations International Drug Control Programme should cooperate and coordinate with the Crime Prevention and Criminal Justice Branch of the Centre for Social Development and Humanitarian Affairs of the Secretariat on activities to counter drug-related criminality, including money-laundering, to ensure, complementarity and non-duplication of efforts.
10 The System-wide Action Plan should be reviewed and updated on a biennial basis.

Finally, the Global Programme of Action called for the implementation of the United Nations International Drug Control Programme. In this context the Assembly welcomed the efforts of the United Nations International Drug Control Programme to implement its mandates within the framework of the international drug control treaties, the Comprehensive Multidisciplinary Outline of Future Activities in Drug Abuse Control, the Global Programme of Action and relevant consensus documents, and urged all governments to provide the fullest possible financial and political support to the United Nations International Drug Control Programme.

Appreciation was expressed of the efforts made by the United Nations International Drug Control Programme to comply with the approved format and methodology of the programme budget of the Fund of the United Nations International Drug Control Programme, in particular with the relevant resolutions of the Commission on Narcotic Drugs.

The Executive Director of the United Nations International Drug Control Programme was encouraged to continue his efforts to improve the presentation of the budget of the Fund. The Assembly finally took note of the reports of the Secretary General presented under the item entitled 'International drug control';[86] and requested the Secretary General to report to the General Assembly at its 49th Session on the implementation of the present resolution.

Comments

It is incontrovertible that the discussion in this chapter clearly shows the concerted efforts of the international community both through the United Nations Organization (through its General Assembly) and through the International Civil Aviation Organization towards controlling the problem of narcotic drug trafficking. A third force – the carriers themselves – have had considerable success in their anti-narcotic drug programme. One of the best examples of carrier action is reflected in the United States Customs Carrier Initiative Agreement Programme which was introduced in 1984. This programme is a purely voluntary arrangement between governments and carriers in which the government allows each airline to create a security programme that is approved by customs. The Carrier Initiative Agreement Programmes are aimed at both prevention and interdiction, covering areas of training, prevention and cooperation.

The enormity of the offence of narcotic drug trafficking by air pervades multifarious delinquencies and criminal offences. These may lead to hijacking of aircraft, destruction of aircraft, interception of aircraft and several other offences leading to loss of life and destruction of buildings and installations. Therefore, in the overall perspective, the offence could be termed 'misuse of civil aviation'.

The problem of 'misuse of civil aviation', 'improper use of civil aviation', 'undue use of civil aviation' or 'criminal use of civil aviation' was raised by several delegations at the 25th Session (Extraordinary) of the ICAO Assembly in April/May 1984 and was mentioned by several representatives on the Council in the context of discussions on the proposed amendment of Annex 2 to the Convention on International Civil Aviation with respect to interception of civil aircraft. In that context, several representatives expressed concern that necessary procedures must be foreseen to prevent the use of civil aviation for unlawful purposes, in particular for drug trafficking which is more and more generally recognized to be a serious crime against humanity. The problem to be addressed is essentially how to reconcile the protection of civil aircraft in situations of interception with the protection of the law and order of states concerned and with the enforcement of such applicable laws. The scope of the problem encompasses in particular the concern of several states whether Article 3 *bis* of the Chicago Convention and the amended Annex 2 leave sufficient safeguards for states to prevent, prosecute and punish and deliberate use of civil aircraft for unlawful purposes.

Article 3 *bis* provides *inter alia* that every state must refrain from resorting to the use of weapons against civil aircraft in flight. The worlds 'refrain from' do not provide the necessary strength to the provision as it does not explicitly prohibit the use of weapons against aircraft in flight.

Article 4 of the Convention on International Civil Aviation

Article 4 of the Chicago Convention is the only provision in the Convention explicitly using the words 'misuse of civil aviation'; even there, however, the expression is used only in the heading (in fact, in the margin in the original signature copy) and not in the substantive text of the Article. The first paragraph of the Preamble to the Convention refers to 'abuse' of international civil aviation without any attempt at a definition of that term.

Article 4 of the Convention has never been the subject of nor involved in a decision or interpretation either by the Assembly or the Council. Therefore, Article 4 is of no relevance to the problem since it refers only to the obligations of states and to the acts of states. The drafting history of this Article indicates that the underlying intent of Article 4 was to prevent the use of civil aviation by states for purposes which might create a threat to the security of other nations. The intent of Article 4 originated in the Canadian 'Preliminary Draft' which stated as one of the purposes of ICAO (or PICAO, as was then envisaged), was 'to avert the possibility of the misuse of civil aviation creating a threat to the security of nations and to make the most effective contribution to the establishment and maintenance of a permanent system of general security'. In the further drafting development ('Tripartite Proposal' presented to the Conference by the Delegations of the United States, United Kingdom and Canada) the wording was changed to read: 'Each member state rejects the use of civil air transport as an instrument of national policy in international relations'. This wording practically repeated the text of the Treaty for the Renunciation of War of 27 August 1928 (commonly known as the Briand-Kellog Pact) in which the signatories renounced war 'as an instrument of national policy in their mutual relations'. The words 'purposes inconsistent with the aims of this Convention' in Article 4 therefore essentially mean 'threats to the general security'.

Article 4 does not offer any solution to the problem of 'misuse of civil aviation' within the scope of paragraph 2 above, namely, the status of an aircraft which is used for criminal purposes or other unlawful purposes.

Other Provisions of the Convention on International Civil Aviation

The Chicago Convention in general does not contain any provisions which would foresee the specific situations when an aircraft is used for or involved in criminal activities or other activities violating the law and public order of the state. However, there are numerous provisions in the Convention which offer effective safeguards to states that their applicable laws and public order are observed by foreign aircraft (with respect to aircraft of its own registry, the state concerned has unrestricted jurisdiction). Articles 11, 12 and 13 of the Convention in essence confirm the rule of general international law that foreign aircraft, its crew, passengers and cargo do not enjoy any 'extraterritorial' status while in the airspace or on the ground of another state; such aircraft are fully subject to the applicable laws of the state concerned. Under the Convention, the state may require the landing of a foreign aircraft involved in a non-scheduled flight (Article 5), may prohibit or restrict foreign aircraft from flying over certain parts of its territory or over the whole territory (Article 9), may require landing of foreign aircraft at a designated customs airport (Article 10), may search the foreign aircraft (Article 16) and may regulate or prohibit the carriage of certain articles in or above its territory (Article 35 (b)).

It is submitted that all states possess within the existing framework of the Chicago Convention full jurisdiction in the application of their respective laws to prevent or prohibit the use of civil aircraft for unlawful purposes. The practical problem therefore does not appear to arise in the field of the applicability of particular laws but in the field of practical enforcement of such laws with respect to aircraft, particularly aircraft in flight.

Enforcement of Legal Obligations in General

The practical enforcement of legal obligations involves a **legal** procedure which in the case of criminal acts would include the arrest and taking into custody of the suspected offender, collection and presentation of pertinent evidence, judicial evaluation of the evidence and evaluation of the points of defence, judicial conviction, sentencing and execution of the judgement. All aspects of such legal procedure are governed by *lex fori* that is, the domestic law of the court seized of the case. That law would determine *inter alia* what degree of force (including the possible use of weapons) may be legally employed in the process of arrest of the suspected offender; as a rule, that level of force is to be proportionate and adequate to the level of public danger created by the suspected offender and by the level of force used by the suspected offender in resisting arrest.

The applicable legal procedure is determined by the sovereign states and 'the general principles of law recognized by civilized nations' as reflected in Article 38, 1 (c) of the *Statute of the International Court of Justice*. These are elements of the general international law, including the general concept of human rights and specifically the protection of human life, presumption of innocence in criminal procedure, etc. The principles of modern general international law in this field reflect the requirement of 'due process' in the procedure for the enforcement of laws.

Article 3 bis

Problems of the interception of and other enforcement measures with respect to a civil aircraft in flight are directly addressed in Article 3 *bis* adopted by unanimous consensus on 10 May 1984 by the 25th Session (Extraordinary) of the ICAO Assembly. The drafting history of this Article supports the conclusion that Article 3 *bis* is declaratory of the existing general international law with respect to the following elements:

a obligation of states to refrain from resorting to the use of weapons against civil aircraft in flight;
b obligation, in case of interception, not to endanger the lives of persons on board and the safety of aircraft;
c right of states to require landing at a designated airport of a civil

aircraft flying above its territory without authority or if there are reasonable grounds to conclude that it is being used for any purpose inconsistent with the aims of the Convention.

While Article 3 *bis* accepted in paragraphs (b) and (d) the terminology 'for any purpose inconsistent with the aims of the Convention' exactly as it is used in Article 4 of the Convention, the drafting history indicates conclusively that the scope of the phrase is different in Article 3 *bis* than in Article 4. At the 25th Session (Extraordinary) of the Assembly this phrase was meant to cover not only violations of the 'aims' of the Chicago Convention as spelled out in the Preamble to the Convention and in its Article 44 (which deals with the aims and objectives of the organization rather than the Convention), but any violation of the law and public order of the state concerned. In the Assembly discussions specific references were made to transport of illicit drugs, contraband, gun running, illegal transport of persons and any other common crimes.

It should be stressed that the scope of applicability of Article 3 *bis* is subject to significant restrictions; the protection of this Article is reserved only to:

a 'civil aircraft'. Consequently, 'state aircraft' would not enjoy the same protection; and
b civil aircraft 'in flight'. While the Convention does not define the concept 'in flight', it is likely that this phrase will be interpreted in harmony with the Rome Convention on Damage Caused by Foreign Aircraft to Third Parties on the Surface, 1952 (Article 1, paragraph 2) and the Tokyo Convention of 1963 (Article 1, paragraph 3). An aircraft shall be deemed to be in flight from the moment when power is applied for the purpose of take-off until the moment when the landing run ends. Consequently, aircraft which are not 'in flight' do not enjoy the special protection of Article 3 *bis*.

It is also submitted that the protection of Article 3 *bis* is reserved to 'foreign' aircraft and does not include aircraft of the state's own registration. After discussions in the Executive Committee of the Assembly, the reference to aircraft 'of the other contracting state' was dropped for the specific reason that the protection was to be recognized as mandatory with respect of aircraft, whether belonging to contracting or non-contracting states. At no stage of the deliberations and drafting did the Assembly (in the Plenary, in the Executive Committee or in the Working Group) contemplate regulation of the status of an aircraft in relation to the state of its own registration; such regulation would have exceeded the scope of the Convention which deals with international civil aviation. Again, the purpose of the Chicago Convention is to establish conventional rules of conduct in the mutual relations of sovereign states but not to govern matters of their exclusive domestic jurisdiction. Consequently, Article 3 *bis* will not apply to the treatment of aircraft by the states of their registration. This conclusion does not imply that a state is free to treat aircraft of its own registration without regard to any rules of international law; other sources of international law (for example, the International Covenants on Human Rights) may be relevant for the conduct of states (protection of the right to life, requirement of due legal process, presumption of innocence, etc.).

When requiring the landing of a civil aircraft flying above its territory or when issuing other instructions to the aircraft to put an end to a 'violation', contracting states may resort to any appropriate means consistent with relevant rules of international law, including the Chicago Convention and, specifically, paragraph (a) of Article 3 *bis*. Consequently, Article 3 *bis* does not exclude enforcement against foreign aircraft in flight and does not rule out the use of adequate and proportionate force and does not rule out interception as such. Any act of interception or other enforcement measure not involving the use of weapons against civil aircraft in flight and not endangering the lives of persons on board and the safety of flight is legitimate and acceptable. Any interception procedures consistent with the applicable Standards and Recommended Practices adopted by the Council of ICAO pursuant to Articles 37, 54 (1) and 90 of the Chicago Convention would be 'consistent with relevant rules of international law'.

Two additional provisions of Article 3 *bis* are likely to deter the occurrences of 'misuse' of civil aviation. Firstly, civil aircraft are unconditionally obliged to comply with an order to land or other instruction; contracting states are accepting, under paragraph (c) of Article 3 *bis*, an obligation to establish all necessary provisions in the national law or regulations to make such compliance mandatory for aircraft of their registration or operated by operators having their principal place of business or permanent residence in that state. Contracting states are also accepting an obligation to make violation of such laws or regulations punishable by severe penalties and to submit the case to their competent authorities. This provision may offer a practical safeguard that no violators would go unpunished; even if they were to escape from the jurisdiction of the state where the unlawful act was committed, they should be prosecuted and punished by the state of the registration of the aircraft; in practical application this provision may be reinforced by existing or future arrangements for the extradition of offenders. Secondly, all contracting states are accepting an unconditional obligation to take appropriate measures to prohibit any deliberate 'misuse' of any civil aircraft of their registration or operated by operators having their principal place of business or permanent residence in that state. Legislative implementation of such a prohibition will no doubt be accompanied by appropriate penalties.

Other Legal Aspects

States can exercise criminal jurisdiction over foreign aircraft in flight over their territory as well as over the territory not subject to sovereignty of any state (for example, the high seas) also under the conditions set forth in the Tokyo Convention of 1963. Article 4 of that Convention permits 'interference' with an aircraft in flight in order to exercise criminal jurisdiction over an offence committed on board in the following cases:

- the offence has effect on the territory of such state;
- the offence has been committed by or against a national or permanent resident of such state;
- the offence is against the security of such state;
- the offence consists of a breach of any rules or regulations relating to the flight or manoeuvre of aircraft in force in such state;
- the exercise of jurisdiction is necessary to ensure the observance of any obligation of such state under a multilateral international agreement.

Since the Tokyo Convention has been accepted by many of ICAO's contracting states, this provision represents an important additional clarification to Article 3 *bis* of the Chicago Convention with respect to the interpretation of the phrase 'any purpose inconsistent with the aims of this Convention'. It is submitted that any offence foreseen in Article 4 of the Tokyo Convention gives right to the state concerned to 'interfere', that is, to require the landing or give the aircraft other instructions and to resort to proportionate and adequate use of force against such aircraft.

The United Nations Convention on the Law of the Sea does not foresee the right of hot pursuit of aircraft; the target of hot pursuit may be exclusively a ship but the procedures of hot pursuit may be effected by an aircraft (Article 111, paragraph 6).

Conclusions

The study of the problem of 'misuse' of civil aviation and of its consequences for law enforcement with respect to civil aircraft in flight leads to the following conclusions:

- Although the term 'misuse of civil aviation' is a legally imprecise term which has no firm basis in the Convention on International Civil Aviation apart from the title of Article 4, it still reflects the overall threat posed by unlawful interference with civil aviation.
- The phrase 'any purpose inconsistent with the aims of this Convention' has historically a different meaning in Article 4 of the Convention and in paragraphs (b) and (d) of Article 3 *bis*.
- The concept of 'misuse of civil aircraft' should best be referred to as 'deliberate use of civil aircraft for unlawful purposes'.
- The Chicago Convention contains effective provisions safeguarding full jurisdiction of states to prevent or prohibit the use of foreign aircraft for unlawful purposes in their territory.

The above conclusions may be use the relevant provisions of the Chicago Convention as a base to formulate other legal documents that would enforce more stringent control over this offence. Some recommendations as to the measures that could be adopted in this regard follow in Chapter 6.

Notes

1 United Nations (1987), *Report of the International Conference on Day Abuse and Illicit Trafficking*, Vienna 17–26 June 1987. New York, United Nations at 7.
2 Bell, R. (1991), 'The History of Drug Prohibition and Legislation', *Interpol International Criminal Police Review*, September–October, at 2.
3 Old unit of weight equal to 62.5 kg.
4 A/40/771 and A/40/772.
5 A/C 3/40/8, annex.
6 A/C 3/40/8.
7 *United Nations, Treaty Series*, vol. 520, no. 7515, p. 204.
8 Ibid., vol. 976, no. 14151, p. 4.
9 United Nations (1981), *Official Records of the Economic and Social Council*, Supplement no. 4 (E/1981/24), annex II.
10 United Nations (1981), *See Official Records of the Economic and Social Council*, Supplement no. 4 (E/1981/24), Chap. XI, sect. A.
11 See United Nations (1985), *Official Records of the Economic and Social Council*, Supplement no. 3 (E/1985/23 and Corr.1), Chap. IX, sect. A.
12 See A/40/773, annex.
13 As illustrated, by, *inter alia*, the following meetings and initiatives:

- The Inter-American Programme of Action against the Illicit Use and Production of Narcotic Drugs and Psychotropic Substances and Traffic Therein, adopted by the Inter-American Specialized Conference on Traffic in Narcotic Drugs, held at Rio de Janeiro, Brazil, from 22 to 26 April 1986.
- The Tokyo Declaration entitled 'Looking forward to a better future', issued at the Tokyo Economic Summit, held from 4 to 6 May 1986 (see A/41/354, annex I, para. 5).

- The 19th Ministerial Meeting of the Association of South-East Asian Nations, held at Manila on 23 and 24 June 1986.
- The recommendations of the first Interregional Meeting of Heads of National Drug Law Enforcement Agencies, held at Vienna from 28 July to 1 August 1986 (see A/41/559, para 10).
- The Economic Declaration of the Eighth Conference of Heads of State or Government of Non-Aligned Countries, held at Harare from 1 to 6 September to 2 October 1986.
- The Puerto Vallarta Declaration, adopted at the Regional Meeting of Ministers of Justice and Attorneys-General, held at Puerto Vallarta, Mexico, from 8 to 10 October 1986 (A/C.3/41/5, annex).
- The Meeting of Ministers of Interior and Justice of the 12 member states of the European Community, held in London on 20 October 1986.
- The recommendations of the Interregional Conference on the Involvement of Non-Governmental Organizations in Prevention and Reduction of the Demand for Drugs, held at Stockholm from 15 to 19 September 1986 (A/C.3/41/7, annex, para. 84).

14 A/41/665 and Add.1.
15 A/CONF. 133/PC/6.
16 See A/41/559, para. 10.
17 *United Nations, Treaty Series*, vol. 976, no. 14152, p. 106.
18 *Ibid.*, vol. 1019, no. 14956, p. 176.
19 United Nations (1987), *Report of the International Conference on Drug Abuse and Illicit Trafficking*, Vienna, 17–26 June 1987 (United Nations publication, Sales no. E.87.I.18).
20 *Ibid.*, chap. I, sect. B.
21 *Ibid.*, chap. I, sect. A.
22 United Nations (1987), *supra*, note 19, chap. I, sect. B.
23 *Ibid.*, chap. I, sect. A.
24 A/43/678.
25 See United Nations (1987), *Official Records of the Economic and Social Council*, Supplement no. 3 (E/1988/13).
26 United Nations (1987), *supra*, note 19, chap. I, sect. B.
27 *Ibid.*, chap. I, sect. B.
28 *Ibid.*, chap. I, sect. A.
29 *Ibid.*, chap. I, sect. B.
30 *Ibid.*, chap. I, sect. A.
31 A/43/684.
32 A/43/679.
33 United Nations (1987), *supra*, note 19, chap. I, sect. B.
34 *Id.*, chap. I, sect. A.
35 See United Nations (1989), *Official Records of the General Assembly*, 44th Session, Plenary Meetings, 13th Meeting (A/44/PV.13).
36 See United Nations (1987), *supra*, note 19, chap. I, sect. B.
37 *Ibid.*, sect. A.
38 E/CONF.82/15 and Corr. 2.
39 See E/1990/4, sect. III.
40 See United Nations (1987), *supra*, note 19, chap. I, sect. III.
41 *Ibid.*, sect. A.
42 See E/CONF.82/14.
43 See A/44/321, annex.
44 See E/CN.7/1990/2.
45 A/44/572 and A/44/601.

46 Convention against Traffic in Narcotic Drugs and Psychotropic Substances and Related Substances, Article 2.
47 *Id.*, Article 3.
48 *Id.*, Article 10 A 1.
49 *Id.*, Article 10 A 2.
50 *Id.*, Article 10 A 3.
51 *Id.*, Article 10 A 4.
52 *Id.*, Article 10 B 2.
53 *Id.*, Article 10 B 3.
54 *Id.*, Article 11.
55 *Id.*, Article 12.
56 *Id.*, Article 13.
57 *Id.*, Article 14.
58 *Id.*, Article 16.
59 *Id.*, Article 17.
60 *Id.*, Resolution 217 A (III).
61 These tables are not reproduced in this book.
62 See C-WP/2372 7/3/57 at p. 1.
63 See C-WP/2372.
64 See AN-WP/1984, 1/12/58 at 1.
65 Doc. 7866, A11–P/3 at 21.
66 E/RES/689 (XXVI) 29 July 1958.
67 See AN-WP/1604; XXIV-11, 25/2/57.
68 See AN-WP/1984 Appendix B.
69 The Economic and Social Council (ECOSOC) in Resolution 770E (XXX) approved certain recommendations to governments on safeguards to prevent abuse for the carriage of narcotic drugs in first-aid kits of aircraft engaged in international flights.
70 Doc. 7970.
71 A recommendation of the Customs Cooperation Council dated 17 June 1985, recognizes 'that the proper balance between the needs of customs enforcement and the facilitation of legitimate trade and travel can best be achieved if customs enforcement is selective and intelligence-based and that it is therefore essential that every effort be made to develop and exploit the best possible intelligence'. (Recommendation on the Development of Coordinated Enforcement and Intelligence Operations aimed at Identifying and Interrupting Concealed Illicit Drugs).
72 C-WP/8099.
73 International Convention on Mutual Administrative Assistance for the Prevention, Investigation and Repression of Customs Offences, signed at Nairobi in 1977 and administered by the Customs Cooperation Council.
74 International Convention on the Simplification and Harmonization of Customs Procedures, Kyoto, 1973.
75 A precursor is a product used as a nucleus, reagent or solvent which can be used for producing drugs covered by the Single Convention on Narcotic Drugs, New York, 1961 as amended and the Convention on Psychotropic Substances, Vienna 1971. Examples of precursors and essential chemicals are acetic anhydride, which is used in the production of heroin, and ethyl ether which is used for cocaine.
76 As reported to the Committee in connection with the triennial review of the implementation of Annex 9 (AT-WP/1467, Revised), recent studies by UNCITRAL (United Nations Commission for International Trade Law) have confirmed the acceptability of machine-readable data as evidence in legal proceedings.

77 *Official Records of the General Assembly,* 39th Session, Supplement no. 1 (A/39/1).
78 A/39/194.
79 See A/41/559, para. 10.
80 See United Nations (1986), *Official Records of the Economic and Social Council,* Supplement no. 3 (E/1986/23), chap. X, sect. A.
81 United Nations (1971), *United Nations, Treaty Series,* vol. 976, no. 14152, p. 106.
82 *Ibid.,* vol. 1019, no. 14956, p. 176.
83 *Ibid.,* vol. 1019, no. 14956, p. 176.
84 See United Nations (1987), *Official Records of the Economic and Social Council,* Supplement no. 3 (E/1988/13).
85 A/39/407, annex.
86 A/43/678.

6 Conclusion

An Overall View

The ICAO Committee on Unlawful Interference, in its sessions in January 1996 noted that there had been 11 acts of unlawful interference with civil aviation in 1995 which had been reported officially to ICAO[1]. Two other incidents had been unofficially made known to ICAO. It was suspected that four other additional incidents had taken place during 1995. The Committee noted that the number of reported acts of unlawful interference with civil aviation fell from 42 in 1994 to 17 in 1995. More important than this decline was the geographical distribution of occurrences. No official reports had been received in 1995 from contracting states in North America, Central America, the Caribbean, South America, Western and Central Africa[2]. Also, during 1995, no passenger or crew member was killed as a result of those incidents. Nevertheless, the Committee concluded that there were reasons to believe that international civil aviation continues to face the threat of unlawful interference.

The single existing flaw in the regulatory structure applicable to terrorism generally and unlawful interference with civil aviation particularly is the deplorable state to which the legal structure has sunk. Taken collectively, the Tokyo, Hague and Montreal Conventions would appear to ensure the peaceful, orderly, and expeditious conduct of international air transport and the administration of swift and appropriate justice for those who unlawfully interfere with such operations. Unfortunately, this has not been the case as there is no uniformity in states' actions regarding adjudication and extradition of offences. No state can act alone – yet states have demonstrated that they cannot act collectively either. An international law which fails to implement its policies and requirements through states is impotent. In the words of Judge Abraham Sofear:

> The law applicable to terrorism is not merely flawed, it is perverse. The rules and declarations seemingly designed to curb terrorism have

> regularly included provisions that demonstrate the absence of international agreement on the propriety of regulating terrorists actively. On some issues, the law leaves political violence unregulated. On other issues the law is ambivalent, providing a basis for conflicting arguments as to its purposes. At its worst the law has, in important ways, actually served to legitimise international terror, and to protect terrorists from punishment as criminals. These deficiencies are not the product of negligence or mistake. They are intentional.[3]

Traditionally, responses to terrorism have been classified as peaceful and coercive. The United Nations Charter provides in Article 2 (3) that all members shall settle their international disputes by peaceful means in such a manner that international peace and security, and justice, are not endangered. This is reiterated, and given content in, *inter alia,* the 1970 Declaration on Principles of International Law concerning Friendly Relations and Cooperation among states, which states:

> States shall ... seek early and just settlement of their international disputes by negotiation, inquiry, mediation, conciliation, arbitration, judicial settlement, resort to regional agencies or arrangements or other peaceful means of their choice ... The parties to a dispute have the duty, in the event of failure to reach a solution by any one of the above peaceful means, to continue to seek a settlement of the dispute by other peaceful means agreed upon by them.[4]

It follows that only after every effort has been made to deal with a terrorist attack by peaceful means should states resort to military action.

This view is, of course, by no means universal. In some cases – for whatever reasons, ideological, political or military – states do opt immediately for a coercive response to terrorist activity and receive no greater admonition from the rest of the international community than a verbal condemnation. But these 'deviations' do not detract from the general rule that peaceful remedies should be exhausted first. This is one of those areas where one cannot expect to find an absolutely consistent practice.

There is another respect in which the peaceful and coercive responses are not on the same plane. This relates to the sources of the international law respectively governing them. The rules governing the coercive responses are part of the law on the use of armed force. For the most part this is customary international law (even though, of course, its roots may lie in treaties, particularly the UN Charter). It follows that these rules are binding on all subjects of international law, with the theoretical exception of those who 'opted out' at the inception of the rules.

By contrast, the rules governing the peaceful response are contained in treaties. This means that they have the advantage of being clearer and less ambiguous than the customary law on the use of force but it also implies one important shortcoming: these rules are binding only on those states that have ratified or acceded to the relevant treaties and, even then, only on a strictly reciprocal basis; in other words, they are not universally applicable.

What we are left with, then, is a rule which, in effect, says that peaceful measures must be tried and exhausted before coercive measures are used, but then fails to compel states to try to exhaust any particular peaceful measures. In the absence of advance agreement, we are presumably thrown back on *ad hoc* negotiations, which may be more or less wholehearted.

The Problem with Treaties and Peaceful Responses

All treaties enshrine the universal principle, *aut dedere aut judicare*, which means essentially that contracting states on whose territory those reasonably suspected of terrorist acts happen to be must either try them or hand them over to whichever other contracting state requests their extradition in accordance with the treaties. They cannot, according to the treaties, allow terrorists to go scot-free. Contracting states also have universal jurisdiction, in that all have jurisdiction to try, within their territories, those suspected of acts of terrorism. However it does not always happen that way.

There are four major problems with these treaties. Firstly, is the usual problem that not enough states are party to the multilateral treaties. And, in particular, not enough states that actually count in this field are party – that is, those states on whose territory terrorists seem consistently to end up. Italy, for instance, was not a party to the 1979 New York Convention on the Taking of Hostages[5] at the time of the *Achille Lauro* affair. There was also the 1984 incident where the hijackers of a Kuwaiti aircraft were allowed to escape because Algeria was not a party to the relevant treaties and, accordingly, could not be compelled to 'extradite or punish' them.

Secondly, there is the problem, which is by no means unusual, that both the multilateral and bilateral treaties contain no effective enforcement provisions. If a party fails to comply with the treaty – refuses to hand over a suspected terrorist, for instance – the other parties can do no more than apply the traditional peaceful sanctions authorized by the international community; not the kind of sanctions that could be expected to deter a firmly recalcitrant state. Again, mention may be made of the *Achille Lauro* case, where Egypt failed to comply with the 1979 Convention on the Taking of Hostages (New

York) and Italy failed to abide by its 1983 extradition treaty with the United States, without, in each case, there being any relevant consequences.

A third problem with these treaties is that hardly any of them specifies that terrorist-type acts are not to be deemed 'political offences' and thereby exempted from extradition. This needs clarification because most terrorist acts are, of course, inspired by political motives, it is simply that the methods used are such that the advantages normally accorded to political offences should not apply.

Finally, there is a fourth problem with these treaties: that the obligations of the state parties to search for, and arrest, suspects are treated in an insufficiently rigorous way. These obligations are crucial because the 'extradite or prosecute' rule can obviously be rendered meaningless if states allow suspects to remain hidden or to abscond.

The 1988 Maritime Convention,[6] a significantly analogous instrument on the subject, imposes no specific obligation to search for suspects believed to be present in the territory of a state party. As regards arrest, the Convention merely requires a state to arrest suspects 'upon being satisfied that the circumstances so warrant' and 'in accordance with its law'. In this, it repeats the language used in a number of the earlier treaties, the Hague Convention, the Montreal Convention, and the 1973 and 1979 New York Conventions. States are thus left a large measure of discretion to decline to arrest suspects for reasons more 'political' than 'evidential'.

On the positive side, it could be said that we have now reached a situation when there is general consensus among the international community that terrorism is to be condemned. The Peace Accord of 1995 between the Palestine Liberation Organization (PLO) and Israel, and the NATO presence in Bosnia-Herzegovina are recent results of universal attempts at recognizing the futility of violence and terrorism.

A further positive development is that the international community seems to be moving closer toward consensus on a definition of terrorism. This is important because, once we have an accepted definition, those who commit terrorist acts will no longer be able to escape the consequences of those acts by 'defining them away', claiming they are legitimate forms of national liberation warfare or other legitimate 'irregular' warfare. A compelling example of this development is a resolution on terrorism which was adopted by the UN General Assembly in 1985 by consensus. The resolution unequivocally condemned as criminal, 'all acts, methods and practices of terrorism wherever and by whomever committed'.[7] It also gave, in its preamble, certain clues as to what is encompassed by the term 'terrorism' as acts ... which endanger or take innocent human lives, jeopardize fundamental freedoms and seriously impair the dignity of human beings ... acts covered by the existing conventions relating to various aspects of the problem of terrorism', including those already mentioned above.

In 1987, a further resolution condemning terrorism was adopted by the UN General Assembly, though this time with opposing votes from the United States and Israel. This resolution actually proposed that a conference be convened to agree on a definition of terrorism.[8] The United States and Israel were opposed to this proposal, fearing that a definition might emerge distinguishing terrorism as something intrinsically different from the activities of national liberation movements.[9] And indeed, it is clear that a number of Third World and other states have long taken precisely this view, that it is quite legitimate for those fighting for self-determination to resort to terrorist action.[10] Our goal of consensus on the question of what constitutes terrorism is, therefore, still some way off.

Another heartening factor is that we have at least some conventional framework for rational peaceful responses to terrorist activity. We also have rules limiting resort to military responses, which at least puts some brake on those who would favour simply 'eliminating' all those whom they characterize as terrorists. It is also encouraging, in addition, that the idea that hijackers are pirates has never been accepted. Such an idea – at least in the way it has been advanced – would serve only to legitimize the use of force against anyone ideologically or politically opposed to the state purporting to exercise 'universal jurisdiction' and to escalate the spread of violence in the world. Whilst it is true that terrorists are in a way 'modern enemies of mankind', and every state should endeavour to search for, try and punish them on its own territory, this does not include a licence to use force in the territory of other states or against ships or aircraft of other states. If such a licence were given by international law, our present conditions of relative anarchy would be at risk of turning into one of absolute anarchy.

Notwithstanding the above, it is disheartening that in an overall sense, the existing structure of law relating to terrorism has failed to provide the international community with an effective system of control of the offence from a legal perspective. As a first step, states should take serious note of United Nations General Assembly admonitions:

> States should contribute to the progressive elimination of the causes underlying international terrorism and to pay special attention to all situations, including, *inter alia*, colonialism, racism and situations involving mass and flagrant violations of human rights and fundamental freedoms and those involving alien occupation, that may give rise to international terrorism and may endanger international peace and security.[11]

The above provision refers to some elements of structural violence which are believed by the General Assembly to stand in the way of the lasting elimination of terrorism.

The problem of terrorism and the need for a practical approach to the problem was eloquently highlighted by the Ghanaian representative in the Security Council in the debate following the Israeli interception of a Libyan aircraft in February 1986. He stated:

> The international community, including the [Security] Council, must summon the necessary political will to delve into the reasons why the frustrations of the dispossessed are vented in this manner. A glib condemnation of terrorism alone, without a scientific and impartial study of its origins will not, we are afraid, eradicate the phenomenon.[12]

An Enhanced Role for ICAO in Aviation Security

In the absence of legislative strength, one of the progressive measures towards assuring aviation security lies in a re-examination of the role played by ICAO in the field of aviation security. ICAO has adopted, through its 184 contracting states, Annex 17 to the Chicago Convention which lays down Standards and Recommended Practices (SARPs) on international cooperation. Standard 3.2.1 requires each contracting state to cooperate with other states in order to adapt their respective national civil aviation security programmes – which are required to be established by Standard 3.1.1 of the Annex. The Annex contains several provisions which are calculated to ensure aviation security, only if they are followed by all states. Unfortunately, this does not happen in reality.

As a further means of ensuring states' compliance with its SARPs in critical areas such as aviation security, ICAO has developed its Strategic Action Plan (SAP) which will, when implemented fully, ensure more cooperation among states in areas critical to civil aviation, such as security. It is necessary therefore to dispel the myth that state sovereignty grants states the absolute right to refuse to follow their international obligations as enshrined in the principles of international law.

The ICAO Strategic Action Plan

The ICAO Strategic Action Plan (SAP) is primarily aimed at promoting the principles enshrined in the Chicago Convention[13] in the most efficient manner so that the challenges posed by modern exigencies of civil aviation are met. The SAP would accomplish the following:

1 ensure that ICAO maintains its position as the main standard-setting body for international civil aviation;
2 encourage national ratification of instruments of international air law and implementation of ICAO Standards and Recommended Practices to the greatest extent possible so as to maintain a common aviation system world-wide;
3 ensure that ICAO continues to focus on the exploration and development of aviation issues of a multilateral nature in the fields of legal, economic and technical regulation and thereby remains a world forum for these issues;
4 identify priorities for ICAO and seek to ensure that sufficient resources are made available to respond to the major challenges concerned; and
5 develop a continued efficient and cost-effective mechanism in ICAO for the management of technical cooperation activities.[14]

The issues that have been identified by ICAO for the triennium 1996–1998 as requiring the above action are:

1 Communications, navigation and surveillance/air traffic management (CNS/ATM).
2 Airport and airspace congestion.
3 Commercial developments and economic regulation.
4 Financial resources.
5 Unlawful interference.
6 Human factors in flight safety.
7 Environmental protection.
8 Human resources.
9 Enhancement of ICAO Standards.
10 Safety oversight.
11 Legal aspects of the challenges.

The legal aspects of these issues form separate studies by themselves and have largely been addressed elsewhere.[15] Of primary relevance are the legal issues that underline the above objectives of ICAO in introducing the SAP to the international aviation community and seeking their cooperation in its implementation. Such an analysis would enable states to acquaint themselves with their legal responsibilities and duties towards compliance with the international regulation of aviation security.

It is an incontrovertible fact that the SAP cannot be implemented unilaterally by ICAO without the cooperation of its member states. Fundamentally, and from a legal standpoint, the position of ICAO in the international aviation community is not one that is compatible with being absolutely legislative in capacity. ICAO sets guidelines on civil aviation and facilitates the adoption of treaties and regulations, with the approval of its member states. It is then up to the member states themselves to implement them. The SAP is therefore essentially a two-sided issue and may be adequately subsumed by the adage 'one cannot clap with one hand'. The obligations of ICAO member states are paramount in giving teeth to ICAO's Standards and Recommended Practices and other guidelines, as much as in satisfying or otherwise accepting treaties of air law that they themselves have adopted under ICAO auspices.

Origin of the Strategic Action Plan (SAP)

During the 1988–1990 triennium, as a measure to meet the challenges faced by civil aviation in the 1990s, the ICAO Council drew up a tentative inventory of the major challenges facing civil aviation and their implications for the work of ICAO. The 27th Session of the Assembly reviewed this inventory and, noting the need for states and the organization to keep pace with the rapidity of change and developments in civil aviation, decided that the Council should develop a global strategy of implementation priorities for the economic, technical and legal fields for the next decade. The Council took up this matter again in 1990 and decided that, in order to prepare a cohesive response to the critical issues concerned, it would develop a strategic action plan looking beyond the traditional triennial programming process. Also, in order to obtain a clear position of states and their views on major challenges facing aviation, the Council decided to seek the views of states and the industry. A State Letter was accordingly issued on 16 January 1991[16] attaching information on each of the challenges identified and seeking views on the objectives, scope and framework of the strategic action plan.

According to information given by ICAO to the 29th Assembly, responses to the State Letter were received from 47 states and from the Airports Association Council International (AACI), the International Air Transport Association (IATA) and the International Coordinating Council of Aerospace Industries Associations (ICCAIA). Support for the Council's initiative for the development of a strategic action plan was widespread. The identification of the challenges concerned was also widely accepted and substantive and extensive comments were made by a large number of respondents regarding these challenges and the proposed action on them.

The Council consequently established a Working Group, comprising representatives of 10 states from all ICAO regions, to give detailed consideration to the challenges identified and the responses to the State Letter and develop a strategic action plan 'to provide a structure and monitoring mechanism for the Organization's priority activities'. This Group worked intensively in both formal and informal meetings over the period August 1991 to June 1992, in close cooperation with a multidisciplinary Secretariat team formed especially to participate in the activity concerned.

The Working Group placed particular emphasis on consultation with the industry, as well as with states, so as to ensure that the strategic action plan would be relevant, practical and contemporary. The Group accordingly not only reviewed in depth the views of states, AACI, IATA and ICCAIA, as expressed in their replies to the State Letter but also received presentations by the Directors General of AACI and IATA as well as the IFALPA Representative to ICAO on their perceptions of the major challenges facing international civil aviation and of ICAO's future role.

As a preliminary step, the Working Group classified the major challenges to international civil aviation into three basic types in a format which would provide flexibility for coverage of a broad range of issues. The currently identified challenges for international civil aviation at large were classified into these three types as detailed in Table 6.1:[17]

Table 6.1 Challenges facing international civil aviation

Technological/ Techical	Economic/Financial	Human/Social
• Communications, navigation and surveillance/air traffic management (CNS/ATM) • Airport and airspace congestion	• Commercial developments and economic regulation • Financial resources	• Unlawful interference • Human factors in flight safety • Environmental protection • Human resources

However, while noting that the role of ICAO in these challenges was essentially one of an operational or regulatory nature, the Group made its observation clear that most of the challenges had some legal content. When considered together with other issues and challenges reflected in the above format, the legal issues concerned were of considerable importance for civil aviation in general and ICAO in particular, which led the Group to establish a fourth classification which related to legal aspects of the challenges.

The Working Group also proceeded to analyse the nature of each of the individual challenges concerned and their legal aspects; the related action already in hand by ICAO; the views of states and the industry; and the relevant activities of other bodies, including some which are not aviation-based but which are increasingly having implications for the work of ICAO (for example, the European Community and the ITU). Finally, the Group considered the need for additional action, if any, by ICAO in relation to each of the challenges concerned, as well as the more general need for increased emphasis on ratification or implementation of instruments of international air law, Standards, Recommended Practices and related material.

This analysis both established a basis for action in relation to each of the currently identified challenges and provided a framework for developing an overall strategy for ICAO.

The Strategic Action Plan (SAP)

On the basis of the conclusions of its Working Group, the Council has now developed a structure for ICAO's Strategic Action Plan (SAP), which, although in an embryonic stage, basically represents a blueprint for the Organization which has to be developed over the 1996–1998 triennium.

Council firstly noted there were a number of forces at work which underlined the need for leadership by a strong and effective ICAO. Firstly, it was observed that there is the increasing involvement of non-aviation sectors (for example, satellites and communications) in civil aviation and an increasing consideration of aviation within the context of wider policy initiatives (for example, the trade negotiations under the auspices of the General Agreement on Tariffs and Trade (GATT) or the environmental protection measures agreed both within and outside the United Nations system). Secondly, there is increasing 'globalization' of civil aviation itself, exemplified by foreign and multinational ownership and alliances of airlines, joint marketing arrangements and computer reservation systems, and multinational approaches to both technical and economic regulation of air transport services, along with increasing interaction between domestic and international air transport services. Thirdly, there are increasingly intense economic, political, environmental and other social pressures on civil aviation policy or operations, particularly on a national or regional basis, including rapid transitional changes in socio-economic systems in some regions which are having global effects. At the same time, in many states civil aviation still has to be considered as an essential public utility, contributing at a fundamental level to socio-economic development and, in some areas, providing service to otherwise inaccessible points.

It was recognized at this stage that given the need to respond to these pressures and the increased complexity and cost of aviation equipment which is continually being enhanced, there were also increasing financial constraints on civil aviation. The SAP was therefore designed to address these constraints which are believed to have a significant bearing on a fundamental concern of the Council, the continuing divergence among individual states and regions in the level of conformity with existing Standards and Recommended Practices (SARPs), with potential global implications for the safety, regularity and efficiency of civil aviation.

The importance of the changing context for civil aviation has repeatedly been echoed in the presentations to the Council Working Group by representatives of the industry, who stressed *inter alia* that in their view ICAO needed to revise its role, structure and functioning or risk being overtaken, either by technology or by the emerging roles of other global or regional bodies.

In the light of the above considerations, the Council formulated the following premises as the basis for development of the Strategic Action Plan by ICAO:

1 There is a need for ICAO to place greater emphasis on bridging disparities among states and regions by assisting states in addressing the implementation of facilities, services and procedures required for consistency in the application of SARPs.
2 There is also a need for ICAO to promote consistency between SARPs and the provisions applying to domestic services where these provisions have implications for international services.
3 It is necessary for ICAO to develop new SARPs in a timely manner, but only where these are essential to a globally coordinated approach to the introduction of new equipment or techniques and/or where they have positively identified economic benefits.
4 ICAO should place greater emphasis on timely ratification of instruments of international air law.
5 ICAO should also assign more meaningful priorities to work programme tasks and to focus on issues of greatest priority.
6 In order to accomplish the above, ICAO should project a higher public profile and play a stronger and more catalytic role in coordinating and representing international civil aviation.
7 ICAO should also develop improved communications with its contracting states and establish closer relations with other organizations, including both public and private sector bodies in civil

aviation and non-aviation bodies where relevant, to ensure effective and timely consultation, proper coordination and avoidance of duplication of effort.

8 There is also a continuing need for ICAO to review the working procedures of the Council and all subordinate bodies as well as the structure and functioning of the Secretariat, to ensure greater efficiency, flexibility and speed of reaction, to release resources for priority tasks, and to reflect the increasingly multidisciplinary nature of many of these tasks.

Progress of the SAP

The Council intended very early in the 1992–1994 triennium, to translate the blueprint of broad strategy contained in the existing structure of the Strategic Action Plan into specific implementation programmes. This was expected to be done by linking the Plan directly to the Programme Budget, defining specific tasks, determining priorities and allocating responsibilities for these tasks, and setting target dates for their implementation.

The Council was conscious that the tasks concerned represented only new challenges or ones with over-riding priority, and it did not underestimate the importance of the large volume of traditional recurring work not covered by the Strategic Action Plan. However, the Council was of the view that there was a need for a critical review of all traditional tasks to ensure that only those essential for the future were retained. The Council therefore intended to undertake such a review on the basis of broad objective criteria such as:

1 the current or future relevance of the task;
2 the direct relevance and interest of the task to a substantial number of states in different regions;
3 whether the task had a clearly defined output which would make an effective contribution to the safe, regular, efficient and economical development of international air transport services;
4 whether the output of the task provided an effective contribution by international air transport services to the socio-economic development of states;
5 whether the task partly or wholly duplicated work which was being performed satisfactorily elsewhere; and,
6 whether the output of the task warranted its fully allocated costs in relation to the overall Programme Budget.

The Council also intended to study and modify as necessary the structure and functioning of the Organization including, *inter alia*:

1 continuing review of the working procedures of the Council and its subordinate bodies, including the functioning of the Secretariat, with an emphasis on multidisciplinary programme management;
2 consideration of adapting existing work of other bodies for incorporation into Annexes or advisory material;
3 continuing review of policy regarding technical cooperation activities; and
4 a substantive review of all Assembly Resolutions in force with a view to assessing their continuing relevance, to streamlining and to clarifying the current and future roles and activities of the Organization.

Apart from carrying out the above work, the Council intended to continue to develop the Strategic Action Plan itself, which was to be reviewed, updated and rolled forward periodically to reflect developments regarding the major challenges as presently defined and new priority challenges that may arise.

Given the fact that while all this activity would require some diversion of increasingly scarce resources from other tasks, the Council believed that the benefits to be achieved from identification of priorities and increased productivity and efficiency would more than justify the effort, and that the work concerned is of fundamental importance if ICAO was to continue to respond effectively to, and not be overtaken by, the rapidly changing civil aviation context.

Therefore, in the final analysis the Strategic Action Plan is intended to provide a framework for the priority activities of the International Civil Aviation Organization within the context of the major challenges facing international civil aviation as a whole into the next century. In the context of this objective, ICAO believes that, of necessity, the Strategic Action Plan can highlight only immediate and direct efforts focused on key issues. The many other activities of the Organization, because of their recurring nature or currently lower priority, do not feature specifically in the Plan, although they are of considerable importance and often underpin the strategic objectives of ICAO as reflected in the Chicago Convention and developed accordingly by the international aviation community at Assembly Sessions of ICAO and other relevant gatherings.

The basic structure for the Strategic Action Plan was adopted by the Council in July 1992. The Council has now developed the Plan further to incorporate a more detailed programme of action on each issue, to monitor these programmes on a continuous basis, and to update and roll the Plan forward periodically to reflect new developments regarding the major challenges facing international civil aviation as presently defined as well as new priority challenges that may arise.

At the 31st Session of the ICAO Assembly, held in Montreal from 19 September to 4 October 1995, ICAO contracting states adopted Resolution A31-2[18] on increasing the effectiveness of ICAO. The Resolution *inter alia* recognizes the new and rapidly evolving technological, social, economic and legal challenges in the field of civil aviation and directs the ICAO Council and Secretary General, within their respective competencies, to intensify efforts to develop a Strategic Action Plan for the Organization. The Plan is required to be implemented by a systematic planning process which draws the financial progress and utilization of the Organization. It also directs the Council *inter alia,* to ensure the effectiveness of the ICAO safety oversight mechanism.

On 22 May 1997, ICAO officially launched its Strategic Action Plan in accordance with the directives of the Assembly in Resolution A31-2. At the launch, the President of the ICAO Council, Dr. Assad Kotaite, renewed calls for increasing powers which would enable ICAO to oversee the implementation of aviation safety and security standards world-wide.[19] Dr. Kotaite identified ICAO's role in the present context succinctly when he said:

> Never has there been a greater need for a strong and active ICAO ... In civil aviation, globalization, commercialization of government service providers, liberalization of economic regulation, increasing environmental controls and the emergence of new technologies all have significant implications for safety and security. Addressing these issues effectively requires an unprecedented level of cooperation among countries and a corresponding level of global coordination which extends beyond borders.[20]

Status of ICAO Regulations Relating to the SAP

The above discussion leads to the inexorable question as to whether ICAO can reasonably expect the implementation of its Strategic Action Plan by its member states. The inherent difficulty of course, which effectively precludes one from answering this question with an unreserved 'yes', lies in the intrinsic fact that the implementation of ICAO Standards and Recommended Practices is by no means a legal obligation on the part of states, at least from the standpoint of international law. Notwithstanding the fact that international law itself has been the subject of criticism on the question of its mandatory powers and the effect of sanctions under international law, obligations of states towards ICAO Standards and Recommended Practices (SARPs) seemingly occupy a much lesser profile than those which are attendant upon the adherence to principles of international law.

The 29th Session of the ICAO Assembly, which was held in Montreal in 1992 noted that there were widely expressed and fundamental concerns regarding, *inter alia,* the inadequate and often non-representative level of responses to State Letters regarding the implementation of ICAO (SARPs); the costs (to ICAO and states) of implementation; the potential for differing interpretation by individual states of ICAO SARPs; and, underlying all these concerns, the need to assure no dilution of safety standards for civil aviation anywhere in the world. In order to address these concerns, the Assembly adopted Resolution A29-3, which recognizes *inter alia* that:

1 The interdependence of international civil aviation makes aviation a prime candidate for benefits to be derived from the concept of globalization, of which global harmonization of national rules for the application of ICAO standards is an important element.
2 International aviation now comprises: mega-air carriers, both national and multinational, and various alliances of airlines for global operation; transnational ownership of airlines; and multinational manufacture of aeronautical products.
3 States have agreed in the Aircraft Agreement of the General Agreement on Tariffs and Trade (GATT) to ensure that civil aircraft certification requirements and specifications on operating and maintenance procedures are not barriers to trade.
4 Global harmonization of national rules in international civil aviation is desirable for effective implementation of the GATT obligation.
5 Individual states interpret and apply the ICAO safety standards differently resulting in dissimilar operations which can be costly.
6 A relatively small number of states generally reply to the ICAO Secretariat's requests for comments or agreement on ICAO proposed standards, resulting in decisions being based on a relatively small number of responses with consequences which are neither helpful to achieve rule harmonization nor in the best interest of the safe and orderly development of international civil aviation.
7 Global rule harmonization could facilitate the implementation of the Protocol Article 83 *bis* of the Convention on International Civil Aviation that authorizes states to transfer to each other by agreement certain safety functions.
8 Certain states have initiated bilateral and multilateral programmes in the interest of harmonizing national rules, to correct costly incompatibility problems and to facilitate more effective competition in international civil aviation.

Accordingly, the Resolution urges states and groups of states, which have not already done so, to take positive action to promote global harmonization of national rules for the application of ICAO standards and to use in their own national regulations, as far as practicable, the precise language of ICAO regulatory standards in their application of ICAO standards and seek harmonization of national rules with other states in respect of higher standards they have in force or intend to introduce. The Resolution also urges all states to respond to the ICAO Council's requests for comments and agreement or disagreement on proposed standards of ICAO to prevent decisions being taken on the basis of a small number of responses. Finally, the Resolution requests the ICAO Council to pursue the enhancement of ICAO Standards and to study the feasibility of establishing a multilateral monitoring mechanism.

Resolution A29-3 is inextricably linked to ICAO's Strategic Action Plan, and ties in the compelling need for states to conform with ICAO Standards – which is clearly a central strategic issue for the achievement of success of the Plan. The question of compliance with, or notification of differences from international Standards is one which has concerned the Organization for many decades, and since 1950 the Council has regularly addressed the implementation of the Annexes to the Convention in relation to the provisions of Article 38 of the Chicago Convention. Nevertheless, previous efforts to improve the situation have tended to focus on specific aspects of the various problems, and the Council has felt that a more fundamental and far-reaching evaluation should be undertaken. Accordingly, the enhancement of ICAO SARPS has now become a critical issue and continues to be subject to sustained discussion in the ICAO Council.

The substantive conclusions from the Council's consideration provide the comprehensive response of the Organization to Resolution A29-3, more specifically regarding the statutory situation of ICAO Standards, the challenges in implementing Standards, and a strategy for improvement of their implementation.

Statutory Status of ICAO SARPS

Basically, ICAO promulgates its SARPs through its 18 Annexes to the Chicago Convention. Article 54 (l) of the Chicago Convention prescribes the adoption of International Standards and Recommended Practices and their designation in Annexes to the Convention, while notifying all contracting states of the action taken. The fundamental question which has to be addressed *in limine*, in the consideration of the effectiveness of ICAO's SARPs, is whether SARPs are legislative in character. If the answer is in the affirmative, then at least theoretically, one can insist upon adherence to SARPs by states.

The adoption of SARPS was considered a priority by the ICAO Council in its 2nd Session (2 September–12 December 1947)[21] which attempted to obviate any delays to the adoption of SARPs on air navigation as required by the First Assembly of ICAO.[22] SARPs inevitably take two forms: a negative form, for example, that states shall not impose more than certain maximum requirements; and a positive form, for example, that states shall take certain steps as prescribed by the ICAO Annexes.[23]

Article 37 of the Convention obtains the undertaking of each contracting state to collaborate in securing the highest practical degree of uniformity in regulations, standards, procedures and organization in relation to international civil aviation in all matters in which such uniformity will facilitate and improve air navigation. Article 38 obligates all contracting states to the Convention to inform ICAO immediately if they are unable to comply with any such international standard or procedure and notify differences between their own practices and those prescribed by ICAO. In the case of amendments to international standards, any state which does not make the appropriate amendment to its own regulations or practices shall give notice to the ICAO Council within 60 days of the adoption of the said amendment to the international standard or indicate the action which it proposes to take.

There is no room for doubt that the Annexes to the Convention or parts thereof lay down rules of conduct both directly and analogically. In fact, although there is a conception based on a foundation of practicality that ICAO's international standards identified by the words 'contracting states shall' have a mandatory flavour (imputed by the word 'shall'), while Recommended Practices identified by the words 'contracting states may' have only an advisory and recommendatory connotation (imputed by the word 'may'), it is interesting that at least one ICAO document requires states under Article 38 of the Convention, to notify ICAO of all significant differences from both Standards and Recommended Practices, thus making all SARPS regulatory in nature.[24]

Another strong factor that reflects the overall ability and power of the Council to prescribe civil rules of conduct (and therefore legislate) on a strict interpretation of the word is that in Article 22 of the Convention each contracting state agrees to adopt all practical measures through the issuance of special regulations or otherwise, to facilitate and expedite air navigation. It is clear that this provision can be regarded as an incontrovertible rule of conduct that responds to the requirement in Article 54 (l) of the Convention. Furthermore, the mandatory nature of Article 90 of the Convention – that an Annex or amendment thereto shall become effective within three months after it is submitted by the ICAO Council to contracting states is yet another pronouncement on the power of the Council to prescribe rules of state conduct in matters of international civil aviation. *A fortiori*, it is arguable that the ICAO Council is seen not only to possess the attribute of the term 'jurisfaction' (the power to make rules of conduct) but also the term 'jurisaction' (the power to enforce its own rules of conduct). The latter attribute can be seen where the Convention obtains the undertaking of contracting states not to allow airlines to operate through their airspace if the Council decides that the airline concerned is not conforming to a final decision rendered by the Council on a matter that concerns the operation of an international airline.[25] This is particularly applicable when such an airline is found not to conform to the provisions of Annex 2 to the Convention that derives its validity from Article 12 of the Convention relating to rules of the air.[26] In fact, it is very relevant that Annex 2, the responsibility for the promulgation of which devolves upon the Council by virtue of Article 54 (l), sets mandatory rules of the air, making the existence of the legislative powers of the Council an unequivocal and irrefutable fact.

Academic and professional opinion also favours the view that in a practical sense, the ICAO Council does have legislative powers. Milde says:

> The Chicago Convention, as any other legal instrument, provides only a general legal framework which is given true life only in the practical implementation of its provisions. Thus, for example, Article 37 of the Convention relating to the adoption of international standards and recommended procedures would be a very hollow and meaningless provision without active involvement of all contracting States, Panels, Regional and Divisional Meetings, deliberations in the Air Navigation Commission and final adoption of the standards by the Council. Similarly, provisions of Article 12 relating to the rules of the air applicable over the high seas, Articles 17 to 20 on the nationality of aircraft, Article 22 on facilitation, Article 26 on the investigation of accidents, etc., would be meaningless without appropriate implementation in the respective Annexes. On the same level is the provision of the last sentence of Article 77 relating to the determination by the Council in what manner the provisions of the Convention relating to nationality of aircraft shall apply to aircraft operated by international operating agencies.[27]

Milde concludes that ICAO has regulatory and quasi-legislative functions in the technical field and plays a consultative and advisory role in the economic sphere.[28] A similar view had earlier been expressed by Buergenthal who states:

> The manner in which the International Civil Aviation organization has exercised its regulatory functions in matters relating to the safety of international air navigation and the facilitation of international air

> transport provides a fascinating example of international law making ... the Organization has consequently not had to contend with any of the post-war ideological differences that have impeded international law making on politically sensitive issues.[29]

Dempsey endorses in a somewhat conservative manner the view that ICAO has the ability to make regulations when he states:

> In addition to the comprehensive, but largely dormant adjudicative enforcement held by ICAO under Articles 84-88 of the Chicago Convention, the Agency also has a solid foundation for enhanced participation in economic regulatory aspects of international aviation in Article 44, as well as the Convention's Preamble.[30]

Unfortunately, in practical application, SARPs do not carry the full import that is theoretically expected of them. As illustrated by Figure 6.1[31], the compliance of states with the requirement of Article 38 for the notification of differences from the standards subsequently adopted is far from adequate and fails to reflect the true position of states in regard to SARPs.

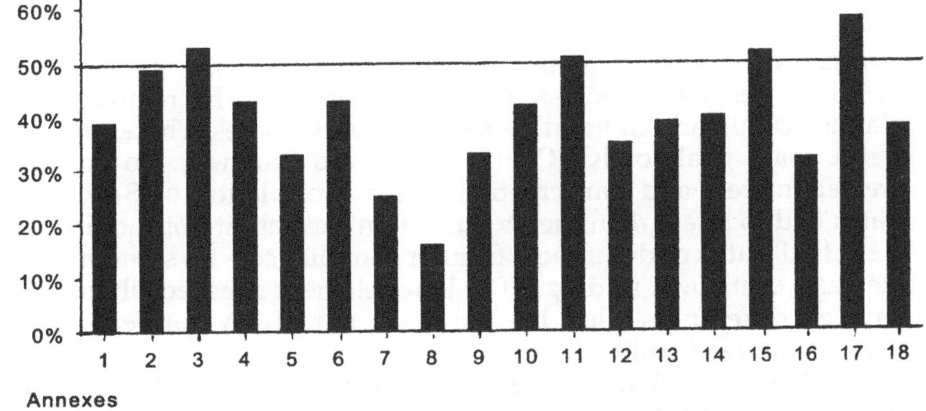

Figure 6.1 States notifying compliance or differences to amendments of ICAO Annexes 1984–1994

Figure 6.1 reflects the position of responses by states with regard to the provisions of each Annex by percentage at the end of 1994. This is based on states' notifications to ICAO of their compliance or differences over the 10-year period 1984–1994. The response level shown varies from 58 per cent (Annex 17) to 16 per cent (Annex 8). According to ICAO:

> this is using a generous measure, since it includes for example a State which has responded in the case of one Amendment to an Annex but not in the case of several other Amendments to the same Annex. A more accurate measure would be one relating to each individual Amendment, but this is very difficult to obtain at present due to the format in which the responses are recorded. As an indication of current response levels, however, the most recent figures on notification of compliance or differences with the latest (pre-1994) Amendment to each of the eighteen Annexes show that an average of only 25 per cent of contracting States have responded.[32]

It is, therefore, impossible at the present time to indicate with any degree of accuracy or certainty what the state of implementation of regulatory annex material really is. This is because a large number of contracting states have not notified ICAO of their compliance with or differences to the standards in the annexes for some considerable time. ICAO observes that it would probably be incorrect to assume that all of the non-responding states have not incorporated the standards of the relevant annexes in their national regulations; it would certainly be equally incorrect to assume that the non-responding states have fully implemented the relevant standards.[33]

Challenges in Implementing ICAO Standards

One of the issues that is being addressed by ICAO is the need for a formulation by the Organization of a comprehensive response of ICAO to Resolution A29-3, taking into account the related tasks planned or already in hand by the subsidiary bodies. Therefore, one of the main goals of ICAO at present is to find ways to create a greater interest and participation in the formulation of SARPs by states and to strengthen the Organization's capability of monitoring the actual status of differences from or compliance with standards on the basis of its own findings. The latter element is especially important, as differences filed by states do not always appear to be representative of reality.

ICAO believes that there are a number of reasons that prevent states from indicating their compliance, or otherwise, with ICAO SARPs. These may include:

1 Insufficient communication between ICAO and recipient states; loss of documentation by recipients and delays in delivering the documentation to the responsible party beyond the target date for replies; organizational structures of civil aviation authorities which render difficulties in identification of, and routing to, the responsible party.
2 Insufficient resources within states to consider expeditiously and process ICAO documentation and to implement the relevant standards into their national legislation.
3 Difficulty in comprehending and interpreting annex material as well as subject matter which is beyond the level of expertise of the recipient administration.
4 Possible lack of understanding about the role of states in the consultation phase of the development of ICAO standards.[34]

More fundamentally, it is always a possibility that states may have insufficient resources either to implement standards or to advise ICAO of non-compliance with the relevant standards. It should be noted in this context, that recent initiatives by states, in an effort to address the concerns raised by the 29th Session of the Assembly and to assure the safety of their citizens, have raised fundamental questions about the effectiveness of the multilateral safety assurance afforded by the Chicago Convention.

ICAO feels that the need to remind contracting states on an ongoing basis of their obligation to notify the Organization of any differences to the standards in the annexes to the Convention remains a critical factor in its advances towards more state participation in its regulatory process. Furthermore, the level of implementation of those standards by states into their national legislation and procedures has to be improved. These two elements complement each other; if too many states simply notify ICAO of their non-implementation of the safety standards, states could no longer assume a mutual level of minimum safety standards and would have to resort to a bilateral or regional approach in order to ensure an acceptable safety oversight between themselves.

Some catalysts for the global implementation of standards and the harmonization of national rules have been identified as the bilateral and multilateral cooperation of states. Organizations such as the European Civil Aviation Conference, the African and Latin American Civil Aviation Commissions, the Conference of Directors General of Civil Aviation of the Asia and Pacific Regions, the Commonwealth of Independent States, and other groups, including trading blocs, may be considered as effective vehicles for the promulgation and adoption of agreements and understandings in this regard.

Another significant issue is that there is an increasing need for cooperation in the regulatory field for states in a particular geographic setting and with certain common regulatory needs which are dictated by technical, operational and environmental needs and motives. Recent years have witnessed the growing significance of regional organizations that are addressing traditional ICAO activities such as technical harmonization, standardization and regulatory matters. These activities are likely to intensify in the near future and may well affect the role of ICAO as the principal intergovernmental organization responsible for the regulation and coordination of international civil aviation.

ICAO's strategy for the development and implementation of ICAO Standards and Recommended Practices purports to make use of available modern technological tools but at the same time aims at more basic issues, that is, to:

1 ascertain and document the actual status of implementation of ICAO SARPs and the extent of differences to standards, improving communication channels among headquarters, regional offices and states to facilitate this objective;
2 improve the awareness on the part of states of the vital role they play in the multilateral safety assurance provided for in the Chicago Convention, which is founded upon the effective implementation of ICAO SARPs;
3 similarly, create or improve the awareness on the part of states of their role in the development of ICAO SARPs, with a view to encouraging more states to be actively involved in the formulation process;
4 pursue systematic analysis of the reasons for any non-implementation of SARPs and differences to standards;
5 develop realistic programmes, including the ICAO Technical Cooperation Programmes, and their funding, to assist states in implementing SARPs, where necessary; and
6 establish adequate coordination and cooperation with states in a regional context in the field of rule harmonization and the implementation of standards.

ICAO claims that such a strategy can be implemented by applying the following measures:

- enhance the role of its regional offices in assisting states with the implementation of standards, raising awareness of responsible officials at all levels, to ensure that the objectives of paragraphs 1, 2, and 3 above are met;

  a implement measures specifically designed to deal with the development and implementation of SARPs, including the publication of relevant articles in the ICAO Journal and by using slide and video programmes shown as part of missions and during ICAO familiarization courses;

b make annexes more comprehensive and accessible and provide, where necessary, guidance material related to individual annexes;

c expand the foreword of annexes to include more basic information, for example on the interpretation of Article 38 of the Chicago Convention, and on what kind of differences should be published in the Aeronautical Information Publication (AIP); and

d continue to make sure that bodies responsible for the development of SARPs formulate them in simple, clear language and in a speedy way.

Simultaneously, it has been proposed that efforts should be further strengthened to find out from states the reasons for them not responding to State Letters in general and for not communicating their status of implementation.

ICAO's Statutory Status Relating to SARPs

The United Nations was created, in more senses than one, during World War II. Although originally questions were asked by the international community whether this war-time union of states could satisfactorily and appropriately be converted into a peace-time organization for international cooperation, these questions were answered by the creation within the Economic and Social Council (ECOSOC) of the United Nations of various specialized agencies – ICAO being one – which were brought into a relationship with the United Nations.[35] The ECOSOC may enter into agreements with any of these specialized agencies; coordinate activities of the agencies through consultation; and define terms on which the agency concerned would be brought into a relationship with the United Nations.[36]

Therefore, ICAO conceptually shares the same international status as the United Nations, while members of the ICAO Secretariat are international civil servants. The establishment of ICAO as the specialized agency of the United Nations which is responsible for regulation of international civil aviation brings to bear the need to inquire as to why such specialized agencies are created instead of conferring functions which are to be performed by them upon the United Nations itself. One of the reasons is perhaps that the general organization of the United Nations and its personnel could not take on all the specialized activities that are handled by the various specialized agencies. Another is that a single organization with greatly increasing administrative personnel would have been too cumbersome a bureaucracy.

Be that as it may, the question as to what status ICAO holds in the international community, which in turn would shed some light as to the status of its regulations, would largely lie in the definition of the word 'agency'. On the term 'specialized agency' one commentator has observed:

> [t]hey are Specialised as to subject-matter, of course, but the implications of the second term may not be so clear. These Agencies are in fact, as the general UN is not, examples of international administrative agencies ... whose chief function is the administrative one, although the conference or representative organs associated with them (or with which they are associated), and the legislative or policy determining activities of the latter, are not to be disregarded ...
>
> The relationships to be developed between Specialised Agencies and the UN constitutes a major problem of international statesmanship. As in the case of regional organizations, whatever the value of the special institutions of the situation would be difficult and dangerous unless adequate measures for coordination of the various elements could be worked out. This is a problem for searching analysis in principle and for careful application in practice. If the Specialised Agencies are created by the UN suitable coordination should be possible, but if it be a question of coordinating with the UN an Agency created independently the task is more difficult.[37]

The above comment supports the view that a certain coordination exists between specialized agencies and the United Nations on the basis of their relationship *ipso facto*. Hence, it may be inferred by this argument that the regulations promulgated by a specialized agency should have similar status and leverage as any created by the parent United Nations.

In the present context of international relations, however, the status of a specialized agency and its regulations cannot be dismissed in such a simplistic manner. The answer to the question would inevitably lie in an analysis of state sovereignty; the character of international law; and international government.

International Law

The Provisional International Court of Justice (the predecessor to the International Court of Justice) decided in the famous *Lotus* case of 1927:

> International law governs relations between independent States. The rules of law binding upon States therefore emanate from their own

> free will as expressed in conventions or by usages generally accepted as expressing principles of law and established in order to regulate the relations between those co-existing independent communities or with a view to the achievement of common aims. Restrictions upon the independence of States cannot therefore be presumed.[38]

The aftermath of World War II saw the advent of the United Nations and the United Nations Charter, the latter of which proclaims that the United Nations is based on the sovereign equality of all members. The Charter also provides that less powerful nations recognize the pre-eminence of the Great Powers as guardians of international peace and security.[39] With the exception of this predominant innovation of post-World War II accord, the rest of the Charter seems complacently to accord with the basic framework of international law which existed under the Peace of Westphalia. Judicial recognition of the United Nations as a subject of international law was given by the International Court of Justice (ICJ) in 1949, in the *Reparation for Injuries Case*,[40] where the ICJ pronounced the end of the old orthodoxy that states are the only subjects of international law, and advised that the United Nations, though not a state, had the capacity to bring certain kinds of claims directly against a state under the rubric of international law.

The many contributions of the United Nations to the development of international law have been both significant and sustained, ever since the United Nations General Assembly convened its first session in 1946. The General Assembly has been prolific in adopting numerous resolutions, declarations and conventions through diplomatic conferences. Guided by Article 13 of the United Nations Charter which places an obligation on the General Assembly to initiate studies and make recommendations for encouraging the progressive development of international law and its codification,[41] the Assembly established in November 1947 the International Law Commission whose members were entrusted with the formulation of principles of international law. One of the first tasks of the Commission was to write a Draft Code of Offences against the Peace and Security of Mankind, which the Commission completed in 1954. The draft code provided that any act of aggression, including the employment by the authorities of a state of armed forces against another state for any purpose other than national or collective self-defence or in pursuance of a decision or recommendation of a competent organ of the United Nations, was an offence against the peace and security of mankind. The code also stipulated that any threat by the authorities of a state to resort to an act of aggression against another state was a similar offence.[42]

The sense of international responsibility that the United Nations ascribed to itself had reached a heady stage at this point, where the role of international law in international human conduct was perceived to be primary and above the authority of states. In its Report to the General Assembly, the International Law Commission recommended a draft provision which required:

> Every State has the duty to conduct its relations with other States in accordance with international law and with the principle that the sovereignty of each State is subject to the supremacy of international law.[43]

This principle, which forms a cornerstone of international conduct by states, provides the basis for strengthening international comity and regulating the conduct of states both internally – within their territories – and externally, towards other states. States are effectively precluded by this principle of pursuing their own interests untrammelled and with disregard to principles established by international law.

International Government

There are several players performing the drama of international discourse and regulation. The roles played by each of these players have a compelling effect on the specialized agencies of the United Nations. While it is not disputed that the international community comprises a number of separate states which form a community of nations, and that the existence of these independent states is essential to the existence of international organization, unquestionably, the multiplication of states makes the task of international cooperation more complicated and more difficult. Often, states tend to pursue their national interests and legislation relentlessly, purely on the grounds that their sovereignty requires of them to hold their own in international gatherings. This attitude may frequently tend to cloud the need to take collective international measures in an issue that requires a certain degree of homogeneity in the international community. Potter observes:

> It is a familiar observation of political science that a moderate amount of homogeneity is indispensable as a basis for law among units of any order. Some common denominators among nations must be found in the intercourse among them. If there are no common interests and standards there can be no legal community ... At this point arises the thought that a substantial international spiritual unity or community must precede any effective international organization and the denial that any such thing exists ... The two elements – spiritual community and practical organization – interact one upon another moreover to produce results not anticipated by an oversimplified analysis.[44]

The premise that a common denominator between states is essential to coalesce them into one conceptual group in implementing international regulations is admittedly the starting point. In the final analysis, the effectiveness of regulation would lie only in adherence by states on a collective basis of those regulations. The challenge is therefore to find a common basis that would add credence to Potter's premise of homogeneity. This basis has been provided by Wassenbergh who observes:

> To find a solution to conflicts between States with regard to regulation of international civil aviation and notably between a big and small State, one should perhaps approach the problem by bearing in mind that the States are the *locum tenentes* of their nationals in the international sphere, not only representing their citizens as a national group but also, and more importantly, representing each individual as a subject of international society as well as of his State. In other words, a government must consider the interests of its citizens also as members of a society beyond that governments own bounds.[45]

Wassenbergh's proposal imputes to states an ineluctable international responsibility towards their citizens, requiring states to align their local policies to be in consonance with international policy, thereby assuring their citizens a certain participation in the international law-making process. This argument is consistent with the sense of international responsibility that the United Nations ascribed to itself in recognizing that the role of international law in international human conduct was primary and above the authority of states. It also cleverly binds the role of states – as units of the international order – to the role of international law in the international community of states. According to this premise, the right of a carrier to operate air services anywhere in the world; and the duty of a state to enforce international regulations on air safety, security, facilitation and airport planning *inter alia*, may be viewed as internationally recognized and enforceable rights and duties.

One of the most perplexing questions that remains unanswered concerns the fact that states have seemingly regarded ICAO's Annexes to the Chicago Convention – which are all of a technical nature – as non-binding. The standards contained in the annexes all carry explicit requirements wherein states 'shall' comply with regulations. Moreover, the Chicago Conference of 1944 which was the precursor to the Chicago Convention, also explicitly recognized that ICAO would exercise power over states in requiring adherence to its regulations in the technical field. In the words of the United States delegation at the Conference:

> It is generally agreed that it is true, in the purely technical field, a considerable measure of power can be exercised by, and indeed must

> be granted to, a world body. In these matters, there are few international controversies which are not susceptible of ready solution through the counsel of experts. For example, it is essential that the signal arrangements and landing practice at the Chicago Airport for an intercontinental plane shall be similar to the landing practice at Croydon, or Le Bourget, or Prague, or Cairo, or Chungking, that a plane arriving at any of these points, whatever its country of origin, will be able to recognise established and uniform signals and to proceed securely according to settled practice ... A number of other similar technical fields can thus be covered; and, happily, here we are in a field in which science and technical practice provide common ground for all.[46]

Figure 6.1 reflects the responses of states to the annexes and clearly shows that this is not so. Over the years, some states have not even responded with their differences to the standards contained in the annexes.

Annexes are adopted by the Council[47] which is appointed by the ICAO Assembly – the governing body of ICAO – and as such they emanate from the highest authority in ICAO. Unfortunately, this *status quo* also gives rise to an anomaly where states make their own regulations with regard to international civil aviation and disregard them at the same time – as some states do in disregarding the requirements of Articles 37 and 38 of the Chicago Convention.

The International Court of Justice (ICJ), in the *North Sea Continental Shelf Case*,[48] held that legal principles that are incorporated in treaties, such as the one in Article 37 of the Chicago Convention calling for each state to collaborate in securing uniformity in ICAO regulations, become customary international law by virtue of Article 38 of the 1969 Vienna Convention on the Law of Treaties. Article 38 recognizes that a rule set forth in a treaty would become binding upon a third state as a customary rule of international law if it is generally recognized by the states concerned as such. Article 37 of the Chicago Convention which designates that ICAO will adopt international Standards and Recommended Practices – for the common good of humanity – therefore arguably becomes a principle of customary international law, or *jus cogens*. Obligations arising from *jus cogens* are considered applicable *erga omnes*, which would mean that states owe a duty of care to the world at large in adhering to Article 37 of the Convention. The ICJ in the *Barcelona Traction Case* held:

> [A]n essential distinction should be drawn between the obligations of a State towards the international community as a whole, and those arising *vis à vis* another State in the field of diplomatic protection. By their very nature, the former are the concerns of all States. In view of the importance of the rights involved, all States can be held to have a legal interest in their protection; they are obligations *erga omnes*.[49]

The International Law Commission has observed of the ICJ decision:

> [I]n the Courts' view, there are in fact a number, albeit limited, of international obligations which, by reason of their importance to the international community as a whole, are – unlike others – obligations in respect of which all States have legal interest.[50]

The views of the ICJ and the International Law Commission, which has supported the approach taken by the ICJ, give rise to two possible conclusions relating to *jus cogens* and its resultant obligations *erga omnes*:

1 obligations *erga omnes* affect all states and thus cannot be made inapplicable to a state or group of states by an exclusive clause in a treaty or other document reflecting legal obligations without the consent of the international community as a whole;
2 obligations *erga omnes* pre-empt other obligations which may be incompatible with them.

If it can be accepted that a principle of *jus cogens* creates obligations *erga omnes*, it becomes an undeniable fact that Article 37 of the Chicago Convention could be considered a peremptory norm of international law.

In the light of the above, it is appropriate to reconsider the legal position of states in terms of their obligation at international law when it comes to their responsibilities towards the standards of the annexes. As was discussed, ICAO has proposed numerous practical steps towards achieving the enhancement of its standards, in order that a more effective approach towards encouraging states to comply with the requirements of the Chicago Convention be adopted. The ICAO Strategic Action Plan, which addresses current challenges posed by civil aviation, is heavily reliant upon the success of the implementation of these standards. It is now up to the states themselves to consider how they could contribute to ICAO's efforts in this regard. The importance of the role of states in relation to aviation security cannot be over-emphasised.

A Revision of the Concept of Sovereignty

In keeping with emerging trends in civil aviation, a radical look at state sovereignty would have to be taken if other legal measures towards the curbing of the threat of terrorism are to be pursued. As Jennings pointed out in 1945, during the first decade of aviation:

> There were three principle schools of thought: the first held that this airspace, like the airspace over the open sea, was entirely free; the second held that it was subject to the territorial sovereignty of the subjacent state, the third held that there was a lower zone subject to absolute sovereignty and an upper zone of free airspace.[61]

The second view has held sway over the last 50 years, bringing with it the strong conviction of states that they are masters of their own destiny even in international policy making and issues involving international crimes. Ironically, jurists and courts have not endorsed this deep-seated reliance by states on their sovereignty.

The Philosophy of Sovereignty in Airspace

The philosophy of air law is based entirely on the concept of state sovereignty in airspace and is essentially related to land. The concept dates back to early Roman times where:

> States claimed, held, and in fact exercised sovereignty in the airspace above their national territories ... and that the recognition of an existing territorial airspace of States by the Paris Convention of 1919[62] was well founded in law and history.[63]

The Roman state adopted an all-embracing approach in ensuring the protection of the private and public rights of its citizens. It could not have assumed full jurisdiction to lay down rules for its citizenry unless it exercised rights of sovereignty in airspace as well as on land. The genesis of the concept of sovereignty in airspace is traced to Justinian's *Corpus Juris Civilis* where the concept seemed rather to be the work of some gloss upon a passage in the Digest.[64] Accordingly, airspace at that time became, in international law, a contentious issue when it came to justifying the removal of projections from adjoining property over a place of burial.[65] Bouve added the view that airspace was new space added to accommodate man's ability to fly.[66] Thus, the right bestowed by the private law maxim, *Cujus est Solum, Ejus est Usque ad Coelum* was firmly entrenched as an absolute right of a person under ancient Roman law. This maxim, which means that a right of land ownership brings with it rights of ownership of airspace above the land, was later found to be unacceptable as an absolute rule. Blacklisted as a 'product of some black letter lawyer'[67] the rule was later adapted to mean that no nation acquired any domain in what was known as navigable airspace until such domain was needed to protect subjacent territory.[68]

The doctrine of sovereignty was introduced to the Western world by the French philosopher Bodin. At a time when political attitudes were in transition from the dominance of the universal church to a universal legal order, Bodin introduced sovereignty as a supreme power over citizens and subjects that was not itself bound by laws.[69] Bodin elaborated that every independent community had to consider that while acknowledging the authority of the law, a state was above the law if it wished to govern successfully. Other jurists who supported the theory of exclusive sovereignty were Hugo Grotius, who maintained that sovereign states were independent of foreign control, and Thomas Hobbes, who said that sovereignty was absolute and its misuse was unthinkable. John Locke attempted to compromise the absolute quality of sovereignty by opining that sovereignty was not absolute and unquestionable in that it was an exchange of social trust between the government and the people. Accordingly, there was an inarticulate premise that a breach of the social trust between the two parties would erode the concept of sovereignty. John Austin in his *Province of Jurisprudence Determined* (1892) defined sovereignty to emanate from a person when:

> A determinate human superior not in the habit of obedience to a like superior, receives habitual obedience from the bulk of a given society, that a determinate superior is sovereign in society and that society is therefore sovereign and independent.[74]

The important question is how is sovereignty determined? Both juristic and judicial opinion favour the view that sovereignty of airspace should be determined on the role played by the importance of subjacent airspace in its relation to land and sea. In other words, a symbolic possession of the airspace is necessary in order that states can claim sovereignty over their airspace. Therefore, the concept of sovereignty becomes compatible with the concept of ownership of property with possession by the owner, to the exclusion of others. To determine sovereignty in airspace, three elements would have to be resolved: the use of airspace; the nature of its possession; and the nature of its control to the exclusion of others.

The use of airspace is inextricably linked to the social needs that the airspace in question would subserve. Roscoe Pound envisaged that one of the fundamental bases for the control and use of property was its sociological importance.[71] There is no difficulty in establishing a nexus between the sociological value of territorial land and sea and the protection offered to them by the subjacent airspace of a country. The next element – symbolic possession – has its roots in the early Roman law concept of *traditio longa manu*[72] where possession was transferred by a symbolic act such as the handing over of a key to a premises when continued and consistent access was impracticable. Savigny elaborates on this classical theory by infusing three elements to the concept of possession: detention with *animus domini* or the will to hold as owner, *animus possidendi* or the will to exclude others from one's property, and *animus rem sibi habendi* or the will to hold for oneself. Savigny's concept of the need to blend detention with *animus* (intention) for the establishment of possession is satisfied by the modern concept of sovereignty in airspace, since all these elements can be seen in a state's claim to sovereignty over airspace where the three elements impute the physical fact of *de facto dominium* to the intention to retain possession of the object.[73] Jhering went a step further by claiming that detention was not necessary; only the will of the possessor was. Weber and Erlich both contended that the law is not a formal set of rules but a prime method of establishing order in society and accordingly required a person merely to show incontrovertible reason for the need to possess property. The final element – the nature of control of airspace – can be subsumed in modern juristic thought; that the modern interpretation of the concept of sovereignty is not the ability to make war or to exploit others, but to legislate over a given state or community.[74]

Perhaps the most convincing justification for the acceptance of sovereignty in airspace as the fundamental legal norm in air law is seen in Hans Kelsen's pure theory of the law.[75] Kelsen considered that all international laws derived their basis from a *grundnorm* or a basic legal postulate derived purely from law and not from morality. This basic norm was international custom. In this context, the philosophy of air law is founded on the concept of sovereignty in airspace and would sustain its credibility through this customary concept. The basic idea of sovereignty is then taken to its final conclusion and ultimate justification by Pound when he states:

> Men must be able to assume in civilized society that they may control, for purposes beneficial to themselves, what they have created by their own labor and what they have acquired under existing social and economic order. This is a final postulate of civilized society.[76]

The linkage between the use of airspace and the protection of a subjacent territory was supported by American and English decisions[77] where the *ad coelum* maxim was called:

> ... a fanciful phrase ... a glittering generality which has not arisen out of contested law suits and not therefore received close judicial scrutiny.[78]

American judicial opinion is exemplified in the decision in *Hinman* v. *Pacific Air Transport*[79] where the court said:

> Title to the airspace unconnected with the use of land is inconceivable. Such a right has never been asserted. It is a thing not known to the law.[80]

The court in this instance applied the overall doctrine as modified and ruled that the plaintiff, who claimed ownership of 150 feet above his land, had no rights in superjacent airspace over the defendant who operated his plane 100 feet above the plaintiff's land. The *ad coelum* maxim was therefore no longer regarded as the law. On the one hand, the formula that it extended from the centre of the earth to the skies was judicially tenuous. On the other, the fact that a landowner had unlimited rights relating to the airspace above his land was considered retrogressive and indefinable. There was no evidence of customary acceptance of the maxim for jurists to consider it as a scholastic doctrine of practical acceptance. As Blackstone said:

> The only way of proving that this or that maxim is a rule of common law is by showing that it has always been the custom to observe it.[81]

The *ad coelum* formula therefore became a figurative phrase, never to be taken literally but to express complete ownership of land, and the right to superjacent airspace only to the extent as was necessary or convenient to the enjoyment of land. The owner of land owns as much of the airspace above him as he uses but only so long as he uses it.

By the end of the 19th century, the private law concept of absolute ownership of airspace over land was antiquated. The beginning of the 20th century saw the emergence of states' sovereignty in airspace. The impetus for public international law to take over the issue of rights over airspace was given by the August 1904 aerial incident where Russian guards shot down the German balloon *Tschudi* when it was flying outside Russian territory and two unrelated but similar incidents that occurred in 1908 and 1910 respectively.[82] The French Government hastened to call a conference of European powers in 1910. For the first time, participating states at this conference recognized airspace as belonging to individual states on the basis that:

> The upper air is a national heritage common to all of the people, and its reasonable use ought not to be hampered by an ancient artificial maxim of law.[83]

The consensus of opinion of the European States in 1910 followed the landmark US decision of *Erickson* v. *Crookston*[84] in 1907 where the court said:

> Common law rules are sufficiently flexible to adapt themselves to new conditions arising out of modern progress, and it is within the legitimate province of the courts to so construe and apply them.[85]

World War I decided the issue of public rights over airspace when Germany alleged that the *casus belli* was the penetration of German airspace by French aviators. The experience of the war (1914–1918) strongly reinforced the view of the British delegation (supported by Holland, Denmark and Switzerland) at the European Air Law Conference of 1910 that states' sovereignty extended *usque ad coelum* and that belligerent aircraft cannot go over the territory of another at will.[86] By the end of the war, air law was regarded as a discipline that accepted air to be a free commodity except when it was connected to owned property (subjacent airspace)[87] and seen to be used to protect that property.[88]

Professor Bin Cheng addresses the principles governing post-World War II sovereignty over airspace as enunciated in Article 1 of the Chicago Convention[89] and concludes:

> The now firmly established rule of international law that each State possesses complete and exclusive sovereignty over the airspace above its territory means that international civil aviation today rests on the tacit acquiescence or express agreement of States flown over.[90]

Shawcross and Beaumont define sovereignty in international law as the right to exercise the functions of a state to the exclusion of all other states in regard to a certain area of the world.[91] In international aviation the concept of sovereignty is the fundamental postulate upon which other norms and virtually all air law is based.[92] Post-1944 attitudes towards the concept of sovereignty in airspace and the philosophy of air law range between the unlimited public law right of a state to exercise sovereignty over its airspace and the idea of free movement of air traffic. Professor Goedhuis identifies the idea of 'free traffic' as opposed to the exclusivity of the sovereignty principle as being considered by jurists as a constructive element of aviation which furthers life and raises it to a higher level.[93] This view is supported by the claim that general principles of international law demand that sovereignty of states should be limited by the principle of freedom of peaceful traffic.[94] Be that as it may, a view advocating the free use of airspace of a country by aircraft of foreign nationalities would give rise to a dichotomy: that there should be freedom of aviation with a minimum of restrictions or none at all, or that international air traffic should be firmly regulated. Professor Lissitzyn analyses the concept of sovereignty in its modern development as having three basic principles: that each state has exclusive sovereignty over its airspace; each state has complete discretion as to the admission of any aircraft into its airspace; and, that airspace over the high seas and other areas not subject to a state's jurisdiction is *res nullius* and is free to the aircraft of all states.[95]

One can observe that air law has bloomed from being a series of exclusive rights – first in private law and then in public law – and has also set parameters within which a host of other progressive objectives may be attained. The concept of sovereignty now entails for each state the responsibility of being conscious of its obligations to the international legal community. The sovereignty principle has therefore evolved to being a cohesive system of co-existence in the air by states which respect the exclusive rights of each state to sovereignty over its airspace. Mutual obligations have sprung up between states bringing as their corollary a deep respect for the principles of international law and the rights of individual states.

The basic concept of state sovereignty has evolved with the commercial exigencies of international civil aviation. To keep up with the world demand for air transport, airlines now share each others' codes and combine their flights to offer the customer a composite package of air transport that would ensure a smooth air trip. The millions who travel are reserved for flight on sophisticated computer reservations systems and their information is sent in advance to their destination electronically. Their passports are read at airports by machine, and their baggage is barcoded. The passenger's comfort is ensured by world-wide regulation on smoking in aircraft, and the effects of aviation on the environment is studied carefully. It is therefore inconceivable that this mature and logical reasoning could not be extended to a much more critical factor in aviation such as aviation security. At the end of the 20th century, aviation has reached sufficient maturity to step into the next century with fortitude and courage. On the subject of the attribution to states of their international responsibility, a more enlightened view of the role of states in civil aviation in the modern era has been offered by Wassenbergh:

> To find a solution to conflicts between States with regard to regulation of international civil aviation and notably between a big and a small State, one should perhaps approach the problem by bearing in mind that the States are the *locum tenentes* of their nationals in the international sphere, not only representing their citizens as a national group but also, and more importantly, representing each individual as a subject of international society as well as of his State. In other words, a government must consider the interests of its citizens also as members of a society beyond that government's own bounds.
>
> Such an approach makes it possible to bridge the gap between States with conflicting interests and obviate both the necessity for smaller

States to have recourse to their sovereignty each time they think their rights are curtailed and for bigger States to ride roughshod over smaller States' interests. By emphasizing the rights and the interests of individuals as subjects of the international community, the conflict between the use of power, on the one hand, and a refusal to cooperate, on the other, could be solved and the further development of international society could be promoted at the same time.[96]

An International Criminal Court

An insurmountable problem in international criminal justice is the question 'Before what court and according to what law should an individual who has committed an international crime be tried?' There are two possibilities:

- an individual criminal may remain at large and unpunished; and
- an international criminal may be tried by the court of any state which can bring him or her physically within its jurisdiction.

The former reflects the present ludicrous state of international criminal law. The latter brings to bear the reversal of established international law, as was seen in the dangerous precedent created in the extradition from Argentina to Israel of war criminal Eichmann and his trial in Israel for international crimes.[97] This would doubtless create international 'vigilantes'.

The inherent defect in the application of municipal law to international crimes lies in the fact that a host of municipal courts, adjudicating on different or separate instances of criminality may find difficulties in maintaining uniformity in application and interpretation. Uniformity of formulation could only be achieved if states followed an authoritative text when incorporating international criminal law into their municipal systems. Although this may be possible, it would certainly be a tedious and devious process. A more expedient method would be for states to except such a text in the form of an international code or convention, to be administered by one international body on the principle of international citizenship of people, irrespective of their nationality. To achieve this goal, the concept of state sovereignty as it exists today has to be revisited along the lines of the foregoing discussion.

Another factor that has to be taken into account in the creation of an international court of criminal justice is that, as a condition precedent, states should form a consensus on definitions relating to critical terminology. For instance, an international crime would have to be clearly defined and universally agreed upon. The word 'aggression' would also have to be clearly spelled out.

During World War II the idea of an international criminal court gained increasing significance and it is often not realized how much effort was devoted to the practicalities of the creation and organization of such a court. The work of a number of official and unofficial bodies[98] paved the way for the deliberations of the International Conference on Military Trials which resulted in the establishment of the International Military Tribunal at Nuremberg.[99]

Although the International Military Tribunal, *functus officio*, ceased to exist, the question of the creation of an international criminal court was actively taken up by the United Nations. It was raised in connection with the formulation of the Nuremberg principles in 1948[100] and with the genocide convention.[101] The General Assembly eventually invited the International Law Commission to investigate the desirability and possibility of the creation of a international criminal court.[102] Although this task was successfully completed the matter went no further. In 1954 the General Assembly resolved that considering the relationship between the question of the definition of aggression, the draft code of offences against the peace and security of mankind and the creation of an international criminal court, further discussion of the latter should be deferred until the other two matters had been settled. The General Assembly reaffirmed this view in 1957. This ambivalence on the part of the United Nations reflects that as long as the solution of the problem of defining aggression remains a condition precedent to the creation of an international criminal court no further progress will be made.

The formation of an international court may be based on the simplistic truism that as there are international crimes, so there should be an international court of justice to adjudicate on those crimes. States should, in this context, adopt a more universal attitude that recognizes the following premise:

> International law pierces national sovereignty and presupposes that statesmen of the several States have a responsibility for international peace and order as well as their responsibilities to their own States.[103]

The fact that the successful formation of such a court is possible may be attenuated from the existence of the International Court of Justice and the successful conclusion of the Nuremberg trials at the Nuremberg Tribunal. It cannot be denied that at Nuremberg, agreement was reached by lawyers from nations whose legal systems, philosophies and traditions differed widely. They circumvented technical difficulties at the trials with 'a minimum of goodwill and common sense'.[104]

The philosophy of the court should be totally flavoured with international interests, as opposed to national interests. Therefore, prosecution should not be relegated to a national entity or authority. It should be left to an international authority such as the United Nations.

Judges of the court should be selected from jurists world-wide, as in the procedure followed in the election of judges to the International Court of Justice. A rigid screening system would have to be built into the rules of court to obviate adjudication of issues which are of a tendentiously political nature. An international convention or code should govern such principles as custody of offences pending trial, whereby contracting states would guarantee to arrest criminals and deliver them up for trial.

An International Convention/Code

One of the responsibilities that would devolve upon the international community towards developing an international convention or code would be to revisit the Bonn Declaration, with a view to expanding its scope to cover acts other than hijackings or unlawful seizure or control of aircraft. The Bonn Declaration is the only instrument so far which has infused a reasonable element of compulsion that would effectively deal with the threat of terrorism and unlawful interference with civil aviation in an international perspective.

An international convention should also include elements such as those incorporated in the Tokyo Summit Statement in International Terrorism of May 1986 whereby state parties agreed:

1 to refuse to export arms to states which sponsor or support terrorism;
2 to enforce stringent limits on activities and size of diplomatic and consular missions and other official bodies overseas of states which engage in or condone criminal activities; and,
3 to introduce stringent and improved extradition procedures within the process of law for bringing to trial those who have perpetrated acts of terrorism.

The convention or code should, in addition, enforce the following:

1 introduction and implementation of strict visa and immigration requirements and procedure in respect of materials of states which support, sponsor or condone terrorism;
2 monitoring all persons, including those of the diplomatic corps, who have been expelled or excluded from states on suspicion of

involvement in international terrorism and refusing to let them enter those states;

3 establishing multilateral, plurilateral and bilateral liaison and co-operation of police authorities, security and military authorities of states;

4 in the light of the foregoing discussion on ICAO's role in aviation security, strengthening ICAO's regulatory role in the promulgation and disseminating SARPs and requiring states compliance thereof;

5 providing adequate sanctions against states who fail to comply with SARPs of ICAO related to aviation security; and

6 recognizing the judicial nature of the ICAO Council within the parameters of the Chicago Convention.

Conclusion

The offence of unlawful interference with civil aviation should be addressed on the basis that individuals have international duties which transcend the national obligations of obedience imposed by an individual state. By the same token, it must also mean that individual states owe their citizens and the world at large a responsibility for maintaining world security. The philosophy of these two premises has to be vigorously employed in bringing to fruition the above measures. It is only then that a substantial legal contribution could be made to the controlling of this offence.

Notes

1 UI-WP/331 Restricted, 03/01/96 at 2.
2 *Id.* at 4.
3 Sofear, A. (1986), *Foreign Affairs*, 64, at pp. 902–903.
4 Annex to GA Res. 2625 (XXV) adopted without vote 24 October 1970, GAOR, 25th Session, Supp. 28 (A/8028).
5 UNGA Res. 34/146, GAOR 34th Session.
6 *Convention for the Suppression of Unlawful Acts Against the Safety of Maritime Navigation*, 1988.
7 UNGA Res. 40/61 of 9 December 1985, (adopted without vote), para 1.
8 UNGA Res. 42/159 of 7 December 1987, para. 12.
9 See UN Docs A/C.6/42/SR.31, 29 October 1987, pp. 6–7, and A/C 6/42/SR.33, 6 Nov. 1987, pp. 6–9.
10 See for example, the debates surrounding the adoption of Res. 40/61 and 42/159.
11 See UNGA Res. 40/61 of 9 December 1985, para 1. Also UNGA Res. 42/159 of 7 December 1987, para 12.
12 UN Doc. S/PV. 2655/Corr. 1, 18 February 1986 at p. 31.

13 *Convention on International Civil Aviation*, opened for signature at Chicago on 7 December 1944, entered into force on 4 April 1947. ICAO Doc., 7300/6.
14 A29-WP/39 EX/8 Appendix at p. 8.
15 See Abeyratne, R.I.R. (1994a), 'Aircraft Engine Emissions and Noise', *Environmental Policy and Law*, vol. 24 no. 5, September, pp. 238–250. See also Abeyratne, R.I.R. (1994b), 'General Principles of Liability of States as Providers of Space Technology in the Field of Air Navigation', *European Transport Law*, vol. XXIV no. 5, pp. 553–569; Abeyratne, R.I.R. (1994c), 'The Evolution from FANS to CNS/ATM and Products Liability of Technology Producers of the United States', *Zeitschrift für Luft-und Weltraumrecht* (German Journal of Air and Space Law), vol. 43, no. 2 June 1994, pp. 156–186; Abeyratne, R.I.R. (1994d), 'The Liberalization of Air Transport Services with GATT – Some Legal Issues', *Trading Law and Trading Law Reports*, January–February 1994, pp. 165–181; Abeyratne, R.I.R. (1993a), 'The Challenge of Airports and Planning Laws', *Environmental Policy and Law* (IOS Press) vol. 23 no. 2, April 1993 at 262–274; Abeyratne, R.I.R. (1993b), 'Legal Aspects of the Unlawful Interference with International Civil Aviation', *Air and Space Law* (Kluwer) vol. XVIII, no. 6 1993 at 262–274; Abeyratne, R.I.R. (1995a), 'The Effects of Unlawful Interference with Civil Aviation on World Peace and the Social Order', *Transportation Law Journal*, vol. 22, no. 3, Spring 1995, pp. 449–494; Abeyratne, R.I.R. (1993c), 'The Air Traffic Rights Debate – A Legal Study', *Annals of Air and Space Law* (McGill), vol. XVIII, part 1 1993 at 3–44; Abeyratne, R.I.R. (1994e), 'The Economic Relevance of the Chicago Convention – A Retrospective Study', *Annals of Air and Space Law*, vol. XIX, part II, 1994, pp. 3–80; Abeyratne, R.I.R. (1995b), 'The WorldWide Air Transport Conference and Air Traffic Rights, – A Commentary', *European Transport Law*, vol. XXX, no. 2, 1995, pp. 131–147; and Abeyratne, R.I.R. (1993d), 'Tobacco Smoking in Aircraft – A Fog of Legal Rhetoric?', *Air and Space Law* (Kluwer), vol. XVIII, no.2 1993 at 50–60.
16 EC2/65-91/6.
17 Table 6.1 has been reproduced from ICAO Assembly working paper A 29-WP/39 EX 8, p. 8.
18 See 'Resolutions Adopted by the Assembly – 31st Session', Montreal, 19 September–4 October 1995, ICAO: Montreal 1995 at p. 2.
19 See 'ICAO Releases Strategic Action Plan – President Renews Call for Empowerment', *ICAO News Release* PIO 10/97 at p. 1.
20 *Ibid.*
21 Proceedings of the Council 2nd Session 2 September–12 December 1947, Doc. 7248-C/839 at 44–45.
22 ICAO Resolutions A-13 and A-33 which resolved that SARPS relating to the efficient and safe regulation of international air navigation be adopted.
23 ICAO Annex 9, Facilitation, 9th ed., July 1990, Foreword.
24 *Aeronautical Information Services Manual*, ICAO Doc 8126-0 AN/872/3. ICAO Resolution A 1-31 defines a standard as any specification for physical characteristics ... the uniform application of which is recognized as necessary... and one that states will conform to. The same resolution describes a Recommended Practice as any specification for physical characteristics ... which is recognized as desirable ... and one that member states will endeavour to conform to ... Buergenthal, T. (1969), *Law Making in the International Civil Aviation Organization*, Kluwer, Dordrecht, p. 10 also cites the definitions given in ICAO's Annex 9 of SARPS.
25 Article 86 of the Convention.
26 Article 12 stipulates that over the high seas, the rules in force shall be those established under the Convention, and each contracting state undertakes to

insure the prosecution of all persons violating the applicable regulations.

27 Milde, M. (1984), 'The Chicago Convention – After Forty Years', *Annals Air and Space L.* McGill, Montreal vol. IX, 119, at 126. See also Schenkman, J. (1955), *International Civil Aviation Organization*, Geneva, at 163.

28 Milde *supra*, note 27, at p. 122.

29 Buergenthal *supra*, note 24, p. 9.

30 Dempsey, P.S. (1987), *Law and Foreign Policy in International Aviation*, Dobbs Ferry, New York, Transnational Publishers Inc., at 302.

31 Figure 6.1 is reproduced from ICAO Assembly working paper A 31-WP/56 EX/19, 1/8/95.

32 See ICAO Assembly Working Paper A31–WP/56 EX/19, p. 4.

33 *Ibid.*

34 *Id.*, at 5.

35 *Charter of the United Nations and Statute of the International Court of Justice*, New York, United Nations, Article 57.

36 *Id.*, Article 63 (1) and (2).

37 Potter, P.B. (1935), *An Introduction to the Study of International Organization*, (5th ed.), New York and London: Appleton Century-Crofts Inc., pp. 273–274.

38 *PCIJ* (1927), Ser. A, No. 9 at 18.

39 Article 24 of the United Nations Charter provides that the members of the United Nations confer on the Security Council primary responsibility for the maintenance of international peace and security and recognizes that the Security Council would act on behalf of all member states of the United Nations. Article 23 of the Charter provides that the Security Council shall consist of 15 members of the United Nations. The Republic of China, France, Russian Federation (then the U.S.S.R.), the United Kingdom of Great Britain and Northern Ireland and U.S.A. are permanent members. Article 25 provides that members of the United Nations agree and accept to carry out the decisions of the Security Council in accordance with the provisions of the Charter.

40 *ICJ Report*, (1949), 174.

41 See *Charter of the United Nations and Statute of the International Court of Justice*, New York, United Nations, Article 13.1.a.

42 Article 2 of the Draft Code at 64–65.

43 *Report of the International Law Commission to the General Assembly on the Work of the 1st Session, A/CN.4/13*, 9 June 1949, at 21.

44 See Potter, P.B. (1935), *An Introduction to the Study of International Organization*, (5th ed.), New York and London, Appleton Century-Crofts Inc., note 23, pp. 8–9.

45 Wassenbergh, H.A. (1970), *Aspects of Air Law and Civil Air Policy in the Seventies*, Dordrecht, M. Nijhoff, p. 5.

46 *Proceedings of the International Civil Aviation Conference*, Chicago, Illinois, November 1–December 7 1944, Washington, United States Government Printing Office, 1948, p. 59.

47 Chicago Convention, *op. cit.*, Article 54 (l).

48 *ICJ Reports* 1970, at 32.

49 *Barcelona Traction, Light and Power Company Limited, ICJ Reports, 1974*, 253 at 269– 270.

50 *Yearbook of International Law Commission* 1976, vol II, part 1 at 29.

51 *Schaake* v. *Dolly*, 85 Kan. 590., 118 Pac. 80.

52 *People* v. *Bradley*, 60 Ill. 402, at 405. Also, (1914), *Bouviers Law Dictionary and Concise Encyclopedia* (3rd ed.), vol. 11, New York, Vernon Law Book Co.

53 ICAO Doc. 7670 vol. 1.

54 *Aeronautical Information Services Manual*, ICAO Doc. 8126-0 AN/872/3.

55 ICAO Doc. 8528, A15-P/6.

56 Article 86 of the Convention.
57 Article 12 stipulates that over the high seas, the rules in force shall be those established under the Convention, and each contracting state undertakes to insure the prosecution of all persons violating the applicable regulations.
58 Sochor, E. (1991), *The Politics of International Aviation*, London, Macmillan, at 58.
59 *Ibid.*
60 Tobolewski, A. (1979), 'ICAO's Legal Syndrome', *Annals Air and Space L.* vol. IV, 349 at 359.
61 Jennings, R.Y. (1945), 'International Civil Aviation and the Law', *BYIL*, 194 at 191.
62 The 1919 Paris Convention established the International Commission for Air Navigation (ICAN), which set up standards on technical matters and provided for the collection and exchange of information on international civil aviation among member states. Later, in 1928, the Pan-American Convention on Air Navigation was drawn up at Havana but unlike the Paris Convention, no attempt was made at this Convention to include in it uniform technical standards. Both these Conventions, although serving a useful purpose, were not considered adequate to serve the needs of post-World War II aviation.
63 Cooper, J.C. (1968), 'Roman Law and the Maxim "*Cujus Est Solum*" in International Law', cited in *Explorations in Aerospace Law*, McGill, Montreal, 55, 102.
64 42 tit. 24, pr 22 S.4.
65 Kuhn, A.K. (1910), 'Beginnings of an Aerial Law', *American Journal of International Law*, vol. 4, 109 at 123.
66 Bouve, (1930), 'The Development of International Rules of Conduct in Air Navigation', *Air Law Rev.* vol. 1, 1, 6.
67 Baldwin, S.E. (1910), 'The Law of the Airship', *American Journal of International Law*, 95 at 97.
68 Cooper *supra*, note 63, p. 29.
69 Weeramantry, C.G. (1982), *An Invitation to the Law*, Australia, Butterworths, 175.
70 *Id.*, 176.
71 Pound, R. (1961), *Introduction to the Philosophy of the Law*, (New Haven, Yale University Press, 114.
72 Weeramantry *supra*, note 69, 165.
73 Pound, R. (1959), *Jurisprudence*, vol. 5, part 8, St. Paul, Minnesota, West Publishing Co., 95.
74 Lloyd, D. (1964), *The Idea of the Law*, Middlesex, England, Penguin Books, 171.
75 See Fuller, Lon L. (1949), *The Problems of Jurisprudence*, Brooklyn, The Foundation Press Inc., pp. 109–113.
76 Pound, R. (1961), *An Introduction to the Philosophy of Law*, New Haven, Yale University Press, 192–193.
77 *United States* v. *Curtiss-Wright Export Corp et. al.* 299 US 3904 (1936), *United States* v. *State of California* 322 US 19 (1947), For English law see *Wandsworth Board of Works* v. *United Telephone Company* 13 Q.B. 904. See also Right, Robert R. (1968), *The Law of Airspace* New York, Bobbs-Merril Co., p. 11 at 65 for comments on the *ad coelum* principle as used in the USA and UK. In English law the *ad coelum* principle at private law can be traced to Lord Cooke (Liber 1, S.1 p. 4). This doctrine was approved in *Fay* v. *Prentice* (1845) 1 CB 827, *Corbett* v. *Hill* (1874) 9 L.R. Eq 671 and *Ellis* v. *Loftus* (1874) L.R. 10, C.P. 10.
78 *Wandsworth Board of Works* v. *United Telephone Company, supra* note 16, at p. 905.
79 84 F. 2d. 411 (2d Cir. 1937).
80 *Id.*, 417.
81 *Blackstone Commentaries*, Book 1, 68.

82 Gunatilaka, V.C. (1972), *Problems of Airspace Sovereignty in the Seventies*, May 1972 LL.M Thesis, Institute of Air and Space Law, Montreal, McGill University, 6.
83 Davis, W.J. (1930), *Aeronautical Law*, London, Parker Stone and Baird Co. Ltd., 27 at 43.
84 100 Minn. 481 (1907).
85 *Id.*, 484.
86 Mollere, N.H. (1963), *The Law of Civil Aviation*, London, Sweet and Maxwell Ltd., 4.
87 Zollman, C. (1927), *Law of the Air*, Milwaukee, Wisconsin, The Bruce Publishing Co., 3.
88 See McNair (1964), *The Law of the Air*, (3rd ed.), London, Stevens and Sons Ltd., pp. 4,5.
89 ICAO (1944), *Convention on International Civil Aviation*, 7 December 1944, 15 UNTS 295; ICAO Doc. 7300/6.
90 Cheng, B. (1962), *The Law of International Air Transport*, London, Stevens and Sons Ltd., at 3. See also pages 3–17 for a discussion on the manner in which air rights devolve upon air carriers under the sovereignty doctrine of the Chicago Convention.
91 Shawcross and Beaumont (1977), *Air Law*, London, Butterworths & Co. Ltd., at 15.
92 *Ibid.*
93 Goedhuis, D. (1947), *Idea and Interests in International Aviation*, quoted in Gertler, Z.J. (1979), 'Order in the Air and the Problem of Real and False Options', *Annals of Air & Space Law*, vol. IV at 100.
94 *Ibid.*
95 Lissitzyn, O.J. (1983), *International Air Transport and National Policy*, New York and London, Garland Publishing Inc. at 365.
96 Wassenbergh, H.A. (1970), *Aspects of Air Law and Civil Air Policy in the Seventies*, Dordrecht, M. Nijhoff at 5.
97 See Green, L.C. (1968), 'The Eichman Case', *MLR* at vol. 23, 507–509.
98 Such as the London International Assembly created in 1941 by Viscount Cecil of Chelwood under the auspices of the League of Nations Union; the International Commission for Penal Reconstruction and Development organized at Cambridge in 1941; and the United Nations War Crimes Commission set up in 1943.
99 See Jackson, R.H. (1945), *International Conference on Military Trials*, (London 1945) (Washington, US Dept. of State Publication 3080).
100 See *Historical Survey of the Question of International Criminal Jurisdiction* (U.N. Document A/CN.4/7/Rev. 1), p. 25 *et seq.*
101 Two draft statutes for courts were produced, see *ibid.*, 30–46 and 120–147.
102 *Ibid.*, 5, 6 and 44–46.
103 Jackson, R.H. (1945), *International Conference on Military Trials*, (London 1945), Washington, US Department of state: Publication 3080, Preface, at ix.
104 Schwarzenberger, G. (1943), *International Law and Totalitarian Lawlessness*, Butterworths, London at 76.

Bibliography

Adams, J. (1989). *The Financing of Terror*, New York, Simon & Schuster.

Aerial Piracy and Aviation Security (1990). Yonah Alexander and Eugene Sochor (eds.), M. Nijhoff, Dordrecht, The Netherlands.

Aggrawala, N. (1971). *An International Perspective*, New York, Carnegie Endowment for International Peace.

Aggrawala, S.K. (1973). *Aircraft Hijacking and International Law*, Bombay, N.M. Tripathi; Dobbs Ferry, N.Y., Oceana Publications.

Arey, J.A. (1972). *The Sky Pirates*, New York, Scribner.

Bennet L.A. (1983). *International Organizations, Principles and Issues*, Englewood Cliffs, New Jersey, Prentice Hall.

Bielenski, E. (1978). *The Role of Law in the Suppression of Terrorism against International Civil Aviation*, Montreal, McGill University Thesis, LL.M.

Bodin, J. (1955). *Six Books of the Commonwealth*, Oxford, Oxford University Press.

Bouvier's Law Dictionary and Concise Encyclopedia (1914). (3rd ed.), Vol. II, New York, Vernon Law Book Co.

Brownlie, I. (1990). *Principles of Public International Law*, (4th ed.), Oxford, Clarendon Press.

Carlston, K.S. (1962). *Law and Organization in World Society*, Urbana, University of Illinois Press.

Cheng, B. (1953). *General Principles of Law as Applied by International Courts and Tribunals*, London, Stevens and Sons Ltd.

Cheng, B. (1962). *The Law of International Air Transport*, London, Stevens and Sons Ltd.

Chiavarelli, E. (1984). *The KAL 007 Incident: The Legal Effects of ICAO Decisions*, Montreal, McGill University Thesis, LL.M..

Christol, C.Q. (1991). *Space Law Past, Present and Future*, Deventer, Kluwer Law and Taxation Publishers.

Clutterbuck, R.L. (1975). *Living with Terrorism*, London, Faber & Faber.

Clyne, P. (1973). *An Anatomy of Hijacking*, London, Abelard-Schumann.

Cooper, J.C. (1968). *Exploration in Aerospace Law*, I.A. Vlasic (ed.), Montreal, McGill University Press.

Corbett, P.E. (1971). *The Growth of World Law*, New Jersey, Princeton University Press.

Dempsey P.S. (1987). *Law and Foreign Policy in International Aviation,* Dobbs Ferry, New York, Transnational Publishers Inc.
Dorey, F. C. (1983). *Aviation Security,* New York, Van Nostrand Reinhold Co.
El Amin M., Abdel Salaam M. (1981). *Concerted Action towards Combating Terrorism with Special Emphasis on Air Transport,* Montreal, McGill University Thesis, LL.M.
El Harudi, El-Muner (1989). *New Developments in the Law of Aviation Security,* Montreal, McGill University Thesis, LL.M.
Eustace, M.D. (1976) *Aerial Hijacking: Stimulus to International Collaboration,* Kingston Ontario, Centre For International Relations, Queen's University.
Freitas, J.A. de Souza (1962). *Jurisdiction over Events Aboard Aircraft,* Montreal, McGill University Thesis, LL.M.
Fuller, L.L. (1949). *The Problems of Jurisprudence,* Brooklyn, N.Y., The Foundation Press Inc.
Ghosh, S. (1985). *Aircraft Hijacking and Developing Law,* New Delhi, Ashish Pub. House.
Gist, F.J. (1961). *The Aircraft Hijacker and International Law,* Montreal, McGill University Thesis, LL.M.
Gist, F.J. Jr. (1968). *The Aircraft Hijacker and International Law,* Montreal, McGill University Thesis, LL.M.
Goodrich, L.M. and Hambro, E. (1972). *Charter of the United Nations, Commentary and Documents,* Boston: World Peace Foundation.
Goodrich, L.M. and Simonds, A.P. (1955). *The United Nations and the Maintenance of International Peace and Security,* Washington, D.C., Brookings Institution.
Graham, D.G. (1981). *The Role of International Civil Aviation in the Promotion of Human Rights,* Montreal, McGill University Thesis, LL.M.
Guldimann W. and Kaiser, S. (1993). *Future Air Navigation Systems, Legal and Institutional Aspects,* Utrecht Studies in Air and Space Law, Dordrecht, The Netherlands, M. Nijhoff.
Henkin, L. (1979). *How Nations Behave: Law and Foreign Policy,* New York, Praeger.
House of Representatives (1989). *Aviation Security, Hearings before the Subcommittee on Aviation of the Committee on Public Works and Transportation,* House of Representatives, 101st Congress, 1st Session, 21 March 1989, Washington, D.C., USPGO.
International Civil Aviation Organization (1987). *Aviation Security, Digest of Current ICAO Policies and Actions on the Subject of Unlawful Interference with International Civil Aviation and its Facilities* (4th ed.), Montreal, ICAO.
International Civil Aviation Organization (1995), *Aeronautical Information Services Manual,* Montreal, Doc. 8126-AN/872.

International Conference on Air Law (1970). Proceedings of the International Conference on Air Law, The Hague.
International Institute of Air and Space Law (1987). *Aviation Security: How to Safeguard International Air Transport?* International Institute of Air and Space Law, Leiden, The Netherlands.
International Labour Organization (1977). *Tripartite Technical Meeting for Civil Aviation*, Geneva, ILO.
Jefferson, D.W. (1930). *Aeronautical Law*, New York, Parker Stone and Baird Co. Ltd.
Jessup, P.C. (1948). *A Modern Law of Nations*, New York, The Macmillan Co.
Joyner, N.D. (1974). *Aerial Hijacking as an International Crime*, Dobbs Ferry, N.Y., Oceana Publications.
Kelsen, H. (1944). *Peace Through Law*, Chapel Hill, N.C., University of North Carolina Press.
Kelsen, H. (1951). *Recent Trends in the Law of the United Nations*, London, Stevens and Sons Ltd.
Kelsen, H. (1951). *The Law of the United Nations*, New York, Praeger.
Lachs, M. (1972). *The Law of Outer Space, An Experience in Contemporary Law Making*, Leiden, Sijthoff.
Lissitzyn, O.J. (1951). *The International Court of Justice – Its Role in the Maintenance of International Peace and Security*, New York, Carnegie Endowment for International Peace.
Lissitzyn, O.J. (1983). *International Air Transport and National Policy*, New York and London, Garland Publishing Inc.
Lloyd, D. (1970). *The Idea of the Law*, Middlesex, England, Penguin Books.
Lyman, M.D. (1989). *Gangland: Drug Trafficking by Organized Criminals*, Springfield, Illinois, Kendall, Hunt.
Margo, R.D. (1987). *Aviation Insurance*, (2nd ed.), London, Butterworths.
McNair, L. (1956). *International Law Opinions, Selected and Annotated*, Vol. II, Cambridge, Cambridge University Press, England.
McNair, L. (1964). *The Law of the Air*, (3rd ed.), London, Stevens and Sons.
McWhinney, E. (1971). *Aerial Piracy and International Law*, Leiden, Sijthoff; Dobbs Ferry, N.Y., Oceana Publications.
McWhinney, E. (1975). *The Illegal Diversion of Aircraft and International Air Law*, Leiden, Sijthoff.
McWhinney, E. (1987). *Aerial Piracy and International Terrorism: The Illegal Diversion of Aircraft and International Law*, (2nd rev. ed.), Dordrecht, The Netherlands; Boston: M. Nijhoff.
Merari, A. (1988). *International Terrorism in 1987*, Boulder, Westview Press.

Mollere, N.H. (1963). *The Law of Civil Aviation,* London, Sweet and Maxwell Ltd.
Moore, K.C. (1976). *Airport, Aircraft and Airline Security,* Los Angeles, Security World Pub. Co.
Morrison, W.L. (1982). *John Austin,* Stanford, C.A., Stanford University Press.
Mutz, W. (1981). *Civil Aviation Security and the Law,* Montreal, McGill University Thesis, LL.M.
Nussbaum, A.A. (1947). *A Concise History of the Law of Nations,* New York, The Macmillan Co.
Office of the President of the Republic of Bogota (1988). *The Fight against Drug Traffic in Colombia,* (*Bogota*), Office of the President of the Republic.
Pound, R. (1959). *Jurisprudence,* Vol. V, Part 8, Saint Paul, Minnesota, West Publishing Co.
Pound, R. (1961). *Introduction to the Philosophy of the Law,* New York, Yale University Press.
President's Commission on Aviation Security and Terrorism (1990b). Report to the President, Washington, D.C., USGPO.
President's Commission on International Aviation Security and Terrorism (1990a). Report to the President, Washington, D.C., USGPO.
Rajan, M.S. (1958). *United Nations and Domestic Jurisdiction,* Bombay, India, Orient Longmans.
Reuter P. (1989). *Introduction to the Law of Treaties,* London and New York, Pinter Publishers.
Right, R.R. (1968). *The Law of Airspace,* New York, Bobbs Merril Company.
Ritchie, M.E. (1958). *Crimes on Board Aircraft.* Montreal, McGill University Thesis, LL.M.
Rossenne, S. (1989). *The World Court* (4th ed.), Dordrecht, The Netherlands, M. Nijhoff.
Schwarzenberger, G. and Brown, E.D. (1976). *A Manual of International Law,* (6th ed.), Oxford, Professional Books Limited.
Shannon, E. (1988). *Desperados: Latin Drug Lords, U.S. Lawmen and the War America Can't Win,* New York, Viking.
Shawcross, and Beaumont, (1991). *Air Law,* London, Butterworths & Co. Ltd.
Shorter Oxford Dictionary on Historical Principles, (1980). Vol II, Oxford, Clarendon Press.
Shubber, S. (1973). *Jurisdiction Over Crimes on Board Aircraft,* Dordrecht, The Netherlands, M. Nijhoff.
Sochor, E. (1991). *The Politics of International Aviation,* London, The Macmillan Co.
Sohn, L.B. (1976). *Cases on United Nations Law,* Brooklyn, N.Y., The Foundation Press.

Starke, J.G. (1984). *Introduction to International Law*, London, Butterworths & Co. Ltd.
Taylor, A.H. (1969). *American Diplomacy and the Narcotics Traffic, 1900–1939; A Study in International Humanitarian Reform*, Durham, N.C., Duke University Press.
The Evolving United Nations: A Prospect for Peace (1971). Kenneth J. Twitchett (ed.), London, Europa Publications.
The Latin American Narcotics Trade and U.S. National Security (1989). Donald J. Mabry (ed.), New York, Greenwood Press.
Tullis, L. (1991). *Handbook of Research on the Illicit Drug Traffic: Socio-economic and Political Consequences*, New York, Greenwood.
United Nations (1946). *The United Nations Conference on International Organizations – Selected Documents*, Washington, D.C., Government Printing Office.
United Nations (1970). *The United Nations: The Next Twenty Five Years – Twentieth Report of the Commission to Study the Organization of Peace*, Dobbs Ferry, New York, Oceana Publishers.
United Nations (1985). *The United Nations at Forty – A Foundation to Build On*, New York, United Nations.
United States Congress (1977). *Tactical Air Warfare: Hearings Before the Task Force on National Security and International Affairs*, United States Congress, House Committee on the Budget, Washington, D.C., U.S. Government Printing Office.
United States Congress, Senate, Committee on the Judiciary (1972). *World Drug Traffic and its Impact on U.S. Security*, Sub-Committee to Investigate the Administration of the Internal Security Act and Other Internal Security Laws, Washington, D.C., U.S. Government Printing Office.
United States Dept. of Transportation (1971). *Hijacking – Selected Readings*, Washington, D.C., Library Services Division.
United States Federal Aviation Administration (1969). *Hijacking – Selected References* (ed. Ann O'Brien), Washington, D.C., Library Services Division.
Villamin, M.L. (1962). *Piracy and Air Law*, Montreal, McGill University Thesis, LL.M.
Walker, T.A. (1989). *A History of the Law of Nations*, Cambridge, England, Cambridge University Press.
Weeramantry, C.G. (1982). *An Invitation to the Law*, Sydney, Australia, Butterworths & Co. Ltd.
Winston, M.W. (1973). *The Role of Extradition in International Civil Aviation*, Montreal, McGill University Thesis, LL.M.
Zellman, C. (1927). *Law of the Air*, Milwaukee, Wisconsin, The Bruce Publishing Co.
Zussman, E.A. (1971). *International Law Regulating Unlawful Seizure of Aircraft*, Montreal, McGill University Thesis, LL.M.

Zuzack, C.A. (1990). *Liability for Breaches of Aviation Security Obligations: A Canadian Perspective*, Montreal, McGill University Thesis, LL.M.

ICAO Documents

Aviation Security

ICAO Head Office

- Assembly Resolution A 26-7
- C-WPs/8753, 8540, (and Add.) 8581, 8656, 8714, 8660, 8789, 8801, 8817, 8848, 8872, 9001.
- C-Mins. 119/1, 120/14, 123/18, 125/17.
- State Letters: LE 3/32 – 86/102 (26/11/86)
  LE 3/32 (14/9/87)
  LE 3/32 – 87/86 (28/10/87)
  LE 3/32 and LE 3/32 – 88/63 (29/7/88)
  LE 3/32 – 89/12 (11/1/89)

ICAO Regional Offices

- C-WPs 8476 and Add., 8616, 8663, 8773, 8826.
- C-Dec. 124/14, 123/8&9.

Technical Cooperation Programme

- C-Dec 126–7
- C-WPs 8811, 8863, 8910, 8945.

Organization of the Secretariat

- C-WPs 8813, 8868, 8893.

Voluntary Assistance Programme

- C-WPs 8652 and Add., 8736, 8845, 9001.

PAN-AM 103 Incident

- ICAO (1989). *Security*, 4th ed, Annex 17, October.
- C-WPs 8752, 8754 and Add. Rev., 8772.
- C-Dec. 126/3.
- *Security Manual*, Doc 8973/3 (Restricted).

- *Aviation Security Manual,* Doc 8849 – C/990/4

Destruction of Civil Aircraft

- C-WP 8782

Detection of Explosives

- C-Min. 128/4 (Restricted)
- C-WPs 8954 Rev., 8846, 8814, 9003, 9000, 8924, 8930.

Research Publications

Books

LEGAL AND REGULATORY ISSUES IN INTERNATIONAL CIVIL AVIATION, Transnational Publishers: New York, April 1996. 420p

LEGAL ASPECTS OF CODE SHARING AGREEMENTS AND COMPUTER RESERVATION SYSTEMS, Editiones Frontieres: March, 1996. 270p

AVIATION SECURITY – LEGAL AND REGULATORY ISSUES, Ashgate Publishing Co. Ltd., Aldershot: January 1999. 500p

THE IMPACT ON SAFETY OF COMMERCIAL STRATEGIES IN AVIATION, Ashgate Publishing Co. Ltd., Aldershot: 1999. 500p

Journal Articles

The Effect of Unlawful Interference With International Civil Aviation on World Peace and the Social Order – *Transportation Law Journal* – Volume 22 Number 3 Spring 1995

General Principles of State Liability for the Provision of Space Technology in the Field of Air Navigation – *European Transport Law* – vol. XXIV No. 5 1994

NAFTA – a Legal and Economic Analysis – *Trading Law* – December 1994

Proposals and Guidelines for the Carriage of Elderly and Disabled by Air – *Journal of Travel and Tourism* – August 1994

Legal and Economic Effects of NAFTA on Canada, Mexico and the United States – *World Competition* – Vol. 18, No. 2, December 1994

The ICAO World-Wide Air Transport Conference – a Commentary – *European Transport Law* Vol. XXIV No. 6 1995

Recent Developments in Taxation of Air Transport – An ICAO-IATA Symbiosis – *Air and Space Law*, Vol. XX No. 2. April 1995

The Role of Automation in Facilitation of Air Transport into the 21st Century – *Annals of Air and Space Law*, (Special Issue) April 1995

Some Issues of the Warsaw Convention: Still Some Debate Left? – *German Journal of Air and Space Law,* Volume 4, 1995
Dispute Resolution in Trading in Civil Aircraft and Related Aviation Issues – a Comparative Study, *Trading Law and Trading Law Reports,* May 1995
Legal Aspects of the Unlawful Interference with International Civil Aviation – *Air and Space Law* (Kluwer: Netherlands) Vol. XVIII No. 6 1993
The Evolution From Fans to CNS/ATM System – *German Journal of Air and Space Law* (Carl Heymanns Verlag KG: Germany) Vol. 43 No. 2 June 1994
The Inclusion of Air Transport Services in GATT – a Legal Study – *Trading Law and Trading Law Reports* – March 1994
Freedom From Arrest and Detention in Sri Lanka the Veeradas Case – *International and Comparative Law Quarterly* Vol. 43 July 1994
Sydney's Third Runway – a Global Perspective – *Journal of Environmental Law and Policy* – Vol. 10, No. 5, October 1993
Liability of Airlines for Off-Loading of Passengers – *Sri Lanka Bar Review* – December 1994
Aviation and the Environment – Regulatory and Legal Issues – *Environmental Policy and Law* – September 1994
Relief Flights – Perspectives in International Law – *German Journal of Air and Space Law* – August 1994
Evidentiary Issues in Electronic Data Interchange – The Anglo-American Response – *Trading Law* – April 1994
Some Recent Trends in the Taxation of International Civil Aviation – *Air and Space Law* – August 1994
Taxation Consequences Attendant Upon Privileged Travel of Airline Employees – a Potential Problem – *Lloyd's Aviation Law* – Vol. 13 No. 4 February 15 1994
Evidentiary Issues in Electronic Data Interchange – The Anglo-American Response – *Tolley's Computer Law and Practice* – April 1994
The Economic Relevance of the Chicago Convention – *Annals of Air and Space Law* – December 1994
The Legal Status of the Chicago Convention and its Annexes – *Air and Space Law* – June 1994
The Air Traffic Rights Debate – a Legal Study – *Annals of Air and Space Law,* (McGill: Canada) September 1993
Pepper v. *Hart* and Airline Fringe Benefits – *Annals of Air and Space Law,* (McGill: Canada) September 1993
Smoking in Aircraft – a Fog of Legal Rhetoric? – *Air and Space Law,* (Kluwer: the Netherlands) April 1993
The Challenge of Airport Congestion and Planning Laws – *Environment Policy and Law,* (IOS Press: The Netherlands) April 1993
The Effect of Taxation of Aviation on the Tourism Industry – a Legal

Study – *Annals of Tourism Research* (Pergammon Press: USA) March 1993
Law Making and Decision Making Powers of ICAO – a Critical Analysis – *German Journal of Air and Space Law* – (Carl Heymanns Verlag KG: Germany 4/1992) January 1993
The Philosophy of Air Law – *The American Journal of Jurisprudence* – (Notre Dame: USA) January 1993
The Development of the Machine Readable Passport and Visa and the Legal Rights of the Data Subject – *Annals of Air and Space Law* (McGill: Canada) December 1992
The Pan Am Case and the New World Order – *Annals of Air and Space Law*, (McGill: Canada) December 1993
United Nations Decade of International Law – a New Dimension? – *Journal of Social Policy and Law*, Science Press: New York, Spring, 1992
Facilitation and the ICAO Role – a Prologue for the Nineties – *Annals of Air and Space Law*, – (McGill: Canada) December 1990
The Carriage of the Disabled by Air – a Legal Dilemma for the Airlines? *Air Law*, (Kluwer: The Netherlands), September 1991
Taxation of International Air Transport – Legal Aspects – *Air Law*, (Kluwer: The Netherlands), June 1991
Hong Kong and Air Traffic Rights in 1997, Some Legal Issues – *Air Law*, (Kluwer: The Netherlands), April 1990
The Invasion of the Maldives and International Terrorism – Definitions and Solutions – *Terrorism – an Annual* (Martinus Nijhoff: The Netherlands), 1990–1991
Civil Liability of Airlines for Death or Injury to Passengers, the Last Frontier, *The Colombo Law Review*, (University of Sri Lanka) September 1990
The Human Stress Factor and Mental Injury in Modern American Tort Law – a Patchwork Quilt? *The Anglo-American Law journal* (Barry Rose Publishers, U.K.) Vol. 15, No. 4, (1986)
The Liability of the Actual Carrier in the Carriage of Goods by Air and in Multi-Modal Transport Transactions – *Air Law* (Kluwer: The Netherlands) March 1988
The Ekanayake Hijacking Appeal in Sri Lanka – a Critical Appraisal – *Air Law* (Kluwer: The Netherlands) April 1989
Skyjacker Gets Life Imprisonment in Sri Lanka – *Lloyds Aviation Law* (Condon & Forsyth: USA) December 1983
Hong Kong and Air Traffic Rights After 1997 – *Lloyds Aviation Law* (Condon & Forsyth: USA) December 1986
The United States as a Defendant in the Korean Airlines Incident, published in *Lloyds Aviation Law* (Condon & Forsyth: USA) May 1984

Airline Tariff Fixing and Pricing Laws of the European Community – *Lloyds Aviation Law* (Condon & Forsyth: USA) December 1986
The Intrusion into Sri Lankan Air Space by Indian Aircraft – *Lloyds Aviation Law* (Condon & Forsyth: USA) August 1987
Legislative Responses to Terrorism – a Book Review – *The American Journal of Comparative Law* (USA) September 1987
Aerial Piracy and Extended Jurisdiction in Japan – *The International and Comparative Law Quarterly* (UK) July 1984
Hijacking and the Teheran Incident – a World in Crisis? – *Air Law* (Kluwer: The Netherlands) December 1985
The General Sales Agency Agreement in the Airline Industry – Changing Perspectives – *Air Law* (Kluwer: The Netherlands) December 1985
The Fair and Equal Opportunity Clause in the Air Services Agreement and Developing Countries – *Air Law* (Kluwer: The Netherlands) August 1987
Revision of the Aviation Laws of Sri Lanka – a Compelling Need – *Law Bulletin,* (Law Comm. SL), 3rd Quarter 1989
The Rights of the Child in Sri Lanka – *Comparative and International Law Journal of Southern Africa* – November 1984. (Co-authored with Anoma Abeyratne)
Land Acquisition, is it Justifiable? – *JURA* (University of Colombo) 1978
Contractual Liability Arising out of Computer Reservation Systems in Air Transport, *Tolley's Computer Law and Practice,* Volume 11 Number 4 1995. Also published in *Trading Law and Trading Law Reports,* January – February 1996, Volume fifteen, Number One
Legal and Regulatory Aspects of Code Sharing and Computer Reservation Systems in Air Transport, *Trading Law and Trading Law Reports,* November 1995
Recent Trends on Legal Liability of Airlines for Denied Boarding of Passengers, *European Transport Law,* March 1996
Measures Taken by the International Community in the Control of Terrorism Against Civil Aviation, *Transportation Law Journal,* July 1996
Olympics 2000 and Sydney's Airport Policy – Legal Aspects, *Annals of Air and Space Law,* December 1995
The Air Traffic Rights Debate – Where Does Everyone Stand? *Lloyd's Aviation Law,* Vol. 14, No. 17, September 1, 1995
Dispute Resolution in Trade in Civil Aircraft and Related Services – a Comparative Study With Other Aviation Issues, Part 1, *Trading Law and Trading Law Reports,* July-August 1995, Volume 14, Number 4
Competition Rules in Commercial Aviation and WTO Competition Rules – a Comparative Analysis, *World Competition,* March 1996

International Attempts at Regulating Unlawful Interference With Civil Aviation (Part 1), *German Journal of Air and Space Law*, March 1996

International Attempts at Regulating Unlawful Interference With Civil Aviation (Part 2), *German Journal of Air and Space Law*, August 1996

The Role of the Flight Attendant in Air Carrier Liability, *Korean Journal of Air and Space Law*, Summer 1996

The Settlement of Civil Aviation Disputes Under the General Agreement on Trade in Services and the ICAO Council – a Comparative Study, *International Trade Law and the GATT – WTO Dispute Settlement System*, Published by the International Trade Law Committee of the International Law Association, Kluwer: Summer 1997

The Application of Multiple Systems of Law to Professional Negligence in Sri Lanka – The *de Soyza* Case, *Tolley's Professional Negligence*, July 1996

Air Carrier Liability for Negligent Acts of Cabin Crew Members, *European Transport Law*, No. 5 October 1996

Would Competition in Commercial Aviation Ever Fit Into WTO? *Journal of Air Law and Commerce*, July 1996

Air Carrier Liability for Denied Boarding of Passengers – Recent Developments, *European Transport Law*, March 1996

Dispute Resolution in Trade in Civil Aircraft and Related Services – a Comparative Study With Other Aviation Issues, Part 2, *Trading Law and Trading Law Reports*, July-August 1995, Volume 14, Number 4

Liability for Personal Injury and Death Under the Warsaw Convention and its Relevance to Fault Liability in Tort Law, *Annals of Air and Space Law*, December 1996

International Politics and International Justice – a Lesson in Unity in Diversity? *Journal of Social Policy and Law*, Science Press: New York, Vol. 10, No. 2, Winter 1996

Regulatory Management of the Warsaw System of Private Liability of Air Carriers, *Journal of Air Transport Management* (October 1996)

Liability of States for Collusion With Extra Terrestrial Intelligence in the Sharing and Use of Space Technology, *Annals of Air and Space Law*, December 1996

The Use of Nuclear Power Sources in Outer Space and its Effects on Environmental Protection, *Journal of Space Law*, Volume 25, Number 1, 1997

The Legal Status of ICAO's Strategic Action Plan, *German Journal of Air and Space Law*, August 1996

The State and International Aviation in India (Book Review), *Zeitschrift für Luft-und Weltraumrecht, German Journal of Air and Space Law*, 45 Jg. 3/1996

The Aerospace Plane and its Effects on Air Traffic Rights, *The Aviation Quarterly*, January 1997

Liability Issues and Professional Negligence of Air Crew, *Tolley's Professional Negligence*, Tolley: London, April 1997

Legal and Scientific Aspects of Exposure of Air Crew to Cosmic Radiation, *The Aviation Quarterly*, Part 4, April 1997

The Notion of Wilful Misconduct in the Warsaw System: Emerging Trends at Common Law, *Annals of Air and Space Law*, Vol. XXII Part 11, March 1997

Some Recommendations for a New Legal and Regulatory Structure for the Management of the Offence of Unlawful Interference With Civil Aviation, *Transportation Law Journal*, March 1997

Competition in the Air Transport Industry and Preferential Measures for Developing Countries, *World Competition*, June 1997

Environmental Protection and the Use of Nuclear Power in Outer Space, *Environmental Policy and Law*, Vol. 26 No. 6, November 1996

The Impact of Tourism and Air Transport on the Sustainable Development of Small Island Developing States, *Journal of Travel Research*, September 1997

International Initiatives at Controlling the Illicit Carriage of Narcotic Drugs by Air, *Journal of Air Law and Commerce*, Volume 63, Number 2, November/December 1997

Free Trade in Air Traffic Rights and Preferential Measures for Developing Countries, *Trading Law and Trading Law Reports*, August 1997

Recent Attempts by ICAO and the United Nations at Controlling the Illicit Carriage of Narcotic Drugs by Air, *European Transport Law*, January 1998

The Impact of Tourism and Air Transport on Small Island Developing States, *Environmental Policy and Law*, Vol. 27, No. 3, 1997

The Display of Airline Computer Reservations on the Internet, *Tolley's Communications Law*, July 1997

Air Carrier Liability for Exposure of Air Crew to Cosmic Radiation, *Air and Space Law*, Vol. XXII, Number 2, April 1997

The Use of Civil Aircraft and Air Crew for Military Purposes, *Annals of Air and Space Law*, Vol. XXII Part 2 1997, October 1997

Outsourcing and the Virtual Airline – Legal Implications, *Air and Space Law*, September 1997

Trading Practice of Outsourcing in the Virtual Airline – Legal Implications, *Trading Law and Trading Law Reports*, October 1997

Display of Airline Computer Reservations on the Internet – *The Aviation Quarterly*, LLP, October 1997

Current Legal Problems in the Control of the Offence of Unlawful Interference With Civil Aviation, *Current Issues in Criminal Justice*, November 1997

Terror in the Skies: Approaches to Controlling Unlawful Interference With Civil Aviation, *International Journal of Politics, Culture and Society* Vol. 11, Number 2, Winter 1997

The Trading of Airline Services on the Internet, *Trading Law and Trading Law Reports*, September-October 1997, Volume Sixteen, Number Five

The Environmental Impact of Aviation and Tourism on Asia Pacific Small Island Developing States, *Asia Pacific Journal of Environmental Law*, October 1997

Safety in International Civil Aviation, *The Aviation Quarterly*, LLP, December 1997

Legal and Ethical Foundations of Space Law, *Journal of Space Law*, January 1998

The Regulatory Management of Safety in Air Transport, *Journal of Air Transport Management*, January 1998

Franchising in the Airline Industry – Some Implications at Common Law, *Air and Space Law*, Volume XXII, Number 6, December 1997

Franchising as a Competitive Tool in the Airline Industry, *World Competition*, Vol. 21, No. 2, December 1997

Infringement of Copyright in Airline Product Distribution on the Internet, *Journal of World Intellectual Property*, Vol. 1 No. 1 January 1998

The Sensibility of Taxing Environmental Pollution, *Environmental Policy and Law*, March 1998

Canada, Focus on Aviation Safety, *The Aviation Quarterly*, Vol. 1 Part 6, October 1997, pp. 392–394

The Automated Screening of Passengers and the Smart Card-Emerging Legal Issues, *Air and Space Law*, April 1998

Principles of Administration of the International Civil Service – The ICAO Experience, *International Journal of Politics, Culture and Society*, June 1998

The Proposed International Aeronautical Monetary Fund, *Journal of Air Transportation Worldwide*, June 1998

Latin American Initiatives for the Financing of the CNS/ATM System, *Aviation Quarterly*, March 1998

International Obligations as Regards Safety in International Civil Aviation, *The Aeronautical Journal*, December 1997, Volume 101, No. 1010, pp. 457–466

Open Skies and the Icao "Safety Net" – a Comparison with WTO Safeguards, *Air and Space Law*, April 1998

Substance Abuse and Negligence of the Airline Pilot, *Tolley's Professional Negligence*, December 1998

Aeronautical and Human Factors of Safety in Civil Aviation, *The Aviation Quarterly*, Part 1, January 1998

Turbulence and Air Carrier Liability under the Existing Warsaw System, *The Aviation Quarterly*, June 1998

The Exchange of Trade Secrets on Information Technology in the Aviation Industry, *Journal of World Intellectual Property*, June 1998

Canada, Focus on Aviation Safety, *The Aviation Quarterly*, Vol. 1, Part 6 October 1997, pp. 393–394
Competition Rules Governing Market Access in Air Transport – a Comparative Study, *World Competition*, June 1998
Liberalized Trading in Air Transport and the ICAO Safety Net, *Trading Law and Trading Law Reports*, July 1998
Global Trends Confronting African Civil Aviation, *The Aviation Quarterly*, September 1998
Liberalized Trading in Air Transport and the ICAO Safety Net, *Trading Law and Trading Law Reports*, July 1998
Theories of Jurisprudence on the Use of Global Navigation Satellite Systems, *Annals of Air and Space Law*, Volume XXIII Part I 1998
The Principle of "Commonality" in Social Obligations of States with Regard to the Exploitation of Outer Space, *Journal of Politics, Culture and Society*, September 1998
The Millenium Bug and the Aviation Industry – Legal Liabilities, *The Aviation Quarterly*, September 1998
The Future of African Civil Aviation, *Journal of Air Transportation Worldwide*, December 1998
Prudence of Taxing Environmental Pollution, *Bar Association Law Journal*: Sri Lanka, (1997) Vol. VII Part 1
The Protection of the Environment in Sri Lanka by Legislation – a Comparison with Asean and the West, Published among papers of the 10th LawAsia Conference, 1987
Substance Abuse and Negligence of the Airline Pilot, *Tolley's Professional Negligence*, December 1998

Index